Health 1919–1948

Studies in the History of Medicine

Edited by Charles Webster, All Souls College, Oxford

Volume 2

PETER LANG
Oxford · Bern · Berlin · Bruxelles · Frankfurt a.M. · New York · Wien

Jacqueline Jenkinson

Scotland's Health 1919–1948

PETER LANG
Oxford · Bern · Berlin · Bruxelles · Frankfurt a.M. · New York · Wien

Bibliographic information published by Die Deutsche Bibliothek
Die Deutsche Bibliothek lists this publication in the Deutsche Nationalbibliografie; detailed bibliographic data is available in the Internet at ‹http://dnb.ddb.de›.

British Library and Library of Congress Cataloguing-in-Publication Data:
A catalogue record for this book is available from *The British Library*, Great Britain, and from *The Library of Congress*, USA

ISSN 1424-7933
ISBN 3-906768-34-1
US-ISBN 0-8204-5622-5

Hochfeldstrasse 32, Postfach 746, CH-3000 Bern 9, Switzerland
info@peterlang.com, www.peterlang.com, www.peterlang.net

Printed in Germany

This book is dedicated to Belinda, Sean and Stephen.

Contents

Acknowledgements

I take this opportunity to thank my two research assistants, Brenda White and Megan Davies, who helped prepare the groundwork for this book. Their sterling efforts in archives uncovered invaluable source materials for this work. Their dedication, enthusiasm and fresh ideas at times injected new life into this project. Thanks should also go to Stephen Mungall who provided additional research assistance.

I would like to provide a general, but deeply-felt, thank you to all the archivists and librarians, too numerous to mention individually, who offered their expertise with the primary and secondary resources utilised in the preparation of this book.

Also, my thanks go to Anne Crowther, Helen Dingwall, Charles Lee, Rodney Lowe, George Peden, and Charles Webster who offered advice and guidance on parts or all of this manuscript.

I acknowledge the generous support in the form of a research grant which I received from the ESRC, without the grant this book would not have been possible.

I also thank the Carnegie Trust for the Universities of Scotland for its liberal financial support towards the publication costs of this book.

November 2001

List of Abbreviations

BMJ	*British Medical Journal*
CBE	Clyde Basin Experiment
DHS	Department of Health for Scotland
DMO	District Medical Officer
EMJ	*Edinburgh Medical Journal*
EMB	Empire Marketing Board
EMS	Emergency Medical Service
GMC	General Medical Council
GMJ	*Glasgow Medical Journal*
HIMSB	Highlands and Islands Medical Services Board
HOC	House of Commons [*Hansard Parliamentary Debates*]
HOL	House of Lords [*Hansard*]
IMR	Infant Mortality Rate
ISIPS	'Incapacitating Sickness of the Insured Population of Scotland'
MH	Ministry of Health
MOsH	Medical Officers of Health
MMR	Maternal Mortality Rate
MSS	Morbidity Statistics Scheme
NAPT	National Association for the Prevention of Tuberculosis
NAS	National Archives of Scotland
NHS	National Health Service
PEP	Political and Economic Planning
PRO	Public Record Office
PUS	Parliamentary Under Secretary
PUSH	Parliamentary Under Secretary for Health
RCPSG	Royal College of Physicians and Surgeons of Glasgow
RCPE	Royal College of Physicians of Edinburgh
RCSE	Royal College of Surgeons of Edinburgh
RMO	Regional Medical Officer
SBH	Scottish Board of Health
SED	Scottish Education Department
SMMB	Scottish Milk Marketing Board
SMO	School Medical Officer
TO	Tuberculosis Officer

List of Tables, Figures and Plates

Tables

Figures

Plates

Introduction

The intention of this study of the Scottish health services is to discover how far Scotland was successful in establishing and maintaining a health administration that was distinct from the Ministry of Health. A further aim is to evaluate how far this parallel, Scottish, health administration responded to health issues in a manner which took into account the unique history and health concerns of the Scottish people. To achieve these twin targets, the focus is on both the administration of Scottish health care and the impact of this service on the health trends of the Scottish population. It is the 'personal' health services with which this book is concerned. The examination of personal health services covers: infant and maternal welfare, the treatment of tuberculosis, school health provision, and also the health of the insured population. Other areas of Scottish health administration such as hospitals, housing, sanitation, public assistance and related local government affairs are generally not included. In selecting the personal health services, the study follows the lead of the Department of Health for Scotland's memorandum *Outline of Scottish Services – Health* submitted to the War Cabinet Committee on Social Insurance and Allied Services (Beveridge Committee) in 1941. The memorandum commented:

> Those health services which are the subject of the memorandum are for the most part personal rather than environmental. They comprise the medical and allied services which have mainly grown up in the last thirty years – since, in fact, the passing of the Education Act of 1908, which started the school health service, and the first Health Insurance Act of 1911 which revitalised the tuberculosis campaign on a national basis. The Great War period saw the start of the maternity and child welfare scheme [...] and since that time the communal medical services have developed gradually but steadily into a health

organisation which at one time or another touches the lives of the majority of citizens.[1]

The development of the personal health services in Scotland from 1919 to 1948 has not, to date, formed a significant part of the body of secondary works on the history of twentieth-century health policy and health care. Many of these works have been of value in the preparation of this book in regard to the context of the medical and bureaucratic debates surrounding health provision, but few have considered the Scottish aspects of British health administration as a distinct system of government. Historians have said little about, or completely excluded, the history of Scottish health administration and policy in their work. For example, Frank Honigsbaum in his book *The Division in British Medicine* (1979) has one reference to the Scottish Board of Health and six items in total under Scotland and Scottish in his index.[2] In contrast, the 1920 Dawson Report alone merits 48 references.[3] Taking this comparison further, Honigsbaum's study on the National Health Service, *Health, Happiness and Security: The Creation of the National Health Service* (1989), deliberately rules out consistent reference to Scotland and Northern Ireland.[4] While it does mention the 1936 DHS Committee on Scottish Health Services Report (the Cathcart Report), Honigsbaum's book provides no background information on how this significant three-year enquiry came to be convened. He merely links it to contemporary concerns with the operation of national health insurance services.[5] That the distinct system of Scottish health policy and care might add to the picture of the creation of the NHS *because* of the differences to the situation in

1 PRO, CAB 87/76, War Cabinet Committee on Social Insurance and Allied Services (Beveridge Committee), Department of Health for Scotland Memorandum, *Outline of Scottish Services – Health*, August 1941.

2 F. Honigsbaum, *The Division in British Medicine* (Kogan Page, 1979), 441. Note – where not given in footnote, place of publication is London.

3 Ibid., 430.

4 'Attention is focused on planning in England and Wales; proposals for Scotland and Northern Ireland are cited only where they had relevance to negotiations in England and Wales.' Frank Honigsbaum, *Health, Happiness and Security: The Creation of the National Health Service* (Routledge, 1989), Introduction, xv.

5 Ibid., 10–11.

England and Wales is not considered. Meanwhile, Maurice Bruce's classic work, *The Coming of the Welfare State* (1968), specifically omitted Scotland from what is an English study.[6] A more recent textbook, Anne Hardy's *Health and Medicine in Britain since 1860* (2001), contains only three references to Scotland in the index.[7]

Some historians have sought to tackle this imbalance in recent considerations of the development of British health services. For example, Rodney Lowe apologetically excluded both Scotland and Northern Ireland from his study *The Welfare State since 1945* (1993).[8] However, in the second edition of the book, published in 1999, Lowe frequently acknowledged the differences in administrative structure and policy development in both countries. Referring specifically to Scotland, Lowe noted: 'the conventions of "parallel administration" or "technocratic autonomy" gave Scotland an equal – or even greater – freedom to develop a distinctive welfare policy.'[9] Other historians, notably Charles Webster in *The Health Services since the War Vol. 1: Problems of Health Care – The National Health Service before 1957* (1988) have successfully integrated the distinct Scottish health administration into their work on British health services. For instance, Webster provides figures for Scotland and often lists specific Scottish legislation, (as on page 7, which covers developments in infant and maternal welfare).

6 'Reference throughout the book is almost entirely to English experience [...] and, although there is [...] much in common with Scotland and Ireland, there are many differences, especially in Scottish traditions and administration [...] The author hopes that his fellow citizens [...] will excuse the omissions that have been made under the demands of concentration and in the interests of clarity.' Maurice Bruce, *The Coming of the Welfare State* (Batsford, 1968 ed.), 9.

7 Although Hardy comments, 'the current volume, inevitably, follows the inherent bias of the existing historiography by focusing on England and Wales', the book is about England. Why else would there be eight references in total to Wales in the index and none at all for England? Anne Hardy, *Health and Medicine in Britain since 1860* (Basingstoke: Palgrave, 2001).

8 'I should also apologise to readers in Scotland and Northern Ireland who will immediately perceive, with resignation, that this is yet another book which focuses essentially on England and Wales.' R. Lowe, *The Welfare State since 1945* (Basingstoke: Macmillan, 1993), x.

9 Ibid., (2nd edn, 1999), 94–5.

The neglect or omission of Scottish material from many studies of health policy in the first half of the twentieth century can lead to statements which, while accurate as regards the position in England and Wales, contradict administrative practice in Scotland. For example, the chapter by Davidson and Lowe entitled 'Bureaucracy and Innovation in British Welfare Policy 1870–1945' in *The Emergence of the Welfare State in Britain and Germany 1850–1950* (1981), edited by W.J. Mommsen, has no reference to Scottish administration. This chapter states:

> [...] Specialists had minimal access to policy-making in other areas of social administration. Precedent and the presence of second or third generation Oxbridge-educated, classically trained civil servants [...] placed a premium on the application of formal rules and consultation procedures to domestic policy [...].[10]

Yet, the Scottish Board of Health (which sat from 1919 to 1928) contained two medical members, a legal expert, a woman member and two former health insurance commissioners. There were no higher-grade civil servants on its six-person Board. Experts continued to play a crucial role in Scottish health policy formulation even after the Department of Health for Scotland in 1929 replaced the SBH. For example, John Boyd Orr's scientific investigations into nutrition were often funded by the SBH (and later the DHS) in the late 1920s. These enquiries and others initiated from within the DHS, led to the introduction of 'milk in schools' schemes and are described in chapter four.

There are, of course, a number of books written from a Scottish perspective which relate to the subject of Scottish health policy and practice in the first half of the twentieth century. The work of Ian Levitt is most notable in this area. In both *Poverty and Welfare in Scotland 1890–1948* (Edinburgh, 1988) and *The Scottish Office: Depression and Reconstruction 1919–1959* (Edinburgh, 1992), Levitt produced an assessment of general social policy developments and a wealth of documentary evidence invaluable to the historian of Scottish

10 W.J. Mommsen, ed., *The Emergence of the Welfare State in Britain and Germany 1850–1950* (Croom Helm, 1981), 271.

health policy. *Improving the Common Weal: Aspects of the Scottish Health Services 1900–1984* (Edinburgh, 1987), edited by G. McLachlan, specifically addresses the history of Scottish health services, but is a narrative rather than analytical account. For examining the level of autonomous control over Scotland's general welfare agencies there is no better starting-point than Lindsay Paterson's provocative and insightful *The Autonomy of Modern Scotland* (Edinburgh, 1994).

The approach of this book is that of micro-politics. The study of specific health policy decisions allows for the exploitation of official and private primary source materials. The sources used in this study are, in the first instance, drawn from government records. While these records are an essential source for the study of health policy, in examining policy-*making* the use of official records poses some difficulties for historians. At many points in the period 1919–1948 there are only scanty records of the decision-making process in Scottish health policy. This is not due to the absence of records, but to the type of formal record retained by Government departments.

There is a wealth of material on the creation and early meetings of the Scottish Board of Health (SBH) in 1918/1919. The full run of detailed minutes of the SBH (covering the years 1919–1928) was recovered in 1999 and deposited in the National Archives of Scotland.[11] Although the, often detailed, papers of related Cabinet committees were not retained in the long term by the Scottish Office, but were transferred to the Cabinet Office in London, copies of Cabinet papers were deposited in the NAS in 2000.[12] However, formal minutes rarely give an indication of the debates behind the decisions. The problem of a lack of detailed information on the process of policy-formulation is

11 The name of the archive was changed in January 1999 from the Scottish Record Office to the National Archives of Scotland.

12 One difficulty in using these papers is that, while Scottish proposals to Cabinet are evident in the memoranda submitted for Cabinet discussion, the papers and debates within the Department of Health for Scotland are rarely included. Once again policy-formulation, rather than decision taking, is the hardest part to identify. For more on this see Ian Levitt, ed., *The Scottish Office – Depression and Reconstruction 1919–1959* (Edinburgh: Scottish History Society, 1992), 5.

not confined to the study of health policy.[13] The detail of policy decisions was not recorded at the highest levels, but by junior officials, whose records were rarely retained. This means the process of decision-making can often only be inferred. Finally, not all official records relating to Scottish health policy are held in Scotland. For example, vital negotiations with the Treasury over financial restrictions that dominated early SBH activity are not available in Scotland. However, these and other records for the period covered in this study are accessible in the Public Record Office in London.

The other main research resource for this book has been a wide range of local archival materials. These include published annual reports from local Medical Officers of Health and School Medical Officers, the minutes and relevant committee records of local authorities, and the archives of the Scottish Royal Medical Colleges. Personal accounts of major players have also been used where available. As well as a diverse range of records consulted, a wide geographical spread of archives was visited. In addition to records covering health administration and practice in Scotland's four largest cities – Glasgow, Edinburgh, Aberdeen and Dundee – archives were consulted and useful materials uncovered in the Highlands and Islands, the Borders, Argyllshire, Perthshire, Lanarkshire and Stirlingshire. This wide-ranging study was essential in order to present a range of health experience in Scotland from the rural to the small town as well as the large urban conurbations. This range of materials helps illustrate the input of local government in Scottish health administration. Local records also add further insight into the process of inter war health policy formulation. Finally, extensive use was made of printed materials, including parliamentary reports in Hansard, government statutes, Scottish Board of Health, Department of Health for Scotland and Ministry of Health annual reports and circulars, professional medical journals, and national and local newspapers.

The motivations of Scottish health bureaucracy in these years and their influence over policy form a crucial aspect of this study. The Scottish Board of Health, created in 1919, was itself the culmination

13 See B.W.E. Alford, et al, ed,. *Economic Planning, 1943–1951* (HMSO, 1992), xi.

of late nineteenth-century developments in the Scottish policy-making process under the system of autonomous expert Boards. For example, there were already Boards for Education, Agriculture, and Prisons, and the SBH saw the amalgamation of the Local Government Board for Scotland with the Highlands and Islands (Medical Services) Board with other related agencies. MacDonagh, writing in 1958, first examined how far Scottish policy-making under the Board system was designed to correlate social policy with administrative remedy.[14] Ellen M. Immergut's 1992 work on comparative health policy formulation[15] reinforced MacDonagh's views on multiple influences on the decision-making process.

In Scotland, the procedural framework of health administration was different from the rest of Great Britain. The influence of expert advice in policy decision-making, first noted by MacDonagh,[16] is here considered in relation to Scottish inter-war health policy and practice. Uniquely in British health policy-making, the Scottish Board of Health was made up of politicians (the Scottish Secretary and the Parliamentary Under Secretary for Health were ex-officio members) and expert opinion in the fields of medicine, national health insurance and the law. These expert Board members did not always pull in the same direction as the government representatives. Within a few years of its formation, administrative remedy was sought through parliament to rein in the SBH. Successive Scottish Secretaries described the Board system as anachronistic and contrary to the requirements of executive government. Interest groups too sought to influence the Scottish health administration. For example, the medical profession exerted sustained pressure on the government to influence the constitution of the Scottish Board of Health and to obtain adequate

14 O. MacDonagh, 'The 19th-Century Revolution in Government: A Reappraisal', *Historical Journal,* 1 (1958), 55.

15 E.M. Immergut, *Health Politics: Interests and Institutions in Western Europe* (Cambridge: Cambridge University Press, 1992), 3.

16 MacDonagh noted that the impulse to bureaucratic activity was 'prone to be distorted by accidents of personality or ideology or politics, or finance or the state of expert opinion, at the moment when the remedy is debated.' MacDonagh 'The 19th-Century Revolution in Government: A Reappraisal', 55.

representation and formative input into its operation. This pressure group activity is discussed in chapter one.

The activity of government institutions is at the heart of the enactment of social welfare programmes. Immergut[17] synthesised three possible levels of government involvement in the creation of health programmes. The first level of intervention is based on the idea of the 'nation-state'. There are two aspects to this. The first is the connection between warfare and welfare: that is, expanded health programmes follow or occur during warfare (a theory closely associated with the work of Richard M. Titmuss and discussed separately below). The other is the economic aspect. According to Immergut, the more 'open' an economy, that is the more dealings a government has with an international economy, the greater the tendency to expand the welfare state. The reverse view, that is, of economic restraint militating against health programmes, is more in evidence in the years covered by this work.

The second level of government institutional impulse towards state health programmes considered by Immergut is the role of the bureaucracy and other organisations. Immergut has stated that: '[...] no program was ever introduced without the very active participation of high-level bureaucrats.'[18] In this model, reforms tend to be prepared initially by the executive government. This is followed by a period of consultation with interest groups. In other words, it is government agencies and not interest groups that initiate health policy. Policy reforms are, furthermore, built upon pre-existing programmes and administrative structures. This is a persuasive argument. However, Immergut's additional remark that, in the realm of national health insurance, bureaucrats and bureaucratic structures are generally indifferent to making policy does not hold good for the study of national health insurance in the Scottish context as discussed in chapter six.

The final model of government institutional activity outlined by Immergut, the 'executive-centred' approach, is the one most favoured in her international study of national health insurance. The 'State'

17 Immergut, *Health Politics*, 22–23.
18 Ibid., 23.

(here defined as the executive branch of government) plays the key role. Government politicians with an interest in stabilising their regime, i.e. in keeping power, determine health policy. Interest groups only have influence in this model depending on the institutional context of decision-making. For Immergut, access to 'political veto points' is crucial. Without these opportunities, interest groups have little influence. This final model appears the most persuasive in the light of the Scottish health policy topics here considered.

Further insight into the issue of administrative motivation is provided by Keith Dowding's 1995 book on the British Civil Service. Dowding outlines a number of possible interpretations of the administrative relationship between government and the civil service. In the 'constitutional-representative government' model the civil service is a neutral agency maintained by an elected government. The government is itself answerable to a parliament that is in turn elected by the people.[19] The 'pluralist account' sees the civil service and other policy-making agencies acting as neutral informers of politicians of the day, with policy emerging from a balance of the various interest-group pressures.[20] The final theory, the 'autonomy of the democratic state' perceives group organisations influencing policy only when their views coincide with those of government. Otherwise their views only influence government in areas where there are no clear policy parameters outlined.[21]

The 'pluralist account' is an appealing description for certain notable health policy developments, for example, the foundation of the Scottish Board of Health, and in the creation of the National Health Service. However, for the purposes of this study, Dowding's final model – the 'autonomy of the democratic state', seems to be most in keeping with the relationships within the various government health agencies examined in the period 1919–1948. The 'state-autonomy' model outlined by Dowding parallels Immergut's 'executive-centred' approach.

---

19 K. Dowding, *The Civil Service* (Routledge, 1995), 3.

20 Ibid., 3–4.

21 Ibid., 4.

The 'state autonomy' cum 'executive-centred' model needs to be refined in the context of Scottish health administration. Scottish health administrators, particularly in the higher levels, were not career civil servants, but 'experts' appointed to the Scottish health bureaucracy. Hence, the idea of outside agencies influencing government policy can be extended beyond the traditional committees, pressure groups and vested interests intimated in the wider theory, to include members of the Scottish Board of Health itself. In other words, the views of interest-group organisations and those of 'government' could at times, in Scottish health administration, be one and the same. Such an argument fits well with Lindsay Paterson's theories on Scottish autonomy in the nineteenth and twentieth centuries.[22]

In Paterson's view, as state welfare provision grew in the course of the twentieth century, Scottish decision-making remained relatively independent under the Board system.[23] Scottish policy formulation benefited from the 'federalist' element in British government. Scottish federalism rested more 'on the way that its bureaucracy interpreted legislation than on the legislation itself. That is what Poggi[24]describes as 'technocracy – rule by experts'.[25] Paterson's argument (which is echoed in Lowe's recognition of Scottish 'technocratic autonomy')[26]

---

22 According to Lindsay Paterson, Scottish Boards had developed autonomous powers since their first formation during the nineteenth century. 'Local government was reformed in 1832 in a largely successful attempt to modernise it for the new age. Equally influential thereafter was the emerging network of boards and committees, which oversaw growing parts of state activities in Scotland – for example, education, the poor law, a rudimentary system of public health and so on.' L. Paterson, 'Scottish Autonomy and the Future of the Welfare State', *Scottish Affairs*, 19 (Spring 1997), 56.

23 'Scotland in the 1920s was the only part of the United Kingdom which continued to be ruled by a system of specialist Boards that were separate from a professional civil service. Despite the existence of the Scottish Secretary and despite the upgrading of that post to a Secretary of State in 1926, the Boards continued to devise and execute policy as if they were wholly autonomous.' Lindsay Paterson, *The Autonomy of Modern Scotland* (Edinburgh: Edinburgh University Press, 1994), 107.

24 A. Poggi, *The Development of the Modern State* (Hutchinson, 1978).

25 Paterson, *Autonomy of Modern Scotland*, 103.

26 Lowe, *The Welfare State since 1945* (2nd edition, 1999), 95.

is persuasive when applied, in particular, to the activities of the Scottish Board of Health. However, both the SBH and its successor, the Department of Health for Scotland, were not always free to pursue distinct policies. Both agencies were, at times, subject to the constraints of the 'executive centre'.

An example that well illustrates the boundaries of independent Scottish health initiative is the early struggle for funds between the Scottish Board of Health and the Treasury. G.C. Peden[27] has drawn attention to the possibility of Treasury encroachment on spending Departments' responsibilities, particularly in the years immediately after World War One.[28] The two British health departments were not alone in their financial struggles with the Treasury. However, when it came to competing for limited financial resources, the Scottish Board of Health faced an additional financial barrier to overcome in the shape of discrimination in salary levels. Administrative differences between the SBH and the Ministry of Health were paralleled in unequal salary structures, in favour of the Ministry. This, in turn, affected the relative standing of the two health departments. Autonomy over health policy did not necessarily lead to equal treatment. Failure to move the Treasury over pay scales was followed by periodic discussion on how best to overhaul first the SBH and later its direct replacement in 1929, the Department of Health for Scotland (DHS). Such discussion and some restructuring continued to the end of the 1930s. The inability of the Scottish Board of Health to influence central government, here in the shape of the Treasury, suggests that Immergut's 'executive-centred' approach (and also Dowding's 'autonomous state' model of the government-civil service relationship) has much merit when applied to Scottish health policy between 1919–1948.

The continued influence of voluntary agencies within an expanding state health system in the inter-war years cannot be discounted in

27 See G.C. Peden, 'The Treasury as the Central Department of Government, 1919–1939', *Public Administration*, 61 (Winter, 1983), 381.

28 The Treasury was strengthened in 1919 in an attempt to create a powerful central government department to control expenditure and cut out waste. Ibid., 376.

this study of Scottish health care developments. The survival of voluntary influence provides a useful counterbalance to the all-consuming theoretical considerations of the role and motivations of the 'State'. This combination of voluntary and state-sponsored care led to what Geoffrey Finlayson identified as 'a mixed economy of welfare'.[29] State involvement in health services by no means represented a linear, far less a planned development. Many voluntary and charitable agencies, rather than wither away, continued in parallel to statutory provision. Sometimes voluntary groups initiated new medical services outside state control. For example, the Carnegie Trust financed the construction of 'model' maternity and child welfare centres in the early 1920s. The model centre at Motherwell, in Lanarkshire, is discussed in chapter three. Another example of important voluntary initiative was the work undertaken by the Scottish National Milk Health Authority. Acting in co-operation with local authorities and the SBH, the SNMHA launched and helped fund scientific investigations into the value of milk in the nutrition of school children. The activities of the SNMHA are discussed in chapter four.

During the period covered by this study, Britain emerged from one, and was involved in a second, global war. Chapter seven of this book examines the impact of World War Two and its aftermath on health policy. The impact of warfare on health policy and provision has been the subject of great debate. One of the first authors to stress the role of war as a motivating factor in social change was Richard M. Titmuss.[30] Titmuss's work related in particular to the effects of war on state intervention and the subsequent affirmative results of this expanded social policy on the nation's health.[31] The formative

---

29 G. Finlayson, 'A Moving Frontier: Voluntarism and the State in British Social Welfare 1911–1949', *Twentieth Century British History*, 1/2 (1990), 185.

30 Titmuss was a leading social scientist and social democratic thinker, and was Professor of Social Administration at the London School of Economics, 1950–1973.

31 Titmuss first made the connection between warfare and welfare in a study on infant mortality: see R. Titmuss, *Birth, Poverty and Wealth: A Study of Infant Mortality* (Hamish Hamilton, 1943). Titmuss extended the connection to include the events of World War Two. In the 'Social Policy' volume of the

influence of the Titmuss view can be seen from the fact that many historians[32] have subsequently dated the beginning of systematic state health provision to the revelation of the ill health of so many of the British recruits in the Boer War. This revelation and the government inquiries that followed, resulted in legislation designed to improve the health of future generations. World War One also acted as a catalyst for further reforms of the personal health services, initially in the field of infant and maternal welfare. The regularisation of health administration under the Ministry of Health and Scottish Board of Health also was a wartime priority, which came to fruition in the year immediately after the War's end. Two decades later, only the special circumstances of the outbreak of World War Two ensured that the promotion of health, rather than the treatment of disease, became a policy option. For example, it took the outbreak of World War Two to force the piecemeal state and local health authority initiatives in the field of supplementary feeding for children into a national scheme. The history of school milk and meals is discussed in chapter four.

The influence warfare had on state health policy was neatly summarised by Fraser who stated 'warfare necessitated welfare'.[33] Yet, not all historians agree with the 'Titmuss' view.[34] As noted

---

official history of the War Titmuss commented: 'The fact that the area of collective responsibility moved out so soon in a wider circle, drawing in more people and broadening the obligations to protect those in need, was to serve the nation well during the following five years of strain and deprivation. Some of the benefits contributed to a good record of national health during these years.' Titmuss, *Problems of Social Policy* [History of World War Two – U.K. Civil Series], (HMSO, 1950), 517. Titmuss later expanded this view to consider the impact of all warfare on British society. In a chapter entitled 'War and Social Policy' in *Essays on the Welfare State* (2nd ed., Allen and Unwin, 1963), 78, he stated: 'The growing scale and intensity of war has stimulated a growing concern about the quantity and quality of the population.'

32 See, for example, D. Fraser, *The Evolution of the British Welfare State: A History of Social Policy since the Industrial Revolution* (Basingstoke: Macmillan, 1973), 164, 195–6.

33 Ibid., 196.

34 'In criticism of Titmuss's thesis there appears to be little evidence that the [Second World] war in itself induced heightened government awareness of social welfare either as a tool of national efficiency or as a means of enhancing

earlier with reference to Immergut's various 'models of the state',[35] it seems that 'warfare to welfare' was not the complete story. The creation of the National Health Service at the end of the period under survey was clearly rooted in the atmosphere of openness to change engendered by the wartime situation. However, various state health schemes had been discussed (but not implemented) since 1920. Not the least of these were the Scottish Board of Health's MacAlister Report of 1920 and the Department of Health for Scotland's Cathcart Report of 1936. These reports are discussed in the first two chapters of this book.

The debate on war as a factor of social change, which has exercised the thoughts of many 'post-Titmuss' historians, has also given rise to an evaluation of the effects of total warfare on the health of the country's civilian population. The health of the nation's population was improved during World War One. From the 'revisionist' viewpoint the general wartime improvement in standards was then augmented as a consequence of the growth in state agencies designed to help sections of the population in need during the 1920s and 1930s. These developments improved health trends amongst all sections of society throughout the inter-war period – including the years of economic depression. This 'revisionist' (or 'optimistic') position has come to be most associated with the writing of J.M. Winter.[36] Winter's view has been challenged by 'pessimistic' social

---

social solidarity. On the contrary, most Ministers were fearful that an over-hasty commitment to social reform would hamper the prosecution of the war and retard post-war economic revival.' Jose Harris, 'Some Aspects of Social Policy in Britain during the Second World War' in Mommsen, ed., *The Emergence of the Welfare State in Britain and Germany 1850–1950*, 258. See also V. Berridge, 'Health and Medicine' in F.M.L. Thompson, ed., *Cambridge Social History of Britain 1750–1950 – Social Agencies and Institutions* (Cambridge: Cambridge University Press, 1990), 239.

35 Immergut, *Health Politics*, 22–23.

36 See, for example, J.M. Winter, 'Infant Mortality, Maternal Mortality and Public Health in Britain in the 1930s', *Journal of Economic History*, 8 (1979), 439:462: '[...] the economic crisis of the 1930s was less disastrous to public health in Britain than previously has been supposed [...]. Because of public provision, medical intervention and long-term improvements in working class nutrition, the 1930s must be seen, therefore, despite the stubborn survival of

historians such as Charles Webster. Webster saw the inter-war period as a time of overriding depression and ill health for significant portions of the population for whom aggregate figures of reduced infant and, latterly, maternal mortality rates, masked the grave inequalities in the state of Britain's health.[37]

This book challenges Winter's optimistic view. The study of Scottish patterns in health statistics suggests that government and other welfare agencies dealt inadequately with the problems of ill health among mothers and infants, school children and the tuberculous (these subjects are discussed in chapters three, four and five). Winter himself acknowledged discrepancies in infant and maternal mortality rates between Scotland and the rest of the United Kingdom.[38] However, he quickly discarded the Scottish figures as not in keeping with the more healthy aggregate figures for the rest of Britain.

---

pockets of terrible deprivation, as a period of major improvement of the health of mothers and infants in Britain' (p. 462). See also Winter, 'Unemployment, Nutrition and Infant Mortality in Britain, 1920–1950', in Winter, ed., *The Working Classes in Modern British History* (Cambridge: Cambridge University Press, 1983), 232:256. In this later work, Winter toned down his optimistic view of the Depression years, noting that the effects of the 1930s depression may have had repercussions for the children and grand children of females born or reaching maturity in the 1930s. Winter, 'Unemployment, Nutrition and Infant Mortality in Britain', 245. For the views of other 'optimist' historians see: C.L. Mowat, *Britain between the Wars* (Methuen, 1968), D.H. Aldcroft, *The Inter-War Economy: Britain 1919–1939* (Batsford, 1970), and J. Stevenson, *Social Conditions in Britain between the Wars* (Harmondsworth: Penguin, 1980).

37 See for example, C. Webster, 'Healthy or Hungry Thirties?' *History Workshop Journal*, 13 (Spring 1982), 110:129. 'The fact of persistent morbidity raises the question of the degree of benefit derived by the lower social classes from the expansion of social welfare services during the inter-war period' (p. 125). Also see, Webster, 'Health, Welfare and Unemployment during the Depression', *Past and Present*, 109 (1985), 204:230. For other 'pessimistic' views see, S. Rowbotham, *Hidden from History – 300 Years of Women's Oppression and the Fight against it* (Pluto Press, 1973), and V. Berridge's useful summary of the optimist/pessimist debate in 'Health and Medicine' in Thompson, ed., *Cambridge Social History of Britain 1750–1950 – Social Agencies and Institutions*, 230–233.

38 Winter, 'Infant Mortality, Maternal Mortality and Public Health in Britain in the 1930s', 441 and 451.

However, Scotland's unique health problems for most of the twentieth century cannot simply be overlooked for the sake of convenience. The latter part of this introduction outlines some of the specific health issues Scotland faced in the first half of the twentieth century.

The findings of the pioneering DHS Morbidity Statistics Scheme published in the 1930s are considered in chapter six. The morbidity figures provide further cause for caution in following an 'optimistic' version of events. These statistics (of insured adult workers) suggest the positive impact of statutory health services on inter-war health trends is far from proved. The Morbidity Statistics Scheme findings reveal the extent of chronic sickness among the working population of Scotland. The figures include the health patterns of those people coming into maturity after the early twentieth-century expansion of personal health services. This group had (presumably) increasingly received the benefits of the growth in statutory health services providing care during birth, infancy and childhood, and in their working lives. The MSS findings suggest that increased statutory health provision made available since the first years of the twentieth century was by no means the safety net that Winter and other 'optimistic' historians suggest.

Investigations such as the Morbidity Statistics Scheme underline that health outcomes are as much a key element in this survey as are health policy formulation and the evolving structure of Scottish health administration. The implementation and tailoring of health directives at the local level are crucial. To help put the policy and administrative developments discussed in chapters one, two and seven in context, a number of case studies examine areas of the personal health services that greatly expanded in scope, public financing and state and local administration in the years between 1919 and 1948. Chapters are devoted to infant and maternal welfare, the health and feeding of the school child, the treatment of tuberculosis, and the health of the insured population. These case studies serve to illustrate the practical implications of Scottish health policy developments in this period.

This book critically examines the attitudes and activities of the SBH and DHS in two crucial respects. The impact of SBH/DHS policies on selected aspects of Scotland's health makes up the core of this book. However, the level of autonomy enjoyed by these two units of Scottish health administration is first examined. The relative powers of the SBH/DHS in negotiations with the Ministry of Health and the Treasury, their relationship with Scottish local authorities, and finally, their interaction with non-governmental agencies, including voluntary organisations and the organised medical profession, are outlined. This detailed examination is crucial, for without knowledge of the shifting administrative framework and policy developments, the effects of major social changes on the realm of Scotland's health in the years 1919–1948 would be of limited value.

Trends in Scottish Economy and Society 1919–1948

Between 1919–1948, Scotland housed around one-tenth of Britain's population (see table 1). Scotland covers one-third of Britain's land area. Although suffering from many of the same economic and social difficulties of the rest of Britain in the years 1919–1948, Scotland had some distinctive aspects. Since the early nineteenth century Scotland suffered from the unique combination of concentrated urbanisation and heavy industry with remote regions of scattered population. In the period 1919–1948 this gave Scotland the unenviable profile of deep-rooted poverty, severe housing difficulties, high unemployment levels and unenviable mortality and morbidity patterns.

Year	Scotland	England and Wales
1911	4.76	36.07
1921	4.88	37.89
1931	4.84	39.95
1941	no wartime census	no census
1951	5.10[39]	43.76[40]

Table 1 British Population Figures, 1911–1951 (in millions)

Almost half of Scotland's population lived in the central belt – in Glasgow or within 20 miles of it. The map of Scotland provided at the end of this book gives some indication of the population concentration around Glasgow.[41] Glasgow and its neighbouring towns in the 'coal belt' of Lanarkshire and Fife presented one problem of dense population in sub-standard housing. These industrial regions were over-reliant on the staple industries which were in decline and fell into depression for much of the period 1919–1948. By the end of World War One, west central Scotland contained double the average proportion of occupations in heavy industry. When depression struck in 1921 this area was hard hit. For example, employment in Clydeside shipbuilding fell from 60,000 to 18,000 in the three years between 1919 and 1921. Employment in this sector did not recover to pre-war levels until the mid 1930s. Similar falls in employment levels were in evidence in coal and steel production across west central Scotland. According to Foster, Scotland did not enjoy the temporary British economic revival of the late 1920s. It suffered again in the general depression of 1931–3. Furthermore, it was not in a position to enjoy the expansion of middle class purchasing power in the mid-1930s which encouraged consumer industries in the south of England.[42]

39 Figures obtained from C. Harvie, *No Gods and Precious Few Heroes: Scotland 1918–1980* (Edward Arnold, 1981), 66.

40 Figures for England and Wales taken from R.K. Kelsall, *Population* (Longman, 1967), 16.

41 See map of Scotland (Appendix 1) at the end of this book.

42 J. Foster, 'A Proletarian Nation? Occupation and Class since 1914' in T. Dickson and J. Treble eds, *People and Society in Scotland vol. 3, 1914–1990* (Edinburgh: John Donald, 1994), 223.

Employment Patterns

In Scotland in 1918, one in six male workers were miners, while one in four males was employed in some aspect of shipbuilding, engineering, iron and steel making and other metal trades. Almost one in four of all women were involved in some aspect of textile and clothing manufacture. These patterns were broadly the same throughout Britain. However, there were some sectional differences between Scotland the rest of Britain. For example, in 1921, there were more miners (8% compared to 6.6%), and more people employed in manufacturing (35% compared to 33.6%) in Scotland, than for Britain as a whole. Although the service sector was the largest employment grouping for both Scotland and Britain, the figure for Scotland was less than one in five, for Britain as a whole it was one in four of all those employed in 1921. Finally, Scotland still maintained a larger rural economy than Britain overall. Almost 12% of Scots were employed in agriculture in 1921, for Britain as a whole the figure was less than 9%.[43]

Unemployment

When economic depression affected Britain in the inter-war years it was the heavy industries which were hardest hit. Within the ranks of the inter-war unemployed, skilled adult male industrial workers predominated. At times, up to 30% of the available workforce in mining, steel, shipbuilding and most branches of engineering were unemployed for periods of two or three years at a time. Meanwhile, the large agricultural sector in Scotland also faced problems. Scottish rural areas (including smaller industrial centres such as the Borders' town of Dumfries) offered distinct problems of their own – rural

43 For complete figures see Foster, 'A Proletarian Nation? Occupation and Class since 1914', 203.

unemployment, poor living standards and little preventive medical care.[44]

Scotland's distinctive employment patterns (with higher than the British average levels of workers in heavy industry) meant that Scottish unemployment levels during the inter-war period were often worse than for Britain as a whole. Between 1923–30 Scottish unemployment averaged 14%, while the United Kingdom average was 11.4%. Between 1931–8 Scottish unemployment averaged 21.9% while the average for the whole of the UK was 16.4%.[45] National figures, although not the complete picture, allow for comparison of broad unemployment patterns across Britain. As table 2 illustrates, during the years 1923–1939, Scottish unemployment levels were higher than the British average rates. The Scottish unemployment figure was not the worst in Britain. Unemployment levels were consistently higher in Wales than Scotland after 1925. Figures for unemployment in Northern Ireland outstripped those for Scotland with the exception of the years 1931–34. Scotland's average unemployment rate was consistently higher than that of all six English regions over the seventeen-year period, 1923–1939. The exception to this was in England's most depressed region: the north east. In this region, unemployment levels exceeded the Scottish rate between 1926 and 1932 (this peak coincided with the General Strike, the longer-term coal dispute and its aftermath, and the worst of the depression years). In all other years, the Scottish average unemployment level was higher.

Table 2 shows that Scotland, as a whole did not suffer the highest unemployment figures within Britain in the inter-war years; however, unemployment was all too often combined with sub-standard social conditions.

---

44 Scottish Board of Health [SBH], *A Scheme of Medical Service for Scotland* (Edinburgh: HMSO, 1920), 9.

45 Harvie, *No Gods and Precious Few Heroes*, 47.

Year	Great Britain	Scotland	Wales	N. Ireland
1923	11.2	13.8	6.3	16.4
1924	9.9	13.3	9.0	15.5
1925	10.7	14.7	16.9	22.8
1926	11.9	15.8	18.2	21.1
1927	9.7	10.4	20.7	12.3
1928	10.8	11.6	23.2	16.3
1929	10.6	12.3	19.9	14.0
1930	16.3	18.7	26.7	22.6
1931	21.4	26.5	32.4	26.4
1932	22.1	28.2	36.8	25.7
1933	20.2	27.1	35.3	25.7
1934	17.2	24.5	33.5	21.2
1935	16.1	23.2	33.3	25.3
1936	13.6	20.2	31.8	23.2
1937	11.2	17.4	24.2	24.6
1938	13.3	17.9	26.6	30.5
1939	11.1	16.1	22.0	26.2

Table 2 British Unemployment Statistics (percentages), 1923–1939[46]

Housing

Scotland suffered badly in terms of poor and over-crowded housing in the first half of the twentieth century. The 1911 census revealed that 45% of the Scots population lived at least two to a room. Improvement in over-crowding was slow. In 1931, 35% of Scots still lived two to a room. The British average at the time was 10%. Scotland's largest city, Glasgow, had a particularly serious over-

46 Department of Employment and Productivity, *British Labour Statistics: Historical Abstracts, 1888–1968,* cited in B.R. Mitchell, *British Historical Statistics* (Cambridge: Cambridge University Press, 1988), 125–6.

crowding problem. Throughout the inter-war period over half of Glaswegians lived in one and two bedroom houses. In 1921, 63.3% of Glaswegians lived in one or two-roomed houses, by 1935 the figure had reduced only slightly, to 55%.[47] As late as 1951, more than half of all Glasgow households were in one and two-roomed houses. The Scottish figure was 31.7%. In England and Wales, there was a considerable variation in patterns of over-crowding. In 1931, Northumberland and Durham in the north east recorded figures of 20.2% of their populations living two to a room. The figure for South Wales was 5.3%, meanwhile in the South Eastern counties of England the figure was as low as 2.8%.[48] Sub-standard housing was not simply an urban Scottish phenomenon. Housing in rural Scotland was often of an inferior quality, such as the 'black houses' of the Islands (turf-walled and lacking windows and any form of ventilation). Poor and overcrowded housing had a serious impact on Scotland's poor health statistics in the first half of the twentieth century.

Morbidity and Mortality Trends

The problematic trends identified in the previous sections on employment, unemployment and housing provide a background to Scottish mortality and morbidity patterns. Comparison of crude death-rates across Britain over the twenty year period 1919–1938 shows the level in Scotland to have been consistently higher than that for England and Wales. More people in lower social classes in Scotland contributed to this sustained differential. As Tranter has noted, in the main it has been those people in higher social classes that benefited

47 Department of Health for Scotland [DHS], *Committee on Scottish Health Services Report* (Cathcart Report) [Cmd 5204], (Edinburgh: HMSO, 1936), 12.

48 M. Abrams, *The Condition of the British People 1911–1945* (Victor Gollancz, 1946), 45.

most from increases in life expectancy during the twentieth century.[49] The average death rate per 1,000 of the population over the period was 13.66 in Scotland and 12.19 for England and Wales. The Scottish average figure was never less than 0.9 greater than that for England and Wales during this twenty year period. The Scottish rate exceeded the England and Wales rate by 1.0 or more in every year between 1919–38, with the exception of 1930 and 1933.[50]

Scotland's average mortality figures in the period masked a pronounced urban/rural divide. The death-rate in Glasgow in 1920–2 was 25% above that of Scottish rural areas. Anderson has noted that the appalling social conditions experienced by much of the urban population led to wide variations in mortality between urban/rural specific occupations. For example, death-rates among iron and steel foundry labourers aged 25–44 in the 1920s were 52% above the average mortality rate for all Scottish males aged 25–44, meanwhile, mortality among fishermen in the same age range was only 1% above the average. Social class also had a dramatic impact on mortality. Scottish solicitor's death-rates were only 41% of the 1920s Scottish average and mortality among ministers and other clergymen were only 38% of the average.[51] Flinn used the existence of the urban/rural divide to illustrate the high differential hidden behind Scotland's average figures for infant mortality. The quinquennial Scottish Infant Mortality Rate (IMR) for the years 1934–8 was 77 per 1,000 live births. However, local rates varied enormously, from figures of 99 for Glasgow down to 39 for the county of Zetland (Shetland). Almost all Scottish towns had figures above the national level, and all counties

---

49 N.L. Tranter, *British Population in the Twentieth Century* (Basingstoke: Macmillan, 1996), 70.

50 Figures derived from *Annual Reports of the Register General for England and Wales and for Scotland, 1919–1938*, cited in B.R. Mitchell and P. Deane, *Abstract of British Historical Statistics* (Cambridge: Cambridge University Press, 1971), 37.

51 M. Anderson, 'Population and Family Life' in T. Dickson and J. Treble, eds, *People and Society in Scotland vol. 3, 1914–1990* (Edinburgh: John Donald, 1994), 20.

came below the Scottish national average.[52] There were of course, some exceptions to this identifiable urban/rural divide. Some rural counties (ranging from the Highland county of Nairn to Wigtown in the Borders) suffered mortality rates over 50% higher than other rural areas.[53] Some heavy industrial towns, including Falkirk, had an infant mortality rate two-thirds that of the Glasgow rate.[54] Yet, overall, urbanisation had a deleterious effect on IMR. In the 1920s, the chances that a child which had survived to age six months would die in the next six months was twice as high in towns with populations over 20,000 than in towns with a population of under 5,000.[55]

Closer examination of infant mortality rates in the years between 1919–1948 provides further evidence that Scottish mortality figures were worse than for the rest of Britain. Flinn noted that in the late 1890s IMR in England and Wales was 21.5% higher than in Scotland. Infant mortality rates in Scotland and England and Wales were similar in 1918. The Scottish rate of 99.8 deaths per 1,000 live births was almost matched by the level for England and Wales at 97.9. Yet, by 1931, the Scottish rate was 25.9% higher than the English rate. From 1919 onwards, although overall national death rates were reducing, the gap between Scotland and England and Wales increased. In 1928 the Scottish rate had fallen to 85.7, while the rate for England and Wales was down to 65.1. In 1938, the discrepancy had widened, the Scottish figures stood at 69.5, while the figure for England and Wales was 52.7. Finally, in 1948, the Scottish IMR fell to 44.7, meanwhile the rate for England and Wales was 34.5.

Improvements in living standards elsewhere in Britain may have played a part in throwing up this discrepancy. For example, IMR from diarrhoea and enteritis fell between 1906–10 and 1936–8 from 13.1 to 9.8 in Scotland, whereas the rates for England and Wales fell from a higher rate, (17.8) to one below the Scottish level (5.1) over the same

---

52 M. Flinn, ed., *Scottish Population History from the Seventeenth Century to the 1930s* (Cambridge: Cambridge University Press, 1977), 386.

53 See map of Scotland – Appendix 1 – for locations of places named here and throughout this book.

54 Flinn, *Population History*, 387.

55 Anderson, 'Population and Family Life', 19.

period.[56] Although falling more slowly than England and Wales, the Scottish IMR declined. This was due to a number of causes: mortality from infectious diseases was halved (chiefly due to a reduction in infant deaths from measles, whooping cough and tuberculosis), deaths due to gastro-intestinal causes fell by a fifth, and deaths from respiratory diseases fell by one-eighth.

Scottish maternal mortality rates per 1,000 live births also outstripped comparative rates for England and Wales throughout the period 1919–1948. While such aggregate figures give a general idea of national trends in mortality levels, they do not give the full picture. More detailed figures on infant and maternal mortality levels can be found in chapter three.

Tuberculosis mortality from all causes was higher in Scotland than in England and Wales. In Scotland, rural as well as urban tuberculosis mortality from the disease was a concern. A high rural incidence of the disease was a long-term feature of Scotland's tuberculosis mortality and remained an issue of obvious concern to the Highlands and Islands medical services. Scottish arrangements for tackling the scourge of tuberculosis are discussed in chapter five.

Deaths from respiratory disease remained consistently high in Scotland. Here again there was a higher incidence in urban areas. The crude Scottish death rate for bronchitis and pneumonia in the 1930s was 13%, in Scotland's large towns and cities it was 15%.[57] As the population aged in the course of the twentieth century, diseases of the heart and circulatory system increased, as did the incidence of cancer. By the 1930s, deaths from the former accounted for 22.3% of all mortality in Scotland, meanwhile cancer accounted for 11.8% of all deaths.

The figures here provided act merely as a taster for the far more detailed analysis of health patterns which follow in the central section of this book. These figures demonstrate that throughout the period 1919–1948, across a broad range of causes Scotland's morbidity and mortality patterns were considerably worse than for the rest of Britain.

56 Flinn, *Scottish Population History*, 416.
57 Ibid., 415.

Conclusion

The figures and trends outlined with regard to employment types, unemployment rates, housing difficulties and health trends have shown that Scotland possessed a combination of some of the worst economic and social problems of any part of the British Isles between 1919–1948. Only a small selection of health statistics has been mentioned in this section to help provide a broader context for what follows. Chapters three and four provide detailed discussions on the health of Scotland's babies, mothers and school children. Chapters five and six examine aspects of the health of the adult population.

Scotland's social and economic problems, while severe, were not much different in kind from those of other deprived parts of Great Britain and Northern Ireland. However, the way in which Scottish health problems were addressed was, to a large extent, independent of London. Before attention is turned to specific aspects of Scotland's health, the development of Scottish health policy between 1919–1948 is first considered.

1: The Scottish Board of Health, 1919–1928

> The present condition of the medical service of Scotland is absolutely chaotic. It is best illustrated by the well-known case of the Scottish family. The husband and father was an insured person and his medical necessities were attended to by the Insurance Commissioners. The wife was an ordinary patient of the medical man. The children were inspected and attended to by the medical officer under the control of the Education Department. The grandfather and grandmother also lived in the house. One of them was an old-age pensioner, whose medical man was the parish officer under the control of the parish council; the other was a pauper lunatic who was under the control of the Board of Control; and last of all, one of the children was suffering from a notifiable disease, and his medical man was the Medical Officer of Health for the district. Any system which permits a condition of affairs of that kind is indeed in need of reform.
> (Lord Forteviot, Second Reading of the Scottish Board of Health Bill, House of Lords debates, Vol. 34, 6 May 1919, col. 471)

Introduction

The path towards the creation of the Scottish Board of Health in 1919 was protracted. The system of Board administration in Scottish affairs was developed in the eighteenth century with the formation of the Board of Manufactures set up to facilitate the Scottish fishery and textile industries. This model was incorporated over decades into various other Boards. One such example, the Edinburgh-based Board of Supervision for the Relief of the Poor in Scotland, established in 1845, was a forerunner of the Scottish Board of Health in relation to its health care provision. Paterson has underlined the importance of the Board model for giving Scotland's nascent welfare services a distinct, native identity.[1] The Board of Supervision touched on many aspects of Scottish social administration with responsibility for destitution and public health. It was absorbed by the Local Government Board for Scotland (LGBS) in 1894. The LGBS was joined in Scottish health administration by the Scottish Insurance Commissioners (1911), and the Highlands and Islands (Medical Services) Board (1913). The Scottish Board of Health, formed in 1919, became the umbrella unit for all these components of Scottish social health administration.[2] Administering the Scottish Boards was the Secretary for Scotland.[3]

The Scottish Board System

The SBH was formed in 1919 in the style of the old Board of Education for Scotland, other Scottish Boards then in existence were Fishery, Agriculture and Prisons. The Board of Health was invested with the powers of the Local Government Board, the Scottish Insurance Commissioners and the Highlands and Islands (Medical Services) Board. It gained Privy Council powers under the Midwives Act, the Secretary for Scotland's powers under the Burial, Alkali, and

---

1 'The national and local boards which oversaw the poor law after 1845 provided such a successful model that it was repeatedly copied, either by giving more and more powers to these boards themselves, or by creating new ones on similar lines. Thus new, intermediate institutions between the people and the state were all thoroughly Scottish.' Paterson, *The Autonomy of Modern Scotland*, 52.

2 Responsibility for the industrial health service (factory inspectorate) remained with the Home Office and Mines Department of the Board of Trade.

3 The office was re-created in 1885 (for the first time since 1746). Until 1892 the Scottish Secretary remained outside the Cabinet. 'Inevitably, Secretaries for Scotland were judged in Scotland on the basis of their accessibility to dignitaries, their willingness to promote petty legislation, their distribution of patronage, and their manners.' H.J. Hanham, 'The Development of the Scottish Office' in J.N. Wolfe, ed., *Government and Nationalism in Scotland* (Edinburgh: Edinburgh University Press, 1969), 51.

Rivers and Pollution Acts, Births, Marriages and Deaths registration. It also assumed the powers and duties of the Scottish Education Department with regard to the medical inspection and treatment of children and young persons. This final power was not included in the original Bill. The Scottish Secretary, Robert Munro[4] was reluctant to disturb the unity of the Education Department which had been achieved only in 1918 in the Education (Scotland) Act. However, pressure from Scottish MPs of all parties ensured that the Scottish Board of Health Act encompassed school health services. Scottish MP's were not so successful in their attempts to invest the Board with authority over Scottish lunacy and mental health legislation, or with the Ministry of Pensions provisions for disabled servicemen. However, the SBH did possess the authority to assume the powers of these and any other departments that affected the health of the Scottish people.

When it was created, the Scottish Board of Health showed strong continuities with the older board system.[5] This is demonstrated by the membership of the Scottish Board of Health. Members of the new board were appointed in much the same way as to the now defunct Scottish Local Government Board – in fact, most of the personnel remained unchanged. The six-member Scottish Board of Health included two former members of the LGBS, and two former members of the National Health Insurance Commission. There was clear continuity too, at civil service level. The former respective Secretaries of the Local Government Board for Scotland, (John T. Maxwell) and

---

4 Robert Munro, Coalition Liberal MP for Roxburgh 1918–1922, previously Liberal MP for Wick Burghs 1910–1918. Munro served as Scottish Secretary from 1916–1922. In 1922, he was elevated to the Lords as Lord Alness. He served as Lord Justice Clerk 1922–1923. Later, he was Chairman of the Select Committee of the House of Lords on the Prevention of Road Accidents and was a member of the Executive Committee of the Child Guidance Council and the National Council for Mental Hygiene.

5 'The typical Scottish office in Edinburgh was headed by a board appointed entirely by patronage from among Scots who had shown some administrative ability and who had influential connections, whether social or political'. Hanham, 'Development of the Scottish Office', 56.

the Scottish Insurance Commission (John Jeffrey)[6] were appointed as Joint Secretaries to the Scottish Board of Health.[7] The appointment of John Jeffrey as Joint Secretary was the beginning of a long association with the SBH and later the Department of Health for Scotland. Jeffrey went on to play an important role in Scottish health policy formulation. For example, on several occasions in the 1920s and 30s he used his previous insurance expertise to great effect in shaping the distinctive Scottish approach to National Health Insurance matters.[8]

All the officials of the Highlands and Islands (Medical Services) Board (HIMSB) retained their posts on the merging of the service with the new Board.[9] In August 1919, Sir James Dodds, Permanent Secretary of the Scottish Office welcomed Lewis McQuibban,[10] the Secretary of the HIMSB into the Scottish Board of Health. Dodds was sanguine that the change in nomenclature would not result in

---

6 John Jeffrey was born in 1871. He was appointed to the clerical staff of the Board of Control in 1892. In 1894 he was transferred to the newly created Local Government Board for Scotland. He became Secretary of the Scottish Insurance Commissioners on the creation of this office in 1911. In 1919 he became Secretary of the SBH, continuing as Secretary of the DHS after its formation in 1929, until his promotion to Permanent Under-Secretary of State in 1933. He was awarded the CBE in 1929 and Knighted in 1934. Jeffrey retired in 1937. He died on 19 July 1947.

7 NAS, HH1/467 Sub-file 13, Memorandum by President of the Scottish Board of Health, Robert Munro, 1 August 1919 on SBH personnel.

8 Health Insurance is discussed in detail in chapter six.

9 The Highlands and Islands Medical Service personnel were transferred to the new Board: 'So far as I can see at the moment there is no objection to a simple and wholesale transfer to the Scottish Board of Health, but I would like to go into the matter carefully over the week-end from the point of view of our agreements with, and obligations to, medical men, hospitals, etc.' NAS, HH1/467 Sub file 11, Lewis McQuibban to Sir James Dodds, Permanent Secretary, Scottish Office, 12 July 1919. See also NAS HH75, SBH minutes, 5 September 1919.

10 Lewis McQuibban had formerly been Head of the Secondary Schools Branch of the Scottish Education Department, before taking up his post at the Highlands and Island Medical Services Board in 1913. Between 1919–1921 he served as Assistant Secretary to the Scottish Board of Health. He was Permanent Secretary at the Ministry of Education in Northern Ireland from 1921–1927. He was also Civil Service Commissioner for Northern Ireland in 1927, the year of his retirement.

redundancies in the HIMSB: 'I hope you will be comfortable in your new post, and I have no doubt that the Board will make suitable provision for yourself and other members of the Medical Service Board's staff.'[11] Jobs were also found or created for those who could not simply transfer their duties to the new Board.[12]

This 'jobs for the boys' approach was not necessarily a negative manoeuvre. The Highlands and Islands Medical Service was an agency well worth preserving. The HIMS was a distinctive and uniquely Scottish entity. It was a statutory medical service established in 1913 (although not fully operational till after World War One) to provide medical care for those in remote Highland regions of Scotland. Many people in these regions had often lacked the medical services of general practitioners, nurses, consultants and clinic facilities due to the remote nature of their environment. The continuation of the Highlands and Islands Medical Service was a boon to those served by it. Moreover, its preservation ensured that the SBH had distinct concerns of its own aside those shared with the Ministry of Health. The HIMS is discussed in more detail in the following chapter.

In the most extreme cases, the Scottish Board of Health (SBH) centralised the haphazard administration of Scottish family health care, as noted by Lord Forteviot,[13] in the quotation at the head of this chapter. Although the creation of a Board to administer Scottish health

---

11 NAS, HH1/467 Sub-file II, Sir James Dodds, Scottish Office, to L. McQuibban HIMSB, 27 August 1919.

12 'Sir George McCrae and Sir James Leishman, who had been authorised by the Board to interview Miss Mary M. Patterson, formerly one of the National Insurance Commissioners, with a view to seeing what post could be offered her under the Board of Health, made verbal reports of their interviews with Miss Paterson and of their investigations of possible suitable offices under the Board.' NAS, HH1/467, Special Minute of the SBH, 15 August 1919.

13 Lord Forteviot (Sir John Alexander Dewar) had been Radical MP for Inverness-shire between 1900–1916. He was Chairman of Whisky firm, John Dewar and Sons, and a former Lord Provost of Perth. In 1912, Dewar chaired the Highlands and Islands Medical Service Committee to the Treasury [Cd 6559]. The Dewar Report recommendations led to the formation of the Highlands and Islands Medical Services Board in 1913. Dewar was appointed to chair the newly created Board.

gave it a separate legal identity aside from the Scottish Office,[14] the Board system itself was criticised because at senior administrative levels it was staffed by outside experts and not by experienced civil servants. In 1914, the existing Scottish Boards came under the scrutiny of the Royal Commission on the Civil Service chaired by Lord MacDonnell.[15] The Edinburgh-system as practised in the Local Government, Fishery, Prison and Agriculture Boards was attacked. The Scottish Boards remained something of an anachronism, when compared to the Whitehall Boards of Education, Local Government, Agriculture and Fisheries, Trade and Works. These boards were described as: '[...] orthodox government ministries in all but name.'[16]

The Board system allowed the Scottish Secretary a certain amount of patronage. If the new health administration had been created as a statutory Department it would have been made more accountable to Whitehall with senior posts filled by career civil servants. The argument in defence of the Board system was that the Scottish Secretary had a much wider remit than his Westminster ministerial counterparts.[17] Moreover, he was based in London 400 miles away from the activities of the Boards. The Scottish Secretary needed the advice of local experts (for example, there were four sea fishing experts on the Fishery Board). To do otherwise and employ permanent officials would be to subjugate Scottish Board activities to

14 G.A. Pottinger, *The Secretaries of State For Scotland 1926–1976: Fifty Years of the Scottish Office* (Edinburgh: Scottish Academic Press, 1979), 15.

15 The MacDonnell Commission also noted political patronage in appointments to both the Welsh and Scottish Health Insurance Commissions set up in 1911, with Lloyd George nominees prominent. See R.K. Kelsall, *Higher Civil Servants in Britain* (Routledge and Kegan Paul, 1955), 108.

16 J.S. Gibson, *The Thistle and the Crown: A History of the Scottish Office* (Edinburgh: HMSO, 1985), 47.

17 In an inaugural address to the Philosophical Institution of Edinburgh, Scottish Secretary Robert Munro described the 'scope and variety of the subjects that fall within the ken of the Scottish Office' and commented that 'he has to live from day to day, to attend Cabinets, to think of Upper Silesia as well as, let us say, Auchtermuchty.' R. Munro, *Looking Back: Fugitive Writings and Sayings* (Edinburgh: Nelson and Son, 1930), 282.

Whitehall interests.[18] For such reasons, it was not until 1928 that the patronage-appointed members of the SBH were finally replaced by a Departmental civil service structure.

The Development of Local Authority Health Administration before 1918

Health administration differed between England and Scotland because of various long-term cultural and legal differences. In both, the position by the beginning of the twentieth century was set by legislation passed in the late nineteenth century. This legislation was related to the medical policing of the urban and rural poor and was designed to protect the interests of other classes in society. Health administration in the period prior to 1900 was controlled by local authority-provided preventive public health measures, directed mainly at tackling infectious diseases. These measures were funded by local taxation and exchequer grants. Meanwhile, Scots poor law authorities provided personal maintenance payments and medical care, in turn funded by parochial levies, bequests and exchequer grants. In addition, there were independent voluntary hospitals which catered for the 'deserving poor' (the 'respectable' working class). The Scottish Royal Infirmaries were free to patients on production of a subscriber's line, in fact, the Royal Infirmary of Edinburgh was bound by its charter not to raise charges from patients. The voluntary infirmaries were funded by private subscriptions. Voluntary hospital funding increasingly incorporated employer and employee donations, as well as endowments and bequests.

---

18 'Administration in Scotland was very largely left to take care of itself [...]. Day-to-day business was left to the Scottish boards in Edinburgh, old and new, each of which functioned as a separate administrative unit, subject to frequent consultation with the Scottish Office in Whitehall.' Hanham, 'The Development of the Scottish Office', 52.

Public health in England became more centralised after 1875, when the Public Health Act created the Local Government Board. In Scotland, the process began after the office of Secretary for Scotland was re-created in 1885 and Scottish health responsibility gradually came under its remit. The Local Government Acts in 1888 and 1889, for England and Wales and Scotland respectively, created County Councils for rural areas. Responsibility for their public health administration later came under the remit of the Local Government Boards (LGB). The Local Government Board for Scotland was instituted in 1894, replacing the Board of Supervision for the Relief of the Poor (established 1845) as the central body for county and district council local health authorities. Large towns, cities and burghs, retained their monopoly of public health administration with local Improvement Acts, but were subject to the central authority of the Local Government Boards via the Home Secretaries for England and Wales, or the Secretary for Scotland. Voluntary hospitals retained their independence through private subscriptions.

By the first years of the twentieth century, there was substantial growth in the environmental and personal services provided by local authority public health departments. This came about through a number of biomedical discoveries related to tuberculosis and typhus, which enhanced the possibilities of medical treatment for such diseases and increased emphasis on the improvement of health by the treatment of individuals. In addition, there was a growing state and public perception of a serious level of ill health among the population. Coming together at the beginning of the twentieth century these developments brought about a new tendency towards a 'curative' approach to health care, replacing the earlier environmental, preventive methods.

Defeats at the hands of the Boers in the South African wars between 1899–1902 when coupled with the discovery that 3 in 5 men who volunteered for army service were declared unfit for duty either at point of entry or within two years of service, led to a questioning of the standards of health in the nation. Major General Sir J. Frederick Maurice (official historian of the South African Wars) made his views clear in two articles for the *Contemporary Review* published in 1902 and 1903. The first was 'Where to get Men' which sketched the difficulties of finding suitable recruits. The second article, 'National Health: A Soldier's Study' identified problems in upbringing as the chief factor dictating the poor health of young adult males who made up the recruits to the British Army.[19]

Two official enquiries followed in the wake of Maurice's revelations. In 1903, the Royal Commission on Physical Training (Scotland) stated that an improvement was needed in the feeding and environment of Scotland's children. These areas had to be addressed or no benefits would come from the proposed introduction of gymnastics in schools. It was believed that the physical education of school children would improve the health prospects of future generations.

> We consider that the question of the proper and sufficient feeding of children is one which has the closest possible connection with any scheme which may be adopted for their physical, and equally for their mental work. It is evident that among the causes which tell against the physical welfare of the population, the lack of proper nourishment is one of the most serious.[20]

The subsequent national Inter-Departmental Committee on Physical Deterioration of 1904 was informed by the findings of the 1903 Scottish Commission. The Inter-Departmental Committee had a much wider remit, which included investigations into infant and maternal welfare. Among its recommendations were that meals be provided for school children and that legislation on registering births should be extended to make such action compulsory in order to monitor the birth and infant mortality rates country wide. The Liberal

19 'Whatever the primary cause of the condition of things to which I have drawn attention, we are always brought back to the fact that, whether for the virility of the nation in civil life or for the supply of an adequate body of recruits to the Army, we have to remember that the young man of 16 to 18 years of age is what he is because of the training through which he has passed during his infancy and childhood [...]. Therefore it is to the condition, mental, moral and physical, of the women and children that we must look if we have regard to the future of our land', Major General Sir John Frederick Maurice, 'National Health: A Soldier's Study', *Contemporary Review*, 83 (1903), 50.

20 LGBS, *Report of the Royal Commission on Physical Training (Scotland)* (HMSO: Edinburgh, 1903), [Cmd 1507], 29.

Government implemented both these measures within a few years of their victory in the December 1905 election.[21]

The poor state of national health identified in the early years of the twentieth century was also evident in 1909, in the report of the Royal Commission on the Poor Law.[22] The National Insurance Act followed in 1911 by the Liberals, piloted through by Chancellor of the Exchequer, Lloyd George. The Act created a new tier of administration in the form of local insurance committees to provide manual and non-manual workers earning less than £160 with medical care and maintenance during periods of sickness. The scheme did not cover dependants. The range of medical care was limited to diagnosis and treatment within the scope of general practitioner services. An anti-tuberculosis campaign was initiated under the Act, but dental and optical treatments were excluded. The scheme of National Health Insurance covered around a third of the whole population, those men, women and children in employment in designated 'insured' occupations. The medical services provided under the scheme excluded specialist and consultant services and institutional care for workers. The Insurance Act was amended in 1914 when parliament voted to extend the legislation to include outpatient and consultant care, but the war prevented the implementation of such action.[23]

The Edwardian era witnessed a growth in demands for Home Rule in Scotland among radical Liberals in order to tackle the twin evils of rural decline and urban squalor. Radical Liberals believed that Scotland's particular problems required devolved intervention if national regeneration was to be achieved.[24] An alteration came in 1914, when the LGBS assumed control over new services such as state-subsidised housing, food regulation, notification of births,

---

21 Key areas of personal health first discussed in the Edwardian era, namely, the health of the school child, tuberculosis treatment, and infant and maternal welfare are individually dealt with in later chapters of this book.

22 *Royal Commission on the Poor Laws and the Relief of Distress* (HMSO, 1909) [Cmd 4499].

23 For more details on the scheme of national health insurance in Scotland see chapter six.

24 For more on the Home Rule issue, see I.G.C. Hutchison, *Scottish Politics in the Twentieth Century* (Basingstoke: Palgrave, 2001), 7.

certification of midwives, care of the tuberculous, venereal disease and child welfare provisions. By such measures administrative health concerns widened, but there was no increase in state or local agencies to cope with these new concerns.

The outbreak of war affected the nascent personal health services and the development of suitable administrative machinery to administer them. Some services, including the recently established school medical service and the Highlands and Islands Medical Service were greatly curtailed by the war. The wartime situation also led to a re-evaluation of government administration. In 1917, a Ministry of Reconstruction was formed to reorganise central government. Also in 1917, Viscount Haldane[25] conducted a review of government departments for the Ministry of Reconstruction. In 1918, the Report of the Machinery of Government Committee[26] recommended the creation of Ministry of Health for England and Wales. The new ministry was to take over the functions of the LGB and the National Health Insurance Commission, and the health remit of other government departments. The process of centralising health policy benefited from a fresh attitude prompted by wartime experience.

---

25 Richard Burdon Haldane was in 1918 a member of the Judicial Committee of the Privy Council. He had been Secretary of State for War 1905–1912, then Lord Chancellor 1912–15. He served as Liberal MP for Haddingtonshire between 1885 and 1911, before his elevation to the Lords as First Viscount of Cloan. He left the Government in 1915 and his political allegiance moved towards Labour. He served as Lord Chancellor in the first Labour Government in 1924.

26 *Report of the Machinery of Government Committee*, [Haldane Report], (HMSO, 1918), [Cmd. 9320].

The Ministry of Health for England and Wales and the Scottish Board of Health

Although first mooted in early 1917, the creation of the Ministry of Health was delayed (partly due to the wartime situation) until 3 June 1919. The reasons for founding a Ministry of Health are generally well documented by Gilbert, Honigsbaum and others in studies dealing with the origins of the National Health Service.[27] Also created on 3 June 1919, by a separate Act of Parliament, was the Scottish Board of Health. The justifications for establishing a separate Scottish Board of Health are generally overlooked in most studies of the 'British' health services.[28]

Dr. Christopher Addison was the first Minister of Health and Sir Robert Morant, the first Permanent Secretary. Addison had been the first wartime of Minister of Reconstruction, Morant a member of the Haldane Committee and chairman of the English National Health Insurance Commission. It was Addison who piloted the Ministry of Health Bill through the Commons. Addison championed proposals for a Ministry of Health from the beginning of 1917. He supported a Cabinet memorandum on the subject by Lord Rhondda, and in a letter to Prime Minister Lloyd George in April 1917 he made an early plea to allow Scotland its own Ministry.

> As Sir George McCrae [Chairman of the LGBS] is becoming Chief Whip, we could now include Scotland in the Bill and let Leishman [Scottish National Health Insurance Commissioner] be Vice-Chairman of the Scottish Ministry of

---

27 See for example, B.B. Gilbert, *British Social Policy 1914–1939* (Batsford, 1970), F. Honigsbaum, *The Struggle for the Ministry of Health, 1914–1919* (Bell, 1970), and his, *The Division In British Medicine* (Kogan Page, 1979), and *Health, Happiness and Security: The Creation of the National Health Service* (Routledge, 1989), and also M. Bruce, *The Coming of the Welfare State* (Batsford, 1968).

28 This point has been addressed in the introduction to this book, which includes a brief review of associated secondary literature.

Health and Local Government Board and responsible to the Secretary for Scotland.[29]

The failure of the Rhondda proposals for a Ministry of Health in 1917 made Addison reluctant to propose a wide ranging Bill himself in 1918. The first draft of Addison's Bill, for a Ministry of Health and Local Government, dealt exclusively to England and Wales. Scotland was mentioned only in the context of the National Health Insurance Scheme. In the draft Bill, circulated to ministers at the end of February 1918, Addison planned to reform and centralise the Joint National Insurance Commissioners Committee which served the four sets of Commissioners for England, Wales, Scotland and Ireland. Under these proposals, the authority of the Scottish Insurance Commissioners was to be transferred to the Secretary for Scotland, Robert Munro, who would be a member of the new committee. Similar arrangements were planned for Ireland with the Chief Secretary for Ireland as member of the reformed Joint Committee.

Scottish Secretary Robert Munro was brought into discussions regarding the Scottish insurance commissioners on 27 February 1918, when Addison sent him a copy of the draft Health Bill.[30] Munro objected to the Bill. Munro wanted the Ministry of Health Bill extended to include Scotland in a more positive sense:

> Upon consideration of the draft Bill, however, I am disposed to take the view that it does not go far enough in the direction of unification of administration in Scotland. There is a strong demand across the border that the present opportunity should be taken to amalgamate departments responsible for public health and for Insurance. You are doing this in England, and I see great advantages in following your example in the same Bill so as to get the benefit of the same pressure of public opinion.[31]

---

29 Bodleian Library, Oxford, Department of Western Manuscripts, Addison Papers, Box 54, Item 647 – private letter from Addison to Lloyd George, April 2 1917.

30 PRO, MH78/70, Memorandum from Addison to Munro, 27 February 1918.

31 PRO, MH78/70, Letter from Munro to Addison, 16 March 1918. (Munro sent Addison two letters on 16 March. This extract and subsequent ones come from the second, longer letter of that date).

Munro put forward an amending clause including Scotland in the Ministry of Health and Local Government Bill. He envisaged a Scottish Board of Health, the nucleus comprised of the existing members of the Scottish Local Government Board and the Scottish Insurance Commissioners.[32]

However, Addison's fear was that wrangling over Scottish and Irish health and local government reforms would harm the progress of the proposals for England and Wales. The 1917 Ministry of Health Bill had been defeated, and since a centralist policy was crucial to his plans, he was preoccupied by the spectre of another failed Health Bill. He feared concerted local authority opposition to relinquishing their powers to a new Ministry of Health might scupper his proposals. Addison saw difficulties ahead if there was a united front against the latest proposals for a Ministry of Health. Consequently, Addison restricted his plan for a new Ministry of Health to England and Wales and disregarded Munro's suggestions.[33]

In the War Cabinet, Addison formally disassociated himself from Munro's new proposals for Scotland. Addison commented:

> The Secretary for Scotland, while not objecting in principle to the proposals as to Scotland in Clause 3,[34] is submitting an alternative proposal for amalgamating the Scottish Local Government Board with the Scottish Insurance Commission, and appointing a Parliamentary Under Secretary to the Scottish Office. This proposal seems to me to involve a constitutional change which is not essential to the main purpose of the Bill, and I should prefer to leave the clause as it stands.[35]

---

32 Ibid.

33 Addison's exclusion of Scotland from the Bill was also based the possible federal and constitutional complications. The formation of separate Ministries of Health for Scotland and Ireland might have added impetus to the rise of nationalism in all the three other nations of the Union. Addison's view was that: '[...] a strong section of Scottish opinion will be directed towards making this Bill the occasion for effecting a constitutional change in the Government of Scotland [...].' PRO, MH78/70, Letter from Addison to Munro, 19 March 1918.

34 Clause 3 of the Bill dealt with the amended position of the Scottish and Irish Insurance Commissioners under a Ministry of Health.

35 PRO, Cab24/49, Memorandum to the War Cabinet by the Minister of Reconstruction [Addison] on the Ministry of Health Bill, April 1918 [no day].

Whilst Munro agreed with the arrangements for the existing insurance commissioners to join those of the Local Government Board under his authority as Secretary for Scotland, he thought the Bill dealt only with Scotland from an English stand-point. Munro felt that the Addison plan did the minimum that was necessary as a result of the new proposals to abolish the Joint Insurance Commission to make way for the new Ministry of Health. His view, clearly stated, was that:

> The Bill should go further, and do for Scotland what it does for England [...] The demand for such a Ministry which is made in England is paralleled in Scotland, and I cannot afford to overlook the difficulties that would arise if the situation were dealt with in England and left as it stands across the border [...] I should find it very difficult to meet Parliamentary and other Scottish criticism taking its stand upon that argument.[36]

No decision was taken on the Health Bill until July 1918 at a specially-convened meeting of the newly-constituted Home Affairs Committee of the War Cabinet. Munro made a presentation to the Committee stressing the support in Scotland for a Health Bill and the need for a Parliamentary Under Secretary (PUS) to aid the Scottish Secretary with the increased workload health administration would place on him. Munro did not himself wish the PUS to deal exclusively with Scottish health, but to cover other areas, such as agriculture, fisheries and prisons, which came under the auspices of the Scottish Office.[37] Munro also requested that the office of Scottish Secretary be raised to an office of state. His plea for superior status was not granted, but that for parliamentary assistance was, although not with the wide-ranging remit Munro desired.[38]

---

36 PRO, Cab24/51, 'Ministry of Health' – Note by the Secretary for Scotland on the Draft Bill, presented to the War Cabinet, 14 May 1918.

37 PRO, Cab24/51, Note by the Secretary for Scotland on the Draft Bill and Memorandum circulated by the Minister of Reconstruction, 14 May 1918,

38 'The Committee approved the Scottish application clause as drafted by the Secretary for Scotland, with the exception of the clause proposing to raise the status of the Secretary for Scotland, which it was thought should form the subject of a separate Bill.' PRO, CAB 26/1, 'Ministry of Health Bill', Home Affairs Committee, 3rd Meeting, 18 July 1918.

One reason why the Cabinet agreed to Munro's proposal and ignored the recommendations of Addison, the originator of the Bill, was the public pressure in support of a distinct Scottish health agency. Representations from outside organisations in support of the Bill influenced the Cabinet Committee's viewpoint.

> In Scotland, the volume of opinion in favour of the Bill was very strong, and important deputations from local authorities and labour organisations were unanimous in pressing upon the Secretary for Scotland the urgency of the matter.[39]

The Royal Faculty of Physicians and Surgeons of Glasgow (RFPSG) for example, threw its collective medical professional weight behind a separate health board for Scotland, in order to conserve the 'autonomy of the several parts of the United Kingdom'.[40] This successful pressure by outside agencies clearly fits the model of the 'autonomy of the democratic state' referred to in the introduction of this study, where outside views influence government in areas where there is no defined policy in place. The minutes of Cabinet Home Affairs Committee, a week before the final decision on the format of the Ministry of Health Bill, recorded:

> With reference to the parliamentary prospects of the Bill, it was suggested that it would be impossible to avoid discussion in the House of Commons of a number of highly controversial issues which were, directly or indirectly, involved in the Bill, *but on which the Government had not made any declaration of policy* [sic]. Before introducing the Bill it was, therefore, desirable that these points should be examined in detail, and the draft amended if necessary in the light of the conclusions reached by the Committee [...][41]

Despite Addison's initial unwillingness to involve himself in potential political wrangling over an expanded Health Bill in July

---

39 Ibid.

40 The Royal Faculty of Physicians and Surgeons of Glasgow (RFPSG) was later renamed the Royal College of Physicians and Surgeons in 1962. Minute book references are abbreviated as RCPSG. Royal College of Physicians and Surgeons of Glasgow, RCPSG 1/1/1/14, minutes of meeting, 4 March 1918.

41 PRO, CAB 26/1, Ministry of Health Bill, Home Affairs Committee, 1st meeting, 9 July 1918.

1918, a diary entry from 17 September 1918 revealed the confidence Addison had by this time developed in the ultimate success of a joint Bill:

> Good progress has been made in the later stages of the Ministry of Health Bill [...]. There appears now to be no difficulty ahead in Scotland. The Bill, therefore, as it stands, has been referred to the War Cabinet. Cave[42] and I are to deal with drafting points and Munro and I with Scottish points [...].[43]

However, the introduction of the Ministry of Health Bill had to await the next session of parliament in February 1919.

'Federalism' and the Scottish Board of Health

The coalition government elected in the post-war 'coupon' election had many major tasks to face, the immediate concern was the peace settlement with Germany and its allies, later the difficult economic situation greatly affected the post-war drive towards 'reconstruction.' Meanwhile, the issue of political devolution was also a live one. Since 1894 the Liberal Party had been committed to 'Home-Rule-All-Round' for all four countries in the United Kingdom. Home Rule for Scotland had been re-stated as official Liberal policy by Prime Minister Asquith in 1910, although its passage seemed less likely in the wake of the split in the Party during World War One. There was also an established Home Rule movement in Scotland, parallel to that of Ireland. In fact, two private members' Scottish Home Rule Bills were laid before parliament in 1920 and 1924.

The Home Rule issue was raised during the 1918 debates on the creation of the SBH in questions to Minister of Reconstruction, Christopher Addison. The Scottish Home Rule Association was re-

42 Sir George Cave was Home Secretary in 1917/8 and Chairman of the War Cabinet Home Affairs Committee.

43 Addison Papers, Box 99, Diary Series, [July 1918–February 1919], Tuesday September 17 1918.

launched in 1918, with members including Independent Labour politicians, Tom Johnston, James Maxton and James Wheatley. The apparent resurgence of nationalism at war's end, coupled with discontent at the way the Scottish issues were dealt with, was further compounded by the election of several Independent Labour Party candidates in Scotland. (In 1918, the Labour Party captured seven Scottish seats and almost 23% of the vote). The ILP members claimed to represent the social and economic plight of the Scottish working class in parliament. These were good grounds for Prime Minister Lloyd George to introduce some element of self-government into the question of addressing the nation's health in the post-war years.

In terms of general election success, the following election in 1922 was the highpoint of the Scottish ILP. In that year, 29 Labour MPs were elected in Scotland. Moreover, ten of the fifteen Glasgow constituencies elected Labour MPs. Among the Clydeside ILP MPs were James Maxton, James Wheatley, Campbell Stephen and George Buchanan. Tom Johnston was among other Scottish ILP MPs elected in 1922, winning the Clackmannanshire and West Stirling seat. Scottish ILP members made critical intercessions in parliament aimed at protecting the health of the Scots population. Most notoriously in 1923, the four Clydeside MPs noted above were suspended from the House of Commons. Their offence was to call those who had presided over SBH budget cuts to local authorities on milk for babies and food for nursing mothers 'murderers'.[44]

---

44 James Maxton outraged the House of Commons with an emotional outburst against Conservative cut backs in local authority health grants on 27 June 1923. Maxton's wife, Sissie, died in 1922 soon after giving birth to an ailing infant. The worries of night and day care for young James led to her premature death within a year of his birth. It was against this traumatic experience that Maxton spoke out against the government as 'murderers'. When Conservative MP, Sir Frederick Banbury objected, Maxton called him the 'worst murderer' of all. Maxton refused to withdraw his remark at the Speakers' request. The other Clydeside MPs supported Maxton's allegation in the Commons and all (Maxton, Buchanan, Wheatley and Stephen) were suspended. At the end of four weeks the banned MPs attempted to re-enter the Commons and were turned away by the police. They were re-admitted two days later after the intervention of Prime Minister, Stanley Baldwin. For more on this episode, see William Knox, ed., *Scottish Labour Leaders 1918–1939: A Biographical Dictionary*

The Clydeside ILP MPs shared a commitment to Home Rule. In 1924, Glasgow Gorbals MP George Buchanan introduced a Government of Scotland Bill. The Bill, calling for an independent Scotland within a federal Britain, gained the support of all Scottish Labour MPs. However, the Bill did not enjoy the support of Ramsay MacDonald's minority Labour Government and it was talked out of time by the Conservative opposition. The issue of home rule led to the creation of a separate party, the National Party of Scotland in 1928.[45] Perhaps due to the formation of a separate party, devolution was dropped from the official Scottish Labour Party programme in 1929. The policy, however, continued to attract widespread Labour support.[46] These developments ensured that Scottish administrative autonomy remained a prominent issue in parliament during the 1920s.

Scotland was not the only member of the United Kingdom to request a separate health agency in 1918. All Home Rule lobbyists sensed the importance of institutional devolution. Government moves to establish outpost ministries could mean a weakening of central administration and provide ready made autonomous administrative bases for future attempts by nationalists to fragment the United Kingdom. Whilst Scottish devolutionists would have preferred a Scottish Ministry of Health, Irish and Welsh home rulers looked enviously at the proposed Scottish Board of Health. Pressed by requests for a Welsh Board of Health during debates on the Health Bill, Addison argued that Wales was to get 'vastly more power than she has now'. But when asked 'Are we giving her as much as Scotland?' Addison erupted:

> No we are not, and for this reason. It has been said many times that we want to create a system of national parliaments in the United Kingdom, and, personally, I believe that that is the only efficient way of dealing with the government of the United Kingdom at the present. But when we want to do that in the House

---

(Edinburgh: Mainstream Publishing, 1984), 204–5. See chapter three for more on the spending cuts which prompted this outburst.

45 In 1932, the Scottish Party was formed. This Party merged with the National Party of Scotland in 1934 to form the Scottish Nationalist Party.

46 J.G. Kellas, *The Scottish Political System* (Cambridge: Cambridge University Press, 1975), 109.

> of Commons we shall do it by the setting up of national parliaments, and not by calling it health. You cannot alter the constitutional government and call it health. It is not health; it is a system of government you are altering.[47]

He added that the only reason for a separate Health Bill for Scotland was that administratively it already had a Scottish Secretary and a Scottish Local Government Board. To a certain extent this also applied to Ireland, but for the time being that country remained within the parameters of the Ministry of Health Act.

During the second reading of the Ministry of Health Bill, Sir Edward Carson, leader of the Ulster Unionists (in pursuit of a distinct political agenda), demanded from Addison some form of centralised health administration for the Northern counties of Ireland similar to that afforded to Scotland. Addison stated that initially he had been asked to create separate Ministries of Health for England, (all) Ireland, Scotland and Wales, however this was taking matters to extremes, and the Scottish example was a limited measure of devolution.[48] A separate Welsh Board of Health was later formed, (its earliest appointments were in December 1919), but although matters such as housing, health insurance and some public health authority duties were transferred to the Cardiff Office, the Welsh Board was administered under the general Ministry of Health Act.

Munro introduced the Scottish Board of Health Bill to parliament on 27 March 1919. On introducing the second reading on 1 April, he explained to the House that the Secretary for Scotland was to be the President of the Scottish Board of Health. Thus health became the direct responsibility of the Secretary for Scotland. This added to his similar position of President of the Boards of Agriculture, Fishery and Prisons. A separate Scottish Ministry of Health with its own minister, and presumably with civil servant staffing, would have relieved the Scottish Secretary of this extra burden, but this had already been rejected by central government in December 1918. In explaining the

---

47 HOC debates, 9–4–19, Vol. 114 col. 2129.
Note – all references to Hansard's published parliamentary debates (for both the House of Commons and the House of Lords) appear in this abbreviated format.

48 HOC debates, 26–2–19, Vol. 112 col. 1835.

measure, Munro stated that although he thought there were 'superficial attractions' in a separate Ministry:

> The head of the new health department should be a Cabinet minister who will have the right to speak in the inner councils of the nation and who will be in close touch with the Treasury. The Scottish Secretary in normal times answers these requirements; a separate minister of health could not.[49]

Regional offices of the Ministry of Health were created for England. The Director for each region was responsible to the Minister of Health. Thus, an extra tier of administration and responsibility was inserted into the Ministry.

The extension of the Scottish Secretary's duties entailed by Munro's presidency of the Board of Health paved the way for the creation of the new office of Parliamentary Under-Secretary (PUS) to be responsible, under the Scottish Secretary, for the administration of the SBH. Clause 3 of the SBH Bill allowed the Scottish Secretary to appoint an Under-Secretary who was to act as Vice President to the SBH. The conditions of appointment went against the general mood of Scottish MPs who, if they could not get a Minister resident in Scotland, wanted more personal contact with the Scottish Secretary in health matters. The Scottish Grand Committee met on 8 April to discuss the Bill and its tabled amendments. Whilst welcoming an extra Scottish minister, the Grand Committee unanimously agreed that the Parliamentary Under Secretary (contrary to Munro's proposals before the Cabinet in May 1918) should be responsible solely for Scottish health matters and the administration of the Scottish Board of Health. The first Parliamentary Under Secretary was John William Pratt,[50] a former Treasury Commissioner. Theoretically, this appointment accorded with Munro's view that the expanded role of the Scottish Secretary needed strong Treasury links. The Cabinet strengthened the role of the Treasury in 1919 in order to create a powerful central department to control the government machine and cut out wasteful expenditure. In 1920, an order in council stipulated that the Treasury

---

49 HOC debates, 1–4–19, Vol. 114 col. 1136.

50 John William Pratt, Coalition Liberal MP for Cathcart Division, Glasgow 1918–1922, previously MP for Linlithgow, 1913–1918.

could make regulations to control the conduct of departments.[51] This measure soon came to have an impact on the working of the SBH.

Despite the appointment of a new PUS, some Scottish MPs feared external control would affect SBH ability to tackle the entrenched problems of Scottish health. The fear arose not only from the possible role of the Treasury, but in doubts about the Scottish Office based at Dover House in London. The remoteness of London from Scotland made some Scottish MPs fear that Pratt, the new Parliamentary Under Secretary for Health (PUSH) would operate entirely from London at Dover House, as did the executive arm of the Scottish Education Department. Liberal MP Joseph Johnstone, went as far to state that Scottish people distrusted 'the influence of the Scottish Office in London, and they want to work this Department apart from the paralysing influence of the Scottish Office here'.[52] Johnstone wanted a minister resident in Scotland but as Pratt was a sitting MP and needed to be in London during parliamentary sessions this was difficult.

The Scottish Board of Health Act[53] stipulated that there should be a legal member who was a member of the Faculty of Advocates or a law agent of not less than 10 years standing, two registered medical practitioners and one or more women.[54] The Ministry of Health Act for England and Wales did not include this positive discrimination stipulation. The extension of the franchise in 1918 to women over

---

51 See G.C. Peden, 'The Treasury as the Central Department of Government, 1919–1939', *Public Administration*, 6 (1983), 376.

52 HOC debates, 1–4–19, Vol. 114 col. 1146. Joseph Johnstone, Coalition Liberal MP for East Renfrewshire from 1918 to 1922. He was Vice Chairman of the National Insurance Commission for Scotland, and was on the Boards of Disabled Servicemen, Tuberculosis Sanatoria, and the War Aims Committee.

53 See Scottish Board of Health Act, 1919, clause 3(2). The new Board's ex-officio membership was made up of the Secretary for Scotland as President, and the Parliamentary Under Secretary for Health as Vice President. Board membership consisted of six officers taken from the Local Government Board, the National Insurance Commission and the HIMSB. The new Board replaced the Local Government Board for Scotland, on which the Secretary for Scotland, the Permanent Under Secretary and the Solicitor General had been ex-officio members.

54 Scottish Board of Health Act, 1919, clause 3 (2).

thirty years of age who were householders was part of a great change in the political and professional status of British women in the early decades of the twentieth century. When the Ministry of Health Bill was under discussion, the role of women as 'medical officers of the home' became an issue and steps were taken to include women on various boards and committees to reflect this. In a sense this was not a new departure. From 1911, the National Insurance Commissions of Scotland, Wales and Ireland contained women to represent the interests of insured female employees, but this was not true for England.

There was some wrangling over sex discrimination for senior civil service posts in the new Ministry during the Health Bill debates. The Bill did not provide equal opportunities, or positive discrimination in favour of women, clause six of the Bill merely stated that: 'The Minister may appoint such secretaries, officers and servants as the Minister may, subject to the consent of the Treasury as to numbers, determine.' During the committee stage an amendment was proposed: 'Provided that, in the making of such appointments, no discrimination be made for reasons of sex between men and women.' When the Report stage was reached, Stanley Baldwin, then Joint Financial Secretary to the Treasury, succeeded in having the amendment withdrawn on the grounds that the clause might prejudice an ongoing enquiry into the position of women in the civil service.[55] Viscount Haldane reinstated the clause (in less positive terms) during the Lords debate on the Bill.[56] It appeared as clause six of both the Scottish Board and Ministry of Health Acts: 'The Minister may appoint one parliamentary secretary and such secretaries, officers and servants [...] and in the making of such appointments shall give equal consideration to the suitability of person of both sexes.'[57]

Although this attempt to introduce positive discrimination in favour of one women in a senior civil service position was negatived for the Ministry of Health, the Scottish Board of Health Act did lead

55 HOC debates, 9–4–19, vol. 114 col. 2132–2134.

56 See HOL debates, 15–5–19, vol. 34 col. 688 for Viscount Haldane's amendment in the Committee stage of the Bill.

57 Scottish Board of Health Act, clause 6 (1).

to the appointment of 'one or more' women to membership of the SBH. Muriel Ritson[58] held this position alone, from 1919 to 1928. Indeed her association with Scotland's health administration continued into the Board's replacement in 1929, the Department of Health for Scotland, where she was woman secretary until 1945, just before her retirement in 1946. The membership of the SBH was therefore, made up of: Sir George McCrae (chairman),[59] Sir William Leslie Mackenzie[60] (medical member), both formerly of the Local

58 At the time of her appointment, Muriel Ritson was prominently associated with social work in Glasgow, especially with health insurance. Her work as secretary of the Women's Friendly Society and Honorary Treasurer of the Glasgow Women's Citizens Association was also closely associated with health insurance work. She had been on several committees dealing with public health and was a member of the Commission of Investigation which visited France in connection with the Women's Army Auxiliary Force. See *Glasgow Herald*, 17 July 1919, 6 col. h. Born in 1885 and educated at Greenock Academy and in Germany, Ritson served as social worker and rent collector for the Glasgow Workman's Dwellings Company from 1908–1911. She was a member of the Ryan Committee of Enquiry into Health Insurance and the Committee of Admission of Women to the Diplomatic and Consular Service and the Beveridge Committee on Social Insurance. She was awarded the CBE in 1936. She was female member of the SBH from 1919–29 and then Controller of Health and Pensions Insurance in the DHS from 1929 to 1945. She was Scottish Controller of the Ministry of National Insurance at her retirement in 1946. She died in July 1980 aged 95 in an Edinburgh nursing home. A photograph of Muriel Ritson is included at the end of this chapter.

59 Sir George McCrae served as Liberal MP for East Edinburgh from 1889 to 1909. From 1909 he was Chairman and Vice President of the Local Government Board for Scotland. He was absent during World War One, where he commanded a battalion which he raised himself in and around Edinburgh. In July 1919 he was appointed Chairman of the Scottish Board of Health. His main interest was in housing while Chairman of SBH. He left the Board to re-enter parliament in October 1922. He died in 1928.

60 William Leslie Mackenzie was born in 1862 in Easter Ross. He graduated MA from Aberdeen University in 1883 and then studied medicine at the same University, qualifying in 1888. He became resident assistant physician at Aberdeen Royal Infirmary. He qualified with a Diploma in Public Health [DPH] in 1890, and was appointed assistant Medical Officer of Health [MOH] in Aberdeen in the same year. He then served as MOH for Kirkcudbright and Wigtonshire from 1891–94. He married Helen Carruthers Spence in 1892. Later, he was MOH for Leith 1894–1901. He gained his MD from Edinburgh

Government Board, Sir James Leishman[61] and Dr John Christie McVail[62] both from the National Health Insurance Commission.

University in 1895. In 1901, he was appointed Medical Inspector to the LGBS, later becoming its statutory medical member. In 1903, he gave evidence to the Scottish Royal Commission on Physical Training. He was appointed a member of the Dewar Committee which investigated the medical services of the Highlands and Islands in 1912. From 1913 he was a member of the Highlands and Islands Medical Services Board. He also served for six years as Crown Representative on the General Medical Council. The author of over 50 works, Mackenzie had a strong interest in the health of children. He wrote two early books on school health: *The Medical Inspection of School Children* (Edinburgh, 1904) and *The Health of the School Child* (1906), and later published *Scottish Mothers and Children* (Dunfermline, 1917), the result of a report for the Carnegie Trust into the issue. He was heavily involved in the Carnegie Trust plans to open a model infant and maternal welfare centre in Scotland (opened in Motherwell in 1922). He was knighted in 1919. He served as medical member on the Scottish Board of Health 1919–1928. In 1929, he was appointed an Honorary Trustee of the Kentucky Frontier Nursing Service. From 1922 until his death in 1935 he was Crown Nominee on the General Medical Council. A socialist and friend of the Webbs, he strongly supported the extension of state medical services. See later chapter on health of the school child for more on his involvement the school medical service. Mackenzie died in 1935.

61 James Leishman was member of Edinburgh School Board in 1903. In the same year he became member of Edinburgh Town Council, where he displayed a special interest in educational matters. In 1909 he was elected to the post of City Treasurer. In 1911, he was appointed Chairman of the National Health Insurance Commission for Scotland. He was knighted in 1914. He continued to serve as Chairman of the NHI Commission for Scotland until July 1919 when it was merged with the LGBS to form the Scottish Board of Health. Leishman served as member of the SBH until March 1928 when he was appointed Chairman. His main involvement with the SBH was in the realms of national health insurance and after legislation in 1925, with contributory pension schemes. He retired in December 1928, as the SBH itself was on the eve of reconstruction, replaced by the Department of Health for Scotland from 1 January 1929. Sir James Leishman died on 27 September 1937.

62 John Christie McVail was born in Kilmarnock in 1849. He studied medicine at St. Andrews and Glasgow University, graduating in 1873. He gained his MD at Glasgow in 1875. He took up general practice in Kilmarnock and then obtained his DPH at Cambridge in 1885. In 1889, he became first Medical Officer of Health for the Counties of Stirling and Dumbarton. He wrote widely on public health matters, and was a special investigator under the Poor Law Commission in 1907. He was appointed deputy chairman of the Scottish National Health

Muriel Ritson joined them as woman member and Ewan MacPherson[63] was appointed the legal member.

'Pressure Group' Campaigns for a new Health Ministry

A common view existed among representative health organisations was that a single Ministry ought to be set up to administer the growing range of state-sponsored health services in Britain after the end of the war. The real debate within these circles was on what form such a new Ministry would take. Both the British Medical Association and local health insurance committees envisaged the new Ministry to suit their purposes. The BMA viewed it as a way of deflecting the introduction of a salaried medical service, while local health insurance committees (which monitored the running of the National Health Insurance legislation of 1911) looked towards an extended Local Government Board acting through the existing health insurance agencies.

The organised medical profession held a unique position in terms of pressure group politics in the first half of the twentieth century. It took on government policy and threatened to make legislation unworkable, gaining concessions over payments and service along the way. This influence was most apparent during negotiations between government and the BMA over national health insurance 1911–13 and

---

Insurance Commission in 1912. He served as Crown Member for Scotland of the General Medical Council between 1912 and his retirement in 1922. He served on the HIMSB from its formation 1913, before joining the Scottish Board of Health when it was founded in 1919. Ill health forced his retirement in 1922 and he died in 1926.

63 Ewan Francis MacPherson was educated at Winchester School and Brasenose College, Oxford where he studied Classics, Greats and Law. He was called to the Scottish Bar in 1880 and served as Legal Secretary to the Lord Advocate 1901–1904. He was legal member of the LGBS from 1904 to 1919, and then was Legal Member of the Scottish Board of Health from 1919–28. He chaired the Board from December 1922 to March 1928 when he resigned due to ill health.

the creation of the National Health Service 1946–48. Immergut puts the success of the organised medical profession internationally down to their ability to move decisions out of the sphere of politics and into areas of exclusive professional jurisdiction, such as how legislation will affect doctors' own practices.[64]

Throughout the protracted discussions on the Ministry of Health Bill, the medical profession was extremely active in expressing its views. In April 1918, the Royal Faculty of Physicians and Surgeons of Glasgow (RFPSG) recommended that representatives of both the preventive and curative branches of medicine be appointed to the new Board.[65] In January 1919, the first meeting of 'Scottish Ministry of Health'(sic) Committee was held in Edinburgh attended by forty-four delegates representing the organised medical profession. Among them were, the eighteen-strong Scottish Committee of the BMA, nine members of the Scottish Branch of the General Medical Council. In addition, one representative of each of the four Medical Faculties of the Scottish Universities, two each from the three medical licensing bodies of Scotland, two representatives of the Medical Officers of Health Association, and one member of the Scottish Association of Medical Women were also included on the committee. Four additional members were later co-opted. The Committee met twice more to consider the Ministry of Health Bills issued in November 1918 and February 1919.[66]

In February 1919, a meeting of the local BMA division for Edinburgh and Leith discussed the plans for a Scottish Board of

64 Immergut, *Health Politics*, 16.

65 RCPSG 1/1/1/14, minutes of meeting, 8 April 1918.

66 The Scottish Ministry of Health Committee came to two main conclusions: '1. That provision ought to be made by direct enactment in the Ministry of Health Bill for the transfer to the Minister of Health of the administration of the Anatomy Acts, and to the Scottish Board of Health of the administrative work of the Highlands and Islands Medical Service Board.
2. That with regard to the constitution of the Scottish Board of Health, the proposed minimum of medical representation – namely, one member – is totally, inadequate, and that not less than one-third of the members of the Board ought to be registered medical practitioners.' *British Medical Journal*, [*BMJ*] 1919 (1), 15 March 1919, 324, see also *Glasgow Medical Journal*, [*GMJ*] 1919 (1), 226–8.

Health. The meeting called for a separate Ministry of Health for Scotland. It endorsed a call by the Royal College of Surgeons of Edinburgh for any Bill to be first submitted to the medical profession for full consideration before it was put before parliament. The meeting also called for medical practitioners to constitute one third of the membership of any Scottish Ministry. On the same theme, a resolution was taken to press for a 'Medical Advisory Council' elected by the profession. Under this proposal, all matters directly affecting public health were to be referred to the Council by the new 'Ministry' of Health for consideration and report.[67]

A similar call for professional medical input and representation in the new Scottish health agency came from the Royal Faculty of Physicians and Surgeons of Glasgow, under the leadership of their President, Dr. Freeland Fergus, who 'deplored the lack of suitably qualified practitioners for the proposed Board of Health'. Freeland Fergus argued that the present medical member of the Scottish Local Government Board, William Leslie Mackenzie, although a prominent medical administrator had no recent experience of general medical practice.[68] Mackenzie's credentials were overshadowed by the outstanding public health career of the other medical member subsequently appointed to the Board, John Christie McVail, both as a teacher and practitioner of public health. Yet then aged 70, McVail was close to retirement age. The feeling was expressed by the RFPSG that the curative as well as the preventive medical services should be represented and that when membership of the Board came up for renewal additional members of the medical profession should be appointed.[69] Despite the strong views of the medical profession over medical representation when McVail retired from SBH membership in 1922 he was not replaced.

The 'Scottish Ministry of Health' Committee was not consulted after the introduction of a separate Bill for Scotland to parliament on

67 See *GMJ*, 1919 (1), 203–4, and *BMJ*, 1919 (1), 291.

68 *Glasgow Herald*, letter to Editor, 10 April 1919, 5 col. c.

69 *BMJ*, 1919 (1), 115 and RCPSG 1/1/1/14, Report of a watching committee of the Faculty, 5 May 1919, reported in minutes of a general Faculty meeting, 6 May 1919.

27 March 1919. The committee had no time to call for a meeting on the new Bill before its swift passage through the House of Commons by mid-April. However, the constitution of the SBH did include the one-third medical representation which had been campaigned for by the Scottish medical profession since the release of the earliest drafts of the Ministry of Health Bill in 1918. Despite this apparent success, the RFPSG deprecated what it viewed as the inadequate medical representation on the SBH and overall lack of consultation with the profession. The RFPSG sent a strongly worded memorandum to Robert Munro in May 1919. The RFPSG was insistent upon the formation of a permanent, medical advisory committee meeting quarterly to advise the SBH.[70] Inadequate medical representation on the SBH was later raised at a meeting of practitioners held to elect representatives to the General Medical Council in October 1919 at the Christian Institute, Glasgow. Dr. Norman Walker, (then directly-elected Scottish Representative on the GMC) rejected complaints that too few doctors had been appointed to the SBH. Walker stated that the various copies of the SBH Bill had always referred to two medical representatives on the six member board. Walker did not feel it fair criticism that no more than two medically-qualified members had now been elected to the SBH.[71] The election of two medical members to the Board marked the high point of medical professional influence over the SBH.

70 *Glasgow Herald*, 7 May 1919, 9 col. e.

71 *Glasgow Herald*, 31 October 1919, 6 col. f.

The first full meeting of the Board took place on 18 July 1919. Both Scottish Secretary Robert Munro (President of the SBH), and John Pratt (PUSH and Vice President of the Board) attended. Sir George McCrae chaired the inaugural meeting.[72] Weekly meetings were initially held on Fridays for the convenience of the Parliamentary Under Secretary for Health.[73] This laid out a pattern for the future, as former Scottish Office civil servant John Gibson remarked:

> Every Thursday evening of the session at Westminster saw the Scottish Parliamentary Under-Secretary for Health making his way from Dover House to Kings Cross for the night sleeper to Waverley so that he might chair the Friday meeting of the Board.[74]

Gibson's account is not quite accurate where the attendance of Pratt at SBH meetings is concerned. From the outset, Pratt attended irregularly. Pratt attended ten of the first eighteen SBH meetings convened between 18 July and 17 October 1919. He then attended no more meetings in 1919, missing eighteen further meetings. He also failed to attend any of the twenty-eight meetings held in the first six months of 1920.[75] Some of his forty-six successive absences were due

72 McCrae gave a formal address to the Scottish Secretary at this inaugural meeting: 'We realise that the new Scottish Board of Health is something more than the fusion of two Departments [The LGBS and the Scottish Insurance Commission]. These two departments have for the last seven and a half years worked in great harmony in matters affecting public health, and specially in the case of tuberculosis, which augurs well for harmonious working in the future. We hope to tackle the great problems which are in front of us with determination and the desire to strengthen your hands in that part of your work which falls to you as President of the Board.' NAS, HH75/1, minutes of the Scottish Board of Health, 18 July 1919.

73 NAS, HH75/1, SBH minutes 18 July 1919, Item 9c.

74 Gibson, *The Thistle and the Crown*, 64.

75 NAS, HH75/1, 75/2, 75/3, SBH minute books, July–December 1919, January–March 1920, April–June 1920, passim.

to ill health. The long-term absence of the Vice President allowed the six Board members to grow into their positions and develop their own, independent, way of working, in co-operation with the permanent administrative staff.

The SBH often met more than once a week, depending on level of business. As the volume of Board business grew, areas of expertise were formalised and the workload divided. The day to day running of the SBH was conducted under seven divisional headings. Joint Board Secretaries, John Maxwell and John Jeffrey devised a scheme of 'office organisation' (set out in table 1.1) in August 1919.

Divisional Committee Number	Section
I	[Health] Insurance
II	Medicine I
III	Medicine II
IV	Public Health, General and Poor Law
V	Housing
VI	Establishment and Intelligence
VII	Finance

Table 1.1 The Seven Divisions of the Scottish Board of Health[76]

In order to administer these subject areas, the Board members grouped themselves into divisional committees. The committees reflected their respective areas of expertise. Each Divisional Committee consisted of three Board members. Each Board member featured on at least three committees, acting as Convenor on one of them. For example, Muriel Ritson sat on three committees: Housing, National Health Insurance and the Establishment Committee chairing the final one. The finance committee consisted of only two Board members, Sir George McCrae and Sir James Leishman. The administrative workload of the Board was divided equally between the two Joint Secretaries. Jeffrey acted as Secretary to Divisional Committees I–III, and Maxwell was Secretary for Divisions IV–VI. Below them Board Administrative

76 NAS, HH75/1, SBH minutes, 26 August 1919.

Officers were appointed to cope with the administrative detail of the divisional offices. Each Divisional Committee reported back weekly to the full Board with recommendations for action and an update on matters under consideration. By November 1919, recommendations from the individual Divisional Committee meetings were incorporated into the formal Board minutes, and by January 1920 the minutes of the Divisional Committees were themselves bound in with the Minutes of the full Board.

The first medical business of the new Board was a decision to give the go-ahead to plans to erect a tuberculosis sanatorium at Muirburn in Lanarkshire, a decision given conditional approval by the old LGBS.[77] As with the Ministry of Health, much of the initial work of the SBH was taken up with housing. Early Board minutes and parliamentary debates on Scottish health matters, show an increasing commitment to providing houses and the difficulties encountered in implementing ambitious housing proposals. Perhaps reflecting the priority given to housing policy, the chairman Sir George McCrae, and his successor in the chair from October 1922, Ewan Macpherson, were both mainly interested in housing matters. Both served, alongside Muriel Ritson, on the SBH Housing Divisional Committee.

When the Scottish Board of Health Bill was issued in March 1919, it contained provision for the setting up of Consultative Councils to advise the Board. The new Ministry of Health already had such Consultative Councils. In keeping with the contemporary desire for expert advice[78] to government departments, Addison appointed four Consultative Councils. The election of such advisory bodies was a new development in public administration. The medical profession recognised that the new bodies had great potential:

> The establishment of this Consultative Council marks an epoch in the relation of the medical profession to the government of this country, and will be accepted by the profession as evidence of a desire to provide machinery through

77 NAS, HH1/472, SBH agenda paper, 18 July 1919.

78 For example, it was at this time that the advisory council on industrial science and technology was founded for the Department of Scientific and Industrial Research.

which it can in its collective capacity be brought into organic relation with health administration, using that term in its widest sense.[79]

The early reports produced by the Ministry's Consultative Councils suggested these new advisory agencies could provide an innovative method of policy formulation. The key Consultative Council on Medical and Allied services contained seventeen medical and three lay members. Its remit was to suggest a scheme to systematise the medical services to provide a more complete service for the whole community. In May 1920 this Consultative Council (under the chairmanship of Lord Dawson of Penn) issued an interim report.[80] The Dawson Report contained an ambitious plan for a more comprehensive state service. The expanded service was to be based on the hospital and health centre, while allowing room for private general practice. The proposals were to be financed through an extended National Health Insurance scheme. However, the new proposals did not survive the economic difficulties of 1920/21, and the Consultative Council issued no final report. The creation of small, well equipped health centres was similarly recommended around this time by the Consultative Committee on Medical and Allied Services to the Welsh Board of Health.[81]

The value of outside expert advice was early recognised in the activities of the new SBH, particularly in regard to the input of the medical profession. The agenda of the first meeting of the SBH on 18 July included discussion on the terms of reference, personnel and the

---

79 *BMJ*, 1919 (1), 4 October, 446.

80 According to Dawson, the Report was designed to secure:
1. The provision of buildings and equipment
2. Services correlated and available to all
3. Opportunity for practitioners to do their best work and further their knowledge
4. Co-ordination of preventive and curative medicine
5. Freedom of action for doctor and patient.
Ministry of Health, Interim Report of the Consultative Council, *The Future Provision of Medical and Allied Services* (HMSO 1920), [Cmd. 693].

81 Political and Economic Planning, *Report on the British Health Services* (1937), 165.

general constitution of the Scottish Consultative Councils.[82] In mid-August, consideration was given to the future proceedings of the Consultative Councils. Clause 5 of the SBH Act stated that all Orders proposed to be issued by the Board had first to be submitted for the consideration of one of the Consultative Councils. The SBH decided that it should have the power to convene combined meetings of the Consultative Councils or committees representing the Councils if the Board so chose. By implication, the advice of the Consultative Councils was to be taken in a form which suited the Board's purposes.[83] Four Councils, (with a maximum membership of twenty, including both men and women, and meeting a minimum three times per year), were appointed by the SBH, their terms of reference having been decided by the SBH divisional committees. The creation and remit of the Consultative Councils were rubber-stamped by the Secretary for Scotland in January 1920.[84] The four councils were divided under the following headings: 1. Medical and Allied Services, 2. National Health Insurance (Approved Societies Work), 3. Local Health Administration and General Health Questions, and 4. Highlands and Islands.

The initial medical professional response to the planned Scottish Consultative Councils was enthusiastic. In late March 1919, the Royal College of Physicians of Edinburgh expressed its approval for the inclusion such councils in the Scottish Health Board Bill through its President, Sir Robert Philip.[85]

> Their establishment will tend to ensure the effective co-operation of the profession with the Ministry of Health, it is essential that these Consultative Councils should be really effective bodies, initiating as well as qualifying proposals, and that they should have ready access to the Minister.[86]

---

82 NAS, HH1/472, SBH, agenda of meeting, 18 July 1919.

83 NAS, HH1/472, SBH minutes, 15 August 1919.

84 NAS, DD1/21, 'list of Standing Advisory Committees at present in existence', March 1936.

85 Philip was Professor of Tuberculosis and Senior Lecturer in Clinical Medicine at the University of Edinburgh. See chapter five for more on Philip's pioneering role in tuberculosis care.

86 *BMJ*, 1919 (1) 29 March 1919, 392.

Sir Robert Philip was later appointed as one of the original members of the Scottish Consultative Council on Medical and Allied Services. Another one of the three candidates nominated by the Royal College of Physicians, Edinburgh,[87] Norman Walker,[88] was also appointed to this Consultative Council.

The experience of the Royal Faculty of Physicians and Surgeons, Glasgow in seeking positions on this Consultative Council was rather different. In December 1919, the Faculty, in response to an invitation from the SBH, nominated three of its fellows as candidates for membership to this Consultative Council. None were successful, much to the chagrin of the Faculty who publicly recorded their view that the rejection of their nominees was a slight on the standing of the Faculty. This provoked a letter of response from the SBH. The letter noted that 45 nominations had been put forward for membership of the CCMAS. The SBH decided that five places on the twenty-member Council should be reserved for representatives of allied medical services, (including veterinary medicine, pharmacy and nursing) which left fifteen positions to be filled by various representatives of the medical profession. Sixteen representative organisations had suggested candidates, and three organisations, including the RFPSG, had been unsuccessful in obtaining representation on the CCMAS. However, the SBH noted that two of those who were appointed to this Consultative Council were also Fellows of the RFPSG.[89] Not satisfied with the SBH explanation, the RFPSG responded with a further protest stating that 'the great medical and surgical interests of Glasgow and the West of Scotland' had been overlooked by this decision. Another area of concern for the RFPSG was that the CCMAS as now constituted, did not contain a single representative of the curative side of the profession, either general practitioners or

---

87 The three RCPE nominations were Robert Philip, Norman Walker and Edwin Matthew. Royal College of Physicians, Edinburgh, RCPE minutes, vol. 14, 4 December 1919.

88 Both Philip and Walker held prominent medical appointments aside from their membership of the RCPE. Philip's posts are noted in footnote 85. Walker was elected Scottish representative of the General Medical Council.

89 RCPSG 1/1/1/14, RFPSG minutes, 3 May 1920.

hospital staff.[90] The SBH replied by noting the Faculty comments, but no further action was taken.[91] The Faculty response was to ignore the activities of the SBH and the CCMAS in its recorded minutes. Even with the death of RFPSG Fellow J.C. McVail in 1926, there was no reference to his membership of the SBH in the minuted tribute.[92]

Eighteen of the twenty original members of this key Consultative Council were medically qualified (although only fifteen practised medicine). Among them were, Archibald Kerr Chalmers, Medical Officer of Health for Glasgow, James R. Drever, Scottish Medical Secretary of the BMA, John Glaister, Professor of Forensic Medicine and Public Health at Glasgow University, Matthew Hay, MOH for the City of Aberdeen, Laura Stewart-Sandeman, late Controller of Medical Services to Queen Mary's Army Auxiliary Corps, Overseas, and Sir James Mackenzie, one of the most prominent practitioners of his day, head of St Andrews Clinical Institute and Consulting Physician to the London Hospital. Sir Donald MacAlister chaired the Committee.[93] MacAlister's appointment reflected the importance attached to bringing the University medical faculties on board in support of the new institutions.

On 12 March 1920, the Scottish Secretary held a joint meeting of the four Consultative Councils. Munro stated it would be the business of the Councils to keep 'in close, constant, and living touch with the opinions and feelings of the people outside.' He further promised that the Board intended the Councils 'to have the fullest opportunity of forming and expressing free and independent judgements.'[94] Not only

90 RCPSG 1/1/1/14, RFPSG minutes, 7 June 1920.

91 Ibid.

92 RCPSG 1/1/1/14, RFPSG minutes, 6 September 1926.

93 Sir Donald MacAlister MD, was then President of the General Medical Council and Principal of Glasgow University. MacAlister was elected fellow of the Royal College of Physicians, London in 1886. He was a Fellow and lecturer at St John's College, Cambridge and worked as a physician at Addenbrookes Hospital. In 1909, he was appointed Principal and Vice Chancellor of Glasgow University. He then became Chancellor of Glasgow University. He served as President of the GMC between 1905–1931. He was knighted in 1908 and given a baronetcy in 1924. He died in 1934.

94 *BMJ*, 1920 (1), 27 March 1920, 452.

were 'a number of important references' submitted to the Councils for their consideration at this first joint meeting, further references were subsequently made to the Councils by the Board during the course of their administration in the first year of their activity.[95] The work of the four Consultative Councils was conducted through sub-committees, which met frequently and also through staging joint meetings. In addition to these, the full Councils met nine, four, seven and three times, respectively.

Consultative Councils played an equivocal role in Scottish health policy formulation. On occasion, their recommendations were acted upon. For example, the advice of the Highlands and Islands Consultative Council was sought on possible post-war expansion of the Highlands and Islands Medical Service. This service was set up in 1913 but its functions were curtailed due to wartime necessity. The recommendations put forward by this Consultative Council were substantially incorporated in the revised schemes drawn up for the administration of the HIMS.

The Scottish Consultative Council on Medical and Allied Services was directed: 'To consider and make recommendations as to the systematised provision of such forms of medical and allied services as should in the opinion of the Council be available for the community.'[96] The Council's interim Report (the MacAlister Report) entitled *A Scheme of Medical Service for Scotland* was issued in November 1920. In some respects it addressed areas identified in the Dawson Report produced by its English counterpart six months earlier under similar guidelines. The MacAlister Report echoed the Dawson Report's emphasis in particular in its focus on the key role of the general practitioner in an extended health service. The MacAlister Report proposed an extension of the National Health Insurance

95 SBH, *Second Annual Report, 1920* (HMSO: Edinburgh, 1921), 257, [Cmd 1319].

96 Scottish Board of Health Consultative Council on Medical and Allied Services Interim Report, *A Scheme of Medical Service for Scotland*, 8 November 1920 4, [Cmd 1039].

Scheme to include wives, children and other dependants of the same economic status as those covered by the existing insurance schemes.[97]

In essence, the Report recommended that the 'Health Service of the Nation' should be based on the family as the normal unit of health care and that the family doctor (general practitioner) be the focus of this health care. The Report stated that a complete medical service could be provided through the extension of national health insurance to all dependants of those currently insured. It also recommended that the service should be expanded to cover all forms of health care required, including preventive monitoring of the whole community, facilitated by a co-ordinated medical service under a unified system of local authorities.[98] The key proposal contained in the Report was for the establishment of a comprehensive health service.[99]

The MacAlister Report also pointed up the distinct nature of Scottish health care. The Highlands and Islands were a special case and had a dedicated Consultative Council, but elsewhere in Scotland there were areas of particular concern different from those in the rest of the British Isles.[100] The Report of the Consultative Council on Medical and Allied Services was received at the end of 1920 for 'earnest consideration' by the SBH.[101] In November 1920, the two Health Divisional Committees of the SBH began a detailed

---

97 'Of primary importance to the Council was that the organisation of a national health service should be based upon the family as the normal unit, and on the family doctor as the normal medical attendant and guardian; that the first essential for efficient treatment of individuals is not institutional but personal service rendered to the people in their own homes'. *BMJ*, 1920 (2), 11 December, 900.

98 SBH, *A Scheme of Medical Service for Scotland*, 6–7.

99 'As a result of our enquiries, we are satisfied that the time is opportune for formulating a general plan, whereby the entire Health Service of the nation may be established on a broad and comprehensive basis, with the object of linking up all the various particular agencies concerned, strengthening and expanding them, and directing their several efforts towards one common end. What is needed is that a complete and adequate medical service should be brought within reach of every member of the community.' SBH, *A Scheme of Medical Service for Scotland*, 6.

100 See the Prologue for more on particular Scottish health issues.

101 SBH, *Second Annual Report, 1920*, 257.

consideration of the MacAlister Report. However, a directive from the Treasury arrived at the SBH in December 1920 which announced restrictions on planned expenditure in many areas of government for the financial year 1921/2. The recommendations of the MacAlister Report were not implemented.

The MacAlister Report was not universally well received by the medical profession. Professor William Russell,[102] a leading figure in Scots medicine, followed a familiar and long-standing conservative line of resistance to any hint of a State medical service. Russell found it difficult to treat the report seriously. He believed that the common sense of the population and parliament would throw out the plan 'to hand over their family doctoring to State officials by an extension of the Insurance Acts at a time when national finances and overtaxed pockets are clamouring for retrenchment and relief.'[103] Meanwhile, the Medical Guild,[104] aiming to prey on general practitioners fears of an imposed State-salaried medical service, produced a circular in response to the MacAlister Report entitled: *A State Socialistic Scheme of Medical Service for Scotland*. It argued that the State – so long as the sick did not pose an infection danger to the community – should stop interfering with the provision of medical attendance for anyone other than paupers.[105]

However, other sections of the medical profession gave strong support to the MacAlister Report. Defending the Report from the charge that it made no attempt to cost an extended scheme of medical

102 Russell was then Emeritus Professor of Clinical Medicine at Edinburgh University, Consulting Physician at Edinburgh Royal Infirmary, a former President of the Royal College of Physicians of Edinburgh, and a member of the General Medical Council.

103 See Professor William Russell's comments in the *Scotsman*, 9 December 1920.

104 The Medical Guild was formed in 1895 to protect the economic interests of 'club' or contract general practice. After the passage of National Health Insurance legislation in 1911, it sought to protect the incomes and interests of panel practitioners.

105 See comments on the circular in *BMJ*, 1921 (1), 5 February 1921, 208.

service, former BMA President, Robert Cochrane Buist[106] stated in a letter to the *British Medical Journal:*

> As the recommendations of the report are not devised for this year or next, and may, indeed, be forwarded where and when practicable, the Advisory Council would have been even less wise than their critics had they attempted such an estimate, and we may leave its omission to balance the fact that the cost of the absence of the scheme is no less real charge on the community than the cost of its fulfilment [...].[107]

A RCPE sub-committee appointed to consider the MacAlister Report thoroughly approved of the Report's general finding that the present provision of medical services was 'inadequate and patchy'. The sub-committee noted with satisfaction 'the definite recognition of the home and the household as the primary centre for medical care.' The RCPE sub committee felt that there was a need for more co-ordination of general practitioner services with the school health service and maternity and child welfare schemes.[108] These prescient views were echoed fifteen years later in the findings of the DHS Committee on Scottish Health Services discussed in chapter two.

The MacAlister Report, like its English counterpart, the Dawson Report, was an innovative document which, while influencing later thinking on the extension of state medical services,[109] was not acted upon, due largely to the financial exigencies facing the government after 1920. The joint report of the Scottish Consultative Councils on National Health Insurance (Approved Societies Work) and Health Administration and General Health Questions on Maternity Benefit and Maternity and Child Welfare Schemes submitted to the SBH on 17 December 1920 was another casualty of the cash-squeeze. The Board gave close consideration to the scope and intentions of the

---

106 Robert Cochrane Buist obtained his medical qualifications at Edinburgh University in 1888. He was gynaecologist at Dundee Royal Infirmary and served as Chairman of the Central Midwives Board for Scotland and was a former President of the BMA.

107 *BMJ*, 1921 (1), 5 February 1921, Supplement, 33.

108 RCPE, minutes vol. 14, minutes of quarterly meeting, 3 May 1921.

109 Such as in its call for unified local authorities, which eventually came with the Local Government (Scotland) Act of 1929.

Treasury's Scrooge-like circular on economy the following week. The meeting took place suitably enough on 24 December 1920.

The fiscal constraints placed on Consultative Councils and their proposals are made clear in the papers of Arthur Greenwood.[110] Health Minister Christopher Addison invited Greenwood to become Vice-Chairman of the Ministry's Consultative Council on General Health Questions during 1920.[111] The minutes of a meeting on 10 December 1920 revealed the shadow of financial restrictions hanging over the activities of the Consultative Councils. In the Chair, Addison:

> Reminded the Council that in the present state of public funding in regard to national finance, any proposals put forward which involved the expenditure of public money on any considerable scale was bound to become the object of close, and often hostile, scrutiny.[112]

As an example, Addison cited the adverse reception the Dawson Report received as being aimed at the introduction of a costly scheme of medical services. For this reason, he felt that to publish the Report

---

110 Arthur Greenwood was educated in Yorkshire and obtained a BSc at Leeds University in 1905. He moved to London in 1916 to take up a civil service career. He was Addison's Assistant Secretary at the Ministry of Reconstruction in 1917. He served as Labour MP for Leicester in 1920. From 1922–31 he was MP for Nelson and Colne, and for Wakefield from 1932 until his death in 1954. In 1924, he was appointed Parliamentary Secretary at the Ministry of Health. From 1929 to 1931 he was Minister of Health. He was elected Deputy Leader of the Labour Party in 1935, and was Treasurer of the Party from 1943–1954. He was appointed to the War Cabinet between 1940–2, as Minister without Portfolio with responsibility for Economic Affairs (1940) and for Reconstruction (1941/2). Under the latter, he appointed the Committee on Social Insurance and Allied Services (Beveridge Committee). He served as Paymaster General between 1946/7 and again as Minister without Portfolio in 1947.

111 The Consultative Council on General Health Questions was the vehicle for patients' views to be represented in the new Ministry. It included 12 female members (out of 19 in total) and also represented the views of the organised Labour movement. Lady Rhondda was its first chair person.

112 Bodleian Library, Oxford, Department of Western Manuscripts, Arthur Greenwood Papers, Shelf 1, Box on Ministry of Health Advisory [*sic*] Council on General Health Questions, 1919–1921, minutes of 20th meeting of Consultative Council, 10 December 1920.

of the General Health Questions Consultative Council recommending a 'complete scheme of services' which had been submitted to him in November 1920 would be a 'grave mistake'.[113] By 1921, the members of this Consultative Council were recording their feelings that their work was not having any influence on the Minister.[114] In November 1921, the new Minster of Health, Liberal MP Alfred Mond, confirmed such fears. Pointing out that the Consultative Councils were still very much at the experimental stage, he made it clear he saw the Council's role as that of providing information for the Ministry, not in policy formulation:

> As the Council were aware, the general position at the moment was that the necessity for economy in public expenditure restricted the development of health services, but council could provide him with information on health questions.[115]

The need for financial economy put paid to any dynamic role for the Consultative Councils of the Ministry and, to an extent, the Scottish Board of Health. Some of the Ministry's Consultative Councils in England and Wales, from early ground-breaking reports on comprehensive health services, fell into abeyance. The Medical and Allied Services Council produced nothing independently after July 1921 and held only periodic meetings with the Ministry down to February 1924, after which it was dormant. The Consultative Council on General Health Questions never recovered from the double blow of its two Reports being quashed and collapsed at the end of 1921.[116]

The Scottish Consultative Councils went through a period of quiescence in the first half of 1921 at the height of concerns over

113 The unpublished report was submitted to Addison on 19 November 1920. 'Our attention has been more particularly directed towards the organisation of services having as their aim the prevention of disease in the community and the individual', *Completed Report of the Consultative Council on General Health Questions* (HMSO, 1920), 4.

114 Arthur Greenwood papers, minutes of 22nd meeting of Consultative Council on General Health Questions, 10 May 1921.

115 Arthur Greenwood Papers, minutes of the 23rd meeting of Consultative Council on General Health Questions, 22 November 1921.

116 Honigsbaum, *The Division in British Medicine*, 63,78.

economy, due in part to the costs of staging the meetings. For example it cost between £70–£80 to stage a meeting of the Highlands and Islands Consultative Council. However, within a few months, the Scottish Consultative Councils resumed meetings and continued to produce new policy proposals. In 1921, the Consultative Council on Local Health Administration and General Health Questions issued an interim report advising the reduction in the number of local health authorities in Scotland by creating larger units.[117] In 1923, the four Councils published joint reports suggesting the reform of local health authorities.[118] The Consultative Council on Local Health Administration produced a final report on the reform of local government health administration in 1923. Its main suggestion was to amalgamate small inefficient local authorities into larger units. The proposal was to create new county councils and burghs of over 50,00 population.[119] The recommendations of the Report, although not immediately acted upon, helped lay the groundwork for the Scottish Local Government Act of 1929.

Economic restraint lay behind much of the failure to act upon recommendations by the Scottish Consultative Councils in their first five years of vigorous activity. In 1923, the final report of the SBH Joint Committee (established in 1920 and representing three of the

117 *GMJ*, 1921 (2), 199–200.

118 SBH, *Reports by Consultative Councils on a Reformed Local Authority for Health and Public Assistance* (Edinburgh: HMSO, 1923).

119 The 1923 Report revealed there were then 201 self-governing burghs in Scotland. 19 of these had a population of less than 1,000 and 108 others with a population of less than 5,000. It was impossible for such units to individually provide the statutory health services required by the 1920s. The Report suggested replacing these units with larger local health authorities of burghs with over 50,000 population and on county councils of a similar size. Reviewing the report, the *BMJ* revealed it had little chance of early success: 'Apart from vested interests, probably the great majority of public health officers will agree that this small number is far better than the present absurd multiplicity, but it seems doubtful whether a Bill to give effect to these proposals has much chance to become law, looking to all the influences which would be ranged against it. Perhaps the report, however, may have the effect of leading to some measure of much needed reform.' *BMJ*, 1921 (2), 18 August 1923, 300.

Scottish Consultative Councils)[120] on the relation of maternity benefit under the Insurance Act and the maternity and child welfare schemes of local authorities was withheld. Again, the reason given was economy: '[...] owing to the expense that would be incurred.'[121] That there was no political will to implement the proposals of the Consultative Councils must also be considered. Immergut has noted that interest groups are often consulted directly in the early stages of policy formulation, but their longer-term importance is dependent on whether they are politically essential. 'Interest group influence thus depends on the institutional context of political decisions.'[122]

The Performances of Political Nominees to the SBH

Lloyd George's coalition government elected in 1918 bridged the period of short-term euphoria after victory in war to the following realisation of the true cost to Britain of world trade dislocation and consequent industrial depression. In 1921/22, the 'Geddes Axe'[123]

---

120 The Joint Committee was composed of representatives from the Consultative Committee on Local Health Administration and General Health Questions and of the Consultative Committee on National Health Insurance.

121 *BMJ*, 1923 (2), 11 August 1923, 256.

122 Immergut, *Health Politics*, 28–9.

123 The name given to the recommendations of the Coalition Government's Economy Committee which was established in August 1921 to curtail spending in the wake of the post-war economic slump. The 'Geddes Axe' was so called after the Economy Committee's chairman, Sir Eric Geddes, himself a recently free-spending Minister of Transport in the wartime Cabinet. In May 1915, Christopher Addison described Geddes, as a 'many £1000-a-year man from the North Eastern Railway Company.' C. Addison, *Four and a Half Years: A Personal Diary from June 1914 to January 1919* vol. 1 (Hutchinson, 1933), 84. The Economy Committee investigations were part of a campaign of 'anti-waste' in Government spending: financial considerations alone now determined the rate and scope of state social welfare and other programmes. The Economy Committee reported to the Government in December 1921 and in February 1922, two Cabinet committees one for defence and the other to review all

resulted in government cut backs. The new restrictions adversely affected both existing health provisions and proposals for new services starting in the financial year 1922/23. This, allied to internal strains within the Liberal Party, disrupted the Coalition consensus and in the general election of October 1922, a Conservative government was returned under Bonar Law. The 1922 election also brought more Independent Labour Party MPs to Westminster, such as Tom Johnston and James Maxton. In terms of Scottish health administration, the Secretary for Scotland, Robert Munro, was elevated to the Lords, taking the judicial title of Lord Alness. His term as Secretary had not been one of dramatic success.[124]

The new Scottish Secretary was Lord Novar,[125] who had recently returned to Britain from a successful spell as Governor General of Australia. Whereas Munro had been based in the House of Commons and could direct his Parliamentary Under-Secretary for Health (when he managed to attend SBH meetings), Novar was isolated in the House of Lords. This change in Secretary had the potential to increase the autonomy of the SBH. Arguably, that autonomy was already considerable.[126] For example, unlike the other Scottish Boards which linked up with the Scottish Office at Dover House, the SBH met in

---

departmental estimates, were appointed to consider how best to implement the cutbacks called for by the Economy Committee. For more on this matter, see K.O. Morgan, *Consensus and Disunity: The Lloyd George Coalition Government 1918–1922* (Oxford: Clarendon Press, 1979), 288–294.

124 History has not been kind to Robert Munro. Harvie described his time as Scottish Secretary thus: 'It was Scotland's tragedy that at this important period the Office fell to the dim representative of a failing political party.' Harvie, *No Gods and Precious Few Heroes: Scotland 1914–1980*, 28.

125 Ronald Craufurd Munro-Ferguson, K.T. 1926. MP. Liberal, Ross and Cromarty 1884–85, Leith Burghs 1886–1914, Governor General Australia 1914–1920, National Liberal Secretary for Scotland 1922–1924 (under a Conservative government).

126 Lindsay Paterson has argued that as the role of the State increased in the twentieth century, so too did the influence of the Scottish bureaucracy in the details of policy making: 'Thus the key debates about education, or housing, or health, or child welfare could take place in a context that was Scottish first and British after that.' Paterson, 'Scottish Autonomy and the Future of the Welfare State', 58.

Edinburgh. The geographic separation between the Board and its President, the Scottish Secretary, increased the autonomy of the Board members. For example, in December 1920 circulars drawn up by the SBH, which contained instructions to local authorities to curtail their expenditure, were sent directly to the Treasury by the SBH for their approval. Novar, SBH President, was not consulted in this process at all. He was merely sent copies of the circulars and 'informed that owing to the urgency of the matter it had been necessary to send the circulars direct to the Treasury.'[127] The separation of the SBH from the Scottish Secretary led to the opening up of a direct line of communication between the SBH and the Cabinet. Even earlier, in June 1921, Scottish Secretary Munro agreed to the Board's request that it be kept informed of Cabinet decisions on memoranda dealing with questions in which they were interested, and instructed that copies of such Cabinet minutes should be forwarded to the SBH.[128]

Distance from the Scottish Office, and from the controlling hand of the Scottish Secretary, helped pave the way to the eventual replacement of the SBH in 1928. Lord Novar soon attempted to curtail the autonomy of the SBH. In January 1923 the Scottish Office, acting on Novar's behalf, approached the SBH to request that communications between the Board and the Foreign Office be channelled through the Scottish Office.[129] The Board's position was that to go through the Scottish Office would cause unnecessary delay, for instance when there was a need to notify the Foreign Office of the outbreak of a serious infection.[130] Eventually, the issue was solved under revised arrangements: 'the Board noted these revised arrangements with satisfaction.'[131] A battle had been won, but the reform campaign from the Whitehall-based Scottish Office was only just beginning.[132]

127 NAS, HH75/1, SBH minutes, 31 December 1920.

128 NAS, HH 75/7, SBH minutes, 24 June 1921.

129 NAS, HH75/14, SBH minutes, 5 January 1923.

130 NAS, HH75/14, SBH minutes, 9 January 1923.

131 NAS, HH75/14, SBH minutes, 23 February 1923.

132 Paterson has argued that the federalist structure of the British welfare system derived partly from the legacy of a distinct Scottish culture and set of distinct political preferences. These allowed the 'Scottish Office and Scottish civil society' to exercise bureaucratic control over Scottish welfare by the mid-

Pratt, a frequent absentee from the Board's meetings since its inception, did not contest the 1922 election.[133] James Kidd[134] replaced Pratt as Parliamentary Under Secretary for Health. Kidd's term of office was short lived, from October 1922 to March 1923, when Walter Elliot[135] was appointed PUSH. Elliot's biographer, dismissed his appointment to the post: 'the job was perhaps not exhilarating, but in those days it was concerned mainly with his speciality – Public Health; and it was Office.'[136] Elliot's first spell as PUSH lasted only nine months. His attendance at SBH meetings (at least once a month) was more frequent than had been the case with Pratt, but soon the Conservative government was replaced by the first-ever, short-lived Labour government. Labour's James Stewart was in office only from January to November 1924.

From 1919 to 1924, often against a background of strict financial control, the four successive Scottish Under-Secretaries for Health each failed to make a mark. John William Pratt (Coalition Liberal), James Kidd (Unionist),[137] Walter Elliot (Unionist) and James Stewart (Labour) seemed to make little impact in terms of parliamentary

---

twentieth century. See Paterson 'Scottish Autonomy and the Future of the Welfare State', 59.

133 Pratt went into retirement in Bordighera, Ireland.

134 James Kidd, a solicitor, was Unionist MP for Linlithgow.

135 Walter Elliot served as Parliamentary Under Secretary for Health between January 1923–January 1924 and November 1924–July 1926. He was then Under Secretary of State for Scotland July 1926–July 1929. At Glasgow University, Elliot gained a BSc in 1910 and then qualified MB ChB in 1913. He served in the RAMC in World War One, gaining two Military Crosses. In 1918 he was elected as Coalition Conservative MP for Lanark and served until January 1924 when the Labour candidate defeated him. Later in 1924 he was elected Conservative MP for Kelvingrove where he served until 1945, and again from 1950 till his death in 1958 (from 1945–50 he was MP for the Scottish Universities). He served as Minister of Agriculture 1934–36, and then as Scottish Secretary of State under the National Government between 1936–38. Elliott was Minister of Health between 1938–1940. He and Addison were the only medical doctors to hold the office of Minster of Health before 1945.

136 Sir C. Coote, *A Companion of Honour: The Story of Walter Elliot* (Collins 1965), 60.

137 The Scottish Conservative Party was known as the Unionist Party in the inter-war period.

initiatives to improve Scotland's health. Arguably, the two Scottish Secretaries, Munro and Lord Novar fared little better.

After 1924, there was a discernible change in the Board's dealings and personnel. In November 1924, when the Conservatives returned to power under Baldwin, Walter Elliot[138] was re-appointed Under-Secretary, under the new Secretary for Scotland, Sir John Gilmour.[139] In late 1925, Prime Minister Stanley Baldwin promised to upgrade the rank of Scottish Secretary to Secretary of State, but made no provision for an increase in salary. Despite the improved status of the Scottish Secretary of State confirmed in 1926, the incumbent still continued to receive £3000 less than other Secretaries of State. Consequently, all SBH staff were paid at a rate lower than were those in the Ministry of Health.

Changes in Scottish Board of Health Membership

Membership changes took place in the SBH within four years of its creation. In early 1922, Dr John Christie McVail retired. McVail's resignation reduced medical representation in the SBH from the statutory two members to one. His retirement precipitated a Bill to amend the Board of Health (Scotland) Act. Driven partly by needs of economy and also partly by government mistrust of the Scottish Board system, in February 1922, a draft Bill to cut the size of the Board was circulated between the SBH, the Treasury and the Scottish Office. The

138 Walter Elliot was the longest serving Parliamentary Under-Secretary involved with health. With the exception of the Labour PUSH James Stewart, (January to November 1924), Elliot represented health in Scotland from 1923 to 1929.

139 Sir John Gilmour was Scottish Secretary from 1924–1926 and thereafter continued as Secretary of State for Scotland until 1929. He had previously been Junior Lord of the Treasury in 1921, and Scottish Unionist Whip 1921/2 and 1924. He was Minister of Agriculture and Fisheries 1931/2 and Home Secretary 1932–35. He was appointed Minister of Shipping in 1939. He served as Unionist MP first for East Renfrewshire 1910–1918 and then for Pollok, Glasgow from 1918 until his death in 1940.

discussions were prompted by McVail's resignation, but also coincided with the Cabinet Economy Committee's attempt to further cap government spending.[140] An amendment was required in law to the SBH Act to reduce the Board membership. At this juncture Munro himself felt a six-member board was '[...] too unwieldy in number; I think three members would be quite sufficient.'[141] The Board membership was split over the constitution of any reduced SBH. Sir George McCrae, Sir James Leishman and Ewan MacPherson all supported a reduced size for the Board on condition that the requirement to have at least one qualified medical practitioner and one woman was removed. Not surprisingly, the remaining medical member and the sole woman on the Board, Sir William Leslie Mackenzie and Muriel Ritson, opposed this proposal.[142]

Robert Munro's views on reducing the SBH to just three members apparently changed in the space of two months. His revised opinion as expressed in a memorandum of April 1922 was that to reduce the medical membership to one was sufficient change in the size of the Board. Both Munro and the Treasury now viewed the presence of a woman on the Board as politically important.[143] Despite these discussions, the 1922 Economy (Miscellaneous Provisions) Bill, followed the recommendations of the Geddes Economy Committee, and included a clause to reduce the Board membership to three and to alter the PUSH duties to cover 'such other public services' as the Scottish Secretary would decide. The Bill gained the support of the Conservative backbench.[144] However, the Economy (Miscellaneous

140 The SBH Treasury estimates for 1923 made '[...] no provision for the vacancies in the Board membership caused by the resignation of Sir George McCrae and Dr McVail.' Further staff reductions included Medical Officers from 9 to 8, Heads of Sections – from 22 to 20, Junior Executive Officers from 51 to 48, Clerical Officers from 145 to 140 and Temporary Clerks from 53 to 33. PRO, T160/147, John Jeffrey, Secretary, SBH, to Treasury, 30 December 1922.

141 NAS, HH1/468, Robert Munro, Scottish Secretary, minute on amending size of SBH, 24 February 1922.

142 NAS, HH1/468, SBH minute, 6 March 1922.

143 NAS, HH1/468, Letter from SBH to Treasury, 24 April 1922.

144 'I am glad to see that, in accordance with the recommendation of the Geddes Committee [...] the Scottish Board of Health is to be reduced from six to three.

Provisions) Bill was not enacted. Instead, various component parts were incorporated into separate Bills.[145] In July 1922, Secretary Munro in answering a question in the House of Commons whether it was possible to reduce the size of the SBH to three without resort to legislation stated: '[...] because these members were appointed by Statute [...] another Statute is required to modify it.'[146]

Further reduction in the Board's size was effected when Sir George McCrae decided to resume an active political career and resigned as Chairman late in 1922. Ewan MacPherson, legal member of the SBH, took over McCrae's position as Chairman. In 1923, McCrae returned to parliament after a gap of fourteen years. He was elected as Liberal MP for Stirling and Falkirk District. The Board was now reduced to four members (excluding the Scottish Secretary and the PUSH).

In the closing days of the parliamentary session ending summer 1923, a Reorganisation of Offices (Scotland) Bill was put before parliament by Munro's successor as Scottish Secretary, Lord Novar.[147] The Bill again proposed to abolish the PUSH and replace the office with a more general Parliamentary Under Secretary for Scotland. In addition, the Bill proposed to cut the ex-officio membership of the SBH to three, and all qualifications (based on medical and legal qualifications and gender) were to be abolished. This suggested alteration of the SBH was viewed as a 'breach of faith [...] and a

---

The Geddes Committee says it is possible, and in the interests of economy it is desirable. If both the Geddes Committee and the Government say it is possible and desirable, why not do it at once? There is one vacancy now. On the Secretary of Scotland's own showing two of these five members are superfluous, and they cannot find work for them. Why not give them a good pension and let them do some other economical work outside instead of going on paying them when there is no work for them to do? It would be cheaper.' Sir John Hope, Coalition Unionist MP for North Midlothian and Peebles, 1918–1922, made these comments. HOC debates, 10–7–22 vol. 156 col. 952. Second Reading of Reconstruction Bill.

145 See HOC debates, 20–2–23, vol. 160 col. 814 and 17–4–23, vol. 162 col. 1899.

146 HOC debates, Oral Answers, 19–7–22, vol. 156 col. 2079. Robert Munro, Scottish Secretary to Lieutentant-Colonel Pownall, (Unionist MP for East Lewisham, 1918–45).

147 HOL debates, 30–7–23, vol. 54 col. 1457, statement by Viscount Novar.

lowering of the status of the medical service'[148] by the BMA. Although this Bill too was lost at the end of the session, the indications of future reform of the SBH were clear. While the medical profession felt a limitation of their influence by the removal of medical expertise from the Board membership, the Reorganisation of Offices Bill had broader aims. It was an early attempt to introduce a more professional administration within Scottish health and replace the 'placed expert' with the professional civil servant, including a Permanent Under Secretary for Scotland who would act as Vice President of the SBH.[149] The Association of Executive Officers and other Civil Servants issued a circular to coincide with the launch of the 1923 Reorganisation Bill:

> Expressing the view that the time has arrived to abolish the Board altogether, and to arrange for the duties of the department to be discharged by a permanent head directly responsible to the Secretary for Scotland and the Parliamentary Under Secretary.[150]

The Bill failed, as did the Reorganisation of Offices (Scotland) Bill of 1924 (this one introduced under of the short-lived Labour minority government by Scottish Secretary William Adamson,[151] who

---

148 *BMJ*, 1923 (2), 18 August 1923, 293.

149 The replacement of 'experts' with professional higher civil servants raises the question of the role of the civil service in policy formulation. According to the Interim Report of Reorganisation Committee of 1920/21, the duties appropriate to the Administrative Class in the Civil Service were those concerned with '[...] the formation of policy, with the co-ordination and improvement of Government machinery, and with the general administration and control of the departments of the Public Service [...].' Cited in G.K. Fry, *Statesmen in Disguise: The Changing Role of the Administrative Class of the British Home Civil Service 1853–1966* (Basingstoke: Macmillan, 1969), 155. This view of increased civil service authority seems to be in keeping with the so-called 'pluralist account' of policy formulation described by Keith Dowding in *The Civil Service* (Routledge, 1995), 3–4. Of course, central government did not necessarily share the civil service understanding of their role.

150 *BMJ*, 1923 (2), 24 November 1923, 1004.

151 William Adamson, Independent Labour MP for Fife (West) 1910–1931, Secretary (later Secretary of State) for Scotland January–November 1924, and

reluctantly accepted the need for some change in Scottish administrative mechanisms under pressure for reform from the Civil Service Union). One reason for the failure of the various Reorganisation Bills at this time was the clear support the existing Scottish Boards enjoyed. The Scottish Office was aware of the popular support in the country for the Board system: 'against the proposal we must consider the national sentiment which is I fancy favourable to the Board system – and, somewhat stronger, the sentiment of an authority actually in session in Scotland.'[152] Another Reorganisation Bill failed in 1927. It was not until 1928 that the long-proposed reorganisation of the Board system in Scotland finally occurred. The remaining original SBH members (Leishman, Leslie Mackenzie, MacPherson and Ritson) continued in office until the Health Board was replaced at the end of 1928.

Conclusion

The formation of a separate Scottish Board of Health owed something to the political reaction against growing nationalist feelings in the peripheral countries which formed the United Kingdom at war's end. This accords with Paterson's theory in regard to how the British welfare state evolved into a federalist structure: 'the implementation of apparently uniform policies has depended everywhere on adaptation to local conditions, many of these shaped by nationalist pressure [...].'[153] Yet, the creation of a separate Health Board for Scotland was not a major break with tradition. Scotland had a history of autonomy over social welfare matters dating back to the Edinburgh-based Board of Supervision for the Relief of the Poor in Scotland in

June 1929–August 1931. Adamson was a 'craggy and crafty' former miner, according to Tom Johnston's *Memories* (Collins, 1952), 100–103, passim.

152 NAS, HH1/521, Minute by J.E. de Watteville, Principal, Scottish Office on the Reorganisation of Offices Bill, 15 April 1924.

153 Paterson 'Scottish Autonomy and the Future of the Welfare State', 55.

1845, right through to the Highlands and Islands (Medical Services) Board of 1913. The formation of the SBH was part of a wider initiative to set up a new health ministry, itself a component of wartime plans for reconstruction.

Popular and political pressure from within Scotland, when coupled with the pressure brought to bear by Scottish Secretary Munro in the Cabinet, forced the issue of a separate Board of Health for Scotland. Munro's stance went against the wishes of Addison, who piloted the new central government department through parliament. However, once conceded by central government, there was considerable debate as to the form of this new Scottish health authority. The old system of bureaucratic Boards seemed out of date in an atmosphere of reconstruction yet it was preferred, due to political pressures from within Scotland, to the apparently more efficient civil service-based departmental structure of a Ministry of Health for Scotland. There was a belief within political and popular opinion that Scotland needed its own distinct health administration. The Scottish Poor Law Board of 1845, its successors, the Local Government Board for Scotland (1894), the Scottish Insurance Commissioners in 1911 to administer national health insurance, and the Highlands and Islands Medical Services Board of 1913, all helped create a tradition of autonomous Scottish technocratic control over health concerns alongside other welfare issues. From a Scottish viewpoint, the creation of a Scottish Board of Health seemed the rational way forward.

Personal considerations no doubt played a part in the favouring of a Board system, staffed by experts. The creation of the SBH had the consequence of maintaining a number of existing high profile administrators in post. Most of the personnel of the main Scottish units of social administration remained intact after the transition. In fact, the only casualty was the Solicitor General. The net personnel gain was the introduction of a Parliamentary Under-Secretary for Health, who, in theory, devoted the whole of his time to the administration of the Scottish Board of Health. However, the position of the Parliamentary Under-Secretary was often akin to that of an absentee landlord. It is clear that it was the Board members (quasi-experts bringing their experience to bear as circumstances arose) and their senior staff, operating through a series of small Committees, who were responsible for the day to day running of Scottish health affairs.

In the first few years of its existence, the ability of the new SBH to tackle the health problems of Scotland's population appeared to be limited. The SBH oversaw one of the most pressing needs of the day, housing. This took up much of its initial energy. In addition, the SBH was, like most government departments, subject to the vagaries of general elections and political ambition, affected by personnel changes in both the office of its main administrator, the Scottish Secretary and of the Parliamentary Under Secretary for Health.

A number of reports generated by the SBH in the 1920s identified an enhanced statutory health service within a reorganised local authority structure as a possible way ahead for meeting the pressing problems of Scotland's health – but implementation was for the future. This was not simply a Scottish health administration problem. The economic depression which affected the whole of Britain between 1921–1924 (and which emerged again in the later 1920s, and continued for much of the 1930s) made it difficult to promote dynamic health initiatives. Meanwhile, broader political will was not in favour of 'experts' or lay advisers dictating policy, as the rapid re-evaluation of the functions of Consultative Councils by the Ministry of Health suggests. Yet, the Scottish Consultative Councils continued to meet and report their findings to a Board of nominated technocrats. The Board continued to meet and awaited a time when political and economic conditions might prove more auspicious towards an expansionist health policy.

Muriel Ritson, member of the Scottish Board of Health, 1919–1928

2: Scottish Health Administration, 1929–1939

Introduction

The transformation of the Board to the Department of Health for Scotland on 1 January 1929 can be interpreted as a triumph of English bureaucratic imperatives over the Scottish tradition of administration through expertise. A fear of external control lay behind strong Scottish back bench opposition in Parliament to the Reorganisation of Offices Bills which were put to the Commons four times between 1923 and 1928, before the implementation of the government whip finally saw the measure safely through.[1] Additionally, there was often bitter opposition to these moves within the Scottish bureaucracy, although professional self-interest played a part in this.

An alternative interpretation is to see these changes as incorporating vital components of a twentieth century bureaucracy into an outdated Scottish system. Such a change was, therefore, necessary if Scotland was to have a strong voice in health policy formation as Britain moved toward a national health system. For example, the staff of the Department of Health for Scotland (formerly SBH) doubled within twenty years, from 400 in 1919 to 800 in 1939[2] to meet the growing needs of an increasingly bureaucratic system. Moreover, the impact of such change was minimalised by the fact that throughout the period there was continuity with the older system in terms of key figures. Muriel Ritson, one of the original Board members since 1919 remained at the Department until 1945. She had begun as women member on the Board in 1919, but was able to transfer her expertise in health insurance within the new administrative structure on the creation of the DHS in 1929. John Jeffrey too, continued in office. He

1 Gibson, *The Thistle and the Crown*, 67.

2 In comparison, Ministry of Health staff was 1,942 in 1919. See *BMJ*, 1919 (2), 609. By 1957, the staff of the DHS numbered 974.

had been Secretary to the Scottish Insurance Commissioners in 1911, then was appointed as Joint Secretary to the SBH in 1919. In 1929, he became Secretary of the DHS.

Arguably, the autonomous system of Scottish health administration put in place when the SBH was created was not completely lost with the reorganisation legislation of the 1920s, but further change came with the administrative modifications of the 1930s. First in 1935, the Department was reorganised along Whitehall civil service lines and in the same year, the local government division of the Office of the Secretary of State for Scotland moved north from Dover House to Edinburgh. This was followed up in 1939, when a new-style Scottish Office was created, and all but Ministerial duties, parliamentary and liaison work, were switched from London to new Edinburgh headquarters. The system of government by local 'experts' characterised by the SBH had gone, but now the remote influence of Whitehall was tempered by the relocation of much of the machinery of the government through the Scottish Office to Edinburgh.

The Change from Board to Department of Health for Scotland, 1926–1929

Under the Secretaries of State Act of 1926, the office of Secretary for Scotland was upgraded to an office of state. However, the Treasury continued to pursue the pay differential between Scottish and other staff, and refused to allow the increase in salary which went with this elevation in status. All SBH appointments remained at lower pay levels than the Ministry of Health. Yet, Sir John Gilmour's enhanced appointment (Gilmour had been Scottish Secretary since 1924) fed down the hierarchy. In keeping with the expansion of the Scottish Secretary's duties as chief of a department of state, Walter Elliot, Parliamentary Under Secretary for Health, was given a wider remit and became Parliamentary Under Secretary of State for Scotland. Elliot was the longest serving Parliamentary Under Secretary involved with health. With the exception of James Stewart, (the Labour PUSH from January to November 1924), Elliot represented health in Scotland from 1923 to 1929. Although his duties widened in 1926, Elliot retained his role of health spokesperson in Scotland.

In March 1927, Gilmour introduced a Bill to transform the Scottish Boards of Health, Agriculture and Prisons into three Departments, answerable to him as Secretary of State. The Departments were to be staffed by administrative civil servants.[3] The Bill was not widely supported in Parliament. William Adamson feared that Government policy was to subordinate Scottish administration to Whitehall to a far greater extent than previously and to '[...] remove from Scotland practically the last vestige of independent Government and nationhood, and to have its centre in London.'[4] The Reorganisation Bill of 1927 did not go beyond a Second Reading. Gilmour introduced a fresh Reorganisation Bill in February 1928. In order to deflect the criticism levied at the previous Bill that control was to be shifted to Whitehall, Gilmour inserted a clause specifying that the new Departments were to be situated in Edinburgh. There was a clear attempt in the new Bill to channel advice along traditional Whitehall civil service lines and away from the 'experts' who dominated the Boards. SBH members were free to act independently, both of each other, and of the government. Whether Board members' policy suggestions were implemented is another matter. What is clear from the various Reorganisation Bills however, was a desire on the part of Scottish Secretary of State Gilmour to receive a common line of advice from a unified body of trained civil servants.[5] In putting

3 'This Bill [...] is designed in the main to alter what is known as the Board system and to set up in its place a system of Departments, following upon the lines both of the Education department which we already have in Scotland and of those other great Departments of State which exist here in England such as the Department of Agriculture and the Ministry of Health.' HOC debates, 23–3–27, vol. 204 col. 465.

4 HOC debates, 23–3–27, vol. 204 col. 436.

5 'The main objective of the first three Clauses of the Bill is to substitute with respect to certain Departments in Edinburgh the ordinary Civil Service system for what is known as the Board system: the change is in accord with recommendations of the Royal Commission on the Civil Service [which reported in 1913] and has the merits of ensuring a more effective responsibility for action and advice, of diminishing the possibilities of appointments being

forward the 1928 Bill Gilmour had the added fortune that several members of the SBH (Leslie Mackenzie and Leishman) and of the Boards of Agriculture and Prisons were due to retire almost simultaneously. It seemed the scene was set to make a fresh start in the administration of Scotland's internal affairs.

Under reorganisation, the make up of the SBH was altered in order to pave the way towards a Departmental set up. Section 2 of the 1928 Reorganisation Bill provided that no vacancies in the SBH or the Board of Agriculture or the Prison Commissioners Office were to be filled. In addition, Section 3 Clause (2) of the Scottish Board of Health Act of 1919 was to be repealed. This clause dealt with the position of experts in the Board. The 1919 SBH Act had stipulated: 'The Board [...] shall at all times include two registered medical practitioners, one or more women, and a member of the Faculty of Advocates or law agent of not less than ten years' standing.' The repeal of this particular clause went to the heart of the change from Scottish Board of Health to Department of Health for Scotland. The special position and assigned role of the expert was removed. Specialist advice was not to be cast aside, but the permanent staff of the new Department was to be trained civil servants and not the Scottish Secretary of State's nominees. Gilmour's standpoint was unequivocal:

> What I am out for is efficiency. I want to get the best man [sic] for a post and I want that man to be there so that he may be absolutely free of patronage of any kind. I want him to get there through the ordinary channels of the Civil Service. The system has proved itself to be of great advantage to the Departments in England.[6]

The role of the expert in the Scottish Board structure was defended by Labour MP Sidney Webb, who suggested that the Government should take care that expert advisers were not smothered in the transfer to a

---

made for political or similar reasons and of facilitating interchange of personnel between the Scottish Office and Departments in Edinburgh. The unified control in each Department will not, of course, in any way preclude recourse being had to expert advice whether from outside or within the Department'. NAS HH1/526, Explanatory Notes, Re-Organisation of Offices (Scotland) Bill, 17 February 1928.

6 HOC debates, 28–2–28, vol. 214 col. 267.

Departmental administrative structure. According to Webb, abolition of Boards was likely to 'subordinate in an altogether improper way' appointees from the professions who had a range of knowledge and experience that the career civil servants could not possibly have.[7]

During the debates on the 1928 Reorganisation Bill it was clear that the Labour opposition feared that even if the Scottish Boards were not moving to Whitehall, the centre of power was. In a year when the Scottish National Party was created, support for home rule was by no means a long-forgotten Liberal pledge, and there was a clear sense among opposition MPs that the Reorganisation of Offices smacked of government of Scotland by remote control. Tom Johnston[8] stated:

> Now we find this Government [...] deliberately attempting to take away the detailed administration of public affairs in Scotland from bodies of presumably skilled men [sic], who have been nominated because of their knowledge of those particular affairs. It is proposed that the direction of these affairs should be handed over to men who, whatever examinations they might have passed in Oxford or Cambridge, have not proved their fitness to conduct those great businesses upon which the lives and happiness of our people depend.[9]

Johnston was also a firm supporter of the Scottish Board of Health itself and despaired of handing over its discretionary powers to a permanent civil service.[10]

---

7 HOC debates, 28–2–28, vol. 214 col. 286–289.

8 Tom Johnston was born in Kirkintilloch in 1881. He was the son of a licensed grocer. Johnston was educated at Lenzie Academy and Glasgow University. In 1906, after inheriting a printing establishment, Johnston founded the Labour weekly, *Forward* which he edited for 27 years. He served as Independent Labour MP for West Stirlingshire from 1922–24, 1929–1931 and 1935–1945 and for Dundee from 1924–9. Johnston was Parliamentary Under Secretary of State for Scotland, 1929–1931. He was appointed Lord Privy Seal in 1931. Between 1941 and 1945 he served as Secretary of State for Scotland in the Wartime Coalition Government In the 1950s and 60s he served as Chairman on many public boards, including the North of Scotland Hydro Electric Board, the Scottish Tourist Board and the Broadcasting Council for Scotland.

9 HOC debates, 28–2–28, vol. 214 col. 271–2.

10 'Here is a Board selected for its skill and knowledge of Health in Scotland. The Right Hon. Gentleman says he cannot always get a unanimous report or advice from it, but why should he? Why does he always want a unanimous report? Is it not his job to get both majority and minority advice, and to decide? But what he

At its Second Reading in March, Labour MP Dr. Drummond Shiels[11] described the Reorganisation Bill as '[...] a triumph for bureaucracy at the expense of their national sentiment.'[12] The Lord Advocate, William McLean Watson[13] replying for the Government, said that presently there was no first-class civil service position open to Scots in Scotland, but the new Bill would make this possible. What was required now was administrative knowledge, and the power of taking a concentrated opinion of all the expert knowledge available. The failure of the Board system to allow this was one reason why Boards were not as efficient as would be a Department. He assured the House that at the outset, and he hoped in succession, the existing members of the SBH would remain in office.

> In form their appointment would be different, but they would be there, and their expert knowledge would be continuously available. There would be no change in that aspect of it and the advisory councils will carry on just the same as they are at present.[14]

---

is proposing to do now is to hand over his decision to a permanent civil servant. He is going to take the advice of a permanent civil servant, who has at some stage in the business to make up his mind upon the conflicting advice which he will get from various quarters. The Right Hon. Gentleman is taking a very serious step indeed when he plans to hand over the complicated and very difficult administration of affairs in Scotland to one civil servant, who may be a Scotsman or who may not, who may have some knowledge of Scottish affairs, or who may not. His sole qualification, so far as we know now, is that he has to pass a Higher Grade examination set by the Civil Service Commission.' HOC debates, 28–2–28, vol. 214 col. 274.

11 Drummond Shiels studied medicine at Edinburgh University, graduating M.B Ch.B. In the First World War, he was awarded the Military Cross and the Belgian Croix de Guerre. He then became a member of Edinburgh Town Council before becoming Labour MP for East Edinburgh from 1924–1931. In 1927, he was a member of the Special Commission on the Constitution of Ceylon. Between 1929 and 1931 he served as Parliamentary Under Secretary of State at the Colonial Office. He was knighted in 1939.

12 HOC debates, 5–3–28, vol. 214 col. 898.

13 William McLean Watson was born in Cowdenbeath and educated at Ruskin College 1906–7. He served as Labour MP for Dunfermline Burghs from 1922–31 and again from 1935–50.

14 HOC debates, 5–3–28, vol. 214 col. 922.

Sir Archibald Sinclair,[15] supporting the Bill stated that he believed the best way to facilitate 'administrative autonomy' was through:

> A departmental organisation under the direction of a skilled civil servant, who knows the ropes, who has been trained at the Treasury and knows his way about, will give Scotland far greater autonomy than she enjoys at present.[16]

In other words, Scotland's best interests lay in employing civil servants who could play the system to Scottish advantage.

At the Third Reading of the Bill, there was a last-ditch attempt to delete the provision to abolish the SBH. This led Gilmour to express in plain terms the problems which he faced with SBH.

> We have heard much about the technical experts. I am not averse from, nor will any regulation which I make prevent intercourse between the experts and those responsible for administration [...]. Parliament must direct policy and control the experts. We know that the expert is often carried beyond the bounds of what is possible in finance or in relation to actual affairs. Is the expert always to have his way? [...] if the medical man had his way, he might possibly impose upon Parliament and the country a system – eminently desirable no doubt in itself – but so extravagant, or so much in advance of the times, that Parliament could not tolerate it.[17]

The intention behind Gilmour's reorganisation proposal is clear. Medical and other expertise within the Board system could lead to the favouring of expensive and radical policy. This ran contrary to the administrative system as it had developed through the professional civil service acting for the government in power. Professional bureaucrats could seek the advice of outside experts. There would be no commitment to act upon such advice. The changes brought about to

---

15 Archibald Sinclair was elected Liberal MP for Caithness and Sutherland in 1922. He entered the army in 1910 and served as Personal Military Secretary for the Secretary of State for War, 1919–21. He served as National Liberal Secretary of State for Scotland between 1931–1932. He was leader of the Scottish Liberal Federation and became Chairman of the Parliamentary Liberal Party in 1935. He also served as a member on the Empire Marketing Board between 1928–30 and was on the Executive Committee of the League of Nations Union.

16 HOC debates, 5–3–28, vol. 214 col. 882.

17 HOC debates, 9–7–28, vol. 219 col. 1986.

Scottish health administration can be compared the system to Immergut outlined for other parts of Western Europe, with the bureaucracy as active participants in health policy programmes. The Scottish bureaucracy, here in the re-modelled Department of Health for Scotland, was now to serve as a filter through which interest group opinions could be conveyed to the Scottish Secretary in a less opinionated manner than in the old Board structure.[18]

Although patronage in appointments was ended by the reorganisation of 1928, with outside experts gradually replaced by recruits from the First Division of the civil service, it was not until the mid-1930s that the Department was reorganised on professional civil service lines. By then, only one original Health Board member remained in office. It is no coincidence that the sole top level survivor of the change from Board to Department was not a medical member nor the legal expert, but Muriel Ritson (now Woman Assistant Secretary of the DHS) who had made a career as an administrator with special knowledge of health insurance.

The Reorganisation of Offices (Scotland) Act was passed on 3 August 1928. It reorganised the Boards of Health, Agriculture and Prisons into three separate Departments under the control of the Secretary of State for Scotland. The 1928 legislation also allowed for continuity with the old Boards. As has been noted, SBH member (Ritson) and some Board staff (including John Jeffrey and John E. Highton)[19] were transferred to the new Department and their salary levels, tenure in office and pension rights were protected. However, their duties in relation to the new Department were directed by the Secretary of State. The Board system which had been so severely criticised in the Civil Service Royal Commission in 1914, and the

18 Immergut, *Health Politics*, 23.

19 John Elborn Highton was born in 1884. He studied Law at Glasgow University. In 1905 he joined the civil service as Assistant of Excise. He became one of the six district inspectors under the National Health Insurance Commission on its creation in 1912. In the early years of the war, he worked in the Ministry of Shipping, then in 1916 returned to the NHIC which was taken under the control of the SBH on its creation. He was Chief Insurance Inspector of the DHS at his appointment to the post of Permanent Secretary in 1933, which he held until 1939. He obtained the CBE in 1935.

Haldane Committee on the Machinery of Government in 1918, and which had survived attempted legislative changes in 1923, 1924 and 1927, was finally replaced.

The fate of the other expert SBH members was determined during the course of 1928. In March, Ewan MacPherson, the Board's legal member, resigned as chairman due to ill health. Sir James Leishman, head of Pensions and Insurance since 1911, first in the LGBS and then the SBH, succeeded MacPherson for the remaining months of 1928. Ill health also brought about the resignation of William Leslie Mackenzie in May 1928 as the Reorganisation Bill was passing through Parliament. Leishman followed him shortly after into retirement. Leishman's retirement was announced at the final meeting of the Scottish Board of Health in December 1928.[20] In the transfer from 'expert' Board to Department with a traditional civil service structure, Muriel Ritson, was the sole surviving Board member. Ritson was appointed as the mandatory woman on the Board in 1919. In 1929, she became one of three Assistant Secretaries (Woman Assistant Secretary) and later became Establishment and Pensions Controller of the DHS – a position she held until 1945.[21]

The Scottish Board of Health held its final meeting on 28 December 1928. It was replaced by the Department of Health for Scotland (DHS) on 1 January 1929. The final meeting of the SBH was an occasion for mutual respect. The two remaining Board members (Leishman and Ritson) received thanks from the staff. The Board members returned thanks for the services of the staff: 'for carrying out the work of the Board during a period of exceptional difficulty.'[22] No one mentioned that many of the difficulties had been caused by central government spending caps and Scottish Office pressures to reform the Board for most of its ten-year history. Two months earlier, in October 1928, similar sentiments were expressed by John Jeffrey whose appointment to the position of Permanent Secretary to the new

---

20 *BMJ*, 1929 (1), 5 January 1929, 36.

21 Ritson served as a member of the Beveridge Committee [Committee on Social Insurance and Allied Services] representing the DHS in 1941/2. In 1945 she moved to the newly formed Ministry of Pensions before her retirement in 1946.

22 NAS, HH75/27, SBH minutes, 28 December 1928.

Department of Health for Scotland, the Board warmly acknowledged. Jeffrey recognised that despite the shift from Board to Department, this did not automatically herald a bright new dawn for those concerned with Scottish health policy formulation:

> He realised to the very fullest [extent] the importance of the position and the difficulties in front of the Department for the next few years [...]. In spite of all the difficulties, the Board had a very loyal staff and he had never seen those difficulties reflected in the quality of the work done.[23]

The new Department no longer had executive Board members, but this did not end expert input into Scottish health policy. John Parlane Kinloch[24] took over Leslie Mackenzie's mantle as medical representative. Parlane Kinloch was appointed as Chief Medical Officer of the DHS in 1929 (as the new Department chose a structure that mirrored the Ministry of Health). The new appointment made the Chief Medical Officer effective head of the medical staff in all its work, subject to consultations with the Permanent Secretary and the Scottish Secretary.[25]

As Chief Medical Officer, Parlane Kinloch organised the medical staff of the Department with the assistance of two Deputy Chief Medical Officers. Together they co-operated with the administrative staff in matters of policy formulation where medical questions were involved and advised the administrative staff as necessary on general medical matters. The main activities of the medical staff by the 1930s

---

23 NAS, HH75/27, SBH minutes, 19 October 1928.

24 John Parlane Kinloch was born in Vale of Leven, Dumbartonshire in 1886. He was educated at Glasgow High School. He studied medicine at Glasgow University and graduated MB ChB in 1909. He obtained his public health diploma from Cambridge the following year. He gained his MD from Glasgow in 1913, and was a Resident Physician at Ruchill Fever Hospital, Glasgow between 1911–1914. From 1914, he lectured in Public Health at Aberdeen University, also serving as Deputy MOH for the city. He served in France in 1918 in charge of a mobile hygienic field laboratory. He was appointed MOH for Aberdeen in 1923. In the same year, he became Head of Aberdeen University Public Health Department. He was appointed as first Chief Medical Officer of the DHS in 1929. He held the position until ill-health forced his premature retirement in 1932. He died the same year aged 46.

25 *BMJ*, 1928 (2), 17 November 1928, 909.

were in the environmental health services, personal health services, and the administration of the municipal hospitals. Parlane Kinloch's legacy in terms of furthering the statutory medical services bore fruit in the realms of morbidity statistics. Annual DHS Incapacity Reports for the insured population were produced from 1930. Parlane Kinloch also demonstrated an interest in the long-term improvement of Scottish infant and child welfare.[26] He also expressed a desire to survey and re-organise Scottish health services into an integrated unit.[27]

Poor health brought Parlane Kinloch's premature retirement and then death in 1932 aged 46, when James Law Brownlie[28] was appointed Chief Medical Officer, in his place. Brownlie served as CMO until his retirement in November 1937. James MacAlister Mackintosh[29] then replaced Brownlie. The reorganisation of the Board as the DHS 1928/9 brought with it the appointment of a Permanent Secretary for Health, John Jeffrey, previously Secretary of the SBH. In October 1933, Jeffrey became Permanent Under Secretary of State at the Scottish Office in London. John E. Highton, another survivor from the SBH, was then appointed in his place as Permanent Secretary at the DHS. Meanwhile in 1934, the Treasury finally agreed that

26 For John Parlane Kinloch's interest in the health of insured workers see chapter six. For his promotion of preventive health care, see comments in infant and maternal health chapter.

27 See discussions on the Cathcart Report later in this chapter.

28 Brownlie graduated from Glasgow in Medicine in 1913 then took a Diploma in Public Health at Cambridge in 1916. In 1918 he obtained his MD. He became a Medical Officer for the DHS in 1930 working closely with Parlane Kinloch, and had previously been Bacteriologist and Pathologist for the County of Lanarkshire.

29 Born in 1891, John M. Mackintosh was educated at Glasgow High School and Glasgow University where he graduated MA in 1911, and then obtained a medical degree in 1916. He became a barrister in Gray's Inn and then during the war served first as a combatant and then in the RAMC. In 1920, he obtained a DPH at London University. He gained his MD at Glasgow in 1923. In 1924, he became Assistant MOH for Dorset and then Burton-on-Trent. In 1930, he became MOH and School MO for the County of Northampton. He served as CMO at the DHS between 1937–1942.

salary scales for the DHS for assistant secretaries, principal and senior executive levels should be on the same level as those for Whitehall.[30]

The new Scottish Departments were each under the direction of the Secretary of State, yet significantly, they retained independent statutory status. The transformation in 1928 of the Health, Agriculture and Prison Boards into Departments more directly under the control of the Secretary of State aroused misgivings that control of Scottish government affairs in Scotland was at risk. Yet in spite of the legislative change, local autonomy was not completely removed. For example, the 1928 reorganisation allowed the new Departments a degree of independence from the Secretary of State. There was no common staffing or ready interchanging of staff between the Departments, which fostered an independent outlook and local loyalty within them. In addition, future reorganisation of the Departments could not be effected by the Scottish Secretary of State but was still to pass through parliament.

The Local Government (Scotland) Act, 1929

The Reorganisation of Offices Act was swiftly followed by the Local Government (Scotland) Act of 10 May 1929 (which came into operation in May 1930). In relation to health services, the 1929 Act was an attempt to increase the co-ordination of statutory medical services under single or unified (re-organised) units of local authority. The legislation attempted to rationalise services, prevent over-lapping and increase the cost-effectiveness of the statutory health services provided. The Local Government Act transformed the units of local health administration from small parish councils to county councils and town councils of large burghs (over 20,000). In addition to the abolition of parish councils, local Education Authorities were disbanded and many of the powers of smaller burghs were removed.

30 NAS, DD1/12, see file on: 'General Policy – Reorganisation of the Department of Health, 1934'.

All existing personal health work undertaken by local agencies (for example, infant and maternal welfare and tuberculosis services), was transferred to the new local health authorities, as was the school health service (previously administered by Education Authorities at local level, although centrally controlled by the SBH). In addition, existing Poor Law arrangements were overhauled, but unlike the English legislation, the Scottish Act did not specifically refer to the municipalisation of Poor Law hospital services. This change was later included in a DHS memorandum at the end of 1929 outlining the service required under the new Act. The new legislation echoed the findings of the MacLean Committee of the Ministry of Reconstruction in 1917 which recommended a transfer of functions from Poor Law authorities in England and Wales to local authority control. The legislation drew upon the proposals of the SBH Consultative Council on Health Administration and General Questions. Two Reports in 1921 and again in 1923 recommended the reduction of the number and a great increase in the size of local authorities. The feeling among leading public health officials was that existing services overlapped were uncoordinated and economically inefficient.[31] The 1923 Report recommended the concentration of all health services in one rationalised local authority for each area based on counties and burghs with a population of over 50,000.[32] These suggestions now came to fruition – albeit in a watered down version, with the minimum

31 'Briefly stated, the position is that money, whether it is provided by employers or employees, by Local Authorities or by the Treasury, is being supplied with a view to providing a comprehensive medical service, ranging from the medical requirements of the Poor Law through the whole system of National Health Insurance to the Public Health Services provided by the local authorities, and it is generally admitted that in many of its aspects, and despite the large expenditure, the service is inadequate.' Lothian Health Board, Edinburgh, LHB24/8/16, *Transactions of the Scottish Association of Insurance Committees, 18th Annual Meeting, 1928*, 41. Address by John Parlane Kinloch, (Head of the Public Health Department and MOH, City of Aberdeen) entitled, 'The Adequacy of the Medical Service, and the Role of the Medical Practitioner in the Official Organisation.'

32 SBH, Consultative Councils on Local Health Administration and General Health Questions and Highlands and Islands Report on *Reformed Local Authority Health and Public Assistance* (Edinburgh: HMSO, 1923).

population for a new local health authority set at 20,000 by Scottish Secretary of State Gilmour.

There was strong dissent from opposition political parties to the intended reform of local government. Scottish Labour politicians were vehemently opposed to the new proposals.

> Although the Right Hon. Gentleman [Scottish Secretary of State Gilmour] was at some considerable pains to attempt to allay the apprehensions about this Bill, it nevertheless remains a fact that this Bill is more drastic, more reckless, more desperate, and more deadly in its attack upon local government and democracy than is the Bill presented by the Ministry of Health.[33]

A key reason for the bitter opposition of the Labour Party to the Bill was the implication of moving funding for health schemes from a percentage grant for local authorities schemes to a block grant system with the sum fixed by the Treasury for all local authority services. According to Neville Chamberlain, Minister of Health in 1928, this would allow local authorities: '[...] that independence and initiative which I think they value above all things.'[34] How local authorities were to afford to maintain (and in some cases create) municipal health services under the block grant system was an open question.

When the 1929 Act was implemented at the local level, it caused a great deal of reorganisation in health provision. In the first instance, the percentage grant to local health authorities was removed causing a reappraisal of the funding of statutory services. The Convention of Royal Burghs issued a memorandum on 9 December 1928 opposing this change, as did individual burgh councils such as Lanark, which sent a memorandum to the Scottish Secretary of State in December 1928 opposing the new funding arrangements.[35] The percentage grant had been the practice in personal health services since the 1915

---

33 See Tom Johnston's speech, HOC debates, 3–12–28, vol. 223 col. 878.

34 HOC debates, 26–11–28, vol. 223 col. 105.

35 'The [Lanark] Town Council is also opposed to the system proposed to be introduced of Block Grants in substitution for the present system of percentage grants, the percentage grants being more equitable in adjusting financial relations as between the Exchequer and the Local Authorities.' Clydeside District Council, Lindsay Institute, Lanark, Royal Burgh of Lanark, minutes, 10 December 1928, 327.

Notification of Births (Extension) Act which allowed Scottish health authorities to claim back 50% of expenditure on infant and maternal welfare schemes from central government. The new block grant allocated to local authorities was based on their actual expenditure for 1927. Yet this was an 'economy' year, hence any future development of existing services would not be met from the Treasury's block grant but would have to be levied by a local rate. Dr. Drummond Shiels suspected that the Treasury had adopted the block grant as a means of checking central funding for rapidly developing services which were likely to expand still more. Some areas had as yet, to develop a full range of personal health services. Drummond Shiels gave the example of Caithness where (as in a number of other districts of Scotland) there was as yet no child welfare service.[36]

Under the new legislation, the general Exchequer contribution formula was designed to adjust differences between the rateable value of particular areas by giving a higher grant to authorities in an area with a low rateable value and high administrative costs, than to more wealthy areas. But this could not make up the shortfall in areas where the rateable value was extremely low. For example, in 1936, a 1d rate in Orkney raised £190, while a 1d rate produced £2,188 in Midlothian. Even with vastly different target populations, it was impossible to expect local authorities in these respective areas to provide a similar range of services. Once again it seemed that reasons of Government economy were impinging on the provision of health services across the country.

The Local Government (Scotland) Act of 1929 was a major achievement and in some respects the culmination of a desire to reorganise the Scottish system of local government which had been in evidence for many years. Parish councils were abolished, small burghs

---

36 'I would like to ask the government whether it is expected that any district which has no child welfare and maternity service at the present time is likely to establish one within the next five years, seeing that to do so would involve a great increase in the local rates? I think it is quite obvious there is no likely development of child welfare and service which could be regarded as excessive, and which would be beyond the needs of the community, in view of the fact that this problem of maternal mortality has been receiving special attention.' HOC debates, 5–12–28, vol. 225 col. 1329–30.

lost their autonomous powers and county councils were re-organised. The massive upheaval caused by the Local Government legislation both in Scotland and in England and Wales, and its modification of local funding for social services, made it unpopular.

The new local authorities were made responsible for former poor law health services including the hospitals, and for maternity and child welfare schemes, and school health (now administered as a local authority health service rather than by local education authorities). In theory this meant linking infant and school health under one agency to provide care for children from birth to the age of fourteen.[37]

The keystone of the new legislation as regards statutory health services was to transfer hospital treatment of the sick poor from the Poor Law to local authority care in municipal hospitals, but this took some time. For, while the new public health powers removed the stigma of the old Poor Law, there remained a two-tier system of hospital provision. The old Poor Law institutions had lower standards of building and equipment than the voluntary hospitals. Such a situation could not be changed overnight. Only five Poor Law hospitals in the whole of Scotland had been converted to local authority general hospitals by 1936.[38]

The fears of those who felt the imposition of a block grant was a way of curtailing local health authority expenditure were apparently realised with the release of the DHS estimates on 29 March 1930. The figures showed a decrease of £318,576 from the previous year. This was directly attributed to substantially reduced state funding following the Local Government (Scotland) Act, 1929 in which grants were replaced by a block Exchequer contribution to the local authorities.[39]

---

37 The implications of the Local Government (Scotland) Act of 1929 for school health inspection are discussed in chapter four.

38 DHS, *Committee on Scottish Health Services Report* (Edinburgh: HMSO, 1936), 234–5 [Cmd 5204]. Glasgow, and other Conservative-controlled local authorities, balked at the costs of plans to reorganise municipal health services, including extended hospital provision and a reorganised general practitioner service. Such plans were delayed until the local election success of the Labour Party at the end of 1933. For more on this see Ian Levitt, *Poverty and Welfare in Scotland 1890–1948* (Edinburgh: Edinburgh University Press, 1988), 162.

39 *BMJ*, 1930 (1), 12 April 1930, 715.

In 1936, the DHS Committee on Scottish Health Services reported that the general Exchequer contribution was not sufficient to 'secure the development of health services on the scale required for national health policy'. The Committee recommended that the Treasury provide further assistance towards local authority health expenditure. The Committee proposed that a 50% grant to run for a 'number of years' should be given in order to create new health services and build up existing ones.[40]

Despite the limiting effects of altered Treasury arrangements for local authority funding after 1929, the Local Government (Scotland) Act gave local authorities the opportunity to combine for the purposes of health service provision. In many cases this was a necessity if any capital health project was required. Municipal health services were expanded in the 1930s and early 1940s. So much so, that discussions on a future 'state health service' in the later 1930s and 1940s tended in the direction of a municipal state medical service. Certainly, this was the view of the Scottish Health Services Committee Report of 1936. The Cathcart[41] Report (as the Report became known) felt that local

40 DHS, *Committee on Scottish Health Services Report*, 289.

41 Professor Edward Provan Cathcart was educated at Ayr Academy and then studied medicine at Glasgow University. He graduated MB ChB in 1900, MD in 1904, and DSc in 1906. He was Lecturer in Chemical Physiology at Glasgow University from 1905–15 and then Professor of Physiology at London Hospital Medical School from 1915–19. He returned to Glasgow in 1919, first as Professor of Chemical Physiology (1919–28), then as Regius Professor of Physiology (1928–47). He was Emeritus Professor until his death in 1951. Cathcart was awarded the CBE in 1924. Cathcart was a member of many Government committees of investigation. These included: the War Cabinet Scientific Committee on Food Policy, Advisory Council on Education in Scotland, Medical Advisory Committee (Scotland), Agricultural Research Council, Medical Research Council (as Chairman of the Nutrition Committee), Army Hygiene Advisory Committee, and the Ministry of Health Advisory Committee on Nutrition. Most notably, he served as member (and from April 1935 as Chairman) of the DHS Scottish Health Services Committee (Cathcart Committee) which was appointed in June 1933 and which reported in July 1936. He represented Glasgow University on the General Medical Council between 1933 and 1945. He formally retired in 1947, but was later appointed as first Chairman of the Western Regional Hospital Board (Scotland) after the

authority health services were: '[...] bound to extend further [...] and [...] influence if not determine the future medical organisation of the country.'[42]

The trend towards larger units of local government was certainly successful in terms of the development of a regional scheme of public health in the Aberdeen area. The administrative changes effected by the Local Government (Scotland) Act, 1929 paved the way for an expanded regional scheme for the Counties of Aberdeen and Kincardineshire, and the city of Aberdeen, to include all medical services (including municipal hospitals and even veterinary services) within the scheme administered by a single chief Medical Officer of Health for the region. The regional scheme was created under the stewardship of then Aberdeen MOH, John Parlane Kinloch. The inauguration of the scheme however, pre-dated the 1929 local government reform. As early as 1920, Matthew Hay, MOH for Aberdeen between 1888–1923, suggested a co-ordinated scheme for the North East. The suggestion was actively taken up in the Aberdeen Medico-Chirurgical Society, which gave the plan intra-professional backing.[43] The regional scheme was initiated in 1925 when Aberdeen

---

creation of the NHS. He was forced to resign after a few months due to ill-health. He died on 18 February 1954 aged 76.

42 DHS, *Committee on Scottish Health Services Report*, 162.

43 The scheme was suggested by Matthew Hay at a special meeting of the Aberdeen Medico-Chirurgical Society on 20 February 1920 to which all medical practitioners in the North of Scotland were invited. A joint conference attended by representatives of the Society, Aberdeen City Corporation, Aberdeen University Court, the managers of Aberdeen Royal Infirmary and the Royal Hospital for Sick Children in April 1920 approved the scheme. By 1922, the decision was taken to build the new Infirmary and other component parts of the regional scheme at the 112 acres Foresterhill site. The new Royal Hospital for Sick Children was opened on the site in 1928 with 134 beds, followed by a new 500-bed Royal Infirmary in 1936. A Maternity Hospital and a new Medical School followed by 1938. For more on the regional scheme see I.D. Lavack and H.A.F. Dudley, *Aberdeen Royal Infirmary: the People's Hospital of the North East* (Bailliere Tindall, 1992), 45–54. For more on Aberdeen Medico-Chirurgical Society's sponsorship of the regional scheme, see J. Jenkinson, *Scottish Medical Societies 1731–1939: their History and Records* (Edinburgh: Edinburgh University Press, 1993), 34

County Council brought all the health services of the county (including school health) under a Joint Health Committee. In 1928, Aberdeen Town Council converted the Poor Law Hospital at Woodend into a general municipal hospital for the region, preceding the 1929 legislative changes by a year.

> In Aberdeen [...] [Parlane Kinloch] was principally known as the creator of a hospital policy for the city which was recognised as pioneer work of a high order and hailed as a precursor in miniature of the Local Government Act.[44]

The implementation of the North East regional scheme did not signal the end of the individual local authority health committees. However, there was pooling of overall costs, and a new liaison committee consisting of both local burgh and county councillors co-ordinated the regional medical services. An indication of the integration of medical services under the regional scheme was the involvement of general practitioners in statutory services, for example in Aberdeenshire general practitioners were admitted as visiting physicians to all infectious disease hospitals in the area, and all were employed as Public Assistance medical officers. The professors of medicine, surgery and midwifery at Aberdeen University were each appointed by Aberdeen Town Council as consultants to the municipal hospitals. This measure widened the clinical scope for the teaching of students at Aberdeen medical school and also improved the staffing levels and status of the municipal hospitals.[45] For such reasons, the unique North East scheme was held up as an ideal model of co-ordination and regionalisation in the 1936 Cathcart Report.[46] Parlane Kinloch's association with the scheme helped facilitate his short-lived appointment as CMO in the DHS (1929–1932).

The 1929 Local Government (Scotland) Act, did not fulfil the intention of the legislators with regards health administration. Partly

---

44 Obituary for Parlane Kinloch by A.S.M. MacGregor, MOH, Glasgow, *Public Health*, 45 (no. 6), March 1932, 165.

45 For more on this see the chapter by Harry Rae, [CMO for the North-East Region], 'Public Health in the North-East', in J.F. Tocher, ed., *The Book of Buchan (Jubilee Volume)* (Aberdeen: P.Scrogie Ltd, 1943), 206–7.

46 DHS, *Committee on Scottish Health Services Report*, Appendix VI, 403–404.

this was due to the time taken to re-organise local authorities and the delicate balancing act that was required, for example, in integrating the school medical service into existing services and in attempting to transform Poor Law hospitals into a municipal service under the shadow of cost efficiency. There were notable exceptions, for example in Glasgow after 1933, where all duties relating to child welfare, school health, tuberculosis and poor law medical services (both dispensaries and former poor law hospitals) were performed under a single Glasgow Health Department, and 500 new beds were provided at the Southern General Hospital. Yet, concerns about local rate levels (particularly against a background of high, sustained unemployment levels) meant local health initiatives remained at a premium. The much vaunted integrated system of health services (strongly supported within the Ministry of Health and the DHS) which was supposed to follow as a consequence of the reorganisation of local government in 1929, remained an unattainable ideal. The aspirations of DHS Secretary, John Jeffrey: 'Under the new Act it will be almost possible to watch over the health of man in his seven ages, with that small gap between school leaving age and sixteen which the raising of the leaving age to fifteen will leave,'[47] awaited fulfilment.

1930s Administrative Changes

Despite the changes in the structure of Scottish health services from top to bottom between 1928 and the mid 30s, the centre of Scottish government, the Scottish Office, remained in London. In 1935 a Scottish Office branch (more properly a branch of the 'Departments of the Secretary of State for Scotland') was finally opened in Edinburgh. In that year, the local government division of the Office of the

47 Lothian Health Board Archives, Edinburgh, LHB24/8/17, *Transactions of Scottish Association of Insurance Committees, 17th Annual Meeting, 1929,* Address by John Jeffrey, Secretary, DHS, 28 September 1929.

Secretary of State for Scotland was moved north from Dover House to Edinburgh. By 1938, 95% of DHS staff was located in Edinburgh.[48]

In 1936, Walter Elliot became Scottish Secretary of State on the death of Sir Godfrey Collins.[49] Elliot had a great deal of experience in Scottish government, and Scottish health in particular. Between 1924 and 1929 as PUSH (later as Parliamentary Under Secretary of State for Scotland) he was given a fairly free hand by first of all Lord Novar (who was of course, in the upper house), and then by Sir John Gilmour. As Scottish Secretary of State in November 1936, in a notable example of role reversal, Elliot appointed a Departmental Committee on Scottish Administration under Gilmour. The Gilmour Committee investigated the functions of the Scottish Office and the Departments and looked at a possible redistribution of offices from London to Edinburgh. Meanwhile, the office of Secretary of State for Scotland was itself belatedly given full recognition in the Ministers of the Crown Act of 1937, which paved the way for all Cabinet ministers to receive an equal salary of £5,000. The office of Scottish Secretary was at last recognised as first-class department of state.

The Gilmour Committee was driven by the desire of the Scottish Office to create a modern professional civil service structure to oversee Scottish administration. There could be no place for fully autonomous Departments within this revised structure.[50] The 1938 Gilmour Report recommended that the statutory Departments should be abolished and their functions should be placed directly in the hands

48 These figures were given by the Scottish Secretary John Colville in HOC debates, 21–7–38, vol. 338 col. 2528–2529

49 Sir Godfrey Collins, Liberal MP for Greenock from 1910–1936, was National Liberal Secretary of State for Scotland from 1932–1936, the year of his death. Collins entered the Royal Navy in 1888 as a midshipman and served at the East India Station. On entering Parliament in 1910, he became Parliamentary Private Secretary to the Secretary of State for War, J.B. Seely until 1914. He was a member of the War Office staff from 1914 until 1915 when he took up active service again and served in Egypt, Gallipoli and Mesopotamia between 1915 and 1917, gaining the rank of Lieutenant-Colonel. He served as Junior Lord of the Treasury 1919/20 and as Chief Liberal Whip between 1924–26. He was a member of the Collins publishing family.

50 For more on the Gilmour Report see James Mitchell, 'The Gilmour Report on Scottish Central Administration' *Juridicial Review*, (1989), pt. 2, 173.

of the Secretary of State for Scotland. There were to be four new-style Departments: a new Home Department (to include Prisons and Fisheries), Agriculture, Education, (with the link to the Privy Council terminated), and Health (which was to assume the duties of the General Board of Control for the mentally ill). Each Department was to have a Secretary, (also to be its Accounting Officer), who had direct access to the Scottish Secretary of State. There was also to be a Permanent Secretary to the Secretary of State, a senior civil servant, superior to the Secretaries, who was to act as an impartial adviser to the Scottish Secretary.[51]

Elliot was appointed Minister of Health in 1936. It was his successor as Scottish Secretary of State, John Colville[52] who finally presented a fresh Reorganisation Bill in November 1938 based on the findings of the Gilmour Committee.[53] The Bill recommended the creation of four Departments[54] each under a Secretary who was to be directly responsible to the Secretary of State for Scotland. The Reorganisation of Offices (Scotland) Act, 1939 excited little debate (unlike so many of its predecessors in the previous decade). The few parliamentary comments were that the Bill did not go far enough in devolving power[55] and on the future role for the Permanent Under

---

51 There is further discussion on these administrative changes in Pottinger, *The Secretaries of State For Scotland 1926–1976*, 18–19 and Hanham, 'The Development of the Scottish Office', 66–67.

52 Colville served as a Captain in the Scottish Rifles in the First World War. His grandfather established Colville's Ltd steel company, and his father served as Liberal MP for North-East Lanarkshire. In 1929, John Colville became Unionist MP for Midlothian. From 1931 to 1935 he served as Secretary to the Board of Trade, then as Parliamentary Under Secretary of State for Scotland. In 1938 he was Financial Secretary to the Treasury, before becoming National Conservative Scottish Secretary of State from 1938–1940. He later served as Governor of Bombay from 1943–48.

53 HOC debates, 10–11–38, vol. 341 col. 307.

54 The four Departments were Home, Education, Health, and Agriculture. Responsibility for Fisheries was to be incorporated into one of the four other main Departments (not specified in the legislation). See Section 1 clause (1) of the Reorganisation of Offices (Scotland) Act.

55 Labour MP Tom Johnston, who sat on the Gilmour Committee, commented: 'what we desire is less bureaucracy and more democracy.' See Pottinger, *The*

Secretary of State whose new duties were not specified in the legislation.[56]

The 1939 Reorganisation of Offices (Scotland) Act allowed Scotland for the first time to have a full-scale Department (the Scottish Office) housed in Edinburgh and employing civil servants of the same administrative class as at Whitehall. The 1920s proposition by Scottish Secretary Gilmour, namely, that it was easier to stake a claim for equal status if the Scottish administration was run along lines clearly recognisable to central Government, could finally be tested. The 'maverick' status of the SBH, with its expert members had militated against this full integration.[57]

The Whitehall model pulled civil servants in the opposite direction to the old 'expert' Boards – towards becoming flexible administrators – able to work anywhere in the system. Expertise in any particular field could be seen as a drawback to promotion prospects. The comment of Sir Warren Fisher, Permanent Secretary to the Treasury from 1919–1939, in evidence before the Tomlin Royal Commission on the Civil Service of 1930/1 made this clear. Fisher stated: 'Let us guard ourselves against the idea that the permanent

---

Secretaries of State For Scotland 1926–1976, 76, and also debates on the Second Reading of the Reorganisation Bill, HOC debates, 13–12–38 vol. 347, passim.

56 'The Secretary of State may appoint such secretaries, officers and servants as he may, with the sanction of the Treasury as to numbers, deem necessary to enable him to discharge the functions vested in him, and may from time to time give such directions as he shall think fit for the distribution of the business of his office among the persons so appointed.' Reorganisation of Offices (Scotland) Act, 1939, Section 1, clause (2).

57 'The Boards and Departments – although based in Edinburgh and identifiably Scottish – had found it difficult to maintain the necessary contact and influence with equivalent English departments and equally important, with the Treasury. The Boards, in particular, with their quasi-autonomous status has been primarily designed for "inward" administration – to monitor and maintain local Scottish institutions.' Levitt, *Poverty and Welfare in Scotland 1890–1948*, 12.

head of a department should be an expert; he should not be anything of the kind.'[58]

All Scottish Departments were unified under the new functions vested in the Secretary of State. In addition, a Permanent Under Secretary, Sir Horace Hamilton[59] (based in Whitehall but with day to day control of the Departments) assisted the Secretary of State. The 1939 Act enabled the Scottish Secretary of State to change the duties or functions of Departments without resort to legislation – one such example was the removal of Fisheries from the Home Department to the newly-titled Department of Agriculture and Fisheries. A result of the new legislation was to increase the staffs of the Departments of the Secretary of State for Scotland. The figure which had risen gradually from 200 in 1885 to 2400 in 1937, now accelerated, amounting to 5500 in 1953.[60] In the DHS, staffing levels stood at 1,005 on 1 January 1940. Of these 112 were from Administrative and Senior Executive Grades.[61]

Yet Scottish Office control was not complete. The Departments, including the DHS, still maintained their individual office procedures and separate identities.[62] On the eve of World War Two, the system of Scottish administration, including health, stood at a crossroads. In one sense, the devolution of duties to St Andrews House in Edinburgh could be seen as a recognition of the autonomy long practised in Scottish bureaucracy, itself a consequence of the distinct nature of Scottish society and politics. Alternatively, since the new administrative structure was a mirror image of Whitehall, the new system could be seen as an attempt at remote control through a Whitehall-

58 Tomlin Royal Commission on the Civil Service 1930/1, question 18, 805 quoted in Fry, *Statesmen in Disguise: The Changing Role of the Administrative Class of the British Home Civil Service 1853–1966*, 57.

59 Sir Horace Hamilton was promoted to Permanent Under Secretary from his former post as Permanent Secretary of the Scottish Office, a post he had taken up on the retirement of former SBH/DHS Secretary Sir John Jeffrey in 1937.

60 Pottinger, *The Secretaries of State For Scotland 1926–1976*, 22.

61 NAS, DD1/21, DHS, Establishment Memorandum Number 242, 23 January 1940.

62 'As a result, Scottish administration retained a slightly old-fashioned bureaucratic flavour.' Hanham 'The Development of the Scottish Office', 68.

trained professional civil service. The outbreak of world war left the issue unresolved.

The Highlands and Islands Medical Service

A key aspect of DHS (and SBH) activity was the administration of health care in the Highlands and Islands of Scotland. The Highlands and Islands Medical Service (HIMS) and its administrative board were created as a consequence of the problems faced in securing a satisfactory medical service in the Highlands and Islands under the National Insurance Act of 1911. In July 1912, a Government committee was appointed to consider:

> How far the provision of medical attendance in districts situated in the Highlands and Islands of Scotland is inadequate, and to advise as to the best method of securing a satisfactory medical service therein, regard being had to the duties and responsibilities of several public authorities operating in such districts.[63]

The Committee presented its findings in December 1912. The existing system of general practitioner care was based on payments from the Poor Law authorities and other payments from local authorities. Because of the low level of payment general practitioners received for their far flung, onerous work, the whole area was lacking in adequate medical cover. The Committee's recommendation for a direct grant from the Treasury to put in place a more organised, better staffed, service, was taken up by the Liberal Government with the passage of the Highlands and Islands (Medical Service) Grant Act, by which an annual fund of £42,000 per year was to be paid into the HIMS Fund:

> [The Fund was created] for the purpose of improving medical service, including nursing, in the Highlands and Islands of Scotland, and otherwise providing and

63 For a description of the early activity of the HIMSB see SBH, *Second Annual Report, 1920*, 99–109.

improving means for the prevention, treatment, and alleviation of illness and suffering therein.[64]

The area covered by the HIMS included over half of the total land surface of Scotland, but less than one-fourteenth of the country's population. The population of the region was recorded at 335,697 in the 1911 census. The material conditions of the area were regarded as some of the poorest in Great Britain, it had poor soil and few viable mineral resources, with agriculture and fishing as the only real employment available. Although introduced in 1913, many of the special services contemplated in the legislation of that year were not at first introduced due to wartime circumstances. Yet this was not seen as an irretrievable situation since the war service record of Highlands and Islands recruits was impressive.[65] Under the new scheme, doctors in the area were contracted to attend defined groups of patients for fees not exceeding an agreed figure and to do so regardless of where they attended them. The groups covered by the HIMS comprised what was known as the 'crofter and cottar' class and their families, and the dependants of those workers covered by National Health Insurance. The HIMS therefore, represented the most wide-ranging state-subsidised service in Britain in the inter-war period.

Initially, the agreed fees for doctors were not more than 5 shillings (25 pence) for the first visit, two shillings and sixpence (12.5 pence) for subsequent visits treating the same illness, and £1 for midwifery visits. These fees were similar to the rates charged by urban doctors for treating patients from these income groups. In return for accepting these fees, doctors received an annual grant from the HIMS Fund. Circumstances dictated the actual rate for each individual practitioner, for example mileage allowance was taken into account. A mileage fee was paid direct to practitioners from the Treasury Grant. In its early years practitioners were guaranteed a minimum income of £300 per year. By 1947, the last full year of the scheme, the

64 Ibid., 100.

65 'It does not necessarily follow that a high standard of physical efficiency is not at present possible, and this is borne out by the war record of the Western Islands and other outlying districts, where material conditions are at their worst.' SBH, *Second Annual Report, 1920*, 101.

guaranteed minimum income for general practitioners had risen to the rate of £800 per year. Doctors were not state salaried servants, but were required to undertake statutory medical services as part of their contract under the HIMS. Among the medical services provided by the HIMS was the treatment of school children identified by medical inspection as in need of medical attention.

The powers of the Highlands and Islands Medical Services Board were transferred to the SBH on 1 September 1919. The Consultative Council set up for the Highlands and Islands in early 1920 played a part in determining the shape of the post-war HIMS. Its remit was 'to consider whether it is desirable to develop as early as conditions permit the services curtailed or put into obeyance due to war conditions.'[66] By 1923, special grants introduced under the HIMS scheme paid for medical and nursing services, accommodation for doctors and nurses, for ambulance and hospital provision, improved telegraph and telephone services, a tuberculosis scheme, and a special emergency scheme. The medical services scheme ensured that the distance of a doctor from a patient should not add anything to the charges paid by the patient, through small fixed fees, subsidised through the annual Treasury grant to the HIMS.

The Scheme proved popular with medical practitioners due to the guaranteed income and special attractions of the location. About 150 doctors were involved in the HIMS. From a dearth of practitioners pre-war, the position by 1923 had reached one of almost full strength. Only some of the most remote areas of the region still lacked sufficient doctors. Often this was due to a lack of suitable housing, such as the on Isle of Lewis. In 1923 Lewis had only two practitioners for a population of 11,000 people covering an area of 354 square miles.[67] Nursing services were given a considerable boost by the Scottish Health Board's implementation of the HIMS after the war. County and district nursing associations were organised to provide district nursing facilities to an expanded population. Nurses were appointed by the local associations but worked in co-operation with

66 NAS, HH75/02, SBH minutes, 6 February 1920.

67 See SBH, *Fifth Annual Report, 1923* (Edinburgh: HMSO, 1924), passim, [Cmd 2156], and *BMJ*, 1923 (2), 7 July 1923, 36.

local practitioners. Nursing associations were financed by the HIMS, supplemented by local subscriptions and subsidised by local authorities.

The relatively successful operation of the HIMS cannot simply be put down to the creation Scottish Board of Health. Yet, the SBH presided over the extension of the services on offer and increased expenditure to fund them.[68] This came at a time when other areas of statutory medical provision were subject to cutback due to government financial restrictions. An example of this is the 1921 SBH estimate to the Treasury which, while making provisions for redundancies among SBH staff, also included an additional grant of £22,000 for expanded tuberculosis treatment in the Highlands and Islands.[69] The need for an immediate cash injection to deal with the higher than average incidence of Tuberculosis in certain parts of the region was clear:

> The disease is most prevalent in the localities where the economic circumstances of the people are at their worst, and in these localities the Public Health Authorities are not in a position to incur expenditure on treatment even with the inducement of a 50 per cent. subsidy from the Tuberculosis Maintenance Grant.[70]

While there were many areas successful aspects of the HIMS, some of its original aims, for example, dental treatment, a wide spread hospital services, and the provision of suitable buildings for medical centres, were held in abeyance. This was initially due to wartime conditions, but later general practitioner and nursing services were prioritised to improve these services from their very low pre-war levels. The cap on Treasury funding for the HIMS was another reason for the need to make stark choices over which elements of the service could be expanded. For example, the Treasury refused the SBH

---

68 The additional funding was obtained by drawing upon money awarded since 1913 under the Highland and Islands Medical Services Act, but left unspent due to the limited nature of the service before 1919.

69 PRO, T160/75, Letter from SBH Secretary, John Jeffrey, to Treasury, 13 January 1921.

70 SBH, *Second Annual Report, 1920*, 106.

attempt to have the annual HIMS grant increased to £100,000 in February 1920.[71]

In the 1920s, the mounting cost of salaries and fuel allowance for general practitioners swallowed up almost all of the HIMS allowance from the Treasury and little was done in the way of the hospital extension and nurse's accommodation envisaged in the 1912 Dewar Report. Although the original sum of £42,00 per year voted by the Treasury in 1912 was not increased, savings accumulated during the war allowed the Service to draw an additional £18,000–20,000 per year to offset the rising costs. This additional sum was soon spent and in the 'economy years' the HIMS lurched from one financial constraint to another. In January 1926, the Treasury awarded £12,000 in grants for the much-needed extension of Lewis Hospital in Stornoway. The money was given on condition that: 'it will not be necessary to approach Parliament for an increase in the present statutory grant of £42,000 before the financial year commencing the 1 April 1929.'[72] Even the decision to fund the hospital extension had consequences for other sectors of the service. Money for improvements to doctors and nurses houses were set aside, as were plans to increase the number of district nurses and to raise the standards of nursing qualifications within the service. Moreover, while improvements for Lewis hospital were approved other Highlands hospitals' appeals were turned down due to lack of funding. Both Bignold Hospital, Wick and the Northern Infirmary, Inverness were told that proposed expansion schemes could not be funded out of the HIMS grant.[73]

In 1927, Parliamentary Under Secretary of State, Walter Elliot, reported to parliament that HIMS resources would be exhausted by the end of the decade.[74] In 1929, the Highlands and Islands (Medical Service) Additional Grant Bill was introduced to allow 'such sum as may annually be voted by Parliament for that purpose' in addition to the original annual Treasury grant of £42,000. The Additional Grant

---

71 NAS, HH75/24, SBH minutes, 12 February 1920.

72 NAS, HH75/24, SBH divisional committee IV minutes, 4 January 1926.

73 NAS, HH75/24, SBH minutes, 29 January 1926.

74 HOC debates, 21–7–27 vol. 209 col. 643.

Act passed with support from all sides of the House in December 1929 did not set aside a specific annual figure to be given to the HIMS. The sum arrived at would take into account development in the Service on a yearly basis. In 1929, as the DHS assumed control of the HIMS, much still needed to be done. Although 174 nurses were in the service more were required and there were no dentistry facilities under the HIMS. Many Scottish Islands required small cottage hospitals in order to prevent patients undertaking hazardous sea journeys when requiring hospitalisation.[75] A supplementary estimate of £10, 650 in addition to the annual Treasury grant of £42,000 was agreed to for 1930.

The DHS Annual Report for 1930 viewed the additional grant as opening up a new chapter in the medical history of the HIMS. The new funds allowed the extension of the district nursing service. For example, grants were paid to nursing associations, such as the Queen's Institute for District Nursing to assist in maintaining this service. The money also helped strengthen new specialist surgical services in Lerwick, in the Shetlands, and Kirkwall and Stornoway, in Lewis.[76] A drawback in the new legislation was that the Additional Grant was not fixed. In 1932, the grant was reduced from £70,000 (this sum included the original £42,000 Treasury grant) to £66,000 due to the economic difficulties of that year. This was viewed as a 'false economy' by prominent Highlands Liberal MP Sir J. Ian MacPherson during the debate on the DHS Estimates in July that year.[77]

---

75 Reported in *BMJ*, 'Medical Notes in Parliament', 1929 (2), 28 December 1929, 1222.

76 *BMJ*, 1930 (1) 24 May 1930, 971.

77 'Mr MacPherson [...] feared that was false economy, and urged the Department of Health to reconsider the housing of Highland doctors and ensure that they had the advantage of surgeries. The Department had dealt with the provision of telephones in doctors' and nurses' houses, but had not dealt with it sufficiently well.' See *BMJ*, 'Medical Notes in Parliament' 1932 (2), 2 July 1932, 39. James Ian MacPherson (1880–1937) was born in Newtonmore, Invernesshire. He served as Liberal MP for Ross and Cromarty from 1911–1935. He was appointed Parliamentary Secretary to the Under Secretary for War in 1914, becoming Under Secretary of State for War in 1916. In 1919, he was appointed Chief Secretary for Ireland. He later served as Minister of Pensions, 1920–1922. He was knighted in 1919 and created a Baronet in 1933. MacPherson died in 1937.

Despite financial difficulties there were some improvements in the service in the inter-war years. An E.N.T. specialist was appointed to the Royal Northern Infirmary (RNI), Inverness in 1929. Ten years later the RNI appointed its first consultant physician. Diagnostic and radiology services were also developed at the Royal Northern Infirmary. These changes were linked to the award in 1930 of a substantial annual grant for a period of ten years to allow the reconstruction and development of the hospital as the central hospital of the Northern Highlands. The RNI's diagnostic services were later extended to cover a postal diagnostic service for the Northern mainland counties and the Western Isles. Orkney and Shetland were covered by a postal service to Aberdeen. In 1933, the DHS developed an air service between the Western Highlands and Glasgow. The responsibility of summoning the aeroplane rested with the local doctor, with the cost defrayed by the Argyll County Council, the HIMS, and the patient (where able to pay). By 1930, a great deal of satisfaction was expressed by general practitioners associated with the scheme in reports back to the DHS.[78] Meanwhile, the HIMS was itself regarded as a model for the creation of health services in other areas of scattered population around the world. 'In Kentucky, in Newfoundland, in South Africa and elsewhere ideas worked out and tested here are being adapted and applied to the cognate problems there.'[79]

By the mid-1930s, over 150 medical practitioners were involved in the service, with remuneration based on annual grant from the HIMS fund in return for the charging of pre-arranged flat fees for medical attendance. Most HIMS doctors also had part-time public

78 'One of them, with 40 years' experience of Highland practice, says: "The terms under which the practitioners work by arrangement with the Department of Health are so reasonably elastic, and in most cases so accurately adjusted to local circumstances, that the Highlands and Islands (Medical Service) is an outstanding example of the success with which a combination of State Medical Service and private medical Service may be worked".' Lothian Health Board Archive, Edinburgh, LHB24/8/18, *Transactions of the Scottish Association of Insurance Committees, 18th annual meeting, 1930*, address by Dr Shearer, DHS, on 'Medical Service in the Highlands and Islands', 24.

79 Ibid., 28.

health appointments with local authorities. They were also free to engage in private practice.[80] In addition, a sum of £10,000 was transferred each year from the Scottish National Health Insurance Fund to the HIMS Fund to meet payments and mileage allowance to doctors who treated insured patients.[81] In 1936, over 200 nurses were subsidised through the HIMS at a cost of £19,000 per year paid direct to local voluntary nursing associations. In this way, the state funds to the Highlands and Islands Medical Service was used to supplement and improve existing services irrespective of whether they were run by local authorities, voluntary organisations or general practitioners. Grants were offered to doctors and nurses to secure suitable accommodation in their area. Other major developments such as the updating of the Royal Northern Infirmary, Inverness, and the appointment of resident surgeons in Shetland, Caithness, Orkney and Lewis were viewed as great advances for the region.

Yet, despite such improvements, by 1936 there were still no dentistry or opthalmological services under the HIMS. The DHS evidence to the Cathcart Committee restated the ultimate goal of the HIMS:

> It has been the aim of the administrators of the Highlands and Islands (Medical Service) Fund to secure a medical and nursing service in these areas approaching so far as practicable that which is available to the people of the Lowlands. It cannot yet be said that that ideal has been achieved, although considerable progress has certainly been made towards it.[82]

The Cathcart Committee set up a sub-committee to visit the Highlands and Islands to investigate the existing state of medical care.[83] The sub-committee which visited the Northern mainland counties and the

80 DHS, *Committee on Scottish Health Services Report*, 165.

81 Ibid., 222.

82 Ibid., 225.

83 'Our general view of the Highlands and Islands Service is that it has fully justified its existence and has returned full value for its cost. In our view, it has brought great benefits to the people of the Highlands and Islands, is administered in an atmosphere of sympathy and understanding between the central department and the doctors, nurses and other parties, and to the satisfaction of all concerned.' Ibid., 227.

Western Isles, found that the hospital service in the region was inadequate, despite the recent initiatives regarding the Royal Northern Infirmary, Inverness. Local authority health services, such as tuberculosis, maternity and child welfare and school medical services, were also considered inadequate and uncoordinated. Such local services were limited by the poverty of the area, meaning that there were insufficient funds raised within the community to expand personal health services adequately to meet local needs. The Cathcart sub-committee felt an additional sum of £50,000 per year should be added to the HIMS grant to properly fund these statutory services.

The sub-committee felt much still had also to be done regarding nursing services: additional nurses were required, more cars for nurses were necessary, nurses' accommodation needed upgrading, and additional provision for nurses to undertake refresher courses was recommended.[84] It also found that telephone and telegraph services connected with the HIMS required extension. Overall however, the sub-committee was well satisfied with what had been achieved to date. In fact, it proposed that the medical services provided under the HIMS should be used as a model for wider application in Scotland, with its unique blend of local and central government control.

> Our study of this service was primarily directed to its suitability to the peculiar conditions of the Highlands and Islands, but we found that it had a wider bearing, and we suggest that further study may provide valuable pointers for consideration of the larger issue of the future of medical service in Scotland as a whole.[85]

This suggestion was quoted in the National Health Service White Paper of 1944,[86] but it was taken no further as the idea of a comprehensive municipal health service was rejected in favour of a state medical service.

In the Highlands and Islands, (and for the rest of Scotland), the Cathcart Report recommended co-ordinating all medical services so that there was no gap between the personal health services and the

84 Ibid., 230.
85 Ibid., 227.
86 DHS, *A National Health Service* (Edinburgh, HMSO, 1944), 72, [Cmd 6502].

general practitioner. One intention of this was so that no person, in whatever financial circumstance, would be unable to call on medical attendance when required. Co-ordination and extension of services were the watchwords for the HIMS as for all health services in Scotland.[87]

In 1937, the DHS estimate for the HIMS was an expenditure of £98,000, an increase of £29,000 over the previous year's estimate. The increase was chiefly down to new capital expenditure approved by the Treasury in respect of expansion of hospital services in Inverness, Stornoway, North Uist and a grant of £15,000 for the Gilbert Bain Hospital, Lerwick.[88] In 1939, the HIMS was awarded a grant of £106,000 which included a sum to assist in the completion of the new general hospital at Lerwick and additions to the hospital at Stornoway. In the twelve months to July 1939, the Western Highlands air ambulance had transported over 30 patients for care to Glasgow hospitals. The air ambulance was funded by block grant allocations from the Argyll and Inverness County Councils.[89] On the eve of the war the HIMS, although incorporating modern advances in air passenger services still had much to do in terms of providing even basic medical services to the whole population of the region.

Policy Initiatives in the 1930s

The replacement of the SBH by a Department of Health brought about the end of 'expert' advice from board members, but little else changed as regards policy advisers. For example, the work of the Consultative Councils in Scotland continued. In 1934, three of the original councils on Medical and Allied Services, National Health Insurance and Local Health Administration continued to meet (between them they met 22 times from 1932–1934). The final Council, for the Highlands and

87 DHS, *Committee on Scottish Health Services Report*, 232.
88 PRO, T160/723, DHS, Expenditure Estimate, 30 November 1936.
89 See *BMJ*, 'Medical Notes in Parliament', 1939 (2), 15 July 1939, 150.

Islands had not met for three years in 1934, but Scottish Secretary of State Collins was 'actively considering' its reconstitution. In contrast, the Consultative Council on National Health Insurance for England had met once in 1933. The other English Consultative Councils no longer functioned.[90] The Scottish Consultative Councils not only continued to meet, they continued to issue policy statements. In 1933, the Scottish Consultative Council on Medical and Allied Services produced a Report on Hospital Services[91] which recommended a co-ordinated hospital service (a call which was echoed three years later in the Report of the Scottish Health Services Committee).

In addition to the Consultative Councils, further advisory committees were set up by the DHS in the early 1930s. Although the Scottish Consultative Councils actively continued in these years, there was nothing radical in the Scottish Secretary of State convening independent committees to consider particular issues. For example, the Hospital Services (Scotland) Committee produced a report for the SBH in 1926. Also, in 1929, the Scottish Secretary of State appointed a Central Liaison Committee to act between the Department of Health for Scotland and the regional committees of the voluntary hospitals.[92] The committee was made up of six executives from various Scottish infirmaries, (three of whom were medical practitioners), an appointed chairman and a representative of the DHS acting as Secretary.[93] Originally to run until March 1932 it was extended to March 1935 due to delays in the progress of a general survey of the hospital services of the country. One reason for the extension of the Liaison Committee

90 HOC debates, 19–12–34, vol. 296 col. 3347.

91 DHS, Consultative Council on Medical and Allied Services, *Report on Hospital Services* (Edinburgh: HMSO, 1933).

92 Although the hospital service is outside the scope of this book, the establishment of this committee (which owed much to the impact of the Local Government (Scotland) Act of 1929 on Scottish hospital services) is a clear example of the DHS continuing to take expert advice in policy formulation. The remit of the Committee was to: 'act in liaison between the Department of Health for Scotland and the regional committees of the Voluntary Hospitals in Scotland, to assist in keeping the Department in touch with voluntary hospital opinion, and, in the development of hospital services in Scotland, to foster co-operation between the voluntary hospitals and local authorities in each region.'

93 *GMJ*, 1932 (2), 44.

was the continued concern for the role of the voluntary hospitals in the 1930s given the increasing financial burden placed on their over stretched privately-funded activities. The assumption of control of the former Poor Law hospitals by the new local authorities under the Local Government (Scotland) Act of 1929 introduced a new municipal element to hospital provision, and with increased consultation in evidence between the DHS and the voluntary hospitals in the 1930s, the path towards a state run hospital service was being tentatively mapped out.

The Committee on Scottish Health Services, 1933–1936

On 22 June 1933, another DHS committee was appointed by Scottish Secretary of State, Sir Godfrey Collins:

> To review the existing health services of Scotland in the light of modern conditions and knowledge, and to make recommendations on any changes in policy and organisation that may be considered necessary for the promotion of *efficiency and economy* [author's emphasis].[94]

The DHS Scottish Health Services Committee Report of June 1936, (the Cathcart Report), is regarded as one of the most complete surveys of the health services undertaken in Britain. The background to its formation and the workings of the Committee between 1933–1936 are rather less well known. The 1936 Report of the Health Services Committee continued the work of the Report of the SBH Consultative Council on Medical and Allied Services in 1920. Indeed, it referred directly to the MacAlister Report as governing its enquiry.[95] The link

94 *GMJ*, 1933 (2), 54.

95 'The Consultative Council on Medical and Allied Services of the Scottish Board of Health, in a Report published in 1920, stated: "We regard it as of primary concern that the organisation of the health service of the nation should be based upon the family as the normal unit, and on the family doctor as the normal medical attendant and guardian [...]". We find that the view expressed

between the Consultative Councils and the Health Services Committee was also shown by the representation of present and former DHS Consultative Council members on the Committee. For example, two current members of the DHS Consultative Council on Medical and Allied Services, Robert W. Craig,[96] and Alexander Miles,[97] were also appointed as members of the Scottish Health Services Committee. In addition, three former members of the Local Health Administration and General Health Questions Consultative Council: lawyer Andrew Grierson, William M. Marshall,[98] and Lady Helen Leslie Mackenzie,[99] were also members of the Committee on Scottish Health Services.

The Committee on Scottish Health Services consisted of a total of eighteen members – fifteen male members and three female. Seven members were medical professionals, including E.P. Cathcart, (Regius Professor of Physiology at Glasgow University, and the University's Representative on the General Medical Council), James L. Brownlie, CMO of the DHS, Andrew S.M. MacGregor, MOH for Glasgow, and A. Mary Chalmers Watson.[100] Two others were members of local government, Provost David Fisher and Bailie Violet M. Robinson (the latter was also County Representative for Perthshire on the Scottish

by the Consultative Council in 1920 is accepted generally by all branches of the medical profession in Scotland.' DHS, *Committee on Scottish Health Services Report*, 151.

96 Robert Craig, MD, was Resident Physician at Edinburgh Royal Infirmary.

97 Alexander Miles was Consulting Surgeon at Edinburgh Royal Infirmary, a member of the GMC and a former President, Secretary and Treasurer of the Royal College of Surgeons, Edinburgh.

98 Marshall was the long-serving Secretary and Treasurer of the Scottish Association of Insurance Committees [SAIC]).

99 Helen Leslie Mackenzie had been involved in health administration and social investigations since the beginning of the twentieth century. She was President of the Scottish National Association of Lady Health Visitors and Woman Sanitary Inspectors. She was also a member of the SBH Consultative Council on Local Health Administration and General Health Questions. As Helen Carruthers Spence, she married William Leslie Mackenzie in 1892 (who served as a member of the SBH, 1919–1928). Helen Leslie Mackenzie was awarded the CBE in 1933.

100 Chalmers-Watson was one of the earliest female medical graduates of Edinburgh University (MB, CM, 1896). A CBE, she was retired from a post as Senior Physician at the Edinburgh Hospital for Women.

Association of Insurance Committees). Other notable members were Joseph Westwood, (Labour MP between 1922–1931, 1935–1948, and Secretary of State for Scotland 1945–47) and John M. Vallance, Chief Accountant of the DHS. Vallance was a significant member of the Committee given the need for economy stressed in its terms of reference. BMA representation on the Committee included Robert W. Craig, (Scottish Medical Secretary of the BMA). In addition to the eighteen members, Niven F. McNicholl, Secretary of the DHS Consultative Councils was appointed as Secretary to the Committee.

The Scottish Health Services Committee produced a Report which became influential in informing policy discussions during and immediately after the war, when the form of a future national health service was under consideration. The convening of the Committee to survey the existing health services in Scotland and to make recommendations for its future reorganisation was the brainchild of John Parlane Kinloch, CMO at the DHS between 1929–1932.[101] In his foreword to the 1931 DHS Annual Report, Parlane Kinloch drew attention to the chaotic and haphazard origin and development of the many agencies concerned with health care and prevention in Scotland. Parlane Kinloch advocated a complete survey of the whole of the Scottish Health Services: '[...] as a basis for future policy and related planning.'[102] The link between Parlane Kinloch's proposals in the 1931 DHS Annual Report and the creation of the Committee on Scottish Health Services is a direct one. The remit of the Committee on the Scottish Health Services noted above, made use of the phrase 'economy and efficiency'. Although this phrase was common civil service language, it bears comparison with Parlane Kinloch's statement in the 1931 DHS annual report: '[...] some more radical changes may be necessary before it can be said that the health policy of the nation is functioning through the most efficient and economical

101 'A word to begin with about the genesis of the Scottish Health Services or Cathcart Committee. It would, I think, be not far from the truth to say that it was conceived in the fertile mind of that brilliant if unstable genius, the late John Parlane Kinloch [...].' E.R.C. Walker, [Scottish Secretary of the BMA] 'The Forgotten Report', *EMJ*, 56 (1949), 494.

102 Walker, 'The Forgotten Report'.

organisation.'[103] Taking the example of existing health services for children, which revealed year after year – 'with monotonous regularity, a mass of disabilities that are eminently preventable' – Parlane Kinloch identified what he felt to be a failure to secure the full benefits of scientific knowledge to prevent illness and disability. The blame, in part, lay with inadequate government health provision: '[...] some of this failure may arise from the present organisation of the health services.'[104]

Parlane Kinloch's call for action was acted upon up only after his premature death in 1932. In June 1933, Scottish Secretary of State Collins convened the Committee on Scottish Health Services. The first Chairman was the Right Honourable Sir John Dove-Wilson, K.C.,[105] who died on 18 April 1935, twenty-two months after the Committee was set up. Edward Provan Cathcart, whose name is forever associated with the report, therefore chaired the committee for the final fourteen and a half months of its forty-eight and a half months of deliberation. Cathcart, a veteran of numerous governmental army, industrial and nutrition committees was an obvious choice to take over the chair of the Committee on Scottish Health Services: 'few men can have served on so many expert committees.'[106] Cathcart's late appointment to the chair helps to explain the apparent anomaly of a well-known conservative[107] chairing a committee which produced

103 DHS *Annual Report, 1931* (Edinburgh: HMSO, 1932), p. xv.

104 Ibid.

105 The Rt. Hon. Sir John Carnegie Dove-Wilson (1865–1935), son of Professor J. Dove Wilson, was educated at Aberdeen and Edinburgh Universities. He was called to the Scottish bar in 1888, and became a King's Council in 1904. In 1904, he moved to South Africa to become Puisine Judge of the Supreme Court of Natal. He served as Acting Chief Justice of Natal in 1907, 1909, 1910. He was knighted in 1918. In 1922, he was President of the Special Court for the Treason and Sedition trials in Johannesburg in 1922. Returning to Britain, he chaired the Departmental Committee on Persistent Offenders in 1931/2. In June 1933 he was appointed chairman of the DHS Committee on Scottish Health Services. He died in 1935.

106 'Obituary – E.P. Cathcart' *BMJ*, 1954 (1), 523.

107 In particular, Cathcart displayed a conservative attitude to the issue of poor levels of nutrition amongst the British population, which he attributed to individual ignorance and fecklessness, rather than inability to afford sufficient

some of the most radical policy proposals of any government health committee convened in the inter-war years. The identification of Cathcart with the report's radical findings struck fellow committee member, A.S.M. MacGregor, as an oddity. In MacGregor's obituary notice for Cathcart he noted 'it may be said that [...] the report was a preamble to the NHS. It was no secret, however, that he [Cathcart] did not like some parts of it.'[108] In fact, Cathcart's conservative views on nutrition and specifically, the ignorance that he believed lay behind the insufficient diets of the poor were widely quoted in the 1930s by establishment politicians and administrators. Cathcart's findings were used as a defence against those such as Cathcart's former Glasgow colleague John Boyd Orr,[109] who claimed that there was widespread malnutrition in Britain due to mass poverty among the population.[110]

Cathcart and before him Dove-Wilson, were at the head of a large committee which brought together a broad spectrum of opinions.

---

food stuffs for an adequate diet. See for example, his comments in September 1932: '[...] the purchase of such a diet of adequate quality does not of necessity entail a high expenditure. It is within the purchasing power of the majority. The problem to-day, as I see it from our many studies of family diets both in Scotland and England, is not the inability to purchase, but the inability to spend wisely and well the income which is available.' LHB24/8/20, *Transactions of the Scottish Association of Insurance Committees Annual Meeting, 1932*, 37. See also *BMJ*, 1954 (1), 524, Professor R.C. Garry's personal obituary of E.P. Cathcart. 'Instinctively, and possibly with some justification, he reacted against the unconfirmed belief that rapidity of growth in childhood and in adolescence and attainment of great stature are inevitably sure indications of individual and social well-being [...]. He cast a kindly, but somewhat critical and sceptical eye on all those who made sweeping claims for progress in medicine and in the social order as a whole.'

108 *Lancet*, 1954 (1), 469, Obituary for E. P. Cathcart: 'Of his work for the last [Committee], known as the Cathcart Committee, A.S.M. writes [...].' 'ASM' was Andrew S. M. MacGregor, MOH for Glasgow and a member of the Cathcart Committee.

109 See chapter four on school health for full biographical details on renowned nutritionist John Boyd Orr.

110 M. Nicolson and D. Smith, 'The "Glasgow School" of Paton, Findlay and Cathcart: Conservative Thought in Chemical Physiology, Nutrition and Public Health' *Social Studies in Science*, 19 (1989), 195:238. See also HOC debates, 14–7–36 vol. 314 [1935/6], col. 1229–1350.

This is shown by the inclusion of nine separate reservations by various committee members to aspects of the Committee's findings, for example, reservations were expressed on the proposals for an extended general practitioner service, and on the proposed reform of maternity services.[111] Cathcart himself signed only one of the published reservations, relating to the suggested transfer of the functions of insurance committees to local authority control. Cathcart and the other four signatories to the reservation (Cox, Marshall, Miles and Robertson) felt that the proposal endangered the intimate relationship between doctor and patient. They believed such a measure would bring 'the family doctor under the supervision of the medical officer of health and in contractual relationship with the local authority.'[112] It is not surprising that this reservation to the Cathcart Report should be made. It was the standard response of most medical professionals when faced with the prospect of any form of public control.

The Health Services Committee met as a group 88 times, as well as convening a number of sub-committees, including the sub-committee on the Highlands and Islands. Other visits were made around Scotland to gather evidence. Sets of questions were also despatched to interested representative groups, such as the Royal Faculty of Physicians and Surgeons of Glasgow.[113] The Committee heard a very wide range of evidence: 76 organisations (including the three Scottish medical licensing agencies) represented by 215 individuals, gave evidence to the Committee, as did 22 individual witnesses, including John Boyd Orr.

The papers of the Scottish Health Services Committee were among the DHS files destroyed for security reasons during World War Two. The full background to the DHS's decision to form the Committee, and how an agreed policy emerged after the Committee reported, unfortunately, now cannot be uncovered. However, there are

111 See DHS, *Committee on Scottish Health Services Report*, 341–356.

112 Ibid., 366.

113 Royal College of Physicians, Glasgow, RCPSG 1/1/1/15, RFPSG minutes, 5 February 1934, Letter from Niven F. McNicholl, Secretary to DHS Scottish Health Services Committee to RFPSG, 3 February 1934.

a number of other sources of information about the work of the Committee. For example, the view of Committee members can reveal the priorities in the final stages of compiling the report:

> When the time came for the report to be written, Cathcart insisted on us assembling on the evenings or at weekends to ensure that the material was fully digested, properly summarised, and clear conclusions reached. He was determined above all to promote a scheme which would uphold the importance and dignity of medical practice in the community.[114]

Copies of papers sent out by the Committee have survived in the minute books of the RFPSG.[115] The Faculty was asked to submit evidence under seven headings. These were: 1. Statutory Medical Services (National Health Insurance, etc.), 2. Hospitals, 3. Voluntary Public Medical Services, 4. Consultative Services, 5. Nursing Homes, 6. Medical Teaching – '(a) in relation to the preventive aspects of medicine e.g. antenatal care, puerperal conditions, child welfare work, care of children of school age, care of adolescents, (b) the utilisation of local authority hospitals for teaching of medical students and nurses', and 7. General Policy – 'the lines along which, in the view of the Faculty, national health policy should be directed so as to secure the best possible results from all the agencies concerned with the health of the people.'[116]

Items six and seven have been noted in some detail since they illustrate two areas of interest in the context of this book. Item six suggests that the Committee was particularly concerned for the existing provisions for mothers, babies and children within the Scottish health services. This concern was shown in questions relating to medical training on these aspects of the personal health services. Since one of the recommendations of the Cathcart Report was to

114 *Lancet*, 1954 (1), 469, Obituary for E.P. Cathcart, by Andrew S.M. MacGregor.

115 'The Committee on Scottish Health Services hope to be in a position after April [1934] to consider the medical and allied services, and they would be grateful if Faculty of Physicians and Surgeons of Glasgow would assist them by submitting evidence on this branch of the enquiry.' Letter from McNicholl, Secretary to DHS Scottish Health Services Committee, to RFPSG, 3 February 1934.

116 Ibid.

expand and co-ordinate the maternity services of Scotland, information on existing training for general practitioners in these fields proved crucial.

Item seven refers directly to developing a national health policy for Scotland. Certainly, the general feeling within the DHS was that the recommendations of the Scottish Health Services Committee would frame the future direction of Scottish health policy, and this seems to have been the feeling within the Committee itself. The Committee's letter to the RFPSG went on to detail some of the initial findings of the Committee in its first few months.

> The evidence so far received on the changes in the social and economic conditions and the trends of vital statistics suggests that fundamental changes may have to be considered if expenditure on health services is to achieve maximum results. It is suggested also in evidence that the development of preventive medicine and advances in biological science may require a re-direction of policy as to aim more directly than at present through educational and other channels at the promotion of mental and physical fitness.[117]

In July 1934, a meeting of the Faculty approved a 'memorandum of evidence' drawn up by four specially-convened sub-committees. The RFPSG memorandum was then forwarded to the Committee on Scottish Health Services.[118] In August 1934, the Committee invited the RFPSG to send four representatives to Edinburgh to give personal evidence in November of that year.[119]

The Health Services Committee took advice from all concerned with the administration of health care in Scotland. In 1934, the Scottish Committee of the BMA produced a memorandum based on its evidence to the DHS Committee which stressed the vital importance of the part played by the general practitioner in the Scottish health services.[120] The BMA was anxious to preserve its traditional professional status and independence, although it broadly supported an extended and co-ordinated medical service.

---

117 Ibid.

118 RCPSG 1/1/1/16, RFPSG minutes, 2 July 1934.

119 RCPSG 1/1/1/16, RFPSG minutes, 28 August 1934.

120 *BMJ*, 1934 (2) 7 July 1934, 25–6.

The account of E.R.C. Walker, a member of the BMA Scottish Committee which gave evidence to the Cathcart Committee, gave an insight into how the BMA's formulated its position. The BMA Committee considered the findings of the two 1920 Consultative Councils for Scotland and England, respectively the MacAlister and Dawson Reports. In addition, it referred to the BMA's own policy statement of 1930 a 'General Medical Service for the Nation' (which recommended an extension of health insurance to workers dependants and a national maternity scheme, and an enhanced role for general practitioners in both), before coming up with the view:

> [...] If health is a matter of the reaction of an individual to his environment, it follows that the person who is to give him expert advice on health should be one who, to the greatest possible extent, is familiar both with him and his environment, and that such a one is to be found in the person of the family doctor.[121]

The emphasis on the importance of general practitioner services, within a co-ordinated health service came out forcefully in the Cathcart Report itself.

The Cathcart Report proposed a national health service for Scotland with a new comprehensive and co-ordinated structure of medical and allied services and an extension of the general practitioner services to all. New statutory services were to be funded by additional Exchequer grants to be made under section 78 of the Local Government (Scotland) Act, 1929, with an extended General Practitioner service to be funded by an extension of the contributory insurance principle. The need for co-ordination and expansion of existing services was one of the main thrusts of the report, which referred back to part of the original remit of the Committee in its 'review of the existing health services [...] in the light of modern conditions and knowledge.'[122]

The Committee did not feel constrained by the wording of the remit to the 'existing health services' to confine its enquiries to the statutory health services and examined conditions of general medical

121 Walker, 'The Forgotten Report', 494.

122 DHS, *Committee on Scottish Health Services Report*, 289.

practice, the work of the voluntary hospitals and the many voluntary agencies involved in delivering Scottish health care.[123] For this reason, a crucial recommendation of the Report was the co-ordination of general practitioner services with existing medical services, such as maternity and infant welfare and school health, to remedy: '[...] one of the principal weaknesses of these services as they are organised at present.'[124] The report also stressed a central role for general practitioners as 'medical officers of the home.' The recommendation for closer involvement of general practitioners as part of an integrated medical service reiterated the view presented in the 1920 MacAlister Report and also reflected the opinion of the late Parlane Kinloch.[125]

The Cathcart Report also recommended the abolition of Insurance Committees and the transfer of their functions to local authorities. However, the Report did not advocate a salaried general medical service and ruled out state control of hospitals. Traditional medical professional resistance to the idea of a state medical service was expressed in the majority of evidence to the Committee. Only the Scottish Trades Union Congress General Council and Glasgow Corporation supported the idea of a full-time salaried service in their evidence before the Committee.

---

123 Ibid., 9.

124 Ibid., 221.

125 'Faced with the reform of whole of our local health administration, it is for local authorities, for the medical profession, and the public generally to determine whether the time is not overdue when the general practitioner would be re-established in his position of full responsibility as family doctor – responsible for watching over the family health, responsible for the prevention of disease, and utilising for that purpose the whole of the official machinery the Local Authorities have provided. I am convinced that it can be done, and just as there must be a complete inter-locking and inter-changing of the work of the statutory health authorities and the voluntary agencies, so the co-ordination of the work of the private medical practitioner and the statutory health officer within a complete medical organisation will provide the adequate medical service that is the desire of everyone interested in social welfare.' *Transactions of the Scottish Association of Insurance Committees, 18th Annual Meeting, 1928*, 41. Address by John Parlane Kinloch, 'The Adequacy of the Medical Service, and the Role of the Medical Practitioner in the Official Organisation.'

Reaction to the Cathcart Report was mixed. The Report found strong support from representative medical organisations. The Scottish BMA supported the notion of increased responsibility for the general practitioner, as did the RFPSG and the two Edinburgh Royal Colleges.[126] The attitude of the Ministry of Health towards the Scottish Health Services Committee Report seems to have been coloured by the pressure then being put on the Ministry to consider an extended plan of health services by the BMA.

The influence of BMA thinking in the report caused an internal Ministry of Health memorandum to comment: '[...] the Scottish Health Services Committee have recommended what is practically the BMA's plan and the Secretary will want a note in the autumn as to any similar proposal for England.'[127] However, as E.R.C. Walker (a member of the BMA delegation that gave evidence to the Committee) noted, the BMA evidence itself was strongly influenced by the findings of the 1920 SBH MacAlister Report. The MacAlister Report placed a great deal of emphasis on the role of the general practitioner within an expanded state health system. The Cathcart Report, although containing much that the BMA representatives to the Committee had proposed, went much further in its recommendations for a co-ordinated health service for Scotland, for example, in the proposals for a complete municipal maternity service for Scotland.

In December 1934, the Ministry of Health pressed the DHS to find out what evidence had been given by BMA representatives to the Scottish Health Services Committee. The Ministry of Health was at this time holding discussions with the BMA to consider the issue of a 'general medical service for the nation'. A joint conference was eventually held with the BMA at the latter's request on 10 December 1935. On 12 December 1934, J.M. Vallance, (Assistant Secretary and Chief Accountant to the DHS and member on the Scottish Health

126 The Royal Colleges of Physicians and Surgeons of Edinburgh both strongly supported the key role of the general practitioner in the health services in their evidence to the Cathcart Committee. See DHS, *Committee on Scottish Health Services Report*, 152–153.

127 PRO, MH58/338, Internal Memorandum A.W. Neville, Assistant Secretary, MH to E.S Hill, Assistant Secretary, MH, 1 August 1936.

Services Committee) received a personal letter from H.A. de Montmorency, Assistant Secretary at the Ministry of Health. The letter requested copies of the evidence taken from 'the doctors' to the Committee on the subject of the BMA's scheme of a medical service for the nation: 'if the shorthand note of the evidence and the cross-examination were available we should be very pleased if we could have a perusal of it. Needless to say it would be treated in strict confidence.'[128]

On its publication, the Cathcart Report did not find much popular support in the press. The two main Scottish broadsheets reacted negatively to its publication. The *Glasgow Herald* noted the importance of the Report without accepting its 'controversial' proposals:

> The report of the Committee on Scottish Health Services is an unusually arresting document, and whatever view may be taken of its particular recommendations, there can be no doubt that it will make social history in Scotland [...]. Practically every proposal of the Committee raises a point of controversy, and the report will provide material for much public discussion for a long time.[129]

Other health agencies also opposed the Cathcart recommendations. The 1937 annual meeting of the Scottish Association of Insurance Committees (SAIC) took great exception to the recommendation that Insurance Committees and their administration of Medical Benefit for insured workers be placed in the hands of local authorities.[130] This recommendation in the Cathcart Report had not gained unanimous support in the Health Services Committee. William M. Marshall, founder member and Secretary to the SAIC was an obvious dissenter. One dissident voice, Mrs Hucheon of Dumfries County, felt that the Insurance Committees had been too complacent in their approach to

---

128 PRO, MH58/238, Ministry of Health, Letter from Sir Walter Kinnear, Controller, Insurance Department, to J.M. Vallance, Assistant Secretary/Chief Accountant, DHS, 12 December 1934.

129 *Glasgow Herald*, 'The National Health' Thursday, 2 July 1936, 10 col. c. See also *Scotsman*, Thursday 2 July 1936, 10 col. b and c.

130 *Transactions of Scottish Association of Insurance Committees, 1937*, debate on the 'Committee on Scottish Health Services', 14–15.

the question of a reorganisation of the health services. Her view was that: 'they would have to consider whether there might not be something in the co-ordination of the Health Services and the handing over of their duties to the Public Health Authority.'[131]

Crucially, the National Government did not welcome the findings of the Scottish Health Services Committee with any obvious enthusiasm. Scottish Secretary of State Godfrey Collins, while publicly acknowledging the efforts of the Committee, refused to be drawn into detailed comment on its findings during a parliamentary debate on the annual estimates of the DHS in July 1936:

> [...] It would be out of order now for me to deal with their proposals. Moreover, the committee sat for many weeks and went into the matter in great detail, and the Government could not yet make any pronouncement upon a report which only reached their hands a few weeks ago.[132]

It is possible that the Cathcart Report, which emphasised the preventive rather than curative aspects of statutory health services was too advanced in its intentions. In a similar vein, the 1937 Political and Economic Planning (PEP) Report on the British Health Services (which itself drew heavily on the Cathcart Report) stressed: 'it is important to therefore to outgrow the attitude of confining the term health services to what are really sickness services.'[133] Both the Cathcart Report and the 1937 PEP Report were extremely influential

---

131 Ibid., 17.

132 'Some years ago I appointed a committee to inquire into our health services in Scotland. That committee recently reported. What was in our minds in 1933 was the question, is the State in its health policy working on right lines? Was the State making full use of modern knowledge and all that that implied? Was also the State gaining full value for its money? If I endeavoured to interpret in one sentence the mind of that committee, to whose labours I am sure hon. Members in all parts of the House would desire me to pay a tribute [...] it would be that the central fact of health policy should be the building up of a healthy race, and that the existing machinery of government, which had done splendid work in the past, was not fully adapted to conditions to-day.' Scottish Secretary, Sir Godfrey Collins, HOC debates, 14–7–36, vol. 314 col. 1903–1904.

133 PEP, *Report on the British Health Services: A Survey of Existing Health Services in Great Britain with Proposals for Future Development* (PEP, 1937), 395.

documents in terms of contemporary thinking about a future state health service. Yet when the NHS was eventually set up, the re-commendations contained in the two Reports were not closely followed.

The shelving of the Cathcart Report was not expected among the higher echelons of the DHS. During discussions on the reorganisation of the Department in 1934/5 (in order to introduce Administrative Grade civil servants to the DHS), the additional workload the implementation of the Cathcart Committee's findings was expected to create was twice cited in internal memoranda.

> In connection with the question of the volume of work in the Department, it has to be noted that so far as the Medical Services Division is concerned it is probable that, when the present Departmental Committee on Health Services issues its Report, a considerable amount of additional work will be thrown on the Division.[134]

Looking back at the organisation of the Department in 1946, the DHS view was that: 'In the 1930s the most important Committee dealing with the Department's work was the Committee on Scottish Health Services whose Report was published in 1936.'[135] The DHS hierarchy confidently expected that the Scottish Health Services Committee's findings would lead to fresh policy initiatives in health matters. This was the view expressed during the months when the Cathcart Committee was in session. In June 1934 an internal DHS memorandum felt that the findings of the Cathcart Committee would provide 'essential information' as to the state of existing municipal health services, a review which the Medical Services Division of the DHS felt ought to be undertaken.[136] However, the Cathcart Report

---

134 NAS, DD1/12, DHS, memorandum 'As to the proposed reorganisation of the Department' (undated), 1935. See also DD1/12, note 'As to causes leading to proposed reorganisation of work of the Department of Health for Scotland', 26 June 1934.

135 NAS, SOE1/234, DHS, Departmental Handbook No. 1, 'The Organisation and Functions of the Department' (1946), 10.

136 NAS, DD1/12, See Paragraphs 6 and 7, 'Note as to causes leading to proposed reorganisation of work of Department of Health for Scotland', unsigned DHS Memorandum, 26 June 1934.

recommendations, despite finding support within the Department, could not influence policy in a direction which was not supported by government. The 'state autonomy' model of bureaucratic control[137] (where group organisations influence policy only when their views coincide with those of government) seemed to be in evidence once again in the guidance of Scottish health policy.

Lack of Government support combined with the predominance of the policy of 'economy' ensured that only the scheme of an extended maternity service[138] was put into operation before the coming of the National Health Service. Despite the limited implementation of its findings, the Cathcart Report helped lay a solid foundation for the operation of a distinctive Scottish service suited to Scotland's health needs in the years before and during World War Two. It also helped open a wider debate on possible reform of health services across Britain. In 1937, the Political and Economic Planning *Report on the British Health Services* gave prominence to a range of the Cathcart Report's findings. For example, the PEP Report noted that the Cathcart Report had 'created lively interest in the regional idea among the voluntary hospitals, especially in the West of Scotland'.[139]

Conclusion

Scottish health policy in much of the 1920s and 30s was affected by twin considerations: continued high unemployment and the need for economy in local and national expenditure. These made for a difficult combination, for the conditions that produced unemployment also created the need for economy. The distress that arose from unemployment normally led to calls for public expenditure on relief and other ameliorative measures. In attempting to steer a course

137 Dowding, *The Civil Service*, 4.

138 See next chapter for more on extending maternity services in the inter-war years.

139 See PEP, *Report on the British Health Services*, 246.

through such seemingly conflicting considerations, the DHS sought to ensure that expenditure was directed wisely, and if possible, to increase the preventive, positive aspects of statutory health provision.

In terms of health, Scotland continued to have one of the worst records of the industrialised world. Much time and effort had gone into making detailed proposals to improve and extend the health services to meet the needs of the Scots population in a variety of Reports. Yet by the end of the 1930s, few proposals had been into operation. The overriding desire for economy in spending on public services was partly behind this inaction. At a local level, the inability of local authorities to raise sufficient funding to expand health services was exacerbated by the introduction of the block grant system under the 1929 Local Government (Scotland) Act which threw more emphasis on income from the rates. The financial burden on local authorities which hampered the extension of services in the Highlands and Islands due to the poverty of the area in these years, was also a consideration in urban areas. For example, the inability of local authorities to properly fund health services in their areas was 'reiterated again and again' in evidence before the DHS Scottish Health Services Committee which met between 1933–36. In fact, the Cathcart Report recommended that there should be more financial balance in statutory health provisions between central government and what was required of local authorities.[140]

In the inter-war years, successive governments placed restrictions on financial expenditure due to the weakness of the economy. This had a deleterious effect on state health service provision. Yet, the great expansion in state health services which occurred between 1946–1948 was conducted in the wake of World War Two – the most expensive undertaking the country had ever witnessed. This suggests that it was political will (or lack of it), which determined the level and nature of statutory health provision in the country at any given period.[141] For the DHS in the 1930s, as with the SBH in the previous decade, perhaps the best that could be realistically achieved in the

140 DHS, *Committee on Health Services Report*, 293.

141 For more on the 'executive-centred' approach see Immergut, *Health Politics*, 23.

inter-war years was to ensure that the 'necessary economies were effected without [further] damage to the physical quality of the people'.[142] The case studies that follow attempt to measure the impact of inter-war policy initiatives on the health of the Scots population.

142 DHS, *Annual Report, 1931*, xiv.

The Highlands and Islands Medical Service in Operation: Nurses in North Uist, the Outer Hebrides, 1926
© National Museums of Scotland

3: Infant and Maternal Welfare

> The basic service that had to be put right was that of maternity and child welfare, and unless that was done, most of the expenditure incurred in ordinary services, and for school children and adults, would be largely wasted.
> (J. Parlane Kinloch, Chief Medical Officer, DHS, at the opening of a child welfare and maternity clinic in Banff, February 1931, NAS, HH61/622, *Aberdeen Press and Journal* cutting, February 1931)

> The figures showing that our Infant Mortality rate is 40% worse than England's and is higher than in any British Dominion or the USA, higher than in Eire, higher than in any nation in Western Europe except Spain and Portugal – these figures have already been the subject of anxious comment.
> (DHS, *Report on Infant Mortality in Scotland*, (Edinburgh: HMSO, 1943). Prepared by a Sub-Committee of the Scientific Advisory Committee, 1)

Introduction

This chapter examines both health policy determinants and the impact of policy implementation on the health of Scots mothers and babies over the period from the end of World War One down to 1948. The development of infant and maternal welfare provision in the twentieth century touches on many of the areas which surrounded the setting up of the Scottish Board of Health and the Ministry of Health. It also well reflects the expanding inter-war role of the State in health care. The question of individual responsibility for health within the personal medical services was also very much to the fore in the area of the welfare of mothers and infants. Public debate on infant and maternal welfare issues coincided with wider fears about the health of the nation. These issues came together at the turn-of-the-century and beyond. This was particularly due to the high public profile of eugenics combined with fears of the implications of a falling birth rate for the future well being of the nation. The health of mothers and babies continued as a concern given the very small recorded rise in the Scottish population level over the whole period covered in this book. Scotland's population fell by 40,000 between the 1921 and 1931 censuses. Between 1931 and 1951 (and well beyond the period covered by this book) the inter-censal growth rate for Scotland's population averaged only one-quarter of a percent.[1]

There has been much historical controversy over how best to interpret inter-war mortality statistics among mothers and infants. This debate will be addressed in this chapter by way of a comparison of Scottish with British and international averages and through an analysis of a wide range of local Scottish burgh and county infant and maternal mortality data.

The Pre–1919 Position

In the main, the birth of the child welfare movement was an event of the twentieth century. Issues of infant and maternal welfare commanded attention at a time when the debate over 'national efficiency' was given much public prominence. The 1903 LGBS *Report of the Royal Commission on Physical Training (Scotland)* recommended that the feeding and environment of children should be actively improved.[2] The first experiments in supplementary feeding of infants were carried out in France through the establishment of milk depots in 1892. The first English depot opened in St. Helens in 1899. The first Scottish depots were opened in Leith in 1903, and Glasgow and Dundee in 1904. Milk depots were the first initiatives to supervise the artificial feeding of infants, and in 1905 an international congress on the subject was held in Paris.[3] The first British conference on child

1 R.K. Kelsall, *Population* (Longman, 1967), 17

2 For more on the LGBS Report on Physical Training see previous chapter.

3 The meeting was attended by delegates from Battersea, Hull and by Glasgow MOH Chalmers and a representative of the Glasgow City Corporation,

life was held in 1906. Archibald Kerr Chalmers, then Medical Officer of Health for Glasgow, and other Scottish representatives attended both of these meetings.[4]

Alongside infant feeding, another early concern was over levels of infant mortality. The 1904 *Report of the Inter-Departmental Committee on Physical Deterioration* uncovered alarming information regarding infant mortality:

> Three facts stand out prominently as the result of this investigation; first, that infantile mortality in this country has not decreased materially during the last twenty-five years, notwithstanding that the general death-rate has fallen considerably; secondly, that the mortality among illegitimate children is enormously greater than among children born in wedlock; thirdly, that about one-half the mortality occurs in the first three months of life.[5]

The findings of the Physical Deterioration Report ensured that infant and child welfare remained prominent on the political agenda in the early twentieth century. In 1907, the Notification of Births Act was passed by which all births were to be registered by the parents or birth attendants.[6] This Act marked the beginning of a steady stream of infant welfare legislation. Appendix 2 lists British and Scotland-only enactments in this field in the first half of the twentieth century.

During World War One the concerns for the nation's health that had first surfaced during the Boer War reappeared to a higher degree, against a background of high war casualties, falling birth rates and rising infantile mortality. In 1915, the Notification of Births

---

Councillor Anderson. Chalmers became first secretary of the National Conference on Infant Life, while Anderson led a deputation of local councillors to Prime Minister Asquith in 1908 to put the case for further government action to protect infant life. See Sir A.S.M. MacGregor, *Public Health in Glasgow, 1905–1946* (Edinburgh: E&S Livingstone Ltd, 1967), 109–110.

4 Strathclyde Regional Archives, Mitchell Library, Glasgow, Corporation of Glasgow pamphlet, 'Public Health Department Scheme for Maternity and Child Welfare', October 1926, 10.

5 *Report of the Inter-Departmental Committee on Physical Deterioration*, (1904), 44, [Cmd 2175].

6 See Appendix 2 for a full list of legislation relating to infant and maternal welfare.

(Extension) Act was passed.[7] The adoptive provisions of the 1907 Notification of Births Act were rendered compulsory, and for the first time local Scottish authorities were empowered to make arrangements for attending to the health of expectant and new mothers and children under five.

Building on turn of the century debates on the 'fitness of the nation' wartime legislative arrangements for infant and maternal welfare brought concerns for these groups to the forefront of developments in the personal health services. According to both contemporary opinion and certain historians, in a way which was not contemplated in the first years of the century, growing concern for the health of mothers and babies coincided with government determination to centralise government commitment to health preservation.[8] Richard Titmuss first cited the importance of war as a factor in social change in the 1940s. Writing specifically on infant mortality, Titmuss identified warfare as a crucial determinant in changing attitudes to social welfare.

> There is perhaps something rather shocking in the idea that it took a war to focus public attention on a wastefully high infant death rate. Whatever our

7 'Any local authority within the meaning of the principal Act may be sanctioned by the Local Government Board for Scotland, for attending to the health of expectant mothers and nursing mothers, and of children under five years of age within the meaning of section seven of the Education (Scotland) Act, 1908', Notification of Births (Extension) Act, 29 July 1915.

8 The view of Scottish Secretary Robert Munro on the importance of state health provision for mothers and babies was expressed in a letter to Edinburgh's Lord Provost in 1918 on proposals for a National Institute of Maternal and Child Welfare for Scotland offered by the Carnegie United Kingdom Trust. Munro stated: 'The ravages of war have compelled us to recognise the problems of maternity and child welfare as of national importance, and manifold activities have developed with a view to their solution.' PRO, MH 55/218, letter from Scottish Secretary to Sir John Lorne MacLeod, Lord Provost of Edinburgh, 29 July 1918. Recent historians have revived this view: 'The introduction of legislation to protect infant and child health may [...] have presaged the establishment in 1919 of the Ministry of Health.' D. Dwork, *War is Good for Babies and other Young Children: A History of the Infant and Child Welfare Movement in England 1898–1918* (Tavistock Publications, 1987), 222–3. See also Honigsbaum, *The Division in British Medicine*, 29–40 passim for more on this view.

reason, it remains true that our concern for national health has followed the course of our military fortunes.[9]

The wartime Maternity and Child Welfare Act, 1918, empowered local authorities to borrow money for the purposes of schemes of maternity and child welfare. In May 1918, the Local Government Board Scotland (LGBS) issued a memorandum to all local authorities reminding them of the availability of grant-in-aid for setting up local maternity and child welfare centres.[10] Also in 1918, two orders empowered the LGBS to require Scottish local authorities to arrange for the supply of food and milk for expectant and nursing mothers and children under the age of five.[11] These measures represented a shift in government attitude towards state involvement in the care of mothers and young children. They also represented the launch of a two-pronged approach by the state to address the worrying morbidity and mortality levels among mothers and babies. This approach, while often severely curtailed by economic constraints, remained the government 'solution' to the problems of the ill health of mothers and babies. Additional nutrition, where freely offered, was a positive development in addressing the health of mothers and babies. However, it is debatable how far providing 50% grants for local authorities to set up maternity and child welfare centres could play a positive role in improving mortality and morbidity patterns among

9 Titmuss, *Birth, Poverty, and Wealth: A Study of Infant Mortality*, 12.

10 'I am instructed by the Local Government Board for Scotland to direct the attentions of the local authority to the appended revised Regulations for the distribution of the grant-in-aid of maternity and child welfare schemes. These regulations came into force as at 16 May 1918, and supersede all those previously issued. In spite of the need for economy in public administration generally, the Board take this opportunity of again impressing on local authorities the importance of securing full provision for maternity and child welfare in their districts'. PRO, MH 55/218, LGBS, memorandum to all Scottish local authorities, 24 May 1918, 'Notification of Births (Extension) Act, 1915: Maternity Service and Child Welfare Schemes'.

11 These were the 'Food for Mothers and Children (Scotland) Order' issued by the Government's Food Controller and the Scottish Secretary, and the LGBS 'Local Authorities Food (for Mothers and Children) (Scotland) Order.' See LGBS, *Annual Report, 1918* [Cmd 230] (Edinburgh: HMSO, 1919), xx.

mothers and babies. Such centres, where instituted, were attended by a minority of mothers and infants, and they chiefly offered educational and diagnostic advice, rather than medical treatment.

Early Financial Restrictions on Infant and Maternal Welfare

In the first months after the end of World War One, the SBH waved through local proposals for infant and maternal welfare schemes, such as those put forward by the local authorities of Edinburgh, Motherwell, Hamilton and Ayr in October 1919, as a matter of course.[12] Moreover, in November 1919, the SBH decided to draft a circular to call the attention of local authorities to their powers in regard to supply milk to mothers and children.[13] The implication was that the level of response for extra feeding was not as high as had been hoped. In January 1920, the SBH agreed a purchase price of £1,000 for a YMCA hut in Bridgeton in the East End of Glasgow for a maternity and child welfare centre and day nursery and approved plans for the provision of food and milk for mothers and children by Glasgow city council. At a single SBH meeting at the beginning of April 1920, local 'maternity and child welfare' schemes for the counties of Selkirk and Zetland, and the towns of Kirriemuir and Kilsyth were approved. Expenses for the expansion of existing schemes in the towns of Wishaw, Grangemouth, St Andrews district, the middle ward of Lanark and the counties of Lanark and Aberdeen were also approved at this Board meeting.[14]

Within a year everything had changed. The first Treasury circular proposing expenditure cuts was discussed by the SBH in December 1920 when it was decided to revise all Board operations at divisional

12 NAS, HH75/1, SBH minutes, 31 October 1919.

13 NAS, HH75/1, SBH divisional committee minutes [not numbered], 11 November 1919.

14 NAS, HH75/3, SBH divisional committee III minutes, 1 April 1920.

level and to consider what projects might be deferred.[15] This review of services came up with a long list of areas relating to the health of mothers and young children where the SBH had involvement.[16] Minutes for 28 December 1920 stated the Board's position on any proposed retrenchment of services:

> It would be deplorable if the Board's activities in regard to the welfare of mothers and children are to be unduly restricted. It is the case that Maternity and Child Welfare Schemes were pushed on, as far as possible and in spite of obstacles, even during the war.[17]

A sign of an enforced change in policy towards infant and maternal welfare expenditure came in April 1921 with the SBH's decision to delay approval for plans for a Maternity Home on Dumfries. The Board informed a deputation from Dumfries burgh: 'the matter was under further consideration within the Treasury and that the Board could not say definitely at this stage whether operations would be allowed to proceed.'[18]

The need for economy led the government to appoint a committee of business leaders to recommend public expenditure cuts. Financial constraints imposed as the nation slid into economic depression were known as the 'Geddes Axe'.[19] Defence spending was cut back even more than health expenditure. In the aftermath of war, however, this was not unexpected. State health provision, especially in

---

15 NAS, HH75/5, SBH minutes, 24 December 1920.

16 'The chief activities in connection with maternity and child welfare are inspection of midwives, provision of midwifery services and maternity nurses, employment of health visitors, provision of child welfare centres and medical attendance at the centres, provision of crèches and day nurseries, schools for mothers and young women, hospital treatment, improvement of home conditions in confinement cases, provision of convalescent homes and homes for children, provision of food and milk for necessitous cases, assistance to voluntary institutions and agencies approved under schemes.' NAS, HH75/5, SBH minutes, 28 December 1920.

17 NAS, HH75/5, SBH minutes, 28 December 1920.

18 NAS, HH75/7, SBH divisional committee III minutes, 5 April 1921.

19 For more on the 'Geddes Axe' see chapter one of this book and also G.C. Peden, *British Economic and Social Policy: Lloyd George to Margaret Thatcher* (Oxford: Philip Allen, 2nd ed., 1991), 51, 74.

areas where government and local authorities were undergoing a period of expansion of services, including infant and maternal welfare, was another matter. As part of the wide ranging Treasury cuts in public services in the early 1920s, the provision of milk and food to necessitous mothers by local authorities allowed under 1918 LGBS arrangements, came under strict financial restriction. These cuts in the feeding of 'necessitous' mothers and babies provoked opposition within the SBH and also outright defiance among some local authorities, notably Glasgow. The situation was made worse by the fact that the expenditure cuts were introduced during a period of high unemployment and coincided with the miners' strike of that year, so that any cut in feeding for necessitous mothers and children would be badly-felt.

The SBH, under pressure from the Treasury, squeezed Glasgow Corporation to cut its costs. However, as John Jeffrey, SBH Joint Secretary pointed out in a letter to the Treasury, in March 1921, the Board wanted to tread carefully in cutting back local authority spending on milk for mothers and babies. Any cutting back of the scheme '[...] is certain to provoke local hostility and questions in Parliament.'[20] The SBH view was that since the milk expenditure was caused by high local unemployment levels it should be regarded as part of a package of relief of the distress of the unemployed.[21] Jeffrey's opinion was proved correct as the Scottish ILP MPs made great play of the Conservative-dominated Coalition Government's financial restrictions on health expenditure.

The Treasury made some concessions to SBH appeals to allow extra expenditure on milk in Glasgow 'in the present circumstances of unemployment' in April 1921, but this was a temporary expedient.[22] Additional spending for milk and meals to expectant and nursing mothers and children under five was also granted to Dunfermline and other mining districts of Scotland at the same time. The SBH also took advantage of this slight easing on expenditure limits to give approval

20 PRO, T161/118, SBH Secretary John Jeffrey to A.W. Hurst, Treasury, 29 March 1921.

21 Ibid.

22 NAS, HH75/7, SBH minutes, 15 April 1921.

to the Dumfries Maternity Home scheme delayed a few weeks before. However, in May 1921 revised Treasury spending proposals were issued setting strict limits on local expenditure on maternity and child welfare among a raft of expenditure cuts across all aspects of health expenditure. In practice the announcement led to a reduction in SBH spending estimates of £700,000.[23] This renewed financial pressure from the Treasury led the SBH to issue a memorandum in August 1921 on the 'Provision of Nourishment for Mothers and Children.' The memorandum set out new financial limits on local authority spending on milk and meals. Supplementary nutrition was to be given by local authorities only where the local Medical Officer of Health was satisfied that extra feeding was essential on health grounds. A scale of income was to be adopted to determine 'necessitous cases' in each area.[24] Glasgow was again a focus for attention during this period of retrenchment. Glasgow Corporation was spending £60 per day on milk for needy mothers and babies (at a cost of £21,000 per year, three times more than the total SBH estimate under this head for 1921).

In October 1921, Edinburgh City Corporation responded to the SBH circular with a revised scheme of milk and feeding plans drawn up by Edinburgh MOH, A. Maxwell-Williamson. Under the revised plans each case was to be considered individually. Where family income was 15 shillings (75p – the level of unemployment benefit), free milk and free dinners were given after a visit to the family from a local health visitor. Free milk and meals (or subsidised meals) were also given where wages were very low or where there were one or more children ill or under the age of five in a household.[25] This revised scheme met with the conditional approval of the SBH, subject to further enquiries of the costs of meals provided.[26]

The position in Glasgow proved to be more difficult to resolve. In November 1921, the SBH sent two investigators to visit Glasgow

23 NAS, HH75/7, SBH divisional committee VI minutes, 27 May 1921.

24 PRO, MH 55/218, SBH Circular, 'Provision of Nourishment for Mothers and Children', 31 August 1921.

25 NAS, HH61/781, Report enclosed with letter from Edinburgh City Corporation Deputy Town Clerk to Secretary, SBH, 27 October 1921.

26 NAS, HH75/9, SBH minutes, 4 November 1921.

Corporation to enquire into the continued much higher cost of milk and meals in the city than elsewhere in the country.[27] The report back to the Board by Dr Watt and Mr Davison suggested various measures in order to cut costs in Glasgow, including that children aged three to five who received free dinners should no longer be given milk. Eventually, the SBH came to an agreement with Glasgow Corporation. High expenditure under this heading was accepted on a one-off basis (the 1921/22 Scottish estimate for spending on maternity and child welfare of £180,00 was projected with an overspend of £80,000). The following year's SBH budget was severely capped under this heading down to a total of £120,000 (£111,000 actual expenditure plus an additional £9,000 to cover some of the carry-over costs of the 1921/22 overspend on milk and meals).[28]

The Treasury assessment of SBH budget limitations for the following year made clear that central government felt the Board had over-reacted in its defence of milk and food for needy mothers and babies during the previous year. A Treasury Memorandum noted: 'The Scottish Board of Health [...] in respect of Maternity and Child Welfare in the current year [...] were alarmed at a possible revolution, and poured out milk in great quantities to soothe the unemployed.'[29] The financial cutbacks planned for 1922/23 had parliamentary repercussions. Matters reached a dramatic climax in June 1923, when James Maxton ILP MP for Glasgow Bridgeton denounced those who had voted for reductions in the Scottish estimates in the grant for milk for babies and food for nursing mothers as 'murderers'.

The Scottish estimates were presented before parliament by Parliamentary Under Secretary for Health, Walter Elliot. Elliot noted that SBH statistics showed that despite the prolonged trade depression, the Scottish population generally was maintaining a good standard of Health. Maxton said that the most depressing feature of the SBH report concerned child health and the withdrawal during a certain

27 Mitchell Library, Glasgow, Strathclyde Regional Archives, minutes of Glasgow Corporation Health Sub-Committee, 21 November 1921, 280.

28 NAS, HH75/9, SBH minutes, 21 December 1921.

29 PRO, T161/118, memorandum by J.B. Beresford, Treasury, 'Limitation of Expenditure by SBH', February 1922.

period when there was an epidemic of measles, influenza and whooping cough, of the grant of milk to babies and food for nursing mothers. Maxton asserted that in the interests of economy hundreds of children living in one apartment houses were condemned to death. 'The men who initiated such a policy are murderers, as are all those who voted for such economy. They have the blood of infants on their hands. To save money they were prepared to destroy children.'[30]

During the commotion that followed, Maxton refused to withdraw his remark on the grounds that the whole matter was historical knowledge. He even resisted Labour leader, Ramsay MacDonald's attempt to defuse the situation. Ramsey MacDonald advised Maxton to limit his charge to the result of the Board's policy without bringing in the personal equation. Maxton stuck to his statement, and was supported by Glasgow Shettleston MP John Wheatley who repeated the 'murderers' allegation. Wheatley stated 'bring back the lives of these Scottish infants and I will withdraw.'[31] A vote was taken during the uproar to suspend Maxton and Wheatley from the Commons. Glasgow Camlachie MP Campell Stephen next began a speech on the same lines and was also promptly suspended. The three MPs were soon joined by Gorbals MP George Buchanan who launched a verbal volley at the unfairness of the treatment of the Glasgow MPs (including another, Emmanuel Shinwell who, while he was speaking, had been subject to murmured comments of 'Jew'). The four Glasgow MPs were suspended from parliament for four weeks for their passionate intercessions during the health expenditure debates. The Labour Party nationally made similar dramatic statements regarding maternal welfare. For example, Party activist Dora Russell spearheaded an inter-war campaign for better maternity care and easier access to contraception. Her starting point was that it was four times as dangerous to bear a child as to work in a mine, and mining was men's most dangerous occupation.

Financial restrictions operated on maternal and infant welfare services between 1921 and 1924. The concern to expand statutory provision for mothers and babies around Britain so much in evidence

30 *Glasgow Herald*, 28 June 1923, 7 col. d.
31 Ibid.

during and after World War One was curtailed.[32] Reference to Appendix 2 shows that in 1918 alone there were three official measures dealing with the welfare of Scottish mothers and babies, namely: the Maternity and Child Welfare Act, the Midwives (Amendment) Act and Scottish regulations which made Ophthalmia Neonatorum a notifiable disease. Yet, after economic problems developed in the early 1920s, there were no other official initiatives or pronouncements for this vulnerable group until the 1927 Midwives and Maternity Homes (Scotland) Act.

The Treasury briefly lifted financial restrictions in 1924.[33] However, further expenditure restrictions under this head were restored for most of 1926. Eventually further spending on infant and maternal welfare was allowed from October 1926. Chancellor of the Exchequer, Winston Churchill in a letter to Scottish Secretary, Sir John Gilmour loosened the purse strings:

> I agree that the restrictive policy in regard to the provision of Maternity and Child Welfare centres in Scotland need not continue in quite so rigid a form as at present. I therefore accept your proposal to approve moderate and well-considered schemes submitted by local authorities where you are satisfied that a case has been made out.[34]

The issue of milk and food for needy mothers and babies was viewed by central government as a question of expenditure. The SBH, working closely with Scottish local authorities, saw it both as a relief measure and a way to preserve public health. Yet the Board was forced to accept the financial limits imposed by the Treasury. The PUSH, Walter Elliot, was then faced with the difficult task of justifying the cutbacks before parliament. Meanwhile, local MOsH were in no doubt that supplementary feeding was not only essential,

---

32 For more on this see J. Lewis, *The Politics of Motherhood: Child and Maternity Welfare in England 1900–1939* (Croom Helm, 1980), 173 and L. Marks, *Metropolitan Maternity: Maternal and Infant Welfare Services in early Twentieth Century London* (Amsterdam: Rodopi, 1996), 140–45.

33 See PRO, T161/118, Draft letter from G.L. Barstow, Treasury, to John Jeffrey, Secretary, SBH, 15 March 1924.

34 PRO, T161/118, Letter from Chancellor of the Exchequer, Winston Churchill to Scottish Secretary of State, Sir John Gilmour, 19 October 1926.

but also a positive boon to these vulnerable sections of the population. Writing in 1935, Stirling County's MOH noted the positive benefits of supplementary feeding during industrial depression:

> During the coal disputes of 1921 and 1926 respectively special machinery was instituted for distributing milk to expectant and nursing mothers and young children in mining areas. That much good resulted was clearly indicated by the fact that infantile mortality for each of these years was remarkably low, it being only 61 per 1,000 live births in 1926, the lowest on record for the County.[35]

Solving the Problem? Infant and Maternal Welfare Centres

Infant and maternal welfare centres remained, alongside the provision of health visitors, the most commonly pursued local authority measure for mothers and babies in the first decades of the twentieth century. However, Scotland's scattered population made it difficult to establish infant and maternal welfare centres except in the large urban centres. For example, examination of the SBH minutes between 1919 and early 1921 when maternity and child welfare schemes were a matter of priority for the SBH show very few counties applying for Board approval to go ahead with such schemes.[36] Aside from the overcrowded central belt, the density of the population of Scotland is much less than in England.[37] Even in large cities, it was a far from an

35 Stirling Regional Archives, SC3/3/41, 'Medical Officer of Health Stirling County, Annual Report', 1935, 63.

36 For example a long list of burgh councils, including Motherwell and Hamilton in Lanarkshire were granted early SBH approval for the expansion of infant and maternity services in their areas, meanwhile only one county council scheme was put forward. NAS, HH75/2, SBH minutes, 24 February 1920.

37 As late as 1961, outside the central belt and in and around the North East cities of Dundee and Aberdeen, Scottish population density was less than 100 persons per square mile. Only the borders and lakes area of England had similarly low population densities. In contrast, in the Clydeside conurbation, population density was 1100 persons and over per square mile. In England, the average

easy matter to find and furnish suitable accommodation overnight. The urban/rural divide, which characterised much of the inter-war statutory Scottish provision for infant and maternal welfare, was also noted for England. The 1934 *Maternal Mortality Report*[38] noted that in England, the Metropolitan councils of London and the urban county councils generally offered a better range of services for mothers and babies than the rural county boroughs.[39]

In Scotland, the conditions of existing voluntary-run and local authority maternity and child welfare centres often left much to be desired. In November 1919, the SBH contacted the Town Clerk of the Edinburgh City Corporation to sanction the opening of three new premises as special treatment centres and the reservation of five beds for expectant and nursing mothers at the Duddingston Convalescent Home. A survey of the existing Edinburgh centres by SBH Medical Inspector, Dr. Mary Jenny Menzies, revealed the unsatisfactory nature of existing accommodation. For example, at the Pleasance Maternity and Child Welfare Centre, Dr Menzies found that undressed infants had to be carried across an open passageway from the waiting and weighing room to the doctor's consultation room.[40]

Perhaps in recognition of the poor standard of existing accommodation, the SBH in 1919/20 made a short-lived commitment to fund a range of local mother and baby services. Money was made available to establish maternity and child welfare centres, arrange extra feeding for children, and provide hospital beds for expectant mothers. The basic tenets of the scheme were three-fold: to provide practical care for mothers and the under-fives, to offer medical examination and preventive advice, and to offer supplementary feeding, through milk and meals schemes.

---

population level for areas outside the main conurbations was 100–299 persons per square mile. Kelsall, *Population*, 106.

38 The Maternal Mortality Committee set up in 1927 was a cross-party pressure group set up by women including trade unionist Gertrude Tuckwell and Lady Iveagh, Chairman of the Conservative Party.

39 Maternal Mortality Committee, *Maternal Mortality Report* (1934), 4–12, cited in Marks, *Metropolitan Maternity*, 196–197.

40 Edinburgh City Archives, Public Health series, File 16, Box 6, Letter from SBH to Town Clerk, Edinburgh Corporation, 5 November 1919.

Gradually, in the areas where maternity and child welfare centres were set up, chiefly the main urban locations, purpose-built accommodation was constructed and the range of services provided was expanded. The Second Annual Report of the SBH for 1920 put the number of health visitors involved in maternity and child welfare schemes at 174 full-time, 188 part-time and 800 voluntary.[41] The 1921 census figures indicated there were 196 maternity and child welfare centres were operating in Scotland, staffed by 132 full-time and 181 part-time nurses and health visitors.

As statutory medical services expanded, the role of health visitors was given more emphasis by the SBH. The preventive nature of health visiting was recognised and more importance placed on the training of health visitors. To this end, the SBH Consultative Councils on Medical and Allied Services and Local Health Administration and General Health Questions jointly compiled reports on the future training of health visitors in 1920. As a result, a programme of training and examination for health visitors was prepared by the SBH.[42]

Voluntary agencies remained a recognised part of the infant and maternity services in Scotland after the creation of the SBH. More voluntary workers were needed after the opening of additional infant and maternal welfare centres funded under the Notification of Births (Extension) Act, 1915.[43] By 1920, there were 29 day nurseries in operation in Scotland, 23 run by local authorities and 6 by voluntary agencies.

Further voluntary effort was very much in evidence in 1921, with the opening a purpose-built health centre in Motherwell paid for by

41 SBH, *Second Annual Report, 1920*, 83.

42 Ibid., 82.

43 'It has been the policy of local authorities in Scotland to incorporate in their schemes the various voluntary institutions and agencies for maternity and child welfare in the area, and, where necessary, to contribute funds to extend and develop their work.' Viscount William Robert Wellesley Peel, Joint Parliamentary Secretary of the National Service Department, HOL debates, 18–7–18, vol. 30 col. 982.

the Carnegie United Kingdom Trust.[44] The new centre included an integrated infant, maternity and child welfare centre, a maternity home, a treatment centre, and provision for mothers' education classes, and was described as a 'model of its kind'.[45] This assessment is certainly borne out when the range of services provided by the Motherwell centre is considered. The Institute was designed to supplement home training and treatment by health visitors, by providing social, educational and a range of medical facilities for mothers, infants and children.

The Motherwell Child Welfare Centre was the first opened of six model centres proposed in 1918 by the Carnegie Trust at various sites around Britain.

> The purpose of these centres is not the treatment of disease, but the instruction in sound principles of those who are in charge of infants and young children [...] On the principle that prevention is better than cure, it is clearly of the first importance that parents and health visitors should have the opportunity of studying under the most favourable conditions the domestic problems of housing, sanitation, clothing and diet.[46]

Although the Carnegie Trust's Child Welfare Centre in Motherwell was a prominent voluntary achievement in Scottish health promotion during the inter war period, it was by no means the only one. The Glasgow Day Nurseries Association provided voluntary care in the

---

44 The original plan by the Carnegie UK Trust – discussed at a conference in Edinburgh City Chambers in July 1918 – was to set up a Maternity and Child Welfare Institute for Scotland in Edinburgh. The institute was intended to serve as a 'national bureau of information and research in all matters affecting the welfare of mothers and children'. LGBS, *Annual Report, 1918* (Edinburgh: HMSO, 1919), xxi, [Cmd 230].
In addition, to providing treatment, the Motherwell Model Centre was set up, as its title suggests, as a model to others in setting up maternity and child welfare schemes. Due to delays in finding suitable premises, the planned Carnegie Trust Maternity and Child Welfare Institute was not constructed.

45 Mary Jenny Menzies 'Maternity and Child Welfare in Scotland', *BMJ*, 1922 (2), 350.

46 Press release from Carnegie United Kingdom Trust on opening of the Motherwell Centre, quoted in the *Motherwell Times*, Friday 22 June 1921, Motherwell District Council, Motherwell Leisure Services.

run down east-end of the city until the mid 1920s. In fact, it was on a site in Bridgeton, transferred from the Association to Glasgow Corporation, that Prime Minister Stanley Baldwin opened the first of Glasgow's new purpose-built maternity and child welfare centres to much fanfare in October 1925. The new building housed both a welfare centre and a day nursery.[47]

By 1927, the SBH claimed that maternity and child welfare schemes were in operation in areas covering 93% of the Scottish population.[48] Yet, the mere recording of the setting up of maternal and infant welfare schemes by local authorities said nothing about the quality of the service offered.[49] In areas with infant and maternal welfare centres, contemporary accounts stress a high attendance rate by mothers as having some positive impact on the local IMR. Commenting on the efficacy of the child welfare service in Edinburgh, the Medical Officer of Health noted that IMR was 123 when the service was established in the city in 1917, by 1941 the figure had fallen to 56.[50] However, in areas with poor attendance or where there were no clinics, there is little evidence to suggest that infant mortality rates were adversely affected.[51]

This raises the question whether attendance at maternity and child welfare centres made much of a difference to the health of mothers and young children.[52] Mere attendance at clinics and offers of

47 MacGregor, *Public Health in Glasgow, 1905–1946*, 115–116.

48 SBH, *Ninth Annual Report, 1927* (Edinburgh: HMSO, 1928), [Cmd 3112].

49 Case studies may illustrate the efficacy of local schemes. For example, Lara Marks has contrasted the range of maternal and infant welfare services in London favourably with provision made elsewhere in the country. See Marks, *Metropolitan Maternity*, 170.

50 'The readiness of the expectant mother to seek medical advice and care at the ante-natal clinics is one of the most potent factors in safeguarding the health of the mother and child and it is a good thing for Edinburgh that, over the years this habit of pre-natal consultation should have become so firmly established.' Edinburgh City Archives, LHB16/2/33, 'Medical Officer of Health, Edinburgh Annual Report', 1941, 3.

51 See discussion later in this chapter on regional variation in Scottish infant mortality rates.

52 As Lara Marks noted: 'the mere presence of an infant welfare centre did not guarantee better health. In North Kensington [a relatively deprived area], for

advice on child rearing did not necessarily provide women, perhaps in poverty, more than likely living in over crowded, insanitary conditions (given Scotland's housing difficulties in both cities and rural areas) with viable alternatives to their current lifestyles. Writing during World War Two, Dugald Baird[53] stated: 'there is a large wastage of child life associated with childbirth in Scotland, intimately connected with unfavourable economic conditions, and malnutrition and fatigue in the mother.'[54]

Setting aside the question mark over their positive impact on infant health for the moment, there was a discernible growth in the number of new-borns being seen at Scottish child welfare centres. Between 1925 and 1934 the attendance figures for all new born Scottish children rose from 22% to 39%.[55] But even this improvement left more than 6 in every 10 infants being born to mothers without any obvious child care advice or treatment. These figures are also much less healthy than the 93% population coverage claimed for existing schemes by the SBH in 1927. Dugald Baird, then visiting obstetric surgeon, conducted research into 999 fatal maternity cases at Glasgow Royal Maternity and Women's Hospital (which admitted working class women) between 1925–1934. As a result of his investigation,

instance, infant mortality remained high despite an abundance of maternal and child welfare provision.' Marks, *Metropolitan Maternity*, 187.

53 Dugald Baird studied science and medicine at Glasgow University. He later worked as visiting obstetric surgeon at Glasgow Royal Maternity Hospital. He moved to Aberdeen in 1937, and served as chief obstetrician to the Aberdeen Maternity Hospital and Regius Professor of Midwifery (later Obstetrics and Gynaecology) at the University of Aberdeen between 1937–1965. He was knighted for his work in 1959. His long and detailed research work at Aberdeen led to the creation of the 'Aberdeen Maternity and Neonatal Data Bank' of maternity case records, which include social data. Baird died in 1986. Baird has been identified as one of a group of elite medical professionals which, before and after World War Two, was increasingly critical about the performance of the existing public health services. See C. Webster, 'The Origins of Social Medicine in Britain', *Bulletin of the Society for the Social History of Medicine*, (June 1986), 53.

54 D. Baird and J.F.B. Wyper, 'High Stillbirth and Neonatal Mortalities', *Lancet*, 29 November 1941, 659.

55 DHS, *Annual Report 1934* (Edinburgh: HMSO, 1935), 71–2, [Cmnd 4837].

Baird stated that an extension of ante-natal supervision – possibly with compulsory notification of pregnancy – was urgently required by the Glasgow local authority to reduce maternal mortality. More hospital accommodation, particularly for ante-natal cases was also required. He also concluded that 9% of maternal deaths examined were among women where there was a clear risk of a fatal outcome in pregnancy. He recommended the immediate creation of a free contraceptive service for women by the local authority.[56]

Baird's call for improved ante-natal supervision for Glasgow was taken up more broadly, elsewhere. The 1937 PEP *Report on the British Health Services,* noted that ante-natal supervision in Scotland compared unfavourably with the aggregate figure for England. In London, 73% of expectant women attended clinics, and 63% of women in county boroughs, meanwhile only 35% of Scots expectant mothers attended ante-natal clinics. The figure for Wales was 36%. Yet, the aggregate Scots figure represented double that of English counties which had only 17% of expectant women attending ante-natal clinics.[57] No separate Scottish burgh and county figures were supplied.

Even encouraging figures hid disquieting undercurrents. The optimistic 1927 SBH claim for wide coverage in maternity and child welfare services was tempered by the recognition that few of the existing schemes provided adequate health supervision for young children aged between 1 and 5 years. In fact, only 7.5% of all such children were visited at home in 1927 and only 3.6% made it into child welfare centres for examination. A report by the Medical Officer of Health for the County of Fife, George Pratt Yule, in 1933 reiterated this deficiency:

> We are dealing increasingly effectively with the problems of maternity and infancy and for a good many years have steadily expanded the scheme for securing the health of the school child. It is all the more difficult, therefore, to realise why the years between infancy and school age, the most profitable period for preventive public health measures, have hitherto been disregarded and neglected. We appear to begin at the wrong age-period with school medical

56 D. Baird, 'Maternal Mortality in Hospital', *Lancet*, 8 February 1936, 298.

57 PEP, *Report on the British Health Services*, 96.

> work, with the result that we are treating defects in school children instead of preventing them at an earlier age.[58]

Within Scotland, clinics and centres were increasingly considered as essential in densely populated areas, but were not practical in sparsely populated locations where advice and treatment was in the hands of general practitioners and health visitors. Home visitation, rather than the creation of welfare centres was often the form of care for nursing mothers, infants and young children in rural areas.[59] This is not to say that rural areas did not attempt to provide a range of maternity and infant welfare services. The Medical Officer of Bute County Council (part of the Argyll and Bute District) reported an impressive range of facilities offered in the county to the DHS in 1931. Services included a consultation and treatment clinic for expectant mothers, infants and pre-school children on the island of Bute, a health visiting service at its capital Rothesay, and arrangements for obstetrical emergencies and consultant services.[60] Yet even within unified district health authorities there could be variations in the type and range of service provided. As late as 1947, the County Council of Argyll relied on home visitation by district nurses because the scattered population

---

58 DHS, *Annual Report 1934*, 71–2.

59 'In the rural areas the difficulty of bringing cases together in sufficient numbers to make the holding of clinics profitable has thrown upon home visitation the whole responsibility for the routine supervision of the health of the child.' SBH, *Sixth Annual Report, 1924* (Edinburgh: HMSO, 1925), 87, [Cmd 2416].

60 'The existing services in Bute Island are a consultation and treatment clinic at the Victoria Hospital for expectant and nursing mothers, infants and pre-school children; a system for the inspection of midwives; the hospital treatment of ante-natal and obstetrical emergencies and of sick infants and pre-school children in the Victorian Hospital; the treatment of puerperal fever, ophthalmia neonatorum and measles, whooping cough, pneumonia and dysentery in the Robertson Stewart Hospital; the services of a consultant specialist for puerperal fever and puerperal pyrexia, and, in the Burgh of Rothesay only, supervision by health visitors of expectant and nursing mothers, infants and pre-school children.' NAS, HH61/616, 'Report on a Scheme of Maternity and Child Welfare Services for the County of Bute', J.R. Currie, MOH for the County of Bute, to DHS, November 1931.

made the provision of infant and maternal welfare centres non viable.[61]

There were parts of Scotland where comprehensive and co-ordinated maternity and child welfare services were introduced. Notably, in the North East region and in Dundee.[62] Meanwhile, another, internationally recognised, scheme of care and screening of infants and school children was introduced in St Andrews. The St. Andrews Maternity and Child Welfare centre was, by the late 1930s, regarded as a model of preventive care. The majority of children in St Andrews attended the Child Welfare Centre until the age of two. Their records were then passed on to the local Sir James Mackenzie Institute[63] where they were seen three times a year by appointment

---

61 'In the area administered by the Local Health Authority the population is too scattered for it to be possible to have clinics which would be accessible to more than a few women and children. The provision of a mother and child welfare service which could serve every mother and child must depend mainly on domiciliary visiting by nurses with sufficient all round qualifications and experience to enable them to give advice and assistance in various fields of midwifery, home nursing and health visiting. It is proposed that Local Authority nurses resident in each area shall visit all expectant and nursing mothers and children up to school age shall give advice and assistance in health matters [...].' Argyll and Bute District Archive, Lochgilphead, ABDA, C06/3/71/10, County Council of Argyll and Bute District, 'National Health Service (Scotland) Act, 1947: Care of Mothers and Children', undated, [1947?].

62 See section on maternal mortality later in this chapter.

63 The St Andrews Institute for Clinical Research (which became the Sir James Mackenzie Institute for Clinical Research) was a voluntary medical centre established by Sir James Mackenzie in 1919 with the emphasis on comprehensive record keeping as an aid to preventive medicine. According to a letter written by Mackenzie on 29 December 1919 'The scheme is essentially intended to make good the defects in the practice of medicine and especially as practised by the Panel doctors. I have at various times placed my ideas and my labours at the service of the government, to have them quietly ignored.' A. Mair, *Sir James Mackenzie MD 1853–1925: General Practitioner* (Edinburgh: Churchill and Livingstone, 1973), 295.

The importance of record keeping, especially among panel doctors was periodically the subject of debate in government circles. At the time of the introduction of the reforming National Insurance legislation in 1920, the Ministry of Health and the Medical Research Council, discussed the possibility of panel practitioners systematically recording insurance cases. Such record-

until they were five years of age. After the age of five, they were seen once or twice a year at the centre and also examined at three-yearly intervals by the school medical officer who submitted her/his records to the Institute. By this, a full history of each child's environment, diet, health, disabilities was available. 'The value of this preventive work alone was very great, and the data in their completeness for the figures for a community must be almost unique in this country.' [64] The comprehensive coverage of the St. Andrews' Scheme remained a novelty on the eve of World War Two.[65] However, later investigators have questioned the research value of the St Andrew's records.[66]

---

keeping was, it was felt, a possible way of furthering medical knowledge and would allow more emphasis to be given the preventive aspects of national health insurance provision. Mackenzie was intimately involved in this discussion. See, for example, Sir James Mackenzie and the staff of the St Andrews Institute for Clinical Research, 'Memorandum on some of the Medical Aspects of the National Health Insurance Acts', 16. This memorandum was attached as an appendix to the Report of the Inter-Departmental Committee on Insurance Medical Records [Rolleston Committee], (HMSO, 1920), [Cmd 836]. In 1921, the MRC awarded the St. Andrews Institute an annual grant of £1300 in recognition of its value as a research centre. In 1930, the DHS 'Morbidity Statistics Scheme' finally brought the plans to produce comprehensive panel practitioner records to fruition. See chapter six for more on the Morbidity Statistics Scheme.

64 NAS, HH61/615, DHS, cuttings file, *Scotsman*, 26 July 1938.

65 'The St. Andrew Child Welfare scheme, whereby children receive medical supervision from birth until they leave school, has been recognised by experts from all over the world as ideal, and a model for Britain.

Infants are supervised in health matters until the age of five, when they pass under the care of the school doctor. It was because of the proved value of this scheme that Dr. Elenora Simpson, of the James Mackenzie Institute, St. Andrews, was included in the sub-committee of the Scientific Advisory Committee set up by the Department of Health for Scotland, which recently reported on Scotland's high infant mortality rate.' DHS cuttings file, *Sunday Mail*, 9 January 1944.

66 'Looking back and taking out case notes at random they would seem to differ little from those one would expect in a good Maternity and Child Welfare Department of a Local Authority. In short, while he had the vision to see the place of medical records in longitudinal research, he [Mackenzie] had not yet perceived that descriptive data, so beloved of the clinician, had to be sacrificed

> The conditions antagonistic to child life are more intense both in the North of England and in Scotland, and they demand steadily increasing preventive efforts. The objective ought to be to secure in Scotland the relatively good results that are obtainable in Southern England.
> (SBH, *Fifth Annual Report*, 1923 (Edinburgh: HMSO, 1924))

> The evidence is overwhelming that the prime cause of excessive infant mortality is poverty; that is insufficiency of purchasing power of the family.
> (Scottish Secretary of State, Tom Johnston, HOC debates, 8 March 1944, vol. 397, col. 2087)

The optimistic view of some historians when dealing with inter-war levels of infant and maternal mortality has led to criticism of local studies as unrepresentative of national trends. However, national aggregates can be subject to political influences, as the 1930s controversy over recorded levels of malnutrition, which is addressed in the following chapter reveals. In addition, other health indices reveal less optimistic trends in the inter-war years. Claims to sickness and disablement benefit under National Health Insurance legislation rose steadily from the mid-1920s. Between 1930 and 1937, a series of annual reports under the pioneering DHS Morbidity Statistics Scheme (to be discussed in chapter six) revealed alarming levels of chronic incapacity amongst the insured workforce in Scotland. Worryingly, almost 72% of chronically disabled in the year 1935/6 were under the age of 55.[67] The conclusion of such findings was that industrial recession had a recognisable impact on levels of sickness and chronic incapacity. These figures do not sit well with the view that overall improved living standards were experienced during the 1930s and can in particular be traced through improving infant and maternal mortality rates.

---

for quantitative data which are the raw materials of the epidemiologist.' Mair, *Sir James Mackenzie MD 1853–1925*, 321–322.

67 DHS, *Report on Sickness Statistics for the Insured Population of Scotland for the year from 1st July 1936 to 30th June 1937*, (Edinburgh: HMSO, 1939), 58.

National IMR rates overlook underlying regional variations. Scottish figures are used in this study to illustrate the wide range of local experience, but other historians including Charles Webster[68] have convincingly used regional statistics to challenge any complacency in attitude towards this type of inter-war health index. Aggregate statistics mask many variations not only based on regional experience, but also on class inequalities.[69]

Class considerations clearly affected infant mortality levels. For example, writing in wartime, Dugald Baird noted that there were clear differences in rates of prematurity between well-to-do mothers and the less well off. Baird fixed the neonatal mortality rate in Aberdeen in 1941 at 20 per 1,000 among the babies of poor mothers and 10 per 1,000 among those of prosperous mothers.[70] An 1946 Edinburgh investigation revealed that of the 490 infant deaths in the city in 1946, 196 (40%) occurred in the first ten days of life. Deaths were chiefly caused by prematurity (102 deaths), gastro-enteritis (104) and bronchitis and pneumonia (96). In other words, prematurity, identified as a class issue by Baird in 1941, was one of the leading factors in causing infant deaths in the 1946 Edinburgh survey. The Edinburgh report went on to note that possible fatal prematurity would not emerge routinely in ante-natal examinations, hence even if an expectant mother attended a maternity and infant welfare centre such defects would not be detected. Infectious and epidemic diseases required early diagnosis to prevent infant and/or maternal mortality.

---

68 Webster, 'Healthy or Hungry Thirties?', 116.

69 In this context it is interesting to note that in a 1964 survey, 60% of Scots described themselves as working class and 33% as middle class. The figures for England were 50% and 42% respectively, and for Wales 54% and 39% respectively. Survey cited in Kellas, *The Scottish Political System*, 13.

70 'In my experience prematurity amongst the prosperous section of the community is rare except where labour is induced because of pre-eclamptic toxaemia. Amongst the poor where the diet is deficient and adequate rest often impossible, premature labour is much more frequent [...]. Surely the solution of this enormous and important problem demands the combined efforts of all those concerned – viz. – general practitioners, local authorities through their maternity and child welfare services, the paediatricians and the obstetrician.' D. Baird, *Lancet*, 1941 (1) 1 February 1941, 160.

The 1946 report concluded that the operation of a more general public medical service was required to deal with such incidences.[71]

In 1955, the Medical Research Council Social Medicine Research Unit published a paper including data from as far back as 1911, which showed that class differences in perinatal mortality had not narrowed. In 1958, Titmuss reinforced the view that social inequality remained in access to health and welfare services.[72] One of the conclusions of Department of Health and Social Security (DHSS) Research Working Group enquiry in 1980 was that issues including class inequality should inform health policy. The subsequent DHSS Report identified childhood as 'the period of life at which intervention would most hopefully break the continuing association between health and class.'[73] The Black Report considered that the abolition of child poverty should be adopted as a national goal for the 1980s. As a modest first step in achieving that goal, the Report recommended the introduction of an infant care allowance for children from birth up to the age of five and the provision of a school meals as a right.[74] Late in the 20th century therefore, class considerations were still felt to play an integral part in health inequalities.

As shown in table 3.1, the aggregate infant mortality rate for Scotland concealed a great deal of variation between local rates over the whole thirty-year period 1919–1948. These extensive figures will be dealt with in detail later. By way of example, selected burgh and country rates for the year 1926 are highlighted in table 3.2. Not unexpectedly, the Scottish burghs in the sample, with the exception of Clydebank and Edinburgh, showed IMR figures in excess of the aggregate Scottish figure of 83.1 infant deaths per 1,000 births. The IMR for England and Wales in this year was 70.2. Of the seven burghs listed, two of Scotland's most heavily industrialised and

---

71 Edinburgh City Archives, 'Medical Officer of Health, Edinburgh, Annual Report, 1946', 75.

72 Titmuss, *Essays on 'the Welfare State'*, 53–5.

73 Department of Health and Social Security, *Inequalities of Health: Report of a Research Working Group* [Chaired by Sir Douglas Black], (Harmondsworth: Penguin, 1982), 194.

74 DHSS, *Inequalities of Health*, 348–350.

Year	1	2	3	4	5	6	7	8	9	10	11	12
1919	101.6	106.9	126.0	117.0	114.0	—	—	74.0	91.0	—	—	83.5
1920	92.0	121.0	131.0	89.0	107.0	—	—	59.0	73.0	—	—	—
1921	90.3	108.0	114.0	96.0	129.0	94.0	—	68.1	70.0	—	80.4	85.4
1922	101.4	133.3	108.8	91.0	120.2	117.1	88.3	62.9	92.9	53.4	89.6	85.5
1923	78.9	103.6	97.6	82.1	89.6	66.0	56.1	76.0	71.8	41.7	71.4	74.9
1924	97.7	122.2	120.1	89.5	118.7	139.0	91.1	81.0	73.9	47.0	84.2	71.7
1925	90.6	108.6	126.4	95.8	102.0	96.1	86.1	68.3	84.6	40.1	88.3	60.5
1926	83.1	96.3	102.6	79.7	104.0	114.0	59.7	39.5	69.7	32.6	66.8	74.6
1927	88.7	105.0	137.9	71.5	107.1	90.5	83.8	24.1	60.5	38.9	79.3	73.5
1928	85.7	94.4	102.0	74.5	106.6	104.6	81.6	23.5	71.6	40.3	84.9	63.5
1929	86.8	95.4	101.8	79.5	107.0	88.8	94.8	55.8	60.8	46.4	76.1	72.3
1930	83.0	80.2	113.5	81.6	101.0	106.5	82.1	61.7	77.4	53.6	67.7	—
1931	81.8	90.4	92.4	68.7	104.4	74.6	62.0	28.6	71.8	63.1	80.3	—
1932	86.2	92.8	72.0	72.8	112.1	104.8	82.1	76.2	83.3	60.5	90.8	67.2
1933	81.1	78.8	98.1	66.3	96.7	99.2	66.3	54.5	73.6	48.3	88.2	64.4
1934	77.7	76.5	74.3	62.5	98.0	85.6	103.1	61.9	70.5	49.6	75.8	67.1
1935	76.8	90.6	68.2	69.6	98.0	88.5	76.2	52.6	71.5	52.3	65.9	71.9
1936	82.3	70.2	80.7	68.3	109.0	85.3	88.6	45.2	73.6	50.3	86.8	60.5
1937	80.3	72.4	87.0	70.0	104.3	93.2	82.0	32.9	69.2	52.7	70.9	63.5
1938	69.5	71.5	77.5	61.2	87.2	76.2	67.7	66.7	53.2	39.2	68.8	64.2
1939	68.5	59.5	74.1	59.2	80.1	91.0	76.1	20.9	62.3	51.0	73.8	52.6
1940	78.3	86.0	66.9	67.5	94.6	114.9	77.6	36.4	73.7	48.0	83.5	70.8
1941	82.7	77.1	88.8	66.5	111.2	116.2	74.6	78.9	51.6	51.2	84.2	59.1
1942	69.3	66.8	67.5	56.2	90.5	96.8	56.6	29.8	62.4	44.8	69.0	53.7
1943	65.2	67.8	69.1	53.5	81.5	80.9	61.5	54.7	58.4	48.0	67.2	56.5
1944	65.0	56.5	59.9	51.0	95.0	80.0	70.7	51.1	55.1	55.3	65.1	52.0
1945	56.2	53.7	57.2	52.0	67.9	75.1	52.4	11.1	54.0	52.1	58.2	40.4
1946	53.8	42.0	47.2	52.4	67.4	56.6	59.1	19.6	57.0	50.0	54.3	45.5
1947	55.8	63.8	69.8	48.7	77.0	62.4	47.8	43.1	48.4	36.5	50.8	48.6
1948	44.7	33.6	47.2	33.7	55.7	56.6	39.6	51.4	41.1	24.5	49.9	35.8

Table 3.1 Selected Scottish Infant Mortality Rates (per 1,000 births), 1919–1948[75]

75 Key – 1: Scotland, 2: Aberdeen, 3: Dundee, 4: Edinburgh, 5: Glasgow, 6: Paisley, 7: Clydebank, 8: Sutherland, 9: Stirlingshire, 10: Argyllshire,

urbanised cities, Dundee and Glasgow, showed figures approximately 20 infant deaths per thousand above the Scottish average. The town of Paisley (a west of Scotland textile centre) showed rates in excess of 30 infant deaths per 1,000 higher than the Scots average.

All of the eight Scottish counties in the 1926 sample recorded IMR considerably lower than the Scottish average. Of the counties, Sutherland in the Highlands recorded a level more than 44 infant deaths per 1,000 below the Scottish average. Meanwhile, the large west coast county of Argyllshire recorded a level over 50 infant deaths per 1,000 lower than the Scottish average, and a massive 81.4 deaths per 1,000 below that of Paisley. Argyllshire, with its mixture of sizeable towns, rural areas and remote islands, provided a patchwork municipal health services for mothers and babies, (i.e. infant and maternity welfare centres in Bute, coupled with health visiting for sparsely populated areas). All the selected Scottish counties had IMR below the 1926 Scottish average. Too much cannot be made of these selected figures for a single year. Yet, the considerable variation in

Scotland	83.1	England and Wales	70.2
Selected Scottish Burghs		*Selected Scottish Counties*	
Aberdeen	96.3	Aberdeenshire	74.6
Clydebank	59.7	Argyllshire	32.6
Dundee	102.6	Caithness	76.9
Edinburgh	79.7	Lanarkshire	66.8
Glasgow	104.0	Ross-shire	58.0
Greenock	90.4	Stirlingshire	69.7
Paisley	114.0	Sutherland	39.5

Table 3.2 Infant Mortality Rates (per 1,000 births) for Selected Scottish Burghs and Counties, 1926[76]

11: Lanarkshire, 12: Aberdeenshire. All figures taken from SBH/DHS Annual Reports and Register General for Scotland Annual Reports, 1919–1948 (all Edinburgh: HMSO).

76 Figures taken from 1926 annual reports from Medical Officers of Health for locations listed and Register General for Scotland Annual Report, 1926.

Scottish infant mortality experience suggested by the 1926 sample is borne out in the more detailed Scottish infant mortality figures given in table 3.1. Two of Scotland's largest cities: Aberdeen and Glasgow experienced varying fortunes in the pattern of IMR between 1919–1948. As noted in the previous chapter, Aberdeen was the centre of a drive during the 1920s towards an integrated health service for the city, and indeed the whole North East region, which culminated in the 1930s in the creation of a single greenbelt location for Aberdeen's hospitals at Foresterhill. Aberdeen city, alongside the counties of Kincardine and Aberdeenshire, was part of a co-ordinated regional health scheme, first begun in 1925, then expanded as a result of the Local Government (Scotland) Act in 1929. The scheme combined local public medical and hospital services under a single Chief Medical Officer of Health for the region.

The North East regional scheme led to the creation of a number of infant and maternal welfare centres in rural areas. This was augmented by the employment of voluntary health visitors to further monitor mothers and infants in remote rural areas.[77] In both the city and County of Aberdeen, a regular programme of lectures on ante-natal care, infant feeding and hygiene were given by medical members of the local Public Health Departments and by general practitioners at the welfare centres. Unusually, the onus in the North East was not on the need for mothers to take the initiative and attend clinics but on the service providers:

> The success of our Mother and Child Welfare Scheme depends largely on two factors, namely, the co-operation of the general practitioners in the area and assistance rendered by the district nurses and voluntary workers.[78]

As table 3.1 illustrates, in Glasgow (Scotland's largest city with a legacy of urban problems dating back over a century) the IMR was never less than 10 deaths higher than the Scottish national average between 1919 and 1948. The trend in IMR in each of the four largest Scottish cities – Glasgow, Edinburgh, Aberdeen and Dundee – was

77 See DHS, *Committee on Scottish Health Services Report*, Appendix VI, 403–4.

78 Grampian Regional Archives, GRHB E2\4\10, County of Aberdeen Medical Officer of Health, 'Annual Report 1930', 27.

gradually downward in the inter-war period, with many sudden upswings. For example, the years 1938 and 1939 were the only ones in the decade to witness a decline in IMR across all four major cities. Any attempt to connect the pursuit of a plan of infant and maternal welfare centres in the Scottish urban conurbations and a decrease in the IMR has to be treated with circumspection. Yet, local MOsH claimed much success for infant and maternal welfare schemes. When the IMR for Glasgow fell to its lowest recorded level, 89.6 in 1923, A.K. Chalmers was in no doubt as to the cause of the reduction (from a figure of 119 in 1922). Chalmers stated: 'This very striking reduction in the infant mortality rate forms a very definite testimony to the value of the work now being carried on in our city under the Infant Welfare Scheme.'[79]

Comparing Aberdeen and Glasgow directly, the fall in the IMR for Aberdeen after 1928 (from a very high rate) is remarkable, but not consistent. Meanwhile the Glasgow figures, (like those of Scotland as a whole), fell gradually. They showed real progress briefly in 1938 and 1939. This trend was abruptly halted during the war. The downward trend was only re-established in the last year of the War (when the rate dramatically fell from 95 in 1944 to 68 in 1945). The improvement in IMR in Aberdeen (alongside Dundee) was noted by J.M. Winter for the decade 1929–1938. Winter used such figures in an attempt to correlate comparative rates of IMR and MMR with contrasting conditions of urban prosperity and squalor. However, the possible impact of the (far from typical) reorganisation of the medical services in these two cities (Dundee's scheme is discussed later) was not considered by Winter.[80]

---

79 'Medical Officer of Health for Glasgow, Annual Report, 1923', 90.

80 Winter, 'Infant Mortality, Maternal Mortality, and Public Health in Britain in the 1930s', 449.

Year	Scotland	England and Wales
1919	101.6	89.0
1920	92.0	84.5
1921	90.3	83.0
1922	101.4	77.0
1923	78.9	69.2
1924	97.7	74.2
1925	90.6	74.5
1926	83.1	70.2
1927	88.7	69.7
1928	85.7	65.1
1929	86.8	74.4
1930	83.0	60.0
1931	81.8	66.4
1932	86.2	65.0
1933	81.1	63.7
1934	77.7	58.6
1935	76.8	56.9
1936	82.3	58.5
1937	80.3	57.6
1938	69.5	52.7
1939	68.5	50.8
1940	78.3	57.4
1941	82.7	59.7
1942	69.3	49.5
1943	65.2	48.9
1944	65.0	44.5
1945	56.2	47.0
1946	53.8	40.9
1947	55.8	41.8
1948	44.7	34.5

Table 3.3 Comparative British Infant Mortality Rates (per 1,000 births), 1919–1948[81]

81 Scottish figures are from Register General for Scotland Annual Reports, 1919–1948, passim. Figures for England and Wales are taken from Register General Statistical Reviews of England and Wales, 1919–1948, passim.

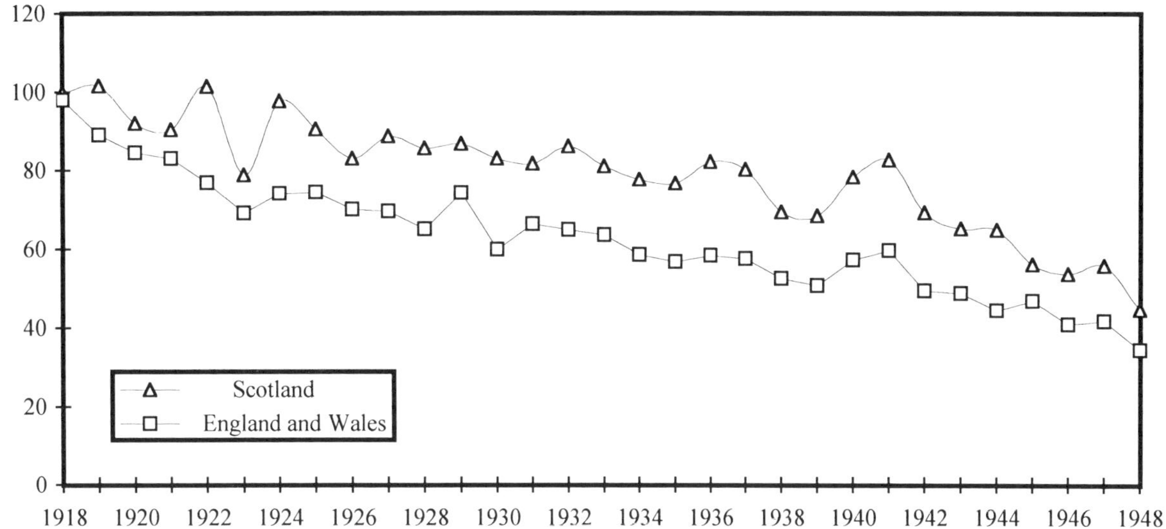

Figure 3.1 British Infant Mortality Rates (per 1,000 births), 1918–1948

Infant Mortality 1919–1948: Some International Comparisons

Scotland as a whole suffered a continuously high infant mortality rate (IMR) in comparison to many other countries in this thirty year period. The aggregate Scottish figures per 1,000 births reached a peak for this period at 101.6 in 1919, but thereafter declined slowly, with many upswings. A confirmed downward trend only gathered pace in the middle of World War Two. (See table 3.3 and figure 3.1) At the same time, the rate for England and Wales, from similar levels to Scotland in 1918 (97.9 compared to the Scottish figure of 99.8) declined more steadily and remained consistently lower than the Scottish figures.[82] This divergence is perhaps why, as Charles Webster has noted,[83] for those portraying an optimistic view of infant health trends in the inter-war years, little attention was paid to Scottish figures at the time, or indeed since. For example, J.M. Winter referred to the 'traditionally higher' Scots IMR following a similar downward trend in the 1930s to that experienced for England and Wales. Yet, the IMR for England and Wales was higher than in Scotland in the late nineteenth century (see table 3.4), and in 1918 the Scottish figure was only 0.9 higher.[84] Moreover, as Margaret Mitchell has shown, the

82 The Scottish rate seemed much more inconsistent than that for England and Wales. For example in the 1920s, the Scottish figures twice rose by over 9 infant deaths per year, this happened once in England and Wales. Meanwhile in the 1930s, the Scottish figure fell by as much as 10.8 in a single year (1938). The most significant fall recorded in England and Wales was 4.9 (also in 1938). In 1940, the Scottish rate increased by 9.8 and the rate for England and Wales rose by 6.6. See table 3 for further details.

83 'To reach the standards of healthier countries or more prosperous areas of Britain, Scotland would have needed to have reduced its post-neonatal mortality by 75% [...]. The most optimistic construction of states of health during the interwar period derives from the general Infant Mortality Rate for England and Wales. A radically different perspective results from finer analysis of the mortality data [...].' Webster, 'Healthy or Hungry Thirties?', 124–5.

84 Winter, 'Infant Mortality, Maternal Mortality, and Public Health in Britain in the 1930s', 440.

trend of falling IMR for England and Wales slowed dramatically in the 1930s compared to the previous and succeeding decades.[85]

The reasons for the high inter-war Scottish IMR lay in a combination of economic and social factors. Long term environmental problems such as the overcrowded, unhealthy conditions of urban Scotland remained a difficult obstacle to overcome. These long-term factors can be inferred from the chief causes of infant deaths given in the DHS Annual Report for 1932, which noted prematurity, births defects and respiratory disease (all more likely to be associated with poor environment) as the main causes of infant mortality:

> In general, the most important causes of death in Scotland under one year of age are congenital causes (congenital debility, premature births, malformations, etc) and all forms of bronchitis and pneumonia, which together are responsible for fully 60% of infant deaths, and, to a lesser extent, digestive diseases (particularly diarrhoea), measles and whooping-cough.[86]

The aggregate trends outlined in figure 3.1 demonstrate that there was no clear down-turn in the Scottish level of IMR until 1938, when it fell by 10 infant deaths (from 80.3 to 69.5) in the space of twelve months. Wartime Scottish IMR figures fluctuated. There was a sharp increase in the early war years of 1940 and 1941, yet after this it never reached above 70, and indeed, fell again by 9 infant deaths between 1944 and 1945 (from 65.0 to 56.2). These figures appear to be at odds with Winter's assessment for the whole of Britain that '[...] the data for 1930, 1932–35, and 1937–9 demonstrate conclusively that infant mortality had diminished during both the upswings and downswings of the trade cycle.'[87]

---

85 Mitchell demonstrated a decennial decline in IMR for England and Wales of 44 for 1900–1910, 26 for 1910–20, 20 for 1920–30, 4 for 1930–40, and 26 for the decade 1940–50. 'The exceptionally poor rate of decline for the decade 1930–40 suggests that a connection between infant mortality and economic crisis is, at the very least, a possibility.' M. Mitchell, 'The Effects of Unemployment on the Social Condition of Women and Children in the 1930s', *History Workshop Journal*, 19 (Spring 1985), 104.

86 DHS, *Annual Report, 1932*, 57.

87 Winter, 'Infant Mortality, Maternal Mortality, and Public Health in Britain in the 1930s', 443.

The Scottish IMR did not only lag behind England and Wales in terms of improvement. Table 3.4 provides a range of international comparisons. These portray a picture of high IMR across six other nations in three continents in the late 19th century (often at a higher level than both Scotland and England and Wales) followed by sharp falls as each country introduced more effective social policies and infant and maternal welfare measures.

It would seem that the introduction of state and extended local authority infant and maternal welfare provision in Scotland after 1915 had far less of an impact in reducing IMR levels. Perhaps the fact that advice and diagnosis, rather than medical treatment, was the main focus of the centres, hampered progress. Personal health measures which placed the onus on the individual to turn up, take advice and be in a position to act upon it, could do little to tackle deep seated problems of poverty, inadequate nutrition and poor housing. For example, in 1931, 35.0% of Scots still lived two to a room. The figures for Glasgow were particularly depressing. In 1921, 63.3% of Glaswegians lived in one or two-roomed houses, by 1935 the figure had reduced only slightly, to 55%. The British average in 1931 stood at 10%.[88] These figures not only show how difficult it was to attempt to counteract the ill-effects of poor social conditions through advice and monitoring the health and welfare of vulnerable sections of the population, it also underlines that national averages do not provide a complete picture of regional diversity.

88 Abrams, *The Condition of the British People 1911–1945*, 45.

	NewZl	Neth	Austral	Norway	Sweden	USA	Eng/Wal	Scot
1881–85	–	181.0	125.0	99.0	116.0	–	139.0	118.0
1886–90	–	175.0	119.0	96.0	105.0	–	145.0	121.0
1891–95	–	165.0	109.0	98.0	103.0	–	151.0	126.0
96–1900	80.0	151.0	112.0	96.0	101.0	–	156.0	130.0
1901–05	75.0	136.0	97.0	81.0	91.0	–	138.0	120.0
1906–10	70.0	114.0	78.0	–	–	–	117.0	112.0
1911–15	54.0	95.0	70.0	–	–	–	110.0	113.0
1916–20	49.0	–	65.0	–	–	93.0	90.0	99.0
1921–25	43.0	64.0	58.0	52.0	60.0	74.0	76.0	92.0
1926–30	37.0	56.0	52.0	49.0	58.0	66.0	68.0	85.0
1931–35	32.0	45.0	41.0	45.0	50.0	59.0	62.0	81.0
1936–40	32.0	37.0	39.0	39.0	42.0	51.0	55.0	76.0

Table 3.4 Selected International Infant Mortality Rates, 1881–1940[89]

Scottish regional differences in the provision of maternity and child welfare services could be accounted for by the differing geographic circumstances of the areas. As previously noted, Argyllshire was a county with better-than-Scots average infant and mortality rates in this period, and yet clinics and welfare centres was not considered practical in parts of the county. Hence much of the welfare work for mothers and children in Argyllshire fell upon the shoulders of health visitors. This of course, need not have been a bad thing, since mere attendance by mothers and babies at a clinic could be no guarantee of improving health. For example, areas of massive poverty and chronic house over-crowding, such as Glasgow, which had an aggressive policy of infant and maternal welfare centre construction, still had some of the worst infant and maternal mortality rates in Scotland and indeed, in the whole of Britain. There were other limiting factors on the overall provision and efficacy of infant and maternal welfare schemes, notably lack of income from the rates to fund comprehensive mother and baby services. In 1936, the DHS Committee on Scottish

89 DHS, *Infant Mortality in Scotland – Report of a Sub-Committee of the Scientific Advisory Committee* (Edinburgh: HMSO, 1943).

Health Services recommended an additional Exchequer contribution of 50% of expenditure for local authorities to provide and build up their local health services, in particular for child welfare.[90] This call for additional Exchequer funds was not heeded. The result was that areas of most need, such as those suffering from high unemployment or those with a small population (which accounted for many Scottish regions), were least able to provide effective health services for their population.

'Blaming' Mothers

The main and lasting aim of infant and maternal welfare centres and health visitors in this field of care was preventive: to educate women in better habits to look after themselves and their babies.[91] 'The primary function of the Centre should be preventive.'[92] Some historians have suggested that this reveals more about the State's desire to control the lives of mothers, rather than with improving infant and maternal mortality rates.[93] The view that high infant mortality was due to maternal inadequacies was as old as the official

90 DHS, *Committee on Scottish Health Services Report*, 289–290.

91 According to Dwork: '[...] the early 20th century insistence upon the "personal behaviour" of mothers as the "predominant determinant" of the health of infants and children has led scholars such as Anna Davin, Carol Dyhouse and Jane Lewis to complain that "medical science and services" were working to control the conduct of women.' Dwork, *War is Good for Babies and other Young Children*, 226.

92 PRO, MH 55/218, SBH, Circular 'Schemes of Maternity Service and Child Welfare, 6 June 1924, 4.

93 'Yet doubt arises over this social control theory over promotion of maternalism [...]. Reading [authors Davin, Dyhouse and Lewis] one begins to doubt the sincerity of official concern with the problem of infant mortality: everyone appears to have been more concerned with controlling women than saving babies[...].' Dwork , *War is Good for Babies and other Young Children*, 228.

concern for infant welfare.[94] Mothers considered culpable were generally from the working class.

Government enquiries 'blamed' parents for neglect or lack of knowledge. This issue was addressed by house visiting (often through voluntary agencies) and through the dissemination of information on better feeding. Poor nutrition, lack of knowledge, cruelty and child neglect by working mothers, were all commonly identified as crucial factors in the high rates of infant mortality. Criticism of unfit mothers came during World War One in relation to the day nurseries scheme in vital war industries. At a conference on infant welfare in Glasgow in March 1917, several speakers criticised the opportunities for neglect which these nurseries provided.[95]

As the IMR remained high into the 1930s and the Scottish Maternal Mortality Rate (MMR) fluctuated at around 6 for the period 1918–1936, criticism of mothers continued. The question now was why, with the expansion in maternity services since World War One, did the Maternal Mortality Rate not show any improvement by the mid-1930s? The Scottish MMR was 6.2 in 1919 and in 1934. In fact, as table 3.5 shows, the Scots MMR fell below 6 per 1,000 on only four occasions between 1918–1936 (1924, 1931, 1933 and 1936). The depressingly high level of maternal mortality was more than matched by bleak morbidity patterns. For example, in 1928 one out of every 150 Scottish mothers died in childbirth. Just as disturbing was the statement by John Parlane Kinloch that for every Scottish maternal death in 1928, twenty other mothers were faced chronic permanent disease or with definite disability, others were left with 'a degree of dis-health that yet made motherhood laborious instead of being a joyous thing'.[96] In a survey report of welfare services of Fife in 1932,

94 *Inter-Departmental Committee on Physical Deterioration*, (1904), 243, Committee Question, with response by A.K. Chalmers, MOH, Glasgow. 'Do you think that the downright neglect of mothers is at the bottom of infant mortality? – We have had evidence that this is so in many cases? – *I am afraid that that is only too true of large sections – that they are negligent in their maternal relations in this matter as in any other.*'

95 *GMJ*, 1917 (1), 231.

96 Lothian Health Board Archives, Edinburgh, LHB24/8/17, *Transactions of Scottish Association of Insurance Committees, 1929,* address by CMO, DHS,

DHS Medical Officer for Maternity and Child Welfare, Charlotte Anne Douglas, clearly identified lack of knowledge on proper nutrition among working class mothers about feeding toddlers as a factor in the poor health of children. Looking at the 'poorer working and mining classes', Douglas noted:

> Unless given free, milk seldom figures in the diet of such households, the usual plaint [sic] being that it is too expensive, yet in every house that I visited on one day there was a toddling child consuming sweets, the cost of which would have paid for sufficient milk for his needs. One is forced to the conclusion that women of this class have little knowledge of food values or marketing and no ideas of 'cooking'. In some instances, however, their difficulties are so overwhelming that they become too apathetic to try to do much.[97]

In the mid 1930s the behaviour of incompetent mothers and their families was again stressed as a possible explanation for the continued high figures for maternal mortality. The findings of the DHS *Report on Maternal Morbidity and Mortality in Scotland*, 1935, determined that 16% (394) of the total registered ante-natal deaths in the period 1929–1933 (2,465) 'were directly attributable to some fault of the patient'.[98] However, this figure is by no means as clear cut as it first appears, as the report itself acknowledged.

For example, the 1935 DHS Report identified a variety of reasons for non-attendance by expectant mothers at clinics. Some women did not consult a doctor despite suffering from illnesses which although not inconvenient in their early stages could and did end fatally in pregnancy, such as kidney and heart disease. Other patients refused to follow advice or ignored it while symptoms were not severe, but in others ethical or religious considerations (such as where therapeutical abortion was recommended) prevailed. In a minority of

---

John Parlane Kinloch on 'The Problem of Maternal Mortality' to 17th annual meeting, 28 September 1929.

97 NAS, HH61/615, 'Report on Fife Maternity and Child Welfare' from DHS Medical Officer for Maternity and Child Welfare to Secretary, DHS, 28 June 1932.

98 DHS, *Report on Maternal Morbidity and Mortality in Scotland* (Edinburgh: HMSO, 1935), 15.

Year	Scotland	England and Wales
1919	6.2	4.4
1920	6.2	4.3
1921	6.4	3.9
1922	6.6	3.8
1923	6.4	3.8
1924	5.8	3.9
1925	6.2	4.1
1926	6.4	4.1
1927	6.4	4.1
1928	7.0	4.4
1929	6.9	4.3
1930	6.9	4.4
1931	5.9	4.1
1932	6.2	4.2
1933	5.9	4.5
1934	6.2	4.6
1935	6.3	4.1
1936	5.6	3.8
1937	4.8	3.3
1938	4.9	3.1
1939	4.4	2.9
1940	4.2	2.7
1941	4.7	2.8
1942	4.1	2.5
1943	3.7	2.3
1944	3.0	1.9
1945	2.5	1.8
1946	2.2	1.4
1947	2.0	1.2
1948	1.1	1.0

Table 3.5 Comparative British Maternal Mortality Rates, 1919–1948[99]

99 All figures taken from SBH/DHS Annual Reports and Register General for Scotland Annual Reports, 1919–1948 (all Edinburgh: HMSO).

cases, ill treatment of patients by ignorance or neglect on the part family members was apparent. In other instances there was refusal to enter hospital. The Report felt this was dictated not so much by fear as by domestic considerations – inability to leave home for the fairly lengthy period of hospital treatment which some such cases often required.[100] However, these mitigating factors noted in the 1935 DHS Report have been over-looked by at least one historian, when considering the causes of maternal mortality in the 1930s.[101]

The 1935 Report's conclusion, while stating that the full co-operation of women was required to improve the mortality rate amongst mothers, placed more emphasis on the inadequacy of the maternity services in Scotland. Too few beds were available for hospital treatment. There was also a poor standard of midwifery care, despite the passage of legislation including the Midwives and Maternity Homes (Scotland) Act of 1927, which strengthened official control over the training and certification of midwives and introduced inspection and licensing of maternity homes.

Inappropriate medical intervention too, was identified as a vital contributory factor in the high Scottish maternal mortality rate, through the combined risks of infection, incompetence or unnecessary intervention. In 1928, the results of a ten years' investigation of all maternal deaths in Aberdeen were published by the SBH in *Maternal Mortality: Report on Maternal Mortality in Aberdeen, 1918–27, with Special Reference to Puerperal Sepsis*. The 1928 Report concluded that the maternal death-rate per 1,000 maternity cases was 2.8 in the practice of midwives, 6.9 in the practice of doctors, and 14.9 in in-patient institutional practice.[102] The later 1935 DHS Report into maternal morbidity and mortality reinforced these findings. 'There is

100 DHS, *Report on Maternal Morbidity and Mortality in Scotland*, 19.

101 'The most likely explanation of the persistence of high maternal mortality rates in Britain in the period is probably that both medical and para-medical care *and* the attitudes of pregnant women to it left much to be desired prior to the mid-1930s.' Winter, 'Infant Mortality, Maternal Mortality, and Public Health in Britain in the 1930s', 456.

102 SBH, *Maternal Mortality: Report on Maternal Mortality in Aberdeen, 1918–1927, with Special Reference to Puerperal Sepsis* (Edinburgh: HMSO, 1928), passim.

no doubt that one of the most disquieting features of present-day obstetrical practice is hurried and unnecessarily meddlesome midwifery.'[103] According to the Report, 12% (296) of the 2,465 maternal deaths investigated were 'directly attributable' to some fault of the doctor, midwife or institution (hospital, maternity home, or ante-natal clinic).[104] The Report proposed a complete maternity service, to include fully trained midwives in attendance before and during birth, with doctors available to deal with any and every obstetrical complication that arose.

The social class of the mother proved to be a factor in maternal mortality rates. Deaths from purely obstetrical conditions could not be linked to 'room overcrowding' (the only measure of social conditions available for both births and deaths in the 1935 DHS *Maternal Morbidity and Mortality Report*). This is not surprising since, unusually, in maternal mortality figures, higher income equated with higher death rates. Women from better-off social backgrounds were generally older at marriage, they were more likely to be experiencing a dangerous first-birth, and most crucially, they were more likely to consult medical advice and thereby run the risk of contracting infection from their medical attendants. However, in cases of maternal deaths from conditions exacerbated by pregnancy, for example, tuberculosis, respiratory, heart, and chronic kidney diseases: 'the impression was gained that at the lower end of the social scale there was an over-average proportion of deaths [...].'[105] This reinforces the view that, as in the case of high infant mortality, poverty and its consequences were important in high Scottish levels of maternal mortality.

Despite the broader conclusions of the 1935 DHS Report, women were often still 'blamed' for high infant and maternal mortality rates. The reason is not hard to find, unlike other average mortality statistics around this time, maternal mortality rates (as table 3.5 shows) were not on the decline. The 1935 Report commented: 'the proportion of maternal deaths in Scotland, in striking contrast with the general and

103 DHS, *Report on Maternal Morbidity and Mortality in Scotland*, 27.
104 Ibid.,15.
105 Ibid., 8.

many specific death rates in the population as a whole, has shown no recorded evidence of improvement over a long period of years.'[106]

Although the issue of individual 'mother blame' was frequently identified as a contributory factor in high maternal mortality rates, the three leading causes of maternal deaths from the mid 19th century to the mid 1930s have been identified as puerperal sepsis, toxaemia and haemorrhage. According to Irvine Loudon, these accounted for around 40%, just over 20%, and a little under 20% of the total death rate respectively.[107]

Reduction in maternal mortality was eventually brought about by three key medical developments, two of these were wartime advances: the increased availability of blood transfusions introduced due to wartime circumstances, and the widespread use of penicillin in the 1940s. The third was the general introduction of sulphonamides in 1937.[108] Andrew Davidson, (Chief Medical Officer at the DHS 1942–1948), attributed the fall in the Scottish MMR in 1937 and 1938 to the reduction in mortality from puerperal sepsis, which in turn, he linked to the widespread employment of the sulphonamide group of drugs.[109] Another factor in the longer-term decline in maternal mortality was the improved diet of pregnant women during World War Two. This was due to the interventionist approach adopted by the Ministry of Food towards vulnerable groups, including babies, children, pregnant women and nursing mothers.

---

106 Ibid., 30.

107 I. Loudon, 'Maternal Mortality: 1880–1950. Some regional and International Comparisons', *Social History of Medicine*, 1/2 (1988), 193.

108 Loudon had commented: 'it is probable that the sulphonamides were the most important factor in the decline in maternal mortality, although other factors played their part.' According to Loudon, over 80% of the total decline in maternal mortality between 1934–1940 was due to a reduction in deaths from puerperal fever (which could be successfuly treated by use of sulphonamides). Loudon 'Maternal Mortality: 1880–1950', 202.

109 Sir A.S. MacNalty, ed., *The Civilian Health and Medical Services vol. II* [History of World War Two], (HMSO, 1955), 236.

As noted in the earlier examination of Scottish infant mortality trends, aggregate statistics mask regional variation. They can also hide any special circumstances which might affect them. For example, the regional figures for the North East of Scotland may well have been influenced by the existence of an integrated health service in the area. Table 3.6 shows Aberdeen to have enjoyed considerably lower maternal mortality rates (deaths of mothers, per 1,000 births) than Scotland as a whole. The comprehensive north-east public health scheme produced some success in the city of Aberdeen. When contrasted with national Scottish figures, it seems to underline the positive effects of co-ordinated municipal welfare provisions on the mortality rates for mothers. However, bearing in mind the earlier caution expressed in examining national aggregates, table 3.6 includes a broad a range of Scottish figures. These include maternal mortality rates from Scotland's three other main cities of Dundee, Edinburgh and Glasgow and for the town of Motherwell in Lanarkshire (which after 1921 had the services of the 'model' Carnegie Trust maternity and child welfare centre).

The figures for Aberdeen show a remarkable improvement. Aberdeen's MMR regularly exceeding some or all of the maternal mortality rates both for Scotland as a whole and of Dundee, Edinburgh, Glasgow and Motherwell for the thirteen years between 1918 and 1930. Yet, in ten of the next sixteen years (between 1931 and 1946), the Aberdeen MMR was lower than all of the other MMR figures. In the years 1934, 1935, 1940, 1945 and 1946, the Aberdeen MMR was at least one death per thousand lower than the comparative figures for the five other series. Most notably, the Aberdeen MMR in 1946 was 0.5 per thousand live births, only Edinburgh at 1.6 and Motherwell at 1.9 came close.

As with Aberdeen, Dundee too, was pioneering in its co-ordination of health services. An investigation by DHS MO Charlotte Anne Douglas in 1931 found much to praise in Dundee's infant and

Year	Scotland	Aberdeen	Dundee	Edinburgh	Glasgow	Motherwell
1919	6.2	6.8	5.5	8.2	6.9	3.3
1920	6.2	6.2	7.1	5.9	7.1	6.1
1921	6.4	5.4	5.6	5.9	6.4	12.0
1922	6.6	6.8	8.5	3.8	7.6	4.5
1923	6.4	5.8	4.8	5.9	7.1	8.0
1924	5.8	4.7	3.9	6.2	5.8	5.0
1925	6.2	5.6	4.6	4.7	7.6	10.0
1926	6.4	5.9	8.9	4.9	6.7	9.0
1927	6.4	6.0	8.0	6.6	7.2	4.7
1928	7.0	6.6	6.9	6.6	8.8	8.1
1929	6.9	6.4	6.9	6.4	8.3	5.6
1930	6.9	4.5	4.3	7.0	8.6	4.8
1931	5.9	3.1	5.2	5.6	6.4	6.4
1932	6.3	7.5	4.6	5.3	7.9	8.8
1933	5.9	5.3	7.7	4.8	5.9	7.5
1934	6.2	3.3	5.4	5.3	6.0	7.4
1935	6.3	3.8	5.6	5.3	7.0	6.9
1936	5.6	3.9	6.9	5.5	5.9	3.1
1937	4.8	4.0	5.1	4.7	5.5	5.2
1938	4.9	4.7	5.8	5.4	5.7	2.3
1939	4.4	1.3	4.4	5.0	4.4	1.5
1940	4.2	2.1	3.3	3.3	4.9	4.5
1941	4.7	2.3	4.4	2.9	5.7	4.2
1942	4.1	4.3	3.4	2.4	5.1	3.0
1943	3.7	2.4	3.4	1.9	5.2	2.1
1944	3.0	1.6	3.3	2.0	4.0	2.7
1945	2.5	1.4	3.4	2.4	3.5	2.4
1946	2.2	0.5	2.0	1.6	2.8	1.9
1947	2.0	1.2	0.9	1.0	2.3	1.8
1948	1.5	1.1	1.3	1.6	1.6	0.7

Table 3.6 Selected Scottish Maternal Mortality Rates, 1919–1948[110]

110 Figures taken from SBH/DHS Annual Reports and Register General for Scotland Annual Reports, 1919–1948 (all Edinburgh: HMSO).

maternal welfare provision. Douglas was impressed by the city's maternity hospital and the health visiting arrangements for expectant and nursing mothers and for children under five. She also commended Dundee's co-ordinated health visiting and school nursery service.[111] The following year, two DHS officials made a special visit to examine the services in Dundee with a view to using the city's arrangements as a possible role model in guidance to local authorities about these services. In 1932, the health service staffs of Dundee's Health Department, Education Authority and Parish Council were combined. This measure also included the amalgamation of the health visiting services. The intention of this measure was to provide a unitary service and a single point of home contact for families in the city. The DHS investigation into Dundee's arrangements noted: 'carrying the responsibility as health visitor for maternity, child welfare, school health, infectious diseases, tuberculosis and venereal disease, the nurses become the "guardians" of the family in the eyes of the Public Health Department.'[112]

The 1932 DHS enquiry found that Dundee's combined public health visiting service worked well, and, crucially, that there seemed to be good understanding between the health visitors and the voluntary district nurses of the city. Dundee's maternity and child welfare service benefited from continuity of direction. In 1917, Dr Scott Dickson was appointed Assistant Medical Officer in the city in Dundee, with a special responsibility for the child welfare service. She continued in this role until her retirement in 1944. In that time, the infant mortality rate fell from 146 per 1,000 live births in 1917 to 70 in 1944.[113]

As with the figures for infant deaths, the Scottish Maternal Mortality Rate outstripped that for England and Wales. It was higher in 1918, and remained higher throughout the years 1919–1948. The

111 NAS, HH61/625, C.A. Douglas, Medical Officer, DHS to Chief Medical Officer, DHS, December 1931.

112 NAS, HH61/625, DHS, internal memorandum, 'Dundee Health Services', 10 February 1932.

113 NAS, HH61/625, Report by Charlotte Anne Douglas, Medical Officer, DHS to Chief Medical Officer, DHS, 6 November 1944.

gap did not narrow to the relatively small difference of below one maternal death until 1945 (see table 3.6). The disparity between the two sets of figures is complicated by differing methods of calculation. As Irvine Loudon has pointed out, Scotland, like the United States and Denmark, included 'associated deaths' e.g. those as a result of a combination of pregnancy and a pre-existing disease such as rheumatic heart disease, in their Maternal Mortality Rates. On the other hand, countries which excluded indirect deaths, including England and Wales and Norway, '[...] showed their MMR in the most favourable light'.[114] Changes in the methods of calculation could also have an impact on the relative rates between cities.[115] As table 3.6 shows, Aberdeen's MMR figures fell markedly in the thirties. This may have been partly attributable to the method of recording of maternal deaths in the city specifically within the Registrar-General's classification of deaths associated with childbirth from 1930.[116] For

114 Loudon 'Maternal Mortality: 1880–1950', 226.

115 There were two significant differences between the way Scottish MMR were calculated compared to the rates for England and Wales, which may have adversely affected the Scottish rates. The first was in the broader classification of 'maternal deaths' in Scotland: 'The Registrar General for Scotland in his Report for 1931, from which the MMR are taken, refers to the differences in methods of classification of causes of death in Scotland and in England and Wales, and points to the need for reserve in formulating deductions from international comparisons. He states, however, that in practically every single group of puerperal causes the Scottish rate is in excess of the corresponding rate for England and Wales, and that it is highly improbable that the observed differences in maternal mortality can wholly be explained on the basis of different methods of classification.' DHS, *Annual Report 1932*, 56–7. Secondly, in Scotland up to 1939, stillbirths were not mandatorily registered, and maternal mortality rates were based on live births only, while (according to the RGS), English statistics were calculated on total births from June 1930. After 1939, with the passage of the Registration of Stillbirths (Scotland) Act, the figures for MMR for both countries were more directly comparable. See Edinburgh City Archives, 'Medical Officer of Health for Edinburgh Annual Report, 1939', 73.

116 The Aberdeen rate until 1929 included all maternal deaths within four weeks of childbirth. See Grampian Health Board Archives, CRWB E2/4/20, County of Aberdeen, Medical Officer of Health, 'Report on the Health and Sanitary Conditions of the County of Aberdeen during the Second World War 1940–1945.'

example, the recorded MMR for Aberdeen in 1930 was 4.5. For the previous three years the recorded rate had been in turn, 6.0, 6.6, and 6.4. The Aberdeen MMR took another dip in 1939, coinciding with the recording of stillbirths in Scotland for the first time as the Registration of Stillbirths (Scotland) Act, 1938 was enforced from 1 January 1939. It fell dramatically from 4.7 in 1938 to 1.3 in 1939 and 2.1 1940. Thereafter until 1948, the Aberdeen figure dropped considerably below that of Scotland as a whole, (with the exception of a high rate in 1942), and continued to decline. Meanwhile, Dundee, a similar industrial city with a slightly higher MMR at the start of the 1940s, remained remarkably constant until 1946, when a noticeable downward shift was noted (see table 3.6). Of course, other factors could have contributed the declining MMR in Aberdeen, including the positive effects of the co-ordinated health service in the north-east referred to previously. In addition, an extended maternity service was in operation in Aberdeen after 1937, with the swift implementation of the Maternity Services (Scotland) Act Scottish of that year. This measure was not at that time introduced to Dundee.[117]

Contrary to Winter's view that the MMR throughout Britain started to decline in 1935,[118] Scotland's MMR of 6.2 in that year was the highest recorded rate since 1930 when it had been 6.9. There was no decisive reduction in the aggregate MMR in Scotland until 1937, when it fell below five for the first time (see table 3.5 and figure 3.3). Loudon has stressed that the down-turn in the figure of maternal deaths corresponded with a decline in mortality levels from puerperal sepsis after 1937, and the Scottish figures bear this out.[119] The increased pace of decline for the Scottish MMR after 1937 coincided with a combination of three developments: improved medical treatment, the introduction of universal nutritional supplements during wartime, and the passage of legislation designed to facilitate an integrated maternity service for Scotland.

117 For more on the Maternity Services (Scotland) Act, 1937 see discussion below.

118 'Starting in 1935, though, the maternal mortality rate throughout Britain declined [...].' Winter 'Infant Mortality, Maternal Mortality and Public Health in Britain in the 1930s', 454.

119 Loudon, 'Maternal Mortality: 1880–1950', 195.

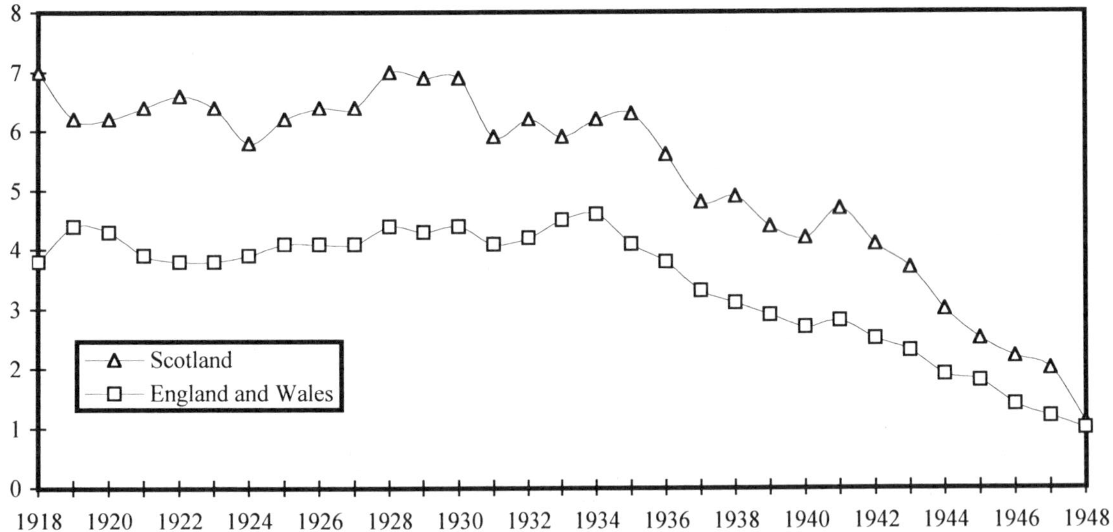

Figure 3.2 British Maternal Mortality Rates (per 1,000 births), 1918–1948

The work of Winter has suggested that the 1930s were 'a period of major improvement of the health of mothers and infants in Britain'[120] owing to state and local authority provision, medical intervention and the impact of longer-term improvements in nutrition. However, much of Winter's argument is based on examining aggregate figures for England and Wales. Winter himself does allow for 'stubborn survival of pockets of deprivation.' Yet, although he deals with Scotland from time to time, his analysis of Scottish trends often appears to be at odds with the overall and local Scottish IMR and MMR figures for the 1930s. Admittedly, part of the difficulty when dealing with local figures, in particular those for causes of MMR, is their lack of consistency. As Loudon has noted, overall rates mask great variations within cause of death, meanwhile areas with high MMR shifted over time.[121] However, this should not mean that Scottish MMR trends are left out as not in keeping with discernible trends for the rest of Britain. At the very least, the Scottish aggregate and local figures in MMR (and IMR) between 1919–1948 suggest that some revision of the 'optimistic' viewpoint is required.

Extension of State Services

> The high maternal mortality rate of Scotland justifies concern. The problem of maternal welfare calls for the provision of a comprehensive maternity service. (DHS, *Report of a Committee on the Scottish Health Services* (Edinburgh: HMSO, 1936), 177–178)

In the 1930s, as previously, the question of infant and maternal welfare was in the vanguard of the debate on the role of the state in the personal medical services. Attempts to extend such care coincided with a growing debate about a state-funded medical service in the

120 Winter, 'Infant Mortality, Maternal Mortality, and Public Health in Britain in the 1930s', 462.

121 Loudon, *Death in Childbirth: An International Study of Maternal Care and Maternal Mortality 1800–1950* (Oxford: Clarendon Press, 1992), 251–252.

1930s. For example, there were calls for an extension of state services in some Government reports, meanwhile BMA reports attempted to head off such a possibility. In Scotland, the theme of the 1936 Cathcart Report was the need for a unified national health policy. The new policy would, it was expected, cover an expanded range of statutory services incorporating general practitioners in the delivery of the enhanced public health services.[122]

However, according to figures for expenditure in Local Taxation Returns (Scotland) for 1932/33, infant and maternal welfare was well down the list of priorities for municipal health services expenditure. As table 3.7 shows, in the tax year 1932/3, out of a total sum of £3,771,418 spent on medical and allied services within overall local authority health services expenditure, just over 8% went on infant and maternal welfare.

	Expenditure	%
Infant and Maternal Welfare	£304,897	8.1
Lunacy and Mental Deficiency	£1,238,195	32.8
Local Authority TB Services	£682,674	18.1
Hospital Services (excluding TB and VD hospitals)	£657,937	17.4
Sick Poor (domiciliary and institutional care)	£509,000	13.5
School Medical Service	£289,387	7.7
Venereal Diseases	£89,328	2.4
Total	£3,771,418	100

Table 3.7 Local Authority Health Services Expenditure, 1932/3[123]

122 'We think it important to stress the fact that the separate services do not constitute a policy but rather a series of policies. They are sectional, addressed to particular conditions or particular classes, and although each of them has undergone change since it was established, and the whole conception of public health has been greatly expanded, there is no co-ordinated national health policy by which effort may be directed [...].' DHS, *Committee on Scottish Health Services Report*, 85.

123 Ibid., Appendix III, 396.

The DHS Health Services Committee which met between 1933–1936, recognised that the problems of maternal welfare called for a radical statutory solution. The creation of a comprehensive maternity service, aimed at preserving the lives of mothers in childbirth, preventing invalidism among mothers and reducing the wastage of infant life was proposed.[124] In addition, for children aged between one and five, the Committee recommended a system of periodic examination by general practitioners and an extension of nursery schools.[125]

The only part of the sweeping changes proposed in the DHS Health Services Committee Report (Cathcart Report) to be introduced pre-1948 was the plan for a comprehensive maternity service in the form of the Maternity Services (Scotland) Act of 1937. The aim was to have midwife, general practitioner, anaesthetist (where recommended by the medical practitioner), and consultant obstetrician to act together to provide a comprehensive and co-ordinated health care package of expectant mothers. A state-funded medical service was created for Scottish maternity care. The 1937 legislation permitted local authorities to provide every woman with a medical examination, treatment in pregnancy, medical supervision in childbirth, and a further medical examination at least once four weeks after the birth. Another aspect of the act was to disbar untrained women acting as maternity nurses for gain. By 1945, 42 local health authorities had enforced this aspect of the legislation, aimed at outlawing the activities of untrained 'handywomen' in the delivery of babies.

The shortcomings of the Scottish maternity services were given much emphasis in the Cathcart Report. However the passage of the 1937 Maternity Services (Scotland) Act can be seen as a response to the cumulative pressure created by the stubbornly high inter-war MMR, combined with findings of the 1928 SBH *Maternal Mortality Report*, and the 1935 DHS Report on *Maternal Morbidity and Mortality*. The 1937 legislation also followed Cabinet discussion on the differences between maternal care in Scotland and England.

124 Ibid., 177–178.
125 Ibid., 182.

In a Cabinet memorandum in May 1936 (two months before the Cathcart Report was published), Secretary of State, Sir Godfrey Collins, stated that the problem of maternal mortality in Scotland was in may ways different from that in England. The maternal mortality rate was higher in Scotland. Meanwhile, midwives attended a much smaller proportion of cases of childbirth than in England – 25%, as against 60% – and doctors attended a correspondingly higher proportion. Collins stressed the practical impossibility of introducing ante-natal and post-natal clinics, suited to an industrial or urban area, to districts such as the Highlands and Islands. Collins told his Cabinet colleagues that it was also essential for Scotland to frame proposals sufficiently broad and elastic to ensure that local authorities were enabled to develop services tailored to the needs of their areas.[126]

The importance of framing proposals that could be made to work in a variety of local circumstances was clearly important in a country where existing provision of infant and maternal welfare services could differ widely according to locality. For example, even the 'model' county of Aberdeen in 1931 (which combined with the city of Aberdeen and the county of Kincardineshire in the north-east regional public health services scheme) provided a limited service. DHS Medical Officer for Maternity and Child Welfare, Charlotte Anne Douglas, noted that with the exception of the town of Peterhead, the county scheme of child welfare rested on the shoulders of district nurses. 'Consequently, little or nothing is done in unnursed areas.' Douglas's report on Aberdeenshire was one of a series of regular reports on maternity and child welfare services delivered to the DHS Chief Medical Officer John Parlane Kinloch, and his successor James Brownlie in the early 1930s. The preventive side of statutory health services particularly motivated Parlane Kinloch.[127] He demonstrated an ongoing interest in the activities of those involved in giving advice to mothers and pregnant women all around Scotland.

---

126 PRO, CAB 24/262, CP (36) 128, Cabinet memorandum by Scottish Secretary of State, Sir Godfrey Collins, on the Extension of Maternal Health Services in Scotland, 7 May 1936.

127 For example, see Parlane Kinloch's comments at the opening of a child welfare and maternity clinic in Banff in February 1931 at the heading of this chapter.

In each local authority visited, Douglas described existing arrangements, and listed services under the headings 'efficient' or 'deficient'. For Aberdeen county in 1931, among the services considered efficient were the existing arrangements for health visiting of children under five years of age and for the supervision of the seven midwives in the county. Among services described as 'not quite efficient, but [...] improving' were educational propaganda in child welfare matters and provision for children suffering malnutrition. Among the services deemed 'deficient' by Douglas were provisions for dental treatment (except in Peterhead), and the absence of immunisation against scarlet fever and diphtheria in the county.[128]

The 1930s SBH investigations showed that in some isolated rural areas, the operation of a maternity and child welfare scheme was of recent origin. For example, in the Highlands County of Sutherland the service had commenced only in 1932, but by 1935 could boast a service monitored by the MOH, Dr Macrae, with monthly visiting of infants in the County carried out by 16 district nurses employed by the Sutherland Nursing Association.[129] In other distant areas, the scheme of maternity and child welfare involved local practitioners in a more practical role than in populous areas. Visiting the Shetlands (Zetland County) in 1935, Douglas noted that there was more ante-natal involvement by general practitioners than in other more populated parts of the country. The education of mothers, for example in stressing the need for early notification of pregnancy, was recognised by both general practitioners and the voluntary-funded (Queen's Institute) district nurses as crucial. Having no institutional maternity provision seriously hampered the Shetland islands. Pregnant women from the Shetlands often made considerable sacrifices to travel to Aberdeen for maternity accommodation. Meanwhile, nurses at the Gilbert Bain hospital (in Lerwick) had no midwifery training and any complicated cases admitted in emergency such as women requiring caesarean sections, were put up in a small room vacated by maids. Meanwhile, infants delivered at the hospital were removed by the

128 NAS, HH61/708, C.A. Douglas, Medical Officer, DHS to Chief Medical Officer, DHS, November 1931.

129 NAS, HH61/618, Report by Douglas, to CMO, DHS, 3 September 1935.

family within hours because their care constituted too 'great a problem at the hospital'.[130]

The varied picture of maternity and child welfare services revealed by Douglas's investigations highlight some of the shortcomings of varied local authority arrangements. They also underline once again that the use of aggregate figures to illustrate trends in infant and maternal mortality and morbidity in the 1930s, can provide only a partial picture of conditions around the country.

The Maternity Services (Scotland) Act 1937 and Beyond

According to the 1937 Political and Economic Planning *Report on the British Health Services*, the Maternity Services (Scotland) Act was 'far more comprehensive than anything yet existing or in preparation in England and Wales'.[131] However, the planned comprehensive Scottish maternity service envisaged in the 1937 legislation was not fully implemented. The delay was due to the cost of scheme (the financial burden was shared equally by local authorities and the state), its permissive character, opposition from general practitioners, and the outbreak of war.

Many general practitioners were reluctant to accept what was seen as the drift towards a salaried medical service.[132] What was worse, the new service was to be administered by local authorities, and involved the development of a government-sponsored ancillary medical service of midwives, while it lessened the opportunities for private practice. The dissatisfaction of the profession was expressed

130 NAS, HH61/717, Report by Douglas, to CMO, DHS, 21 August 1935.

131 PEP, *Report on the British Health Services*, 7.

132 The opposition of the majority of the Scottish medical profession to the expansion of salaried services was apparent much earlier. For example, the introduction of the National Health Insurance scheme between 1911–13 split the Scottish medical profession. As was the case elsewhere around Britain the majority (though not quite so high a number as in other parts of the country) opposed the scheme until the eve of its introduction.

through the BMA. A meeting of representatives for the divisions of the British Medical Association in Scotland was held in Edinburgh on 16 December 1937.

> The meeting expressed profound dissatisfaction with the remuneration suggested by the Department and was also strongly opposed to any proposal which involved the establishment in any area of a service, upon a whole-time basis, which would exclude family doctors from participating in the scheme. A resolution was passed that the British Medical Association could not accept service under the proposed scheme unless considerable improved remuneration was forthcoming.[133]

The stern opposition of general practitioners and the BMA notwithstanding, 45 draft local authority schemes for implementing the permissive maternity services legislation were submitted to the DHS for consideration by the end of 1937. In all the areas covered, the local medical practitioners were invited to undertake the medical services provided under the scheme. In county areas, the service of midwives was provided by local nursing associations with the addition, in some cases, of midwives in private practice, in burghs, midwifery services were mainly in the hands of midwives in private practice.[134]

Two of Scotland's largest cities failed to implement the new permissive legislation. The maternity service proposals were not operated in the cities of Dundee and Glasgow due to wrangling over payment levels to general practitioners. The crux of the matter was the reluctance of general practitioners (particularly in Glasgow) to accept what was regarded as the imposition of a salaried medical service. Other reasons lay behind the non-implementation of the 1937 Maternity Services Act elsewhere in Scotland. In the Outer Hebrides, local antagonism played a part in the reluctance of the Islands' doctors to implement the legislation. The Island doctors were resentful of the mainland local authority Inverness County and there was a widespread belief that the scheme was working on the mainland. When Charlotte

133 *GMJ*, 1938 (1), 90.

134 'Report on the Health of Scotland in 1938', *Public Health*, 52 no. 9 (June 1939), 256.

Anne Douglas informed doctors on the Outer Hebridean islands in July 1946 that the legislation was unpopular in Inverness county, she was left with the distinct impression that local doctors might have put in into operation to spite their mainland colleagues. Douglas wryly commented: 'I gather that a certain amount of emotionalism was at the base of it, and I feel that if they had realised earlier that the local authority were not too keen on the Act they would have worked it themselves just to be different.'[135]

Expanding Scottish public services for infant and maternal welfare in the inter-war years were given added significance by a number of issues in the 1930s. These included the stubbornly high rate of maternal mortality, the enthusiasm of CMO Parlane Kinloch to promote the service as a key to preventive health measures for the country, and the publications of the 1935 Departmental Committee on Maternal Morbidity and Mortality and the Cathcart Report in 1936. These culminated in the passage of the 1937 Maternity Services (Scotland) Act. However, implementation of the legislation encountered professional opposition among general practitioners and also ran into problems due to the difficulties of introducing an integrated maternity service into areas which had very different existing maternity and child welfare schemes.

Wartime Developments

The 1937 Maternity legislation was an early casualty of war. The absorption of doctors and nurses into the armed forces after 1939 was one reason for its slow implementation. Partly for this reason, the problems in Scottish infant and maternal welfare remained a long way from being resolved during World War Two. The war itself led to special arrangements for the care of infants to allow women to undertake war work, in the form of factory crèches and the govern-

135 NAS, HH61/623, memorandum from Charlotte Anne Douglas to William S. Douglas, Secretary, DHS, 12 July 1946 .

ment-sponsored 'war-time nursery scheme'.[136] There are parallels between the decision to provide day nurseries for the children of working mothers during both the First and Second World Wars. However, there was a clear change in emphasis between the two conflicts – no longer were such nurseries regarded as a short-term solution dictated by circumstances, going against nature in taking mothers from their place in the home. This is shown by official willingness to extend the nursery arrangement beyond wartime. In order to prepare for the transition from the emergency wartime provision to peacetime administration, the Treasury agreed to maintain its full commitment to reimbursing local authorities net expenditure on wartime nurseries from the Exchequer until 31 March 1946.[137]

During the war, the diets of children under five and mothers of infants were augmented by supplementary milk, vitamins, cod liver oil and fruit juices, which were provided to vulnerable groups in society through the auspices of the National Welfare (Foods) Scheme set up by the wartime Ministry of Food. In some cases, this superseded local schemes for supplementary feeding already in operation around the country. A scheme had been introduced in Scotland in early 1939, under the auspices of the Scottish Milk Marketing Boards for the provision of a pint of milk for all mothers, expectant mothers, and/or

136 'The disturbance of family life as a result of war-time conditions has inevitably become more widespread as the range of evacuation and of the employment of women has increased, and the problem of making some form of nursery provision for young children is now one of increasing importance in some districts. It has now been decided that the provision of nurseries, to be known as War-time Nurseries both for evacuated children and for the children of women in employment (whether evacuees or local residents), should be regarded as war provision [...]. It will be appreciated that the provision of a nursery is practicable only where a sufficient number of children live within easy reach, as the mothers or guardians will require to make arrangements for bringing the children to and taking them from the nursery. Only exceptionally, therefore, will it be possible to establish nurseries in rural or semi-rural areas.' ABDA, C06/5/355/47, DHS/Scottish Education Department, Joint Circular, 'War-time Nurseries for the Care of Children under Five Years of Age', 9 June 1941.

137 ABDA, CO6/5/355/47, Meeting of the Joint Committee of Argyll County Council and Dunoon Town Council), 29 May 1945.

infants below a certain income.[138] A similar scheme was discussed, (although not then introduced) in England. The Scottish scheme was superseded in September 1940 when a comprehensive cheap-milk policy: 'the National Milk Scheme', was launched to provide milk at a reduced price of 2d (1p) to all pregnant and nursing mothers, and to children under the age of six. The price of a pint of milk to ordinary consumers was meantime raised to 3 and a half pence (nearly 2p). Milk was supplied free of charge to families with an adult income of less than 40 shillings (£2) (an additional 6 shillings (30p) allowed for each child). Nearly three million Britons were eligible for the cheap-milk scheme and the reported take up in Scotland was between 70 and 80%.[139]

Vitamins, cod liver oil and fruit juices were also freely provided during the war for nursing mothers and babies. The Scots take up of the supplementary vitamin initiative was poor[140] – according to the Coatbridge Food Control Committee of the Ministry of Food, only between 30–50% of mothers attended for repeat preparations of cod liver oil and fruit syrup in the Lanarkshire mining town of Coatbridge in January 1942.[141] This disappointing take-up was reflected around the country as many mothers remained to be convinced of the importance of such nutritional supplements. From 1943, food supplements were given to children up to the age of five or in possession of Green Ration Book R.B.2.[142] By this time, the food supplements were incorporated within a National Milk Scheme (which included seven pints of milk per week at subsidised cost for children).

138 *BMJ*, 1939 (2), 93–4.

139 R. Marrack, *Food and Planning* (Victor Gollancz, 1942), 236.

140 In September 1943, the Scottish uptake figure for cod liver oil preparations was 17.5%, compared to the UK figure of 21%. The Scottish uptake of free orange juice was 35.4%, compared to a UK figure of 43%. See DHS, Circular No. 6/1944, 'Welfare (Foods) Scheme – Cod Liver Oil, Orange Juice and Vitamin Tablets', 21 January 1944.

141 Coatbridge Burgh Archives, North Lanarkshire Council, Coatbridge Food Control Committee of the Ministry of Food to Dr Robert Cordiner, Medical Officer of Health, Coatbridge, 26 January 1942.

142 Coatbridge Burgh Archives, DHS Circular 8/1943, 'Simplified Procedure under Combined National Milk and Vitamins Scheme', 23 February 1943.

Improved wartime nutrition for mothers and babies had both short- and longer-term consequences for the health of Scots mothers and babies. Dugald Baird promoted research into social and economic influences on still birth levels and maternal health. Generational studies by Baird in the 1960s and 1970s showed that the health and survival rates of children owed much to the environment and early nutritional experiences of mothers at *their* births. Baird identified economic and social factors as having an influence beyond the immediate health of the new-born baby. This view has been reinforced by the work of Titmuss[143] and Floud.[144]

According to Richard Titmuss, the implementation of wartime supplementary feeding measures demonstrated a dramatic change in government attitude towards mothers and their babies:

> For over a decade many authorities [...] had demonstrated the need for getting more milk into mothers and children [...]. It was, in the main, a problem of purchasing power. This problem was solved for mothers with young children by decision of the Government five days after the evacuation of the British Expeditionary Force from Dunkirk.[145]

Certainly, state action was swift during wartime in both nutritional and institutional arrangements for infants, nursing and expectant mothers. A scheme of 'Wartime Emergency Maternity Homes' was established between 1939–1941. Eleven such homes were equipped. By June 1941, seven maternity homes for evacuated expectant mothers were in operation in Scotland, with the remaining four others held in reserve on a care and maintenance basis.[146] Between 1940–1944, the seven homes admitted 7,803 cases. These resulted in 7, 290 live births and 133 still births. There were a further 78 neonatal deaths

143 Titmuss, *Problems of Social Policy*, 535.

144 '[...] people carry with them, throughout life, an endowment which is acquired during childhood and adolescence but which affects their later health.' R. Floud, et al, *Height, Health and History: Nutritional Status in the United Kingdom, 1750–1950* (Cambridge: Cambridge University Press, 1970), 270.

145 Titmuss, *Problems of Social Policy*, 511.

146 See DHS, *Summary Report: 1939–1941* (Edinburgh: HMSO, 1941), passim.

and 4 maternal deaths. 4,713 admissions were evacuee women, the other 3,090 were local women.[147]

These wartime measures helped improve the life chances of Scottish mothers and babies. However, other pre-war changes in Scotland may have contributed to the later down-turn in MMR in the 1940s, in particular, (where implemented) the operation of the Maternity Services (Scotland), Act, 1937 which aimed at improving and co-ordinating maternity services for all expectant Scotswomen.

DHS Report on Infant Mortality, 1943

Special maternity arrangements were a response to the needs of wartime. Meanwhile spiralling Scots infant mortality levels in 1940 and 1941, (see table 3.1) led Tom Johnston, Secretary of State for Scotland, to convene a sub-committee of the DHS Scientific Advisory Committee in July 1942 under the chairmanship of John Boyd Orr to investigate the issue.[148] The *Report on Infant Mortality in Scotland* was issued in 1943. The Boyd Orr Report emphasised a shocking lack of progress in Scotland's infant mortality statistics in the inter-war period, which had been exacerbated since 1939 by wartime circumstances. In the foreword to the Report, Tom Johnston stated:

> Our infant mortality compares badly with England's; but it is not without significance that so, year after year, do our unemployed figures and our percentage of overcrowded houses. These have been the chief blots upon our

147 Macnalty, *The Civilian Health and Medical Services*, 303.

148 'I have been very concerned, as we all are, about our infantile mortality figures. The [rounded] figures per 1,000 births rose from 68 [...] in 1939 – and that itself was a high figure – to 78 in 1940 and 83 in 1941. I have asked the Department of Health's Scientific Advisory Committee, under the Chairmanship of Sir John Boyd Orr, to consider and report quickly, if they can, the causes of this rise and to suggest remedial measures.' Scottish Secretary, Tom Johnston, HOC debates, 8–7–1942, vol. 381 col. 787.

social arrangements in the past and they have been productive of the most part of the poverty evils from which we have suffered.[149]

The Boyd Orr Report identified a number of areas where the Scottish service could be improved. The Report stressed that Scotland lagged behind in the provision of maternity and child welfare services. Clinic premises were identified as often poor, ill equipped and overcrowded. Nutritional supervision was deemed inadequate. Liaison between the hospitals, the family doctors and the child welfare service was also poor. Health visitors had much larger case-loads than they could efficiently manage. Powers to supply extra food and domestic help which were available under wartime arrangements (noted above) were not sufficiently used by local authorities.[150]

The Boyd Orr Report findings were not surprising bearing in mind the difficulties in funding maternity and child welfare centres for much of the 1920s due to economic constraints. This, coupled with the scattered nature of Scotland's population, placed a heavy burden on health visitors to advise mothers and monitor the health of young children. Scotland's wider problems of poverty, poor housing, and insufficient nutrition levels created a bleak backdrop to the limited and unsuccessful maternity and child welfare service identified in the wartime report.

The Boyd Orr Report noted that although there had been a gradual improvement in attendance at antenatal clinics and centres since the 1920s, there was a clear discrepancy in attendance between Scotland and England. Between 1925 and 1946, clinic attendance among eligible Scottish mothers rose from 8.7% to 51%.[151] In England, the 1945 figure was over 70%.[152] This geographic imbalance had been identified as early as 1933 by the President of the Maternity and Child Welfare Group of the Medical Officers of Health

149 DHS, *Report on Infant Mortality in Scotland*, 1.

150 Ibid.

151 Figures cited in G. McLachlan, ed., *Improving the Common Weal: A History of the Health Services in Scotland* (Edinburgh: Edinburgh University Press, 1987), 419.

152 Winter, 'Unemployment, Nutrition and Infant Mortality in Britain 1920–1950', 251.

Association, Margaret Emslie, in a presidential address published in the journal *Public Health.*[153]

The failure of infant and maternal inter-war provision to meet the needs of the population was explained by the Boyd Orr Committee in terms of the economic situation in Scotland:

> The committee desires first to record its conviction that infant mortality in Scotland is high because a large part of the population, both in towns and rural areas live under poor housing conditions and in poverty. Unemployment has, in the past, seriously aggravated the problem, and recurrence of unemployment on any large scale would add greatly to the difficulty of its solution. There is little use of health education if the principles cannot be practised.[154]

The Boyd Orr Report recommended that specific child welfare services should be extended and improved by increasing the number of qualified health visitors and home helps available to families, to improve the quality and use of clinic services and increase the number of maternity beds. The education of mothers in infant feeding and domestic hygiene was of paramount importance and was regarded in the Report as the primary function of the child welfare service. More broadly, improved housing and sanitary arrangements were also stressed. The Boyd Orr Report noted that child welfare services in Scotland lagged behind those in England and Wales and that expenditure per birth in Scotland was only two-thirds that in England and Wales. In fact, expenditure per birth based on 1935 figures showed that England and Wales was £5.20 per head and £3.50 per head in Scotland. The imbalance was further shown in the poor

---

153 Looking at the attendance figures of 1 to 5 year olds at infant welfare centres in 1931, Emslie observed that in Birmingham (noted as having one of the most well developed maternity and child welfare services in Britain), 12% of children in this age group attended centres. In Glasgow, the corresponding figure was less than 3%, in Edinburgh the figure was 2.5%. These figures were not the worst, however, since less than 1% of Liverpool toddlers attended welfare centres. As well as reinforcing how much had still to be done in ensuring a reasonable coverage in Scottish infant and maternal welfare provision, the figures overall show how far there was to go before an accurate monitoring of pre-school children across the country could be achieved. M. Emslie, 'War in the Family', *Public Health*, 46 no. 12, (September 1933), 389.

154 DHS, *Infant Mortality in Scotland*, 62.

numbers of antenatal clinics and child welfare centres. The number of births in Scotland was one-seventh of the English rate, but the number of ante-natal clinics was only one-ninth of that in England, and that of child welfare clinics was only one-twelfth.

Local authorities all around Britain experienced difficulties in funding health services during times of economic depression and high unemployment. Lara Marks's study of the infant and maternal welfare services in four London boroughs provides one such example.[155] However, few areas could claim to have the unique combination of areas of concentrated urbanisation and heavy industry and remote regions of scattered population, which together gave Scotland its severe housing difficulties, its deep-rooted poverty and high unemployment levels. These were problems which often lay far beyond the capabilities of local authorities to address.

Scottish local authorities generally had lower populations from which to generate rates, and after the introduction of the block grant system in the 1929 Local Government (Scotland) Act an extra burden was placed on local funding of health services. When this was combined with the high level of unemployment in the country (for example, the unemployment rate in Scotland in 1938 was 17.9%, while the British rate was 13.3%)[156] it meant that it was difficult to expand local authority health provision when it was needed most. Such factors help explain the discrepancy in state and public funding per birth noted in the Boyd Orr Report.

The findings of the Boyd Orr Report quickly led local authorities, including Glasgow, to reappraise their schemes of child welfare.[157] On 11 February 1944, the DHS convened a meeting of representatives from all local authorities to discuss the findings of the

155 Marks, *Metropolitan Mortality*, 159–161.

156 Mitchell, *British Historical Statistics*, 125–6.

157 'Councillor John Stewart made reference to the recently published report on Infant Mortality in Scotland [and] agreed that a copy of the said report be sent to each member of the Corporation and that the Medical Officer of Health be instructed to submit his observations on the report in so far as affecting the City, with particular reference to the possibility of implementing any of the recommendations contained therein.' Mitchell Library, Glasgow, minutes of Glasgow Corporation Sub-Committee on Health, 5 January 1944, 363.

Boyd Orr Report. After the consultations, local authorities promised the Scottish Secretary of State that they would do everything they could to improve the situation. Measures to be taken included aiming to improve the intakes of orange juice, and vitamin tablets among mothers and babies[158] (already noted as being less enthusiastically supported by families than expected in the Lanarkshire town of Coatbridge), and by requisitioning large houses in the locality to use as maternity homes.

Such local authority measures under DHS prompting combined with the reduction in unemployment due to war production needs helped retrieve the Scots IMR situation. Speaking in parliament in February 1944, Tom Johnston noted that in July 1939 the Scottish unemployment figure was 11.5%, by January 1944, it had fallen to just one per cent. Johnston believed that higher income and more purchasing power helped to account for the improvement in IMR. The joint efforts of the DHS and local authorities doubled the number of beds in Scottish maternity homes to 2,260 beds during the course of the war. In addition, 108 beds were kept open in rural areas for maternity cases.[159] After witnessing a sharp increase in 1940 and 1941 and a return to pre-war levels in 1942, by 1943, the Scottish IMR fell to its lowest ever level (65.2) and continued to decline, falling to 44.7 by 1948 (see table 3.1).

---

158 As has been noted, the intake of 'welfare foods' in Scotland was lower than in England and Wales. In March 1944, Tom Johnston noted that the intake of vitamin A and D tablets was 20% less in Scotland, that of orange juice 18% less and of cod liver oil, 7% less than in England and Wales. HOC debates, 8–3–44, vol. 397 col. 2087.

159 HOC debates, 17–3–44, vol. 397 col. 311.

On the eve of the introduction of the National Health Service, a number of Scottish services attempted to provide a comprehensive system of maternal and infant care peculiar to the country. The Highlands and Islands Medical Service, jointly funded by government and the local authorities, provided general practitioners with a basic income and a mileage allowance amounting to a basic salary. Specialists, with a guaranteed salary, were also available at key locations. A wide-ranging nursing service and an ambulance service, including an air ambulance, were also available for the region. This level of service was crucial for scattered communities, particularly in relation to the care of mothers and infants where treatment centred on the clinic was impracticable.

The implementation of the 1937 Maternity Act and the relevant provisions contained in the 1945 Education (Scotland) Act, gave the care of mothers and young children a more uniform formulation throughout the country in the lead up to the implementation of the National Health Service (Scotland) Act. The 1945 Education Act extended the Scottish Education Department's responsibility to include nursery schools. The inspection of children attending the nurseries became the responsibility of the school medical service. There was close liaison between Education and Health Departments, and the local Medical Officer of Health was also invariably the School Medical Officer. In 1947, a meeting was held in Edinburgh between local authority Medical Officers of Health and education directors to set up a continuing committee to formulate a plan for future health education in the nurseries and schools.[160]

The advent of the National Health Service in 1948 signalled the end of curative work at local authority child welfare centres (as the local authority health and welfare services were fused) and care became progressively more preventive. Although the Government took over important sections of the health and welfare services formerly undertaken by the local authorities, many of the local

160 MacGregor, *Public Health in Glasgow, 1905–1946*, 123.

responsibilities remained and new ones were added, with the development of home nursing, home help and midwifery services.

Conclusion

Over the period 1919 to 1948, arrangements for the care of mothers and infants were in the vanguard of the personal medical services. In the inter-war period, 'official' care of mothers and infants expanded considerably: supplementary feeding and integrated maternal services came to be considered normal practice. However, the inter-war years cannot be simply characterised as a time of steady improvement in the fields of mother and baby health. Many of the developments in Scottish infant and maternal welfare came towards the end of the 1930s and matters were accelerated by the outbreak of warfare.[161]

Despite the much-vaunted extension of maternity and child welfare services, over the period as a whole, infant and maternal mortality rates were high and slow to improve. Local authority and SBH/DHS initiatives, particularly in the realm of supplementary feeding, came under government scrutiny and ultimate 'capping' in the 1920s. The series of SBH/DHS investigations between 1928 and 1943 demonstrated that Scottish health care in the field of infant and maternal welfare in the inter-war years was patchy, uneven and simply unable to tackle problems on a scale which lay beyond its powers. The problems uncovered touched on the very nature of Scottish society and the long standing problems of the economy. There was less infant and maternal welfare coverage in Scotland than in England, fewer clinics, less money spent per child by local authorities struggling to set

161 'What was remarkable about these war-time developments in the provision of school meals, milk and special foods for certain groups in the community was the unanimity underlying policy and the speed at which decisions were acted on. No longer was it argued (as it often was before the war) that the condition of the people did not warrant such measures, or that nothing should be done until unmistakeable evidence of a deterioration in the public health had shown itself for some time.' Titmuss, *Social Policy*, 514.

low rates, and most crucially, higher mortality (both infant and maternal). Scotland's falling population in the period added urgency to the attempts to improve the health of mothers and babies, but it was also part of the problem. Rural depopulation meant there were fewer local rate payers from which to generate funds for local infant and maternal welfare schemes, meanwhile already overcrowded Scottish cities became more overcrowded. The 'golden age of public health' left many sections of Scotland's most vulnerable population untouched by its rays.

Maternal and Child Welfare in Practice at the Grove St Dispensary, Edinburgh, 1920

4: The Health of School-Age Children and the Nutrition Controversy

> Even when the child is shown to be in need of food, the education authority is required to go through an elaborate procedure before it can supply meals, except as a temporary expedient. The authority must summon either or both of the parents to appear before it, to give an explanation of the child's condition. If the explanation is not forthcoming, or if it is not satisfactory, and the authority finds that the child's condition is due to neglect, it is required to send a copy of its findings to the parents and a copy to the Procurator Fiscal with a view to prosecution. If the authority [...] is satisfied that the parent is not able, by reason of poverty or of ill-health, to supply the child with sufficient or proper food, the authority has next to be satisfied that the necessities cannot be provided by voluntary agencies. Not until the authority is satisfied on that score can it provide free meals to a necessitous child [...]. They render themselves liable to surcharges if they feed children gratuitously without going through this alarming catalogue of difficulties.
> (Tom Johnston, HOC debates, 18 March 1941, vol. 376 col. 1872)

Introduction

This chapter looks at changes in the health, height, and weight of Scottish school children in the period between 1919–1948. It also examines how far the SBH/DHS can be credited for any improvement in these figures. The chapter continues the consideration of a number of issues identified in the previous chapter. Broad concern for the health of future generations, the involvement of the state as providers, and the sometimes uneasy relationship between Scottish and central government in making decisions about the level of service provided are again in evidence. In addition, this chapter covers the role of the expert in influencing policy. Expert influence over Scottish health policy is considered within the broader inter-war nutrition debate. The tenor of this debate was, in turn, influenced by DHS-sponsored enquiries into the value of milk as a food supplement for children.

The realm of child health in schools has been the subject of a number of secondary studies, particularly since the regular inspection of Scottish school children after 1908 generated a series of local school medical officer annual reports containing large amounts of qualitative and quantitative data. These and other related materials have in the main been used here to address the debate on the recorded health of school children (and the wider population) in the period between 1919–1948.[1]

This chapter seeks to add to historical debate on the health of the nation by examining the SBH/DHS pioneering experiments in supplementary nutrition in Scottish schools at the end of the 1920s. The work of John Boyd Orr[2] in this area is of particular importance.

---

1 For more on the controversy over inter–war school medical inspection reports see Floud, et al, *Height, Health and History: Nutritional Status in the United Kingdom, 1750–1950*, and B. Harris, *The Health of the School Child: A History of the School Medical Service in England and Wales* (Buckingham: Open University Press, 1995). See also Webster, 'Healthy or Hungry Thirties?', and Winter's, 'Infant Mortality, Maternal Mortality, and Public Health in Britain in the 1930s', and 'Unemployment, Nutrition and Infant Mortality in Britain 1920–1950'.

2 John Boyd Orr was born in Ayrshire in 1880 and educated at Glasgow University, obtaining MA, MD and DSc degrees. He served in World War One in the RAMC and was decorated with both the MC and DSO. Orr moved from Glasgow to become Director of the Rowett Research Institute, Aberdeen. Orr, like E.P. Cathcart, was also a member of many scientific committees, including the Reorganisation Commission on Fat Stock, 1932, Reorganisation Commission for Milk, 1935/6, Advisory Committee on Nutrition (Ministry of Health), and the League of Nations Technical Commission on Nutrition. He served as Chairman of the Scottish Scientific Advisory Committee (which reported on Infant Mortality in 1943). He was Professor of Agriculture at Aberdeen University 1942–5. In 1945, he became Rector of Glasgow University and then Chancellor the following year. He also served as Independent MP for the Scottish Universities 1945/6. He was awarded the Nobel Peace Prize in 1949 and in the same year was created first Baron Boyd Orr of Brechin Mearns, County of Angus. He later served as Director-General of the United Nations Food and Agricultural Organisation, 1945–8. He published a number of best selling books on the problems of nutrition, the best-

His innovative work in the 1920s helped identify the positive impact of supplementary milk feeding in schools. Boyd Orr's 1930s findings on the inadequate level of nutrition experienced by much of Britain's population in *Food, Health and Income* (1936) are also discussed. Both these sets of investigations were initially given a lukewarm governmental response, but were later used as part of the national 'milk in schools' scheme in the 1930s and influenced wartime nutrition policy.

Pre-1919 Health Care for School Children

As with infant and maternal health, the first national debates on the medical inspection and supplementary feeding of school children took place as part of wider discussions on the ill health of the nation in the wake of the Boer War of 1899–1902. The Royal Commission on Physical Training in Scotland which reported in 1903 made recommendations on the provision of physical training for school children and young adults (with priority to be given to drill and games). The Royal Commission also put forward more wide ranging suggestions for medical inspection and the feeding of school children. These recommendations were based on findings of high aggregate figures of children suffering from disease and under nourishment in studies of Aberdeen and Edinburgh school children reported to the Commission.[3] The Commission did not make any suggestions regarding state intervention in child health, but the implication was clear:

> We are aware that School Boards, as a general rule, have no power at present to deal with this question. They have no power to spend money from the school

known being: *Food, Health and Income*, 1936 and *Food and the People*, 1944. He died in 1971.

3 In Edinburgh, 259 of 299 boys, and 294 of 298 girls examined were suffering from ear or throat defects. *Report of the Royal Commission on Physical Training (Scotland)* (Edinburgh: HMSO, 1903), 27 [Cmd 1507].

fund upon food, clothing, or lodging [...] But we are not on that account deterred from calling attention to the necessity for better feeding, which, in our opinion, has been fully demonstrated, nor from considering a practical remedy.[4]

Taking up the call, the Inter-Departmental Committee on Physical Deterioration in 1904 made some policy statements and recommended selective permissive powers for local authorities to deal with the general health, physical well being and nutrition of school children.[5] These recommendations were given legislative support after the landslide Liberal election victory of December 1905. In 1908, the School Medical Service in Scotland was initiated under the Education (Scotland) Act of that year which provided for the medical inspection of Scottish school children. Individual Scottish local authorities enacted schemes of medical inspection which pre-dated the new legislation. For example, Govan Parish School Board, which covered 30 schools in the burghs of Govan and Partick set up its own school medical inspection service in September 1907.[6] (Both these burghs were later incorporated into the city of Glasgow.)

The 1908 Education (Scotland) Act also empowered local authorities to set up schemes to provide meals during the school day for necessitous children and, where necessary, clothing. The arrangement was extended by the Education (Scotland) Act of 1913 which provided for the medical treatment of needy children, with

4 Ibid., 30.

5 'The Committee are emphatic in recommending that a systematised medical inspection of children at school should be imposed as a public duty on every school authority, and they agree with the Royal Commission on Physical Training (Scotland) that a contribution towards the cost should be made out of the Parliamentary Vote. With the assistance of teachers properly trained in the various branches of hygiene, the system could be so far based on their observations and records that no large and expensive medical staff would be necessary [...]. The Committee recommend that the various Local Authorities should make definite provision for dealing with the question of underfed children [...]. The Committee [...] do not contemplate any one uniform method of procedure, but think that regard should be had to the varying circumstances of different localities.' *Report of the Inter-Departmental Committee on Physical Deterioration* (1904), 91, [Cmd 2175].

6 M. Mayes, *The Stormy Petrel: A Life of Dr Kate Fraser 1877–1957* (Glasgow: Glasgow Wellcome Unit for the History of Medicine, 1995), 65.

costs divided between local school boards and the Treasury. In 1914, a further Education (Scotland) Provision of Meals Act clarified the situation regarding the ability of local authorities to provide meals for children of school age outside the school term.[7] In tandem with such government effort, the voluntary sector remained a main component in the health social services in Scotland.

From the slender beginning of the 1908 Education Act, statistics on the physical condition of school children began to be compiled and a methodology of administering the service was developed. The Scottish Education Department (SED) formally launched the School Medical Service in Scotland in 1909. The SED's memorandum outlining the new medical service noted the unacceptable 'degree of unfitness' among school children and made plain that the nation's health could only be advanced by improving the personal health and environment of the school child.[8]

Many of those appointed as School Medical Officers (SMOs) were already local authority Medical Officers of Health (MOsH). This was because Medical Officers of Health were already responsible for the medical inspection of school children in cases of infectious diseases and all Scottish school buildings were subject to the sanitary supervision of their local authority. The connection between School Medical Officers and Medical Officers of Health was therefore very close. In addition, many of the SMOs were part-time and carried out their duties in conjunction with local authority work. Doctors involved in examining school children formed the Association of School Medical Officers of Scotland in January 1911.[9] Despite the

---

7 The Education (Scotland) Provision of Meals Act, 28 August 1914 sought to 'Remove doubts as to the interpretation of the Education (Scotland) Act, 1908, in regard to the provision of meals for school children.' The feeding of necessitous school children outside the school year was an area of confusion for some local education authorities.

8 SBH, *Memorandum on School Health Administration 1920*, Appendix I – 'Memorandum on School Health Administration 1909', 11 (Edinburgh: HMSO, 1920)

9 NAS, GD1/1022/1, minutes of the Association of School Medical Officers of Scotland passim. The first meeting was held in the North British Station Hotel, Edinburgh, 28 January 1911.

professional organisation of the school medical service, the level of service provided pre-war was far from complete. The treatment of school children, as distinct from inspection, was not authorised in Scotland until 1913, and the School Medical Service was almost totally suspended during the war.[10] The experience of war on school children was not necessarily deleterious according to the most comprehensive study of the School Medical Service in Britain. Bernard Harris's study of school children in twenty-four local authorities (including six in Scotland), revealed that the 1914–18 War had relatively little impact on the average standard of child health.[11]

A consolidating Education Act for Scotland was passed in 1918. The new act set up local education authorities with responsibility for school health. This situation did not survive the reorganisation of Scottish health agencies in 1919. Contrary to Scottish Secretary Robert Munro's wishes, school health provision passed to the new Scottish Board of Health. The 1919 Board of Health (Scotland) Act[12] brought the medical inspection and treatment of school children under SBH control. There was an overlap of responsibility however, and the new SBH worked in conjunction with the Scottish Education Department and local education authorities. The SBH was at pains to point out that the new legislation did not in any way alter the duties of the local education authorities. However, it laid great stress on the need for co-operation between the education authorities and local

10 Only 10 of the 40 Inspection Schemes in Scotland remained in operation in July 1919 when the SBH assumed control for school health administration. A further 15 were greatly modified, and 15 had ceased completely. 'As regards treatment schemes the effect of the war was that from 1916 onwards there was a steady decline in the amount of work performed except perhaps in the larger burghs.' SBH, *Second Annual Report, 1920*, 96.

11 Harris, *Health of the School Child*, 87.

12 Section 4, (1), I of the Scottish Board of Health Act, 3 June 1919 transferred to the Board: 'All the powers and duties of the Scottish Education Department with respect to the medical inspection and treatment of school children and young persons [...]. Provided that [...] the Board may make arrangements with the Scottish Education Department respecting the submission and approval of schemes of education authorities and the payment of grants to education authorities, so far as such schemes and payments relate to, or are in respect of, medical inspection and treatment.'

authority Public Health Committees, since medical inspection, the provision of treatment, and the sanitary supervision of schools were all municipal public health matters.[13]

When the SBH took over the medical inspection and treatment of school children it took over a piecemeal School Medical Service. Despite the widely held view that children were a precious national resource, little had been achieved in protecting, or conserving, the health of school children prior to 1919.

School Health Administration after 1919

After 1919, the responsibility for school health still lay with the local education authorities under the general control of the SBH. The system of inspection was gradually built up after the war. In the course of 1920, 33 Scottish education authorities submitted schemes to the SBH of which 25 had been approved. The type of scheme varied according to circumstance:

> As a rule, the schemes cover the medical examination of routine and special cases, and the re-examination of children previously found to be in need of treatment, and provision has been made for the 'following up' by the School Medical Officers and school nurses of such cases as require further supervision. Measures have also been taken which provide for, inter alia, the cleansing and disinfection of schools, medical supervision of physical education, and practical instruction in personal hygiene.[14]

A further SBH concern was the expansion of physical education provision as a measure of preventive health care. 'Of the various measures of preventive nature that may be adopted none is of more

13 SBH, *First Annual Report, 1919* (Edinburgh: HMSO, 1920), Appendix V, ix. [Cmd 992].

14 'In addition, certain authorities make special provision for the education of physically defective and mentally defective children who are unable to profit from education along with normal children.' SBH, *Second Annual Report, 1920*, 97.

importance than a well considered scheme of Physical Education [...].'[15] However, plans for extending training for schoolteachers to supervise programmes of physical education were among many items of expenditure adversely affected by the financial retrenchment exercise which followed the drift into economic depression in the early 1920s. Nevertheless, within government the view persisted that expanded provision of physical education was a cost-effective step in preventive health.[16]

In 1920, an SBH memorandum unfavourably compared Scottish school medical inspections with those in England and Wales. It noted that since the end of World War One, treatment of children at secondary level had been organised in only five Scottish burghs. These figures were in sharp contrast to England and Wales where, in 1914, 266 authorities out of 318 offered treatment, and 179 provided school clinics. By 1918, this had risen to 287 authorities offering treatment and 169 with their own clinics. Moreover, it was noted that the School Medical Officer remained independent of the Medical Officer of Health in all the large Scottish cities and eight counties. The administrative unity of Medical Officer of Health and School Medical Officer recommended by the SBH had only been achieved in twenty-three counties and one burgh by 1920.[17] Some regularisation in the service was achieved with the issue of an SBH memorandum on the 'Health of the School Child'. This memorandum recommended that each child be examined at four separate stages of the elementary school career.[18]

---

15 Ibid., 99.

16 Newman, CMO at the Ministry of Health argued that if physical education was more universally provided and expanded: 'the less shall we need formal and corrective work in physical training and the *less shall we need medical treatment* [Newman's own emphasis].' See Ministry of Health, *Health of the School Child, 1928*, [annual report on the school health service], (HMSO, 1929), 215.

17 See *BMJ*, 1920 (1), 520, article on 'SBH Memorandum on School Health Administration, 1920.'

18 SBH, *Memorandum on the Health of the School Child* (Edinburgh:, HMSO, 1920), 13.

Despite early limitations, the newly launched, SBH-controlled, School Medical Service fitted clearly into the contemporary notion of personal responsibility for health. For example, there was clear emphasis on the practical involvement of parents in the school medical inspection process. This was highlighted in the 1920 Glasgow education authority annual report. During the course of 1920, 3,672 visits were paid by SMOs to some of the 210 Glasgow schools attended by 198,551 children under its care. Parents or guardians were encouraged to be present at the inspection of the children, and received due notice of the hour of visit. 63% of parents took advantage of this opportunity to receive personal advice in cases of necessity.[19]

While state and local involvement in child health increased after World War One, the voluntary sector continued to play a supportive role. None more so than in the privately funded Carnegie Trust Child Welfare Centre which opened in Motherwell in June 1922.[20] The cost of building the centre was met by grants from the Carnegie Trust at a cost of £18,000, while equipment and furnishing for the centre was provided by the local authority aided by Government grant. As noted in the previous chapter, the Motherwell child welfare centre was built in conjunction with a new local authority maternity home. The integration of resources to cover mothers, infants and children was a move that accorded with the 'anti-waste' stance of the Conservative Government. Walter Elliot, then PUSH, spoke approvingly of the measure at the opening ceremony of the Carnegie Trust Child Welfare Centre:

> The boundary age between the maternity service and child welfare scheme and the school health administration scheme was a purely artificial one, and did not mark any definite stage or problem in the health progress of the child [...] There would thus be that continuity of supervision so essential to the maintenance of health and healthy conditions. Such an arrangement had also an important

19 *Annual Report of Education Authority of Glasgow, 1920*, quoted in *GMJ*, 95, 1921, (1), 277.

20 See chapter three for more on the model Motherwell infant and maternal and child welfare centre.

advantage from the Government's point of view in that it was an *economy that conduced to greater efficiency* [author's emphasis].[21]

While the involvement of voluntary agencies helped establish the medical care of school-age children, within the SBH moves were made to develop the School Medical Service itself. In July 1919, SBH Board member Sir William Leslie Mackenzie[22] began the procedure to recruit Dr Lewis Cruikshank[23] from his position as Medical Officer of the SED to the SBH. This matter took months, even though the Board gave it a high priority.[24] The delay meant that the SBH plan to assess the efficiency of existing measures of the 'Inspection and Treatment' of school children provided by local education authorities within its first year of operation was unduly rushed.[25] After his eventual transfer in 1920, Cruikshank worked closely with Leslie Mackenzie to improve the health of school children during the 1920s.

By 1924, Cruikshank had completely reorganised the system of school medical inspection and treatment. Standard tests were applied to Scottish children at three points of their school career, 'entrants', in mid-school life, and 'leavers.' An additional examination was given to those children who remained at school beyond the age of 14. These schemes of school medical inspection included dental and oculist care.

21 Motherwell District Council, Motherwell Leisure Services, *Motherwell Times*, Friday 22 June 1921.

22 See chapter one for more on the career of William Leslie Mackenzie.

23 Lewis Davie Cruikshank obtained his medical training at Aberdeen University, graduating MB ChB 1902 and MD in 1906. In 1905, he obtained the DPH from Cambridge University. He became Medical Officer and Lecturer at Aberdeen Training College and then Principal of Dunfermline College of Hygiene and Physical Training. Author of a number of books on school clinics and hygiene, he became Chief Medical Inspector of Schools in Dunfermline before his appointment as Medical Officer and Chief Inspector of Physical Training at the Scottish Education Department. In this office, he prepared the Annual Reports on Medical Inspection of School Children in Scotland. He was appointed Medical Officer for the SBH on its creation in 1919. He died in 1927.

24 NAS, HH75/1, SBH minutes, 18 July 1919. Item 6 of the SBH inaugural meeting noted 'It was remitted to Sir W. Leslie Mackenzie to draft a letter for submission to the Education Department as to the taking over of Dr Cruikshank.'

25 NAS, HH75/2, SBH divisional committee III minutes, 13 January 1920.

An increasing supply of dentists and nurses were taken on to augment the growing medical presence. By 1925, the Scottish School Medical Service employed 37 School Medical Officers, 57 Assistant School Medical Officers, and 168 full-time and 416 part-time nurses. Health personnel were employed directly by each education authority, under the general jurisdiction of the SBH.

The Log Book of Motherwell Iron Works School indicates a pattern of regular attendance and follow up visits at the school by the School Medical Officer, Dr Young, between 1922 and the end of the log book entries in 1926. Dr Young was often accompanied by one of several nurses, and latterly, by a school dentist.

> 3 May 1922. Dr Young assisted by Nurse Dobbie examined the newly enrolled pupils in the infant department [...]
> 30 May 1922. Dr Young, assisted by Nurse Dobbie visited the school this afternoon and re-examined certain of the pupils [...]
> 14 November 1924. There are eight exclusions due to diphtheria and scarlet fever. Many pupils are suffering from sore throat.[26]

By 1926, the examination of school children at the Motherwell Iron Works School by the School Medical Officer and nurse Dobbie was taking up four days,[27] whereas in 1922 this had taken place over a two-day period.[28] The implication is that either the inspections were becoming more thorough and wide ranging or that the school roll had increased. The fact that no dentist is recorded as visiting the school until May 1924, is suggestive of the former.[29] The work of the SBH seemed to be having some positive impact, at least in terms of identifying and monitoring child health.

However, this assumption cannot be taken too far. As noted in the previous chapter, in 1927, only 7.5% of all children aged between 1 and 5 were visited at home and only 3.6% attended SBH child welfare clinics. This failure to detect illness early often left the School Medical Service facing chronic conditions among the children they

26 Motherwell District Council, Motherwell Leisure Services, Log book of Motherwell Iron Works School, 1911–1926.

27 Ibid. See entries for 4 and 7 September 1926.

28 Ibid., 3 and 4 May 1922.

29 Ibid., 19 May 1924.

inspected. School Medical Officers made frequent reference in their reports to the high proportion of diseases and conditions found in school entrants that ought to have been treated effectively before school age.[30]

At the end of 1929, the newly created Department of Health for Scotland, produced its first annual report. This first report of the new Scottish health authority examined the achievements in health provision since 1919. In school health, the number of children inspected rose from 258,130 in 1919 to 471,979 in 1929. The number of school children medically treated in 1919 was 68,526 rising to 236,025 in 1929. By 1929, the medical staff involved in school health consisted of 37 chief School Medical Officers (21 of whom were also local MOsH), 64 Assistant School Medical Officers, 47 part-time local practitioners, 82 dentists, 64 specialists in various departments, and, 684 nurses (of whom 481 were district nurses). Yet, behind these apparently healthy figures lay a picture of continuing neglect. Only one-third of the school population received systematic medical inspection, and an average of only seven and a half minutes was spent on each child.[31]

In 1930, a joint memorandum from the Department of Health for Scotland and the Scottish Education Department recognised the care of those between 1 and 5 years old as the 'most serious gap in the national scheme of health [which] must be filled'. The passage of the Local Government (Scotland) Act of 1929 was seen as an ideal opportunity for local authorities to expand the existing infant and maternal welfare provision to now cater for children from infancy, through the pre-school years, right through until the end of the school career.[32] Existing local education authority responsibility for school

---

30 SBH, *Ninth Annual Report, 1927*, 168.

31 DHS, *Annual Report, 1929* (Edinburgh: HMSO, 1929), passim, [Cmd 3520].

32 'The moment is indeed opportune for a great step forward in the building up of a stronger and more vigorous race. Under the provision of the Local Government (Scotland) Act, 1929, the power to supply, or aid the supply, of nursery schools under Section 8(a) of the Education (Scotland) Act, 1918, and the wide powers of a similar nature under statutes relating to Maternity and Child Welfare are now vested in one Authority, which is responsible for all schemes affecting the health, well-being and education of the child from its

health was superseded. The new, re-organised, local authorities were made responsible for school health from May 1930. In theory, infant and school health now were under a single agency which provided care for children from birth to the age of 14. Yet, years later, the 1936 DHS Committee on Scottish Health Services Report (the Cathcart Report) found the absence of continuous monitoring of a child's health still to be a problem.[33]

Section 14 (5) of the Local Government (Scotland) Act, 1929, provided for co-operation between the local health authority and the education authority where these authorities were distinct – i.e. in large burghs. In 1930, the DHS and the Scottish Education Department produced a joint memorandum for County Councils to set out what should be included in any scheme of school health service. The School Medical Service was responsible for 800,000 children (one-sixth of the population of Scotland). The main intentions of the service were to provide systematic medical examination of school children, to supervise those who were physically or mentally unfit, to provide treatment for necessitous children, and to ensure that parents had their children treated either at their own or at the public expense. Other guide-lines stressed the provision of meals and milk at schools as required in the light of recent scientific investigations, and the importance of physical instruction in large open areas. Such open areas were to be provided where possible by Burgh and County Councils.

Procedures as to the method and frequency of examination were set out in the 1930 joint memorandum. Medical inspections were to be on an individual basis. That this was pointed out in the memorandum suggests that group inspection of school children was not unknown. Three routine medical inspections were to be held at three points in a primary school child's education: upon entrance, at age ten, and for children leaving school. Finally, the agency of administration of the new reorganised service was discussed:

---

birth to the end of its school life.' NAS, HH61/613, DHS/SED Joint Memorandum, 'Children under School Age' (Edinburgh: HMSO, 1930), 1.

33 DHS, *Committee on the Scottish Health Services Report*, 175.

> It is said that while there is still doubt as to whether the administration of the services should be in the hands of the Education Committee or the Public Health Committee, it will probably be found that in the case of most authorities it should rest with the Education Committee. To secure unity of control it is recommended that the MOH should always be appointed chief administrative school medical officer.[34]

In practice, the education and health committees of local authorities seemed to share the duties. A meeting to discuss the co-ordination of Health, Education and Public Assistance services in Glasgow under the Local Government (Scotland) Act of 1929 unanimously decided on an allocation of duties. '[...] The feeding and clothing of school children be a function of the Education Committee, and the distribution of milk and meals to necessitous children a function of the Health Committee.'[35]

By the end of the first year of operation of the new local government legislation, the numbers of children medically examined had risen slightly from close to 472,000 in the year 1928/9 to 485,490 for 1930/31. The proportion of children examined remained unchanged at a third of the school population.[36] Routine medical inspection as reinforced by the joint memorandum was the subject of contemporary debate. It was felt that routine inspections did not sufficiently monitor child health. Standards of assessment, moreover were not uniform.

The health of school children continued as a joint concern in the 1930s. In fact, by the mid 1930s it seemed that an increasing number of public agencies were assuming responsibility for an expanding range of health and welfare services for school children. On December 12 1935, a series of meetings on 'Welfare Services for Children' was held in Glasgow. Representatives of the DHS, the Scottish Education Department, and officials from the County Councils and Town Councils of the large Burghs, the Scottish Juvenile Welfare and After-

34 *GMJ,* 1930, (1), 93–6, passim.

35 Mitchell Library, Glasgow, Strathclyde Regional Archives, Glasgow Corporation Minutes of Joint Meeting of the Education, Health and Public Assistance Committees, 3 February 1930.

36 DHS, *Annual Report, 1931*, 48.

Care Office and the Commissioner for the Special Areas[37] in Scotland attended the meetings. The meetings were called to explore the possibility of providing additional services for the health and welfare of school children and pre-school children in the Special Areas in Scotland. The DHS and the SED communicated with the Commissioner for the Special Areas to provide information particularly on services which were dependent to some extent on voluntary effort, such as Toddlers' Playgrounds, Day Nurseries and Nursery Schools for pre-school children, and Play Centres for school children. The Commissioner indicated that he would favourably consider applications which made out a good case for financial assistance – particularly as regards capital expenditure to foster these services.[38]

Play Centres, run either by education authorities or by voluntary agencies with school premises provided free by education authorities, were open for two hours on two or three evenings per week, to children of school age. Play Centres provided a supervised indoor recreational pursuits, principally in the winter months: 'A Play Centre is valuable as a means of keeping children off the streets, in developing the spirit of play inherent in every child, and as an influence in the formation of character.'[39] Within a few months of this series of meetings, the Commissioner for the Special Areas in

---

37 By the Special Areas Act of 1934 (extended in 1937 until 1939), the National Government designated a number of geographic areas in Britain suffering particularly badly due to the economic depression and consequent high and persistent unemployment as 'special areas'. Special Areas were given additional funding by the Scottish Special Areas Commissioner, initially Sir Arthur Rose, (or the equivalent Commissioner for England and Wales) to help deal with some of the consequences of the economic depression, in particular to attempt to expand the narrow industrial base of these areas. In Scotland, the designated area was west central Scotland (excluding Glasgow). Other medical services received grants from the Special Areas Commissioner for Scotland. For example, financial assistance was given to the nursing associations of Ayr, Dumbarton, Renfrew, Lanark, Stirling and West Lothian.

38 North Lanarkshire Council, Coatbridge Burgh Archives, DHS/SED, Notes of Meetings on 'Child Welfare Services for Children', 10 January 1936, quoted in Burgh of Coatbridge, Public Health Committee minutes, 4 June 1936.

39 Ibid.

Scotland awarded a grant of £300 for the provision of a toddlers' playground in Paisley. Other local authorities also considered how best to approach the Commissioner for funds.[40] Yet the designated Special Areas were just that, a special case. Overall, there were still gaps in the range and nature of health and welfare services provided for school age children in Scotland. The questions of comprehensive treatment and preventive health care remained far from resolved.

Nutrition, Under-Nutrition and Malnutrition – Milk and the Supplementary Feeding of School Children

> A nutrition policy should have a prior claim on any funds available for extending the health services.
> (PEP *Report on the British Health Services* (1937), 337)

The merits of a healthy diet have long been the subject of discussion among historians with regard to the health of the wider population. The work of Thomas McKeown[41] suggested that improved nutrition was the main factor to account for the decline in mortality from infectious disease, in particular in the nineteenth century. For McKeown, late nineteenth-century public health improvements in sanitation and hygiene played significant, but clearly secondary roles to the positive effects of improved nutrition in accounting for the fall in mortality levels in the nineteenth and early twentieth centuries. Other historians, including Szreter[42] challenged McKeown's views. In

---

40 Ibid.

41 See T. McKeown, *The Modern Rise of Population* (Edwin Arnold, 1976), 15–16, McKeown, *The Origins of Human Disease* (Oxford: Basil Blackwell, 1988), 9, and McKeown, et al, 'An Interpretation of the Decline of Mortality in England and Wales during the Twentieth Century', *Population Studies*, 29 (1975): 391–422.

42 S. Szreter, 'The Importance of Social Intervention in Britain's Mortality Decline, c. 1850–1914: A Re-interpretation of the Role of Public Health', *Social History of Medicine*, 1 (1988): 1–37. Szreter's view stresses the

the context of inter-war school health, the issue of nutrition chiefly centred on the merits of additional milk in the diet.

After the brief boom period in health care provision in the early twentieth century which helped launch the School Medical Service, it did not take long for economic constraint to put pressure on the services provided for school children. The Treasury periodically imposed financial restrictions upon school health services, such as free or cheap milk for school children. Health spending was cut after 1921/2, due to the financial constraints – the so-called Geddes 'Axe'[43] – imposed as the nation slid into depression. In August 1921, the Scottish Board of Health issued a memorandum on the 'Provision of Nourishment for Mothers and Children' which sought to cut back the rising cost of providing milk and meals for mothers and children.[44] Despite this atmosphere of financial constraint, which here focused on supplementary feeding, the nutritional levels of children of school age remained a keen concern for Scottish health agencies throughout the inter-war period.[45]

Although medical thought had long recognised the connection between nutrition and health, the vitamin content of food was still a novel idea and was not fully developed until the late 1920s and especially 1930s, coinciding with a renewed 'fitness of the nation'

---

importance of improved environment (e.g. through public health initiatives, including sanitary reform). This view is discussed in more detail in the next chapter on tuberculosis.

43 As noted in chapter one, a committee of business leaders, under Sir Eric Geddes was appointed by the Government to recommend public expenditure cuts, bringing an end to a period of expansion in post-war social reform. See chapter three for more on the impact of the Geddes cuts on Scottish health services.

44 PRO, MH 55/218, SBH Circular, 'Provision of Nourishment for Mothers and Children', 31 August 1921. 'Milk and food should be given only where the Medical Officer of Health is satisfied that a supply is essential on the grounds of health [...]. For the purposes of determining whether applicants are generally necessitous a scale of income should be adopted suitable to the circumstances of the locality [...].'

45 In England and Wales too, the nutrition of school children was a live issue. The distribution of free milk to badly-nourished children began with the Education Act of 1921, and in 1927, the National Milk Publicity Council launched the milk-in-schools scheme on a self-supporting basis.

debate. Free school meals were available to needy children through education authority and Poor Law mechanisms from the early 1920s, but the path to such feeding was decidedly narrow.[46] However from 1928, the SBH was actively involved in experiments to measure the physical impact of the supplementary feeding of school children.[47]

At this point the role of the expert was crucial in informing health policy. Scottish policy in the realm of school health was influenced by the findings of scientific investigations into the merits of supplementary feeding of children. It involved politicians at the highest level, including two successive Parliamentary Under Secretaries of State for Scotland, Walter Elliot,[48] and Thomas Johnston,[49] and one of the world's leading scientific medical figures, John Boyd Orr.[50] Boyd Orr had been working on the vitamin values of food, (at what became the Rowett Research Institute in Animal Nutrition near Aberdeen), since before World War One. Elliot himself worked with Boyd Orr at the Rowett Research Institute while preparing for his D.Sc. in the early 1920s during parliamentary recesses. Elliot was a consistent supporter of Boyd Orr's views on nutrition and vitamins.[51]

---

46 Tom Johnston described the tortuous procedure before the House of Commons in 1941. An extract from this speech in HOC debates, 18–1–41, vol. 376 col. 1872, is quoted at the beginning of this chapter..

47 Contemporary scientific surveys into dietary values including Dr H.C. Corry Mann's, *Diets for Boys during the School Age*, published by the Medical Research Council in 1926 suggested milk was the most beneficial additional food to be given to children with no dietary deficiencies. See Corry Mann, *Diets for Boys during the School Age* (MRC, Special Report Series, No. 105, 1926), 56. John Boyd Orr's SBH-sponsored survey of children from a range of family circumstances and varied diets took the research further than Corry Mann's survey of a residential institution for boys near London, were the boys had a consistent and adequate diet.

48 See chapter one for full biographical details of Walter Elliot.

49 See chapter one for biographical details of Tom Johnston.

50 Boyd Orr was then Director of the Rowett Research Institute, Aberdeen. See footnote 2 of this chapter for full biographical details of Boyd Orr.

51 Elliot's review of the Medical Research Council report for 1919–1921 appeared in the Tom Johnston-edited radical journal, *Forward* in 1921. See also *Glasgow Herald* and *Scotsman* 13 March 1925, *Lancet* 21 March 1925 and *BMJ* 27 March 1925 for reports of a speech by Elliot at the Andersonian Medical

Elliot's time as PUSH from 1924–26 and as Under Secretary of State for Scotland 1926–29, gave him almost six consecutive years to consolidate his theories on Scottish health. His appointment to the Empire Marketing Board[52] also gave him access to funding and new ideas on how supplementary feeding could also stimulate British agriculture. Elliot was later appointed Minister of Agriculture in 1932, succeeding former Scottish Secretary Sir John Gilmour, who held the post from 1931–2. In fact, two Agriculture Acts in 1931 and 1933, sponsored by Gilmour and Elliot respectively, were introduced to bring some stability to the price of liquid milk and encourage popular milk consumption. These acts paved the way for the creation of the Milk Marketing Board for England and Wales, and a separate board for Scotland.

The idea of systematically nourishing Scottish school children with milk came first from within the Scottish National Milk and

---

College, Glasgow, on preventive medicine. Cuttings of all reports are in Walter Elliot's papers housed in the National Library of Scotland (NLS) catalogue number, 6721, No. 11.

52 The Empire Marketing Board was established in 1926 as an official executive body on the recommendation of the Imperial Economic Committee for the purpose of developing trade with the Empire. One aspect of the committee was to encourage the sale of Empire produce in Britain. Technically, it was an Advisory Committee of the Secretary of State for the Dominions (Colonial Secretary). However it incorporated ex-officio members. The EMB was a non-partisan committee covering every part of the Empire. The Colonial Secretary chaired it, (initially Leo Amery, then J.H. Thomas). Under the auspices of a Scientific Committee, part of the EMB remit was to finance scientific research in Britain and the Empire through existing scientific agencies – hence its support for the research into milk feeding through the Rowett Research Institute in Aberdeen. Acting through the Ministry of Agriculture, the EMB was also concerned with the marketing, grading and production efficiency of fresh produce such as beef, eggs, and flour and malt products. The EMB's Publicity Committee used newspapers, exhibitions, films and poster advertising to enhance its marketing strategy. It was funded through an annual grant voted by parliament. The EMB was abolished in 1933. For more on the Empire Marketing Board see: Stephen Constantine, 'Bringing the Empire Alive: The Empire Marketing Board and Imperial Propaganda, 1926–33' in John M. Mackenzie, ed., *Imperialism and Popular Culture* (Manchester: Manchester University Press, 1986).

Health Association (SNMHA), also known as the 'Milk Experimental Committee'. The SNMHA was founded in 1924 'to promote the use of milk as a healthy food'[53] and to improve ways of using surplus by-products such as casein, lactose and whey. The SNMHA had a formidable executive committee, consisting of Boyd Orr, A.K. Chalmers (former MOH Glasgow), A.S.M. McGregor (then current MOH Glasgow), and representatives of the Scottish Universities, dairy producers, as well as high-ranking officials from the Scottish Board of Agriculture. After a shaky start, the SNMHA proceeded with plans for research in the USA and for an educational promotion campaign in schools. Boyd Orr formed an SNMHA research committee and visited America to enquire into the uses of milk in industry. A publicity officer, Miss Dewdney, was appointed, and after receiving training in London from the National Milk Publicity Council, she returned with the duty of promoting milk as a healthy food in Scotland.[54] Meanwhile, the National Milk Publicity Council launched the first small-scale subsidised milk-in-school schemes in England in 1923.

In June 1926, Dewdney wrote to the Glasgow education authority (GEA) asking to lecture in Glasgow schools on health and diet as part of the SNMHA educational promotion scheme. In her approach to the GEA, Dewdney stated that similar lectures had been successfully given in United States schools for some time.[55] Whilst her approach was under consideration, Dewdney also asked the GEA to co-operate with the SNMHA in a medically supervised experiment of Glasgow school children to assess the nutritive value of milk. After some discussion, the Association's secretary, Mr Hyslop, and a prominent dairyman, Charles Ross, met the GEA and a class room experiment was agreed, dependent on parental agreement.[56] From this

53 The SNMHA was founded as a direct result of the 1923 Dairy Congress in the USA. Scottish delegates returned with enthusiasm and approached the Scottish Board of Health for support, which it, tacitly, received. For more on this organisation see minutes of meetings of the Scottish National Milk and Health Association, NAS, GD1/41/4.

54 See minutes of meetings of the Scottish National Milk and Health Association.

55 Strathclyde Regional Archives, DED 2/1/8, Glasgow Education Authority minutes, 17 June 1926, 272.

56 Ibid., 2 September 1926.

small initiative, taken by a voluntary organisation, within the space of a few years grew a larger, influential movement for the introduction of milk as a supplementary food. The movement reached a notable high point with the passage of the 1934 Milk Act. The transformation of the small SNMHA initiative to national enquiry involved a momentum-gathering combination of voluntary agencies, scientific expertise, local authorities, the SBH and finally, central government.

Prominent SNMHA member, John Boyd Orr sought government aid for the initial project through the Empire Marketing Board[57] (EMB) Research Grants Committee.[58] Boyd Orr told the committee in 1927 that the problem of the dairy industry in Britain and the rest of the Empire, was the disposal of surplus milk. He suggested a campaign to show the nutritive value of milk and increase the sale of liquid milk (more profitable than dried milk) was needed. Walter Elliot's role in obtaining funds for the milk experimental scheme was a key one. In his autobiography, Boyd Orr[59] referred to Elliot's dealings (as a parliamentary representative of the EMB) with scientists who were reluctant to approach the EMB. Elliot would invite them to dinner, get them talking over the brandy and have a secretary take down the conversations which were then considered by a sub-committee of the EMB, describing the method as 'discussing it in drink and then considering it sober'.[60]

With a budget of £3,850 funded by the EMB, and after meetings with the SBH, the SNMHA Glasgow school-milk project was expanded from a localised, to a Scottish experiment. School children in seven towns and cities were involved in the investigation: Aberdeen, Edinburgh, Peterhead, Paisley, Greenock and Dundee were

57 The EMB (1926–1933) established a number of committees to direct its operations, including the Research Grants Committee and a Publicity Committee. Tom Johnston was a member of the Publicity Committee.

58 According to Boyd Orr £250,000 of the EMB's £2 million budget was set aside for research grants. Sir J. Boyd Orr, *As I Recall* (McGibbon and Kee, 1966), 109.

59 Boyd Orr, *As I Recall*, 110–111.

60 Ibid., 111.

now added to Glasgow for the purposes of the extended experiment.[61] Belfast was later added to the list of seven Scottish cities, too late to be included in Boyd Orr's 'Milk Consumption and the Growth of School-Children – Preliminary Report on Tests to the Scottish Board of Health', which appeared in the *Lancet* in 1928. The *Lancet* report made clear the facilitating role played by the SBH medical member William Leslie Mackenzie, and the close involvement of the leading SBH Medical Officer, Dr Lewis Cruikshank in the experiments.[62]

The Empire Marketing Board-funded exercise was carried out between November 1926 and June 1927 under the auspices of Boyd Orr, and the results were correlated at the Rowett Research Institute. The findings were promising, showing increased heights and weights for children drinking a daily ration of one-third pint of milk per day.[63] Children in three age groups (5–6, 8–9, 13–14) were placed in four categories for the seven month experiment: controls, and those given supplementary biscuits, separated milk, and whole milk. The experiment showed an average monthly increase across the age-groups of 0.17 inches in height and 0.42lb in weight for those who were non milk fed. This was far exceeded by the average monthly increase of 0.21 inches and 0.52lb for the milk-fed groups.[64]

The *Lancet* (commenting on the milk investigation report included in that edition in January 1928) declared:

---

61 NAS, GD1/41/4, Note of meeting between the Scottish Board of Health and the Scottish National Milk and Health Association, 12 November, 1926

62 'The tests were conducted under the auspices of a committee appointed by the Board of Health for Scotland with Sir Leslie Mackenzie as Chairman. The committee consisted of the school medical officers for the cities and towns where the work was carried out. Four women medical officers undertook the collection of data. The late Dr L.D. Cruikshank, of the Scottish Board of Health, and the school medical officers' made the clinical examination of the children.' *Lancet*, 1928, (1), 202.

63 'The addition of milk to the diet of school-children, during the seven months' experimental period, has been accompanied by a rate of growth as indicated by an increase in both height and weight 20% greater than in children not receiving the extra milk.' Ibid., 203.

64 Ibid., 202.

> The investigation of Dr. Orr is of special value because it applies to children who live in their [own] homes. The result is a striking commentary on the glib statement which one hears and reads so frequently that on the whole the dietary of the people in this country is adequate.[65]

The first survey was so successful that the SBH organised a further year's trial in 1927/8[66] administered by its own medical staff, under the organisation of Gerald Leighton,[67] Medical Officer (Foods) to the SBH. Leighton's report in the *Lancet,* stated that the findings of the 1926/27 investigation appeared to the SBH test committee to be so interesting and important that the committee decided to continue the experiment for a further year.[68]

The second report showed further increases in height in weight for children who received additional milk feeding. 'Not only have the same milk-fed children benefited again, but they have done so to a greater extent than before. Their initial improvement has continued over the second year.'[69] These two reports attracted much interest from the medical press at the time.[70] The second report on milk

---

65 Ibid., 40.

66 Funding was again defrayed by the Empire Marketing Board by grant to the Rowett Research Institute, Aberdeen.

67 Gerald Rowley Leighton, born in 1868, was educated at Nelson College, New Zealand and Manchester Grammar School. He obtained qualified MB CM in 1895 at Edinburgh University and obtained an MD in 1901. He moved into general practice in Herefordshire for a year. In 1902, he was appointed Professor of Pathology at the Royal Veterinary College Edinburgh, later Professor of Pathology and Bacteriology. He published a number of books on the meat industry and problems of food preservation. He was appointed Medical Officer (Foods) to the LGBS in 1913, an office he continued under the SBH. He was awarded an OBE and a Honorary DSc by the University of Syracuse, and died in 1953.

68 'Milk Consumption and the Growth of School-children – Second Preliminary Report on Tests to the Scottish Board of Health.' *Lancet*, 1929 (1), 40.

69 Ibid., 43. The second test included figures for Belfast, but not Paisley which did not continue with the study for the second year.

70 '1,425 school children between the ages of 6 and 14 were divided into four groups. One group was given three-quarters of a pint of whole milk daily – the quantity determined by age; one group was given separated milk; one group was given a biscuit ration of the calorific value of the separated milk; and the fourth group acted as controls [...] The home feeding of the children showed

consumption covered 1,425 school children (the figures for 1157 children were incorporated into tabular findings). The two older age groups (9–10 and 13–14) were given an extra pint of milk per day, the

	Number of Children	Height Increase (inches)	Weight Increase (pounds)
Age 13–14			
Whole milk	68	1.45	5.57
Separated milk	69	1.49	5.71
Biscuits	67	1.12	4.42
Control	66	1.27	4.10
Total	270		
Age 9–10			
Whole milk	105	1.42	3.53
Separated milk	83	1.36	3.28
Biscuits	101	1.11	2.04
Control	111	1.11	2.06
Total	400		
Age 6–7			
Whole milk	121	1.56	2.71
Separated milk	121	1.45	2.36
Biscuits	115	1.24	2.16
Control	130	1.24	1.58
Total	487		

Table 4.1 Weight and Height Gain among Scottish School Children in SBH Milk Consumption Survey, 1928[71]

---

ordinary variations. Accurate measurements of eight and weight were taken, and an estimate of the general mental and physical condition made. The extraordinary results confirm Dr Orr's earlier observations [...]. In weight, height, mentality, and nutritional standard the milk-fed children outstripped all the others [...]. Between the milk-fed groups and the controls there was an average difference in growth between 0.2 and 0.3 inches; and in weight of between 1.2 and 1.5 pounds. The teachers of the children, as independent observers, were in no doubt as to the acquired superiority of milk-fed pupils.' *GMJ*, 1929 (1), 107–8.

71 *Lancet*, 1929 (1), 41.

youngest (age 5–6) were given three-quarters of a pint. Each child was measured four times during the course of the yearlong experiment. Measurements were taken on each occasion with children wearing light clothing and without shoes. The positive effects of milk consumption for the school children sampled can be seen in table 4.1.

In 1930, Tom Johnston, Labour Parliamentary Under Secretary of State for Scotland (1929–31), gained EMB funding for an extended study of milk feeding on 20,000 Lanarkshire children (10,000 acted as controls). The DHS report on the survey noted its importance: '[...] for the first time a Government Department, in this case the Department of Health for Scotland, made itself responsible for a daily milk supply to 10,000 children for a period of over four months [...].'[72]

The scheme in Lanarkshire was the largest milk testing experiment to date in Scotland. This was partly in response to peer group complaints that the previous experiments were too small-scale to produce representative findings.[73] The scheme was launched on 15 February 1930. It covered 67 schools in the Lanarkshire area, and had twin aims: to test the value of milk as a food for growing children, and to help relieve distress in Lanarkshire. The scientific aspect of the scheme was stressed in local press reports and public meetings to remove any suggestion of social stigma from participation in the exercise:

> As far as Bellshill is concerned, the following schools come under the scheme: Bellshill Public School, Belvidere Public School, Mossend R.C. School and Mossend Public School. Bellshill Academy is at present outwith the experiment [...]. It, however, must be borne in mind that this is solely an experiment and the public must not deem it as for necessitous children.[74]

72 DHS, *Milk Consumption and the Growth of School Children* (Edinburgh: HMSO, 1930), 5.

73 'Previous experiments on the same lines have been criticised on the grounds that they were on too small a scale to justify the conclusions which were drawn from the striking increased weights and heights of the children after the experiments.' North Lanarkshire Council, Coatbridge Burgh Archives, *Bellshill Speaker*, Friday 14 February, 1930.

74 Ibid.

The scheme covered children aged from 6 to 11 years. It was administered by the DHS assisted by the Lanarkshire education authority. From 17 February until the closing of the schools in July 1930, 10,000 children received a ration of three-quarters of a pint of Grade A tuberculin-tested milk, 5,000 received untreated milk, and the other 5,000 received pasteurised milk. A further 10,000 received no extra milk and were used as controls. All the children were weighed and measured for purposes of comparison. The estimated cost of the experiment was £9,000, to which the Empire Marketing Board contributed £5,000 and the Central Advisory Committee of the Miners' Distress Fund provided £2,000. One intention of the mass experiment was to encourage increased consumption of milk to benefit local agriculture. A sounder medico-scientific goal was the intention to eradicate surgical tuberculosis by popularising tubercule-free milk.[75]

Almost £500 towards the overall cost of the experiment was raised locally by donations from companies and individuals in the dairy industry. The scheme entailed the consumption of 950 gallons of milk per day. The milk was obtained from tubercle-free cattle in Lanarkshire, Ayrshire, Aberdeenshire, and Dumfriesshire. A key feature in the EMB financial support for the Lanarkshire scheme was the publicity it attracted and the hope that this would have a knock-on effect of increasing milk consumption across the whole population. In its coverage of the experiment, the local Lanarkshire press drew attention to low levels of milk consumption in Scotland. The *Belshill Speaker* noted: 'Scotland is one of the smallest milk consuming countries in the world per head of population and an increased consumption, it is held, would benefit the public health as well as the agricultural industry.'[76]

Scottish Secretary of State, William Adamson referred positively to the scheme during the May 1930 debate in the House of Commons on the annual grant for Scottish agriculture.[77] Adamson made the economic argument for increased milk consumption. Adamson

75 *BMJ*, 1930, (1), 357.

76 *Bellshill Speaker*, Friday 14 February, 1930.

77 See report in *GMJ*, 1930 (2), 84.

expressed the hope that the results of the Lanarkshire experiment would demonstrate the value of fresh milk, and particularly of milk from tubercule-free herds, as a food for children. He hoped it would provoke greater consumption of milk and lead to increased production levels in the dairy farming industry.[78]

The Lanarkshire project was discussed at a meeting of the Scottish National Milk and Health Association, (SNMHA) held in Glasgow on 21 February 1930. Dr Gerald Leighton, Medical Officer (Foods) of the DHS said that investigations had originally been carried out with 1,000 children, but this number was not regarded by statisticians as sufficient to warrant generalisations of any significance. He hoped that, as a result of the Lanarkshire experiment with 20,000 children (plus 10,000 controls), they would be able within twelve months to advocate a policy of giving children as much milk as they could digest. W.J. Harvey, Edinburgh-based treasurer of the SNMHA, referred to the public prejudice against milk, particularly as a food for adults. The SNMHA had the support of the medical profession and the local authorities, and Harvey asked the milk industry to use the opportunity of the wide attention given to the Lanarkshire experiment for more intensive propaganda to promote the industry.[79]

The final report of the Lanarkshire experiment was written up by Leighton and Peter McKinlay[80] and was published by the DHS under the title *Milk Consumption and the Growth of School Children* in 1930. The findings were clearly set out in the introduction to the Report by DHS Chief Medical Officer John Parlane Kinloch: '[...] the addition of milk to the diet of children has a striking affect in improving physique and general health and increasing mental alertness.'[81] The investigation showed no difference between the increases in height and weight for those given untreated (raw) milk and those given pasteurised milk. It was a common public misconception at the time that treated milk was less nutritious than

78 HOC debates, 22–5–30, vol. 239 col. 604.

79 *BMJ* 1930, (1), 462.

80 McKinlay was Medical Officer (Statistics) at the DHS in 1930.

81 DHS, *Milk Consumption and the Growth of School Children*, 3.

milk taken in its whole state. Table 4.2 lists the average increases in heights and weights of the children used in the Lanarkshire school experiment. Significant differences in weight and height increases appeared in milk-fed boys of all ages, but for girls the improvement in the milk-fed pupils only became noticeable from the age of seven and above.

	Boys			Girls		
			Weight Increase in Ounces			
Age	Control	Raw Milk	Pasteur. Milk	Control	Raw Milk	Pasteur. Milk
5	11.64	14.88	15.65	7.00	14.50	6.62
6	13.75	13.51	9.96	11.21	10.61	10.05
7	11.17	14.85	15.55	8.90	11.22	12.94
8	11.38	14.21	15.21	9.77	13.40	13.37
9	9.53	13.43	11.83	7.87	13.81	12.52
10	7.10	13.53	10.39	9.51	15.08	18.96
11	6.14	12.74	11.05	12.62	24.92	17.08
			Height Increase in Inches			
5	0.75	0.95	0.94	0.86	0.64	0.87
6	0.80	0.87	0.87	0.80	0.86	0.84
7	0.76	0.87	0.82	0.75	0.84	0.81
8	0.74	0.82	0.79	0.71	0.81	0.78
9	0.69	0.80	0.74	0.66	0.76	0.78
10	0.68	0.76	0.68	0.71	0.79	0.72
11	0.69	0.74	0.70	0.77	0.86	0.81

Table 4.2 Weight and Height Gain among Lanarkshire School Children, 1930[82]

The reorganisation of local health provision under the Local Government (Scotland) Act of 1929 provided fresh impetus for the School Medical Service in general and supplementary nutrition in particular. The Joint 1930 DHS/SED memorandum 'Children under

82 Ibid., 16.

School Age' referred to earlier stressed that proper balance of diet was just as important as the provision of adequate amounts of food.

> The value of milk in supplying this balance has been clearly demonstrated in these experiments. School children, as a rule, do not receive sufficient milk. The improvement in physique which follows the increase in milk dietary has been shown to be accompanied by definite mental improvement. It is pointed out that Education Authorities have the power to supply food to necessitous children, and to provide the accommodation for preparing and supplying meals to pupils. They are strongly urged to take full advantage of these powers.[83]

One tangible result of the scientific investigations into milk feeding was the passage of the Education (Scotland) Act of 1930. DHS Chief Medical Officer John Parlane Kinloch highlighted the findings of the Lanarkshire experiment as giving a special significance to the new powers conferred on local authorities by the Education (Scotland) Act. 'In view of the results of these Scottish tests, it would be difficult to exaggerate the importance of the new powers.'[84] The 1930 Education Act had the sole purpose of allowing local education authorities to provide milk for all school children irrespective of circumstances.[85]

Walter Elliot introduced the legislation as a Private Member's Bill which, when enacted, had the result of extending the experimental Scottish schemes of free (or cheap) milk for school children.[86] A

83 See *GMJ*, 1930, (1), 94 for a report on the 1930 DHS/SED memorandum, 'Children under School Age'.

84 DHS, *Milk Consumption and the Growth of School Children*, 3.

85 'Measures which have been previously brought forward, with regard to the provision of meals and so on, hinge on the question of necessitous children, but in this Bill there is no proposal to differentiate between necessitous and non-necessitous children, for the reason that the experiments have shown that the average school child in Scotland suffers from a shortage of certain vital constituents, which would not entitle a local authority to put it down as a child that was necessitous and that [it] ought to be supplied with meals or food as such.' HOC debates, 23–5–30, vol. 239, col. 710.

86 'It shall be lawful for an education authority, if they think fit, in addition to any powers already vested in them, to incur expenditure and to defray the same out of the education fund in supplying milk in accordance with a scheme approved by the Scottish Education Department and the Department of Health for

similar Act was introduced later in England. As a consequence of the new, permissive, legislation, local authorities in West Lothian and Selkirk adopted short-term small-scale schemes for supplying milk to school children.[87] So, too, did the Edinburgh City Council Education Committee. On 26 January 1931, the committee approved an experimental scheme to provide a third of a pint of milk to necessitous children already on its free food roll in two inner city schools. It also agreed to provide the same milk at a penny a bottle for other children in these schools. The milk was to be of the same Grade A TT milk as had been used in previous experiments.[88] This Edinburgh scheme was continued into 1933 covering 6,000 children, although only 350 of the children received free milk. A similar scheme in Aberdeen involved the parents of 8,000 school children paying a penny a day for milk.[89] In Glasgow, a pilot scheme covering 6,000 children was extended in 1935 to a city-wide 'milk-in-schools scheme' to cover 142,000 children in the city. In the year 1936/7, it was estimated that over 2 million bottles containing a third of a pint of milk were issued free of charge to Scottish school children or at a charge of a halfpenny for non-necessitous children.[90]

With convinced supporter Elliott in place as Minster for Agriculture, the Scottish pilot project became national policy. The 1934 Milk Act instituted a national scheme for the provision of milk in schools. A facilitating Act, it made a £500,000 government grant available for a year to allow the Milk Marketing Boards to extend the various local milk-in-schools schemes, in order to make milk available in third-of-a-pint bottles to all children in schools. The Milk Act also included provisions for improving the quality of milk supply and for increasing the demand for milk. The Treasury agreed to pay up to half the cost of expenditure by Milk Marketing Boards to increase demand for milk.[91]

Scotland to pupils attending schools within their area.' Education (Scotland) Act, 1930 Section 1.

87 *BMJ*, 1931 (2), 228.

88 *BMJ*, 1931 (1), 238.

89 *BMJ*, 1933 (2), 272 .

90 *BMJ*, 1938 (1), 1067.

91 See Milk Act, 31 July 1934, Sections 9 and 11.

The milk scheme was first introduced as a temporary measure, but was prolonged by extending legislation in 1936, and was still in operation at the outbreak of World War Two. The Act also sought to ensure improved milk quality and to safeguard milk prices.[92] The national scheme was delayed in Scotland until 1935, but launched in England in October 1934. Within a month, over 50 million bottles of milk were supplied to school children.[93] By 1935, 13 Scottish local education authorities were operating the 'milk-in-schools' scheme, providing milk to almost 200,000 children, with more planned to follow. The schemes by this time came under the jurisdiction of the Scottish Milk Marketing Board.[94] In 1936, 321,00 children from a Scottish school population of 807,000 were receiving milk.[95] In June 1936, the Scottish Milk Marketing Board opened five milk bars in densely-populated parts of Glasgow to sell milk at one and a half pence (1p) per pint to pre-school children and to school children during school holidays.[96]

Milk was now available in schools free of charge or at subsidised rates. However, the proportion of school children in receipt of school meals remained tiny. Figures for England and Wales in 1938 showed that in terms of free food supplements, 11.5% of school children received free milk, 2.8% received free milk and food, and 1.2% received food only.[97] The discrepancy between the numbers of school children receiving milk and the smaller number receiving meals can in part be explained by the government desire to reduce the milk surplus by encouraging milk consumption in Britain. There was no such government necessity to intervene to support the food industry.

92 *BMJ*, 1936 (1), 345.
93 *BMJ*, 1935 (1), 218.
94 *BMJ*, 1935 (1), 342.
95 *BMJ*, 1936 (2), 129.
96 'At first the bars were a great success, but they seemed to have suffered from the novelty wearing off.' PEP, *Report on the British Health Services*, 329.
97 Board of Education, *Report of the Chief Medical Officer of the Board of Education for 1938* (HMSO, 1939), 28.

Under-Nourishment or Malnutrition?

The nutritional requirements of school children were given further prominence during the years of severe depression in Britain when it was suggested that more children were suffering from under-nourishment than the official records suggested. The *Glasgow Medical Journal* reported in 1934 that the pressure group the Children's Minimum Council[98] had submitted a memorandum to the Unemployment Assistance Board. In the memorandum, the Council claimed that the incidence of under-nutrition requiring treatment among school children was higher than the figure given in Sir George Newman's 1932 Annual Report for the Board of Education.[99] The Council noted that in experiments where additional milk was given to large numbers of unselected children in elementary schools, considerable increases in height and weight resulted: 'among children of whom presumably only a very small proportion are officially suffering from under-nourishment.'[100]

Controversy on the well-being of school children (and the wider British population) in the 1930s extended to the use of terminology. 'Under-nutrition' was the term used by some public health officials to identify the condition of those children and adults who received insufficient calories in the diet to properly function (a condition which could lead to starvation in extreme cases). 'Malnutrition' on the other hand, was used to signify the intake of a faulty diet – that is, an intake of foods deficient in essential minerals and vitamins, which could lead to chronic disease e.g. anaemia, rickets.[101] This distinction could be used to distinguish in nutritional terms between the 'deserving' and the 'undeserving' or to explain inadequate nutrition as simply due to a

98 The Children's Minimum Council was set up in 1934, and included Eleanor Rathbone, (Independent MP for the Combined English Universities, 1929–46, leader of the National Union of Societies for Equal Citizenship and campaigner for Family Allowances), among its members.

99 Sir George Newman was Chief Medical Officer of the Ministry of Health (1919–1935). Between 1907–1919 he was CMO of the Board of Education.

100 *GMJ*, 1934 (2), 215.

101 See PEP, *Report on the British Health Services*, 320.

lack of knowledge of the best foodstuffs to ensure a healthy diet. Improved nutritional education, for example through cookery classes, was, of course, a less expensive government option than embarking on a national food policy to improve the overall health of the nation. To add to the confused contemporary debate on deficient diet these distinctions of 'under-nourishment' and 'malnutrition' were not always used.

Into the contemporary controversy between official and other estimates of the levels of under-nourishment stepped John Boyd Orr with the publication in March 1936, of *Food, Health and Income*. The book revealed a picture of widespread inadequate diet in Great Britain among working class families. There was keen press interest in Boyd Orr's report. This was partly due to his BBC radio broadcast on 26 February 1936. Speaking on the programme 'Our Children's Scotland' Boyd Orr called for an increase in income tax to raise Treasury funds for a 'national food policy.' Boyd Orr thought that such a policy would allow any glut in foodstuffs to be directed to those in need.[102] Boyd Orr's radio appearance prompted the *News Chronicle* to declare:

> A week hence Sir John Orr is to publish his great personal survey of 'Food, Health and Income' that should help to revolutionise our social system [...] The facts revealed should rouse every housewife in the country and create such a demand for a new food policy that the Government will have to capitulate [...].'[103]

Boyd Orr's research indicated that the diets of only 50% of the country's population were completely adequate for health, according to modern standards of nutrition.[104] Boyd Orr's findings indicated that

---

102 Rowett Research Institute Archive, Aberdeen, press cuttings file, *Daily Herald*, 27 February, 1936.

103 Ibid., press cuttings file, *News Chronicle*, Thursday 5 March 1936: 'It is in the mind of Sir John Orr that the amount of money spent by Britain in fighting disease is so colossal and the amount of money spent on organising health so relatively minute, that a fair exchange of cash and attention is not only fair, but essential – and possible.'

104 John Boyd Orr, *Food, Health and Income: Report on a Survey of Adequacy of Diet in Relation to Income* (William Clowes and Sons, 1936), Foreword.

within his six defined income groups, the lowest group contained a disproportionately high number of children – more than twenty per cent of all children.[105] Boyd Orr considered children particularly susceptible to the ill effects of inadequate nutrition, owing to the requirement for new tissue formation in growth. Boyd Orr was convinced that children need a diet richer in first-class protein, in minerals and probably also in vitamins, than adults[106] – milk was therefore an essential nutritional source for children. Boyd Orr showed that milk consumption was very much influenced by income. In the lowest income group the average milk consumption per head per week was 1.1 pints, while in the highest it was 5.5 pints.[107] For the positive effects of additional milk in the diet, Boyd Orr referred directly to the SBH/DHS studies in additional milk feeding in school-children carried out between 1926–1930, which indicated a 20% greater growth rate for those receiving additional milk over those receiving no additional milk. The increased growth rate was accompanied by a noticeable improvement in health and vigour.[108]

Meantime, while poorer children suffered from insufficient nutrition, and notwithstanding the increased milk provision to schools made available from 1934, there still remained a large milk surplus in Britain. In both Houses of Parliament, the debate arising from Boyd Orr's findings focused on whether the existing milk scheme could be extended to provide subsidised milk to include all children, expectant and nursing mothers, and infants.[109]

105 Ibid., Foreword, and 21. This lowest income group [group 1] consisted of 10% of the population with an income per head of 10 shillings per week. The richest income group [group 6], also 10% of the population, had an income per head per week of over 45 shillings. For statistical purposes, Boyd Orr weighted the population by income into four mid range groups each of 20%, with a further 10% at the top and bottom of the income scale.

106 Ibid., 38.

107 Ibid., 29.

108 Ibid., 48.

109 In the House of Commons, the Labour opposition proposed: '[...] that on the grounds of health the Government should provide £7,000,000 a year to ensure adequate milk being brought within the reach of children and others [...]. It was emphasised that the Party's demand for free distribution of milk to those who most need it, but cannot afford to buy at present prices, was made as a practical

In the Lords, the Bishop of Winchester used Boyd Orr's findings published only a few days before in *Food, Health and Income* as evidence for his motion to extend the state provision of milk to other vulnerable sections of the population. He also pointed out that there was an excess milk supply in Britain. While not wanting to enter the well-known 1930s political debate too far,[110] it is clear that the whole question of milk as a supplementary food was in the public eye not simply because of the findings of nutritionists into its qualities as a food, but because of Government policy. There was a degree of hypocrisy in promoting milk consumption to take up the surplus milk production while at the same time side-stepping the much wider, and potentially more costly, issue of addressing widespread under-nourishment in the country as a whole. Tom Johnston who, in July 1936, moved a censure motion criticising government policy specifically on this issue brought the controversy forcefully before the Commons:

> That this House had noted with concern the convincing evidence of widespread malnutrition, is of opinion that the destruction of essential foodstuffs is a crime against society and regrets the continued failure of His Majesty's Government

---

proposal for improving the nation's health.' Rowett Research Institute Archive, Aberdeen, press cuttings file, *Daily Herald,* 18 February, 1936. In the Lords, the Bishop of Winchester: '[...] rose to ask His Majesty's Government if, in view of widespread malnutrition and the existence of a large milk surplus, they will take steps to extend still further the provision already made to supply liquid milk to school children and to initiate a scheme on similar lines for expectant and nursing mothers and for children under five.' HOL debates, 18–3–36, vol. 100, col. 59.

110 Local SMO and national data on school health provided evidence and counter-evidence for the possible scale of under-nutrition (malnutrition in today's terms) among school children. This was debated at the time and has been a subject of debate by historians. For more on the possible under-reporting by national Government agencies of malnutrition in Britain in the 1930s, see Webster, 'Healthy or Hungry Thirties?': 110–129, and 'The Health of the School Child during the Depression', in N. Parry and D. McNair, eds, *The Fitness of the Nation – Physical and Health Education in the Nineteenth and Twentieth Centuries* (History of Education Society, 1983), 70:85.

to take effective steps to deal with this grave and urgent problem of hunger and want in the midst of plenty.[111]

The Minister of Health, Sir Kingsley Wood, urged caution on distorting the views of Boyd Orr for political purposes and instead cited the opinion of another member of the Ministry of Health Committee on Nutrition, E.P. Cathcart, that 'malnutrition' was not so much due to poverty as to ignorance.[112] The predictable Government response was that better education rather than a national nutrition policy was the solution to the problem of 'malnutrition'.[113]

Physical Health and School Nutrition in the later 1930s

At the Empire Exhibition held in Bellahouston Park, Glasgow, in 1938, a 'Fitter Britain' exhibit was staged in the 'United Kingdom Government Pavilion'. The exhibit was jointly organised by the Ministry of Health, the DHS, the Board of Education, the National Fitness Council, and a number of local authorities and voluntary agencies. The exhibit promoted family health and happiness. In the middle of the exhibit was a giant sculpture of a family group, and a working model of a 'Mechanical Man' (the top half of a human body) around four times actual size. Bays around the hall featured sculptures, photographs and diorama illustrating municipal provisions, including maternity and child welfare services, the School Medical Service, and a community centre providing for 'healthful games and recreations'. The whole exhibit was described in glowing terms by *Public Health* (the journal of local MOsH) as '[...] quite outstanding,

111 HOC debates, 8–7–36, vol. 314 col. 1229.

112 HOC debates, 8–7–36, vol. 314 col. 1243.

113 Johnston's censure motion was defeated. Instead, a motion approving the National Government's efforts to secure a equitable food supply (to both consumers and suppliers) and to promote the health and social conditions of the population was passed by almost 200 votes. HOC debates, 8–7–36, vol. 314 col. 1337–1350.

not only for its size, but for the excellence of its presentation and the interest of its component parts.'[114] It was hoped the exhibit (under the auspices of the Central Council for Health Education) would tour the country.[115] Yet the government discussions, belated legislative provisions and exhibits designed to promote health and physical efficiency, especially among the youth of Britain, did not address the wider problem of poverty and chronic under-nourishment which was attracting growing scientific and public attention in these years.

School feeding and poor nutrition re-emerged as a parliamentary issue in March 1937, when Tom Johnston again provocatively questioned Walter Elliot on Government policy regarding the provision of school meals.

> In view of the desirability of having uniformity in this matter, would not the Secretary of State consider the issue of a request to the local authorities to stop a practice whereby poor children may starve for long periods in certain areas?'[116]

In response, Elliot denied that the Scottish Education Department had issued instructions to insist upon a medical certificate proving under-nutrition before food was supplied to school children. Instead, discretionary powers to provide school meals were given to head teachers pending further investigations into the circumstances of the child. The 'starvation' issue he refused to consider.[117]

The Scottish policy outlined by Elliot differed from the position in England in Wales. The separate administration of school meals in Scotland led to a different approach. For example, in September 1934, a circular issued by the Minister of Education restricted English local authorities to provide milk or meals only to those poor children who

---

114 *Public Health*, 58, (1938), 258.

115 The Empire Exhibition in Glasgow contained both the 'Fitter Britain' Exhibit in the UK Government Pavilion and a 'Health, Housing and Town Planning Exhibit' in the Scottish Pavilion. See programme of the 11th Annual Health Education Conference, held at the Empire Exhibition Cinema, Bellahouston Park, Glasgow, 28–29 September 1938, GRHB D10\1\14, Grampian Health Board Archives, Aberdeen,

116 HOC debates, 16–3–37, vol. 321 col. 1839.

117 Ibid.

had been medically-certified as undernourished. According to Elliot, no such certificate was needed for the granting of school meals in Scotland. Yet, in practice, it proved difficult to provide meals for Scots school children, otherwise than for full payment, unless the child was actually showing signs of want of food. Even in these circumstances, payment was sometimes obtained.[118] For example, in the year 1935/6, of the 33,800 meals given Scots school children 'suffering from lack of food', payments were taken from 5,200 children.[119] In a period of severe economic depression, even extreme poverty was not sufficient grounds to allow school children easy access to supplementary nutrition.

In 1937, John Boyd Orr initiated an extended dietary and clinical survey of 1,000 poor families in Scotland and a sample survey of England. The Carnegie Trust funded the investigation. Boyd Orr contacted the Secretary of State for Scotland, Walter Elliot, to solicit DHS involvement in the survey. His overture was based on the fact that the Rowett Research Institute, Aberdeen was at the time already carrying out a dietary survey of 85 families in the centre and north of Scotland for the DHS.[120]

Boyd Orr clearly viewed his survey as having an important role in future Scottish health policy formulation. He later addressed a joint meeting attended by six representatives of the DHS, and single representatives of the Department of Agriculture and the Scottish Education Department, to discuss possible government support for the investigation. Despite declaring an interest in Boyd Orr's survey,

---

118 PEP, *Report on the British Health Services*, 125.

119 Ibid., 328.

120 'It is unnecessary to point out that when completed, it will form the most complete investigation which has ever been carried out, and will yield information which will be invaluable as a guide to public health and social measures, and also yield information of value in connection with the reorganisation of agriculture in so far as it will show the extent to which the consumption of protective foodstuffs is likely to be increased with a rise in the standard of living and the spread of the new knowledge of the influence of food on health.' PRO, MH 56/220, Sir John Boyd Orr, Imperial Bureau of Animal Nutrition, Rowett Institute, Aberdeen to Walter Elliot, Scottish Secretary of State, 16 April 1937.

advice and some statistical assistance was all that was promised by the three Scottish Departments.[121] A DHS minute to the Scottish Secretary of State clearly recognised the importance of Boyd Orr's planned survey and the political use which could be made of it.

> This inquiry breaks new ground by associating with a dietary survey an attempt at assessing the nutritional state of the persons whose diet is examined. An inquiry of this sort may be expected to throw light on the extent to which nutrition is capable of influencing health and physique and may clear up many points in this connection which are at present in doubt.[122]

However, the memorandum came to the conclusion that there should be no formal links between the DHS and Boyd Orr's inquiry. The fear was that the DHS might become formally associated with an inquiry whose procedure and findings might not coincide with Government health policy.[123] In July 1938, Boyd Orr returned to his theme of the importance for the government of sponsoring child health in a public address at the Empire Exhibition held in Glasgow. Boyd Orr declared that the provision of meals and milk in schools, alongside maternity services, and child welfare clinics were 'bearing fruit' in a fitter and healthier 'race'.[124]

---

121 PRO, MH 56/220, minute of meeting of representatives of the Departments of Health, Agriculture and Education with Sir John Boyd Orr, held at the Department of Health, 7 June 1937.

122 PRO MH, 56/220, Minute by J.W. Hamill, DHS, to Scottish Secretary of State, Walter Elliot, 16 June 1937.

123 'One reason why I think we should not be formally associated with the inquiry [...] is that no matter how closely we were associated with the inquiry we could not control the procedure and we would have to accept responsibility for the inquiry and its results in spite of the fact that there might be much in its conduct with which we were dissatisfied.' J.W. Hamill to Walter Elliot, 16 June 1937.

124 'Those who grudge the expenditure of so much public money on the different health services of the country were replied to yesterday by Sir John Boyd Orr when, at a conference at the Empire Exhibition on Glasgow, he asked – "What better dividend could a Government get for the expenditure of public funds than the improved health, physique, and happiness of the rising generation? These are the nation's greatest assets." The maternity services, child welfare clinics, the provision of meals and milk in schools were all schemes that were now beginning to bear fruit in a fitter and healthier race, he declared.' Rowett

The debate in the 1920s and 30s on milk feeding, diet and under-nutrition was a wider one than the issue of milk in schools, and the activities of the SBH, (later DHS), and Scottish scientific evidence were crucial in airing the debate. Looking back, Boyd Orr viewed the years of investigation into milk in the diet to have been a time of positive achievement. However, Boyd Orr felt that it took the outbreak of war and the creation of a separate Ministry of Food to fully implement his (and others) scientific findings in to government policy.

> It was a great satisfaction to all of us when the surplus milk which had been poured down the drains was directed to the empty bellies of poor children. The full fruition of the campaign came when Lord Woolton, Minister of Food in the Second World War, brought in a food policy based on nutritional needs, with priority for health foods for mothers and children.[125]

The Impact of World War Two on School-Age Children

On the eve of World War Two, the 1938 Glasgow education authority annual report confirmed the continuing trend of progressive and definite improvement in the average weight and height of the city's school children. Group measurements for the years 1937/8 showed that figures for the six groups of children – namely, boys and girls at 5, 9, and 13 years – were the highest recorded to date. Yet these averages could not hide marked class-based variations in the overall encouraging picture:

> There are still quite well-marked differences in the average heights and weights of scholars in the better class schools as compared with those attending schools in the poorer districts, nevertheless the gains have been participated in to an

Research Institute Archive, Aberdeen press cuttings file, *Glasgow Herald*, Wednesday 20 July 1938.

125 Boyd Orr, *As I Recall*, 118.

almost equal degree by the children of all social grades. Dental disease is still far too common.[126]

Schemes of additional feeding for children continued during World War Two. The DHS and the Ministry of Health formed a joint Advisory Committee on Nutrition, which included Boyd Orr and E.P. Cathcart among the expert physiologists. The Advisory Committee recommended that milk consumption be encouraged for the population as a whole by reducing prices and that the shortfall in calorific intake due to a wartime sugar shortage be made up with an increased consumption of potatoes.[127]

Initially, the wartime situation disrupted existing milk-in-school schemes (and more widely, the School Medical Service itself). For example, the quantity of milk consumed in Scottish schools had fallen almost by half by the end of 1939 from the pre-war level.[128] However, acting on advice from the Nutrition Advisory Committee and through the agency of the Ministry of Food this trend was overturned, and milk and meals were increasingly supplied in Scottish schools. By 1941, Scottish Secretary of State Tom Johnston estimated that 50,000 Scottish school children were receiving a well balanced meal either free of charge or supplied at cost price for those with the ability to pay.[129] Yet experience showed that supplementary nutrition could be affected by local circumstances. In the middle of 1941, meals (malted milk, cocoa, and soup) were provided to 532 local children and 40 evacuees in the Borders County of Berwick. However, the 'Milk in Schools' scheme was curtailed in April 1941 depriving the children in 21 Berwick schools of supplementary milk. Local milk distributors brought the school milk supply for these schools to a halt. The suppliers' felt the financial allowance they received from the Scottish

126 Glasgow Corporation Public Health Department, *29th Annual Report on the Medical Inspection and Treatment of School Children* (Glasgow, 1938) cited in *GMJ*, 1939 (1), 125.

127 PRO, MH79/374, Note of an Informal Conference called by the Minister of Health and the Secretary of State for Scotland and physiologists, 19 December 1939.

128 Titmuss, *Problems of Social Policy*, 138.

129 *BMJ*, 1941 (2), 252.

Milk Marketing Board [SMMB] was insufficient to cover their costs. This was because the allowance was based on numbers of bottles distributed. Hence, no more allowance was made by the SMMB for distributing milk in an area of 450 square miles to 21 schools than was allowed for its distribution to three or four schools in a town area of only one square mile. Meanwhile this unfortunate group of Berwick children lost out.[130]

In the House of Commons in December 1941, Scottish Secretary of State Johnston in moving the Second Reading of an Education (Scotland) Bill stated its aim was to extend the school meals system as a preventive measure to avoid malnutrition, rather than treat the effects of it.[131] Johnston's emotive comments clearly touched on the contemporary debate on whether state expenditure should be directed towards preventive or curative health provision.[132] The costs of supplementary feeding as a preventive measure to improve the health of the nation was, of course, likely to be much more than the cost of supplying supplementary meals and milk for only those certified as under-nourished after medical examination. The Education (Scotland) Act of 1942 came clearly in to the preventive category. This wartime

---

130 Borders Regional Archive, B/PH/1/25, County of Berwick, 'Annual Report on the Health and Sanitary Condition of the County, 1941/2', 13.

131 'With the Minister of Food helping in every possible way, and the Scottish Education Department prepared to do anything and everything in its power to develop the school meals system, I hope that before long we shall be able to report that 20% of the children attending our schools have a hot midday meal [...]. We hope to reach the highest possible standard, the best possible nutritional standard, at the lowest possible price, for the maximum number of children [...]. *The aim of the Government is to prevent malnutrition instead of trying to remedy it after unmistakeable symptoms have appeared* [author's emphasis]. We desire that where school meals are provided, they shall be available for all school children, whether the parents can afford to pay or not [...]. The question of whether payments can be recovered from the parents is one for the education authority afterwards.' Tom Johnston, HOC debates, 16–12–41, vol. 376 col. 1870–2, passim.

132 Boyd Orr entered this debate in *Food, Health and Income* in 1936, when he stated: 'Reports of School Medical Officers based merely on the appearance of the child show incidences [of anaemia] but an examination based merely on appearance would not show minor degrees of anaemia such as could be caused by lesser degrees of malnutrition.' *Food, Health and Income*, 42.

legislation allowed local education authorities to provide both meals and clothing for any child over the age of five (including outside school days and for children who were not yet attending school) out of the Education Fund. There was no reference to restricting the measure to necessitous children. Financial outlay by the education authorities could, however, be recovered from parents of children deemed able to pay, either in whole or in part.[133]

In a written reply before parliament in January 1944, Johnston revealed further improvement in the supplementary nutrition of Scots school children.[134] By March 1944, Johnston's December 1941 target of 20% of Scots children in receipt school meals had been reached.[135] Yet there remained a gap between Scottish figures for school milk and meals and those for England, (in spite the pioneering work in the field of child nutrition carried out in Scotland since the 1920s). Figures for Scottish schools in October 1943, showed the number receiving milk was 513, 502 (67.6% of all school children). This showed a slight decrease from the figure of 520,124 (68.5% for June 1943, which was the best wartime rate achieved in Scotland – the February 1945 figure was lower again at 501,000, representing 66.1% of school children). The number of Scottish children receiving school meals (dinners and lunches) was close to 160,000 (21.2% of those on school rolls) in October 1943. This showed a increase on the figure of just over 140,000 (18.8%) in June 1943.[136] In comparison, the higher English figures for 1943 showed 78% of school children received milk and 29% received meals. The percentage of those who received milk and meals free of charge were not given.[137] By the end of the war, more than one-third of elementary school children and over 47% of

133 See Education (Scotland) Act, 26 February 1942, Section 1, Clauses (1–3).

134 The number of children receiving school meals (dinners or lunches) rose from 18.8.% in June 1943 to 21.2% by October 1943. HOC debates 18–1–44, vol. 396 col. 45.

135 'The total consumption of liquid milk has risen 34% since 1939. In Scotland 67% of the whole school population is now receiving a milk ration at school [...]. Over a quarter of the children attending school are given a nutritious mid-day meal in Scotland.' HOC debates, 18–3–44, vol. 397, col. 2082.

136 HOC debates, 18–1–44, vol. 396 col. 45.

137 *BMJ*, 1944 (1), 274.

secondary school children in England and Wales were receiving school dinners. The best Scottish equivalent in February 1945, was 201,490 (26.7%) of Scots school children receiving meals.[138] The disparity between Scottish and English aggregate figures reflects a higher expenditure on local authority health care in the more prosperous south than in the north. The 1943 DHS Report on infant mortality produced by Boyd Orr revealed similar disquieting discrepancies between Scotland and England in expenditure on infant and maternal welfare centres.[139]

Wartime medical inspection of the children in Glasgow schools established the fact that the younger generation was not suffering in health and physique due to the prevailing war conditions. On the contrary, School Medical Officers found that in the year 1942/3 the tendency to better height and weight measurements continued. For example, the report on the medical inspection and treatment of school children in Glasgow for the year ended on 31 July, 1943, showed increases in the average heights and weights as compared with the pre-war five-year period 1935–1939. Among children of five years of age, boys had increased in height by 0.40 inch, and in weight by 1.24 lb., while girls had increased in height by 0.28 inch, and in weight by 0.97 lb. Among children of thirteen years of age, boys had increased in height by 0.75 inch, and in weight by 2.90 lbs. Girls in the same age range increased in height by 0.72 inch, and in weight by 2.94 lbs.[140]

In rural Aberdeenshire, the general health of school children was maintained during the war. Apart from a few outbreaks of 'Sonne dysentery' the school children were noted to be singularly free from infectious disease. The school dental service had however, been affected by war due to the reduction of available dental surgeons which curtailed routine inspections and the increase in dental work as a result of the influx of evacuee children to the county (including 348 school children under the Overseas Evacuation Scheme). However, there was no deterioration in overall dental condition, '[...] the

138 Figures quoted in Harris, *The Health of the School Child*, 156–7.

139 The Boyd Orr Committee concluded that poverty and poor housing helped account for this discrepancy. For more on this see previous chapter.

140 *GMJ*, 1944 (1), 98.

introduction of war-time bread, with its increased calcium content and decreased percentage of white flour, may well have been a factor in this satisfactory result'.[141]

These improved health results at a time of limited school medical inspections and disrupted school nutritional programmes suggest that the introduction of a national food policy was paying dividends. The Welfare Foods Scheme was started in 1941 and provided subsidised (and later free) orange juice and cod liver oil tablets for infants and children. The scheme was continued in the immediate post-war period and was linked to the new welfare reforms such as the introduction of Family Allowances in 1945. However, supplementary nutrition was not restricted to those receiving family allowance. The positive effects of food and vitamin supplements had become evident during the War years. A DHS circular to Scottish local authorities in July 1946 drew attention to the Government decision to continue the existing welfare food scheme, with some slight modifications, as a supplement to the new family allowances scheme. The DHS Circular acknowledged that the welfare food scheme had proved beneficial to the health of mothers and children.[142]

Two contrasting surveys examined the state of the Scottish school health services in the 1940s. The DHS submission to the Beveridge Committee in 1941 outlined developments in the Scottish school health service since its creation in 1908.[143] The 1941 survey

---

141 Grampian Health Board Archives, GRHB E2\4\20, 'Report by the Medical Officer of Health on the Health and Sanitary Conditions of the County of Aberdeen during the Second World War 1940–1945', 2.

142 North Lanarkshire Council, Coatbridge Burgh Archives, DHS Circular, D.H.846U, 'Welfare Foods Scheme', 12 July 1946.

143 'The aims of the school health administration have been (1) the systematic medical examination of children throughout their school life, (2) to follow up and keep under supervision all children found to be suffering from physical or mental defects, (3) to provide appropriate treatment for the children of necessitous parents and to encourage parents to have their children treated whether at the public expense or privately, and (4) to secure as far as possible healthy growth and development and the prevention of sickness and incapacity among school children.' PRO, CAB 87/76, Cabinet Committee for Social Insurance and Allied Services [Beveridge Committee], DHS, 'Outline of Scottish Services – Health', August 1941, [no day].

stated that the medical inspection of school children had operated in Scotland since 1909. Since then the service had expanded to include: provision of medical treatment, supervision of physical education, control of school hygiene, co-ordination of services with child welfare and other public health services. The School Medical Service also assisted in the arrangements for the feeding of school children, and the provision of milk-in-schools schemes (which covered almost every Scottish county and had an average take up rate of about 60% of children).[144] According to the list of services supplied to the Beveridge Committee, much had been achieved by an enhanced school health service in Scotland by the 1940s. The end of World War Two brought a further increase in the scope of the service, with the extension of school health inspection to include nursery schools, under the provisions of the 1945 Education (Scotland) Act. Warfare clearly led to welfare in the case of needy school children. Many of the comprehensive measures (such as school milk and meals) identified in the 1941 DHS report were only implemented during crisis war conditions.

Richard Titmuss's 'Social Policy' volume of the official history of World War Two also looked at the 1940s school health service in Scotland. Titmuss drew attention to this decisive change in wartime government policy towards supplementary feeding in schools. The matter became a priority in July 1940 as a relief measure for 'under-nourished' children. In September 1941, poor aggregate health indices in the first two years of the war were revealed. As a result, combined pressure on the Cabinet from the Ministry of Health, the Board of Education and the DHS led to the release of new funds to local authorities to expand the provision of school meals and supplementary milk as quickly as possible.[145] In the inter-war years, the nutritional levels of school children had been a field of scientific investigation, trial study and pilot schemes. Finally, in wartime, the issue became a matter of urgent priority for the State.

144 Ibid.

145 Titmuss, *Problems of Social Policy*, 509.

On the eve of the introduction of the National Health Service in Scotland, the greatest factor in determining the health of school children remained social class. As the research of Boyd Orr forcefully demonstrated in the 1920s and 1930s, children from poorer areas of the country were less nourished, weighed less and suffered more from disease. Having said this, there had been some inter-war achievements, notably, in the supply of milk to most and meals to some school children. By World War Two, supplementary nutrition was becoming a right for all children of school age and not the last resort for the necessitous child identified as suffering from malnutrition (or 'under-nourishment') by a School Medical Officer.

In reaching this position, the pioneering nutrition studies of the SBH and the DHS in the later 1920s and 1930s increased both scientific knowledge of the effects of improved diet, and provided concrete evidence of the beneficial effects of milk and supplementary feeding on children.[146] That such studies were taking place in an atmosphere of increased political debate on nutrition and under-nourishment gave the findings added significance. Once again, it is clear that expert advice played a role in Scottish health policy formation and implementation. In the area of child health, the work of nutrition specialists, funded and/or commissioned by the SBH to inquire into the dietary value of milk, helped influence policy towards extended milk-in-schools provision.

The health of the school child in relation to the future health of the adult was an increasingly influential consideration in the inter-war period. There was a feeling that the levels of chronic incapacity un-

146 The position of children in society was also worth considering in the nutrition debate in these years: 'It is important to remember that the average height of an adult population reflects the conditions which it experienced during childhood, and it may therefore reflect the value which a previous generation attached to childhood as well as the standard of living of the population as a whole.' B. Harris, 'Health, Height and History: An Overview of Recent Developments in Anthropometric History', *Social History of Medicine*, 7/2 (August 1994): 319–320.

covered by the 1930s DHS Morbidity Statistics Scheme – particularly among younger workers – owed much to untreated deficiencies in childhood.[147] The hypothesis ran that the health of the adult was based on the physical constitution of the child. In this view, the first fifteen years of life were considered vital. Such belief led, not only to attempts to co-ordinate municipal health services from infancy to the end of the school career, but also to consider the preventive health aspects of such services in endeavouring to promote the physical efficiency of the adult workforce.

This concern was, of course, nothing new. Turn of the century debates on the fitness of soldiers for the Boer War and subsequent developments in health services for mothers, infants and school children had already demonstrated just such a priority. What was novel by the late 1920s and 1930s, was that the DHS now had a series of statistics to show that the problem of physical inadequacies, principally among poorer school children, remained unresolved.

The SBH/DHS investigations into the relative height and weight of children under controlled nutritional circumstances provided solid evidence for the benefits of supplementary feeding of school children and there were some valuable initiatives in free and subsidised milk feeding in the late 1920s and 1930s. However, it took the outbreak of World War Two to finally elevate the health of children of school age from an issue of Scottish Departmental concern (through the supplementary feeding initiative) to a subject of vital national interest.[148]

---

147 See chapter six for a detailed discussion on the Morbidity Statistics Scheme and morbidity patterns among the Scottish workforce.

148 Dowding's 'autonomy of the state' administrative model is useful here in understanding the process of policy formulation. According to Dowding: '[...] self interest means that civil servants and elected politicians only accede to the wishes of the pressure groups [...] when they already agree with them or are relatively indifferent to their proposals. It may appear that groups affect the policies of departments, but often they carry out their policies regardless of what organisations tell them. Those organisations which tell the department what it wants to hear will appear to be influential but this is simply happenstance'. Dowding, *The Civil Service*, 111.

Ultra Violet Light Therapy,
Sister Street Day Nursery and Child Welfare Clinic, Glasgow, 1926
© Mitchell Library, Glasgow

5: 'The Tuberculosis Problem', 1919–1948

> The tuberculosis problem is associated with everything political, social, economic that effects the life of the people. It may truly be said that tuberculosis is dependent on housing, feeding, wages, habits of the individual, conditions of work, and life generally.
> (Harry J. Rae, Chief Medical Officer, City of Aberdeen, and counties of Aberdeen and Kincardine, 'Some local and general problems in tuberculosis administration', *Edinburgh Medical Journal*, 38 (1931), 158)

Introduction

So far, the examination of the personal health services in this study has concentrated on areas most obviously given special emphasis in the inter-war years – namely, infant and maternal welfare and child health. This is because these areas saw the development of wider government and local authority agencies to deal with a perceived problem of the health of the nation which emerged strongly in the early part of the twentieth century and which focused on improving the health of coming generations. At the same time, tuberculosis was recognised as a chronic debilitating illness, the most potent of all the 'killing' diseases. Tuberculosis disproportionately affected both adults of working age and children.[1] It is not surprising that treatment of the disease was of mounting concern to central government and local

1 Among the 3,733 deaths from respiratory tuberculosis in Scotland in 1925, 25% were in the 15–25 age group. More than two-thirds of the total were aged between 15–45. Of the 1,656 deaths from non-respiratory tuberculosis in 1925, over 63% were children aged under age 15. Nearly 78% of all non-respiratory deaths were aged under 25. SBH, *Seventh Annual Report, 1925*, (Edinburgh: HMSO, 1926), 58–59, [Cmd 2674].

health authorities in this period of growing involvement in the nation's health.

Such was the scale of the problem, that more government funding was spent on tuberculosis 'control' in the years from 1919 to 1948 than was spent on the infant and maternal welfare and school health programmes combined. In a reflection of the early-twentieth century concern for 'national efficiency' previously mentioned in connection with expenditure on these other two services, institutional care for tuberculosis sufferers was greatly expanded after the passage and implementation of National Health Insurance in 1911. Increased state and local authority interest in tuberculosis was also accompanied by an apparent divergence of opinion between central, Scottish and local agency approaches to the containment and treatment of the disease. On occasion in these years, the SBH was in conflict with both the Treasury and with Scottish local authorities over the pursuit of a policy of expanding institutional care.

The years 1919–1948 continued the overall downward trend in mortality from tuberculosis.[2] As there were no real breakthroughs in the medical treatment of tuberculosis until the very end of this period, the influence both of environmental and nutritional factors feature largely in the historical debate on the reduction in tuberculosis mortality in the twentieth century. A further consideration in this wider debate, namely, the possible ameliorating effects produced by the increase in publicly funded medical services is an obvious concern in this book.

2 'Since the year 1870 [...] mortality from tuberculosis has shewn a continuous decline. In that year [...] there was a death-rate of 404 per 100,000, and it took a period of forty years before this death-rate was halved. By the year 1909 the rate had been reduced to 198 per 100,000. In the twenty years since 1909 the death rate has again been halved. While the absolute decline in the mortality rate is of course greater in the earlier period, there has been an acceleration in the relative decline in the later period, and this later period coincides almost wholly with the time that the tuberculosis schemes of local authorities have been in operation, it is not unreasonable to suppose that part at least of the relative decline is due to the special efforts made under these schemes on the lines of prevention and treatment.' DHS, *Annual Report, 1929*, 94.

The work of Thomas McKeown[3] in the 1970s and 1980s was most associated with the view that a substantial proportion of the very significant fall in overall death rates in the late nineteenth and early twentieth century was due to better nutrition. McKeown assigned lesser roles to improved hygiene and sanitation. A fall in tuberculosis mortality made a large impact in this downward trend. According to McKeown, declining tuberculosis rates accounted for 47% of the total decline in mortality in the nineteenth century. Tuberculosis mortality began its downward trend around 1840 in England and Wales and from 1870 in Scotland,[4] before institutional and public health tuberculosis services were in operation.[5] McKeown principally looked at England and Wales. There is some Scottish evidence which supports his argument. A.K. Chalmers,[6] MOH for Glasgow in the early twentieth century, identified improved nutrition as playing a part in reducing tuberculosis deaths in early twentieth century Scotland. Chalmers attributed the 57% decline in pulmonary (respiratory) tuberculosis in the city in the years from 1871 to 1911 to increased consumption of butcher meat.[7]

---

3 See for example, T. McKeown, et al, 'An Interpretation of the Decline of Mortality in England and Wales during the Twentieth Century', *Population Studies*, 29 (1975), 391:422, McKeown and R.G. Record, 'Reasons for the Decline in Mortality in England and Wales during the Nineteenth Century', *Population Studies*, 16 (1962), 94:122, and McKeown's, *The Modern Rise of Population*.

4 The tuberculosis death rate in Scotland was 311 in 1882, 172 in 1912 and 69 by 1939. Figures quoted in C. Clayson, 'Modern Trends in Preventive Medicine and Social Aspects of Tuberculosis', *EMJ*, 50 (1943), 208.

5 According to N.M. McFarlane, 53% of the overall decline in respiratory tuberculosis mortality between 1870 and the advent of effective chemotherapy in 1950 occurred during the thirty years 1870–1900, when there was little parochial or voluntary institutional provision for the disease. McFarlane, 'Tuberculosis in Scotland 1870–1960', Ph.D. thesis, University of Glasgow, 1990, 39.

6 See chapter 1 for biographical details of Chalmers.

7 The introduction of refrigerated ships to Britain in 1882 had increased availability and led to a reduction in the price of meat. See A.S.M. MacGregor, *Public Health in Glasgow 1905–1946* (Edinburgh: E&S Livingstone Ltd, 1967), 86. F.B. Smith provides some equivocal support for the McKeown thesis: 'Yet the beneficent fact stands: the easing of deprivation amongst the

McKeown's opinion was that:

> Improvement in diet was probably the main cause of the decline of mortality from tuberculosis during the nineteenth century. It seems to us that the same interpretation can be accepted for the trend of mortality in this century until the introduction of chemotherapy, although improvements in housing were also important.[8]

McKeown's view that better living standards, including improvements in nutrition mainly accounted for the decline in tuberculosis has been challenged by a number of other historians.[9] One criticism of McKeown's view is that he over-simplified a process, wherein food consumption could be both a negative and positive factor in health trends. With reference to tuberculosis, milk consumption can be used as an example of a nutritious food which, when taken in an infected form could spread, rather than slow, the progress of the disease.[10]

Much of the historical debate on tuberculosis decline has focused on England and Wales, yet the Scottish position should not be overlooked. Scottish tuberculosis rates differed from other parts of the country. Table 5.1 shows that in the years from 1919–1941, death

---

British peoples during the 120 years to 1960 was coincident with a fall in the general death-rate from around 22.3 per 1,000 to around 10.6 per 1,000.' F.B Smith, *The Retreat of Tuberculosis, 1850–1950*, (Croom Helm, 1988), 2.

8 McKeown, et al, 'An Interpretation of the Decline in Mortality in England and Wales during the Twentieth Century', 412.

9 Critics of McKeown's findings base their arguments on the growth of sanatoria and other institutions (including Poor Law Infirmaries) in the late nineteenth and early twentieth centuries, which increased the isolation of patients with respiratory tuberculosis and limited the spread of the disease among the population. In other words, an improvement in public health services helped account for the reduction in tuberculosis levels. See S. Szreter, 'The Importance of Social Intervention in Britain's Mortality Decline c. 1850–1914: A Reinterpretation of the Role of Public Health', *Social History of Medicine*, 1 (1988): 1:37, and L.G. Wilson, 'The Historical Decline of Tuberculosis in Europe and America: Its Causes and Significance', *Journal of the History of Medicine and Allied Sciences*, 45 (1990): 366:396.

10 P.J. Atkins, 'White Poison? The Social Consequences of Milk Consumption, 1850–1930', *Social History of Medicine*, 5/2 (1992), 207.

	Scotland		England and Wales	
	All Forms	Respiratory	All Forms	Respiratory
1919	130	88	123	92
1920	124	86	112	83
1921	126	81	112	85
1922	120	83	111	85
1923	127	82	105	80
1924	116	80	104	80
1925	110	76	102	79
1926	99	69	94	73
1927	100	71	95	74
1928	97	68	91	71
1929	93	67	93	74
1930	88	62	87	68
1931	87	62	85	67
1932	84	61	80	62
1933	80	60	78	62
1934	75	57	73	57
1935	74	57	68	54
1936	73	55	64	51
1937	74	56	64	51
1938	69	52	59	46
1939	70	54	58	46
1940	82	62	67	54
1941	84	63	74	57

Table 5.1 Comparative British Tuberculosis Mortality Rates (per 100,000 of population) , 1914–1941.[11]

11 Figures taken from DHS, *Scottish Health Statistics* (Edinburgh: HMSO, 1958) and the Registrar General's, *Statistical Review of England and Wales for the year 1941* (HMSO, 1945). Series figures end in 1941 since thereafter the methods for calculating tuberculosis mortality for England and Wales was altered. It was not possible to compare the two sets of figures on a like for like basis beyond 1941. See table 5.2 for Scottish tuberculosis levels after 1941.

rates from all forms of tuberculosis were greater in Scotland than for England and Wales.

The only exception was during the depression years 1929–1934 when the levels were similar. Table 5.1 shows that comparative mortality rates from respiratory tuberculosis only were more closely aligned between 1919–1934. The Scottish respiratory tuberculosis rate again outstripped the rate for England and Wales thereafter.

Since improved nutritional standards can, at best, be a partial explanation for levels of tuberculosis incidence and mortality, other factors, principally over-crowded and sub-standard housing must also be considered. The level of overcrowding in Scotland's urban centres and poor housing stock in general, (contrasting with housing improvements elsewhere) was a deep-seated problem. The distinct problems of Scottish housing were identified both by contemporaries and by more recent historians, as playing a crucial part in the overall higher rates of tuberculosis in Scotland than elsewhere in mainland Britain.

The responsibility for inter-war housing policy lay in the hands of the Ministry of Health and the Scottish Board of Health. Housing policy (or rather deficiency in housing policy) is not generally within the remit of this book.[12] It is considered in this chapter because it came to play a crucial role in diverting Scottish health spending on tuberculosis towards institutional care rather than the more expensive alternative of improving urban living conditions. This gave rise to a curative, rather than preventive, emphasis to health policy for tackling tuberculosis.

12 For an account of how housing questions dominated the early years of the Ministry of Health, see Gilbert, *British Social Policy* and Honigsbaum's *Health, Happiness and Security: The Creation of the National Health Service* and *The Division in British Medicine. A History of the Separation of General Practice from Hospital Care 1911–1968.*

Housing Deficiencies and the Emphasis on Institutional Care

> The housing difficulty is perhaps the most outstanding difficulty associated with the eradication of tuberculosis. The problem of slumdom is associated partly with the house and partly with the habits of the tenant. (Grampian Regional Health Board Archives, Aberdeen, GRHB E2\4\8, County of Aberdeen, 'Medical Officer of Health Annual Report, 1928', 73)

In the early twentieth century, the impact of poor housing on the general health of the nation was brought to public attention in the report of the Committee on Physical Deterioration in 1904.[13] The correlation between overcrowding and high death rates was made in relation to respiratory tuberculosis, as early as 1901 by Glasgow MOH, A.K. Chalmers. His findings showed a respiratory tuberculosis death rate of 2.5 per 1,000 of the population living in one bed-roomed houses, dropping to 1.8 per 1,000 among those in two-bedroomed houses. The level was at 1.2 for people in three-bedroomed houses, and decreased to 0.7 deaths per 1,000 for those fortunate enough to live in four-bedroomed houses.[14]

Scottish local authorities soon recognised the need to address the poor environmental conditions among tuberculosis sufferers and their families. Aberdeen County Medical Officer's Annual Report for 1919 questioned the ability of current housing policy to address the housing problems facing the poorest and most vulnerable sections of the population. Meanwhile in Glasgow in 1921, 63.3% of the city's population were identified as living in one and two-roomed houses.[15] Inadequate housing was identified as a factor in the spread of the disease in rural areas also as later comments linking high incidences

13 *Report of the Inter-Departmental Committee on Physical Deterioration*, (1904).

14 Mitchell Library, Glasgow, 'Glasgow Medical Officer of Health Annual Report, 1901', 53.

15 The 1921 census showed that 13.2% of Glasgow's population lived in 1 room, 50.1% in 2 rooms, 21.0% in three rooms, and 15.7% in four or more rooms. Mitchell Library, Glasgow, Corporation of Glasgow, 'Glasgow Tuberculosis Scheme' (1926), 5.

of tuberculosis with poor housing by the MOH for Lewis will illustrate.

A mass of housing legislation was passed in the inter-war years. Measures passed included: the Housing of the Working Class Act, 1919, and the Housing (Finance) Act, 1924 (which aimed at constructing 2.5 million new houses in the United Kingdom within fifteen years). The Housing (Scotland) Act, 1925, the Housing (Rural Workers) Act, 1926, the Town and Country Planning (Scotland) Act followed, and finally, there was the Housing (Scotland) Act, 1935. These Acts resulted in the building of over 200,000 houses in Scotland under State-aided schemes between 1919 and the end of 1935. The construction of these new houses only began to address the chronic housing shortage in Scotland. Another concern was the poor condition of the existing housing stock occupied by the majority of the Scottish population. Merely keeping pace with the shortfall of houses occupied Scottish local authority housing policy for much of the period. In 1932, the DHS spoke of reorienting housing policy towards the issues of slum clearance and the re-housing of those cleared made homeless in the process.[16] ‘A systematic attempt is being made to clear slums and to eliminate the evil influences of bad housing on health, and overcrowding is being brought under control.’[17] Despite this programme, overcrowding remained serious and slum housing was still prevalent, particularly in large cities. At the end of 1935, 55% of the total population in Glasgow still lived in one or two apartment houses.[18] In 1937, the DHS estimated that Scotland still needed 250,000 new houses.[19]

While housing was acknowledged as an important factor in the high tuberculosis rates and general ill health in Scotland, meeting the challenge was another matter. A deputation from the British Legion to the Ministry of Health in 1924 about problems facing tuberculous ex-service personnel (including the administration of tuberculosis schemes in the West of Scotland), elicited a rare admission of doubt

16 DHS, *Annual Report 1933* (Edinburgh: HMSO, 1934), 12.
17 DHS, *Committee on Scottish Health Services Report*, 13.
18 Ibid., 143.
19 DHS, *Annual Report, 1937* (Edinburgh, HMSO, 1938), 12.

regarding sanatorium treatment from the Minister of Health. The fact that Labour MP for Glasgow Shettleston John Wheatley was then Health Minister perhaps accounted for his frankness.

> The Minister in reply to the Deputation said that he had had a long experience of the administration of tuberculosis schemes in the West of Scotland [...]. He shared their doubts as to the value of sanatorium treatment and questioned whether the millions of money that had been spent on the treatment of tuberculosis were not largely thrown away because of the failure to deal with bad housing and under-feeding which were the most potent causes of tuberculosis.[20]

The annual reports of the SBH/DHS clearly identified inadequate housing as a factor in the ill health of the Scottish population. A survey of overcrowding made under the Housing (Scotland) Act, 1935, emphasised the magnitude of the Scottish housing problem. 'Overcrowding in Scotland is relatively six times greater than in England: more than 22 per cent. of Scottish houses are overcrowded and a minimum of 160,000 new houses is needed merely to relieve these conditions.'[21] Given the long-term nature of addressing housing deficiencies, it is no surprise that the inter-war government response to the blight of tuberculosis concentrated on short-term objectives such as local authority tuberculosis schemes and the medium-term 'solution' of a programme of sanatorium construction.

Early Tuberculosis Services – The Voluntary Impulse

Voluntary-run tuberculosis sanatoria pre-dated the advent of municipal and state effort in the early twentieth century. For example, in May 1897, the first of four 'Consumptive Homes' had opened for patients at Bridge of Weir in Renfrewshire funded by philanthropist

20 PRO, PIN15/29, 'Village Settlements for Ex-Servicemen', notes enclosed with letter from F.O. Roberts to William Graham, MP, 24 April 1924.

21 DHS, *Annual Report, 1936* (Edinburgh, HMSO, 1937), n.p.

William Quarrier. By 1907, the 'Quarrier homes' provided accommodation for 140 men, women and children. There were a further seven small charity sanatoria serving rural Scotland by the early twentieth century. The various voluntary agencies supplemented in-patient treatment with dispensary services and educational activities.

These voluntary tuberculosis facilities continued to function after the entrance of central and local authorities into tuberculosis care. For example, in addition to the special SBH arrangements under the Highlands and Islands Medical Service[22] for expanded general practitioner, nursing and institutional care, the National Association for the Prevention of Tuberculosis (NAPT),[23] was responsible for the provision of specially trained nurses in the region. NAPT nurses spent their whole time on tuberculosis nursing and educational work.[24]

The educational activities of the NAPT emphasised individual responsibility. This was very much in keeping with the Government's drive to improve 'national efficiency'. Hence, both private enterprise and state agency educational efforts towards improving understanding of tuberculosis contained an implied measure of censure for those who fell victims to the disease. The NAPT prevention campaign was especially active in the 1920s. In 1927, the NAPT (at the suggestion of Sir Robert Philip, who was then Vice-Chairman of the Association) decided to set up a propaganda organisation in Scotland. Activities were, in the first instance, concentrated in the problem-Highlands and Islands area.

In the Autumn of 1927, J. Harley Williams (MOH for the Island of Lewis), and Medical Commissioner of the NAPT, toured the Highlands and North East Scotland giving a series of talks. His lectures dealt chiefly with the prevention and cure of tuberculosis '[...] in a simple, easily understood and effective manner that was

22 See chapter two for more on the Highlands and Islands Medical Service.

23 The NAPT was first constituted as the National Association for Prevention of Consumption and other forms of Tuberculosis in 1898. In 1959 it was restyled the Chest and Heart Association. For more on the work of the NAPT see J. Harley Williams, *Requiem for a Great Killer: The Story of Tuberculosis* (Health Horizons, 1973).

24 DHS, *Committee on Scottish Health Services Report*, 206.

appreciated by all who had the good fortune to hear him'.[25] In September 1928, Harley Williams gave a further series of lectures, (illustrated, where electricity was available, by an educational film 'The Story of John Macneil'), in seven towns in Aberdeenshire. The optimistic film showed the fictional John Macneil and his family pass through the treatment and prevention routine at the Edinburgh Dispensary. Macneil then received sanatorium treatment, before moving to the Edinburgh Tuberculosis Scheme Farm Colony for remedial open-air work, raising flowers and tending pigs. The film ended with Macneil cured and he and his family settled in a new house.[26]

Public information exercises aimed at reducing the spread of the disease were conducted by both voluntary and local authority agencies. The NAPT lectures and demonstrations were given to school children in the afternoons, and adults in the evenings. A similar pattern was followed when Harley Williams visited Argyllshire in April 1928 and March 1929, speaking to large audiences in both afternoons and evenings. He visited eight towns, including Lochgilphead and Campbeltown.[27] In Aberdeenshire, members of the Public Health Department staff gave other lectures and demonstrations on the disease and local practitioners gave talks at tuberculosis clinics, while other lectures were given at meetings of the Women's Rural Institute and the District Nursing Associations.[28]

---

25 Highlands Health Board Archive [HHBA], Inverness, County of Sutherland, 'Medical Officer of Health Annual Report, 1927', 10.

26 Harley Williams, *Requiem for a Great Killer*, 47.

27 Argyll and Bute District Archives, ABDA, CO 6/9/1/31, County of Argyll, 'Medical Officer of Health Annual Report, 1929', 70.

28 GRHB Archive, GRHB E2\4\8, County of Aberdeen, 'Medical Officer of Health Annual Report, 1928', 74.

Scottish cities with an established public health tradition and active Medical Officers of Health, in particular Edinburgh[29] and Glasgow,[30] led the way in creating public tuberculosis services. This is clear from the work of the 'model' Tuberculosis Scheme in Edinburgh established by physician Robert Philip.[31] Philip was, arguably, the best known specialist in the field of tuberculosis research and care in the late nineteenth and early twentieth century. He was knighted for his services in 1913. Philip's pioneered his care system, the 'Edinburgh Scheme' (more formally, the Co-ordinated Edinburgh Scheme for the Control of Tuberculosis) in the late 1880s. The Scheme was adopted as the Scottish standard by the LGBS, with the issue of a circular in March 1906 to all local authorities pointing out that tuberculosis was an infectious disease requiring action under the Public Health (Scotland) Act of 1897.

The 'Edinburgh Scheme' entailed the recording of a detailed case history for respiratory tuberculosis sufferers, provision of information on how to avoid spreading the disease, identification and examination of contacts, home visits by medical officers and lady health visitors, and the disinfection of an infected person's home. All of this work

29 See article: 'The Edinburgh Tuberculosis Scheme 1887–1937', *EMJ*, 44, (1937): 285–297.

30 See Appendix 3 for an outline of the development of municipal provision for tuberculosis sufferers in Glasgow between 1890–1925.

31 Robert Philip, later (Sir Robert) was mentioned in chapter 1 in his capacity as one-time President of the Royal College of Physicians, Edinburgh. Philip was an active member of the Departmental Committee on Tuberculosis chaired by Lord Astor appointed on 22 February 1912, which produced its final report in 1913. Philip remained an influential figure in government health circles after World War One. He was a member of the SBH Consultative Committee on Medical and Allied Services. He was also at various stages President of the International Tuberculosis Union, Vice Chairman of the National Association for the Prevention of Consumption and Other Forms of Tuberculosis (NAPT), and a member of the Tuberculosis Society (founded in 1918), which consisted of local authority Tuberculosis Officers and Medical Officers to sanatoria, farm colonies and related hospitals.

was carried out through a purpose-built tuberculosis dispensary, staffed by trained medical staff.[32] The 'Edinburgh Scheme' was a case of voluntary and local authority efforts combining to offer a pioneering level of care and monitoring. The scheme was soon viewed as a role model for the treatment of tuberculosis around the world. After the changes to funding local authority tuberculosis schemes with the creation of National Health Insurance in 1911, Edinburgh Corporation purchased Philip's voluntary-run Victoria Hospitals institutions for the city for the sum of £7,000.[33]

Edinburgh also led the way in official notification of tuberculosis cases. Voluntary notification of respiratory tuberculosis began in Edinburgh in 1903. The LGBS followed three years behind. In March 1906 a LGBS circular to local authorities stated that tuberculosis was to be considered as an infectious disease and that local provision was to be made for its control, notification and institutional treatment, under the Public Health (Scotland) Act of 1897 and the Infectious Disease Notification Act, 1889. Edinburgh accepted compulsory notification in 1907 and Glasgow in 1910.[34] By 1911, notifying authorities represented 50% of the Scottish population. In 1912, the LGBS Public Health (Pulmonary Tuberculosis) Regulations introduced compulsory notification for all cases of respiratory tuberculosis, and in 1914 this was extended to all forms of the disease. All forms of tuberculosis became notifiable in England and Wales in 1913. Further guidance on notification came in the shape of the Public

---

32 In 1887, Philip set up the Royal Victoria Dispensary for Consumption in the centre of Edinburgh, and the voluntarily funded (by the Victoria Hospital Trust) Victoria Hospital followed this for Consumption, in 1894. In 1907, the Royal Victoria Hospital's 'farm colony' was opened at Polton. This provided training in rural pursuits for tuberculous patients. Philip acted as physician at all these institutions and was appointed to the first Chair of Tuberculosis at Edinburgh University in 1917 in addition to his involvement in clinical teaching at Edinburgh University. The Chair was funded by the Royal Victoria Hospital Tuberculosis Trust.

33 Lothian Health Board Archive, Edinburgh, John A. Young 'Report on the Evolution and Development of Public Health Administration in the City of Edinburgh from 1865 to 1919', (Edinburgh, 1919), 12.

34 See Appendix 3 for more information on the development of municipal tuberculosis services in Glasgow, 1890–1925.

Health (Tuberculosis) Regulations of 1930, which remained the basis for notification in Scotland until after World War Two.

Compulsory notification did not always mean early notification. Many cases were only notified when they were far advanced or upon death. This was a major problem for both respiratory and non-respiratory cases. In 1924 the SBH reported that 45% of respiratory cases that year were notified upon death or within three months of death. For non respiratory cases the figures were even worse. 70% of non respiratory cases were notified on death or within one month of death.[35] Glasgow Corporation's viewpoint in 1926 was that the fault chiefly lay with general practitioners who failed to notify cases until they were far advanced.[36] This charge was put down to a fear among general practitioners of losing patients to local public health authority services. Yet, in the County of Aberdeenshire, at least, there seemed to be little evidence of such unwillingness among doctors to hand over patients to public health authorities until it was too late to treat them.[37]

In 1937, over 30% of the deaths from respiratory tuberculosis in Stirlingshire were unnotified or notified only upon death.[38] In 1938, of 37 respiratory deaths in the industrial town of Coatbridge, Lanarkshire, seven had either not been notified or notified only at, or after, death.[39] In 1941, 27.7% of all Scots' respiratory tuberculosis deaths were notified upon death or within one month before death. In 1945, the DHS Joint Tuberculosis Council commented:

---

35 SBH, *Sixth Annual Report, 1924*, 61.

36 Corporation of Glasgow, 'The Glasgow Tuberculosis Scheme' (1926), 8.

37 'It is not unusual to find in reports issued by institutions that the blame of not notifying cases until the disease is far advanced is put on the family doctors, but this does not hold good, at any rate in Aberdeenshire [...]. Almost without exception the County doctors avail themselves of the benefits obtainable for their patients through the County Scheme.' Grampian Health Board Archives, GRHB E2\4\35, County of Aberdeen MOH, 'Annual Report on Tuberculosis, 1921', 29.

38 Stirling Regional Archives, SC3/3/43, County of Stirling, 'Medical Officer of Health Annual Report, 1937', 85.

39 North Lanarkshire Council, Coatbridge Public Library Archives, DHS, 1938 report on 'Tuberculosis Scheme in Coatbridge', to Dr Robert Cordiner, MOH, Coatbridge, on, 20 November 1939.

> It is common knowledge that there are wide variations in carrying out the obligation of notification of tuberculosis. Many cases are still 'notified by death' and far more only a short time before death. There is much ignorance amongst practitioners as to their duty in this respect and of the value of notification as a public health measure.[40]

The widespread failure to notify tuberculosis cases until death or when the disease was at an advanced stage did nothing to reduce the chances of the disease spreading.

Scottish Tuberculosis Mortality Rates

Table 5.2 and figure 5.1 provide a long-term perspective on Scottish tuberculosis mortality (all forms). The figures underline that total tuberculosis death rates fell markedly in the late nineteenth century. The rate continued to fall in the first decade of the twentieth century, but on the eve of world war there was still much room for improvement. There was a steep fall in tuberculosis mortality just after the end of World War One. It fell from 158 to 130 between 1918 and 1919. There was never such a large drop thereafter in the period covered in this study. Small reductions were subsequently recorded almost every year after 1919. The downward trend was reversed during and immediately after World War Two (this wartime increase will be discussed later).

---

40 NAS, HH61/593, Joint Tuberculosis Council, 'The Notification of Tuberculosis' (Revised Draft), July 1945.

1871	398	1927	100	1943	83*
1881	306	1928	97	1944	82*
1891	254	1929	93	1945	79*
1901	223	1930	88	1946	79*
1911	177	1931	87	1947	81
1914	163	1932	84	1948	77
1916	160	1933	80	1949	68
1918	158	1934	75	1950	54
1919	130	1935	74	1951	43
1920	124	1936	73	1952	32
1921	126	1937	74	1953	26
1922	120	1938	69	1954	22
1923	127	1939	70	1955	19
1924	116	1940	82*	1956	16
1925	110	1941	84*	1957	14
1926	99	1942	82*	1958	13

Table 5. 2 Total Respiratory and Non Respiratory Tuberculosis Deaths in Scotland (per 100,000), 1871–1958 (selected dates)[41]

*Note – * Civilians only*

Health Insurance and Tuberculosis Services, 1911–1930

One consequence of the passage of the 1911 National Insurance legislation was that all tuberculous cases in the country were entitled to some form of treatment. Section 64 of the National Insurance Act[42] and Section 16 (1b) of the Finance Act 1911, £157,000 was allocated to the Local Government Board for Scotland for dispersal among local authorities to part finance the building of tuberculosis sanatoria, dispensaries and hospitals.[43] The National Health Insurance Act also

41 DHS, *Scottish Health Statistics* (1958).

42 For more on National Insurance legislation see chapter six on the Insured Population.

43 Out of a total of £1.5 million – the money was allocated proportionally around the U.K. based on population size at the 1911 census.

incorporated for general practitioner and tuberculosis dispensary consultations and sanatorium admission (sanatorium benefit) for insured workers. The extension of sanatorium care to dependants of insured workers was discretionary to the Insurance Committees. Pressure from local authorities to extend public health tuberculosis treatment to non insured patients met with success later in 1912. In that year the Treasury agreed to pay half the net costs of all local authority tuberculosis treatment (less the cost of treating insured persons and any covered dependants, which was still to be met by Insurance Committees). Under the 'Hobhouse grant'[44] capital funds from the Treasury to a maximum of £90 per bed were given under the auspices of the National Insurance legislation to local authorities for any sanatoria or hospital built or under construction for tuberculosis sufferers since 1911. In November 1919, this was raised to £180 per bed to encourage completion and erection of sanatoria institutions after wartime interruption. The remainder of the cost was borne by local authorities.

National Health Insurance legislative provisions together with the publication of the Departmental Committee on Tuberculosis (Astor Committee)[45] Interim and Final Reports in 1912 and 1913 paved the way towards a nascent public health service for tuberculosis sufferers. These two events also skewed the emphasis towards sanatorium care above other (more preventive) aspects of tuberculosis schemes. The findings of the Astor Committee stressed the provision of residential treatment by local authorities. It also supported the

44 Henry Hobhouse was Chair of the County Council Association. The Association was one of many groups representing municipal authorities which protested to Chancellor David Lloyd George about the unfairness of the original sanatorium arrangements under the National Insurance legislation. Initially, only the insured tuberculosis sufferer was admitted for care, excluding any dependants who might also have the disease. Lloyd George announced that the remit of the legislation was to be widened in a letter of reply to Hobhouse.

45 The Astor Committee's final report was entitled the *Departmental Committee on Tuberculosis, Final Report* (HMSO, 1913), [Cmd 6641].

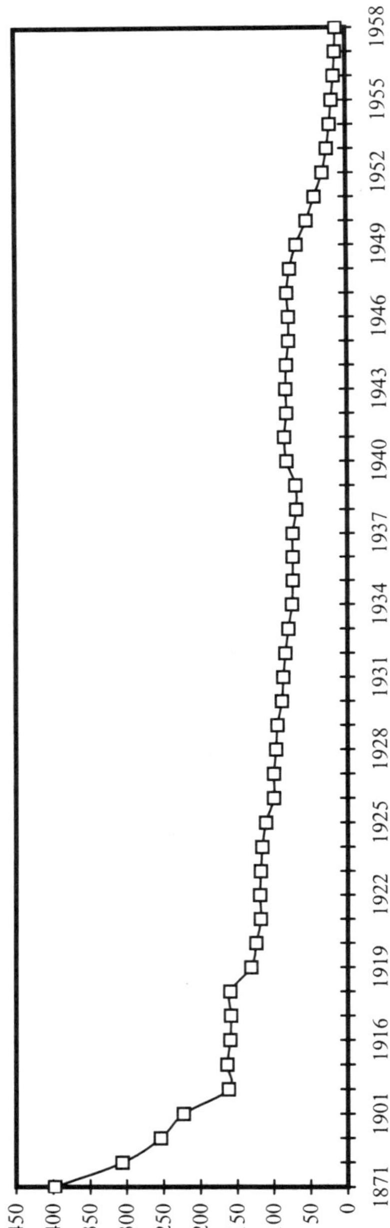

Figure 5.1 Tuberculosis Mortality in Scotland (per 100,000 population), 1871–1958

creation of dispensaries with broad powers. The Committee proposed that dispensaries serve as receiving houses and centres for diagnosis and as clearing houses and centres for observation (treatment in dispensaries was not one of the main priorities). The new provisions were placed under the control of local authority-employed Tuberculosis Officers (TO). The Astor Committee also recommended the creation of voluntary 'care committees' to follow up the work of local dispensaries.[46]

Following the Astor recommendations, the LGBS launched an initiative to facilitate the construction of sanatoria as a key aspect of local authority Tuberculosis Schemes. One consequence of the initiative was the creation of joint sanatorium boards covering groups of Scottish counties and/or burghs to pool resources in sparsely populated areas with had difficulty in raising sufficient funds from their own rate-payers to construct their own sanatorium, even with state subsidies.[47] Joint Sanatorium beds were allotted proportionally by respective size of population. In 1914, Aberdeenshire county council held discussions with the counties of Kincardine, Elgin, Nairn, Banff, Sutherland, Caithness, Orkney and Shetland to select a suitable site for the erection of just such a Joint Authority sanatorium.[48] However, the outbreak of World War One put on hold building plans. After the war, the discharge of large numbers of tuberculous ex-servicemen gave a new impetus towards the construction of local authority institutions. The SBH advised local authorities to proceed with the erection of planned sanatoria, as they believed that many

46 See *Departmental Committee on Tuberculosis, Final Report*, vol. 1, 1–17.

47 Other authorities which combined for the purpose of sanatorium construction were West, Mid, and East, Lothian. These counties, alongside Berwick, Selkirk, Roxburgh and Peebles financed a large sanatorium at East Fortune. Another successful joint project was the Lochmaben Sanatorium, which was built under the auspices of the counties of Dumfries, Galloway, Kirkudbright and Wigtown. For more on these combinations see McFarlane, 'Tuberculosis in Scotland 1870–1960', 110.

48 GRHB, E2\4\36, , MOH, 'Annual Report on Tuberculosis 1914', 18.

more beds would be required in view of the large numbers of ex-servicemen who were discharged suffering from tuberculosis.[49]

The Report of Astor Committee on 'Provision of Residential Treatment for Discharged Tuberculous Soldiers and Sailors' in 1919 estimated 35,000 ex-servicemen had been disabled by respiratory tuberculosis. Aberdeen County 1919 annual tuberculosis report cited a figure of almost 40,000 ex-service sufferers.[50] Overall wartime tuberculosis disablement figures may have been closer to 60,000.[51] Increased civilian mortality from tuberculosis in England and Wales during the war added further weight to the plans for increased sanatoria construction. One example of how far the war impacted on Scottish local authority tuberculosis provision may be taken from the rural North Eastern county of Banff, where of the 66 cases notified in 1919, 22 were former service personnel – 15 ex-army and 7 ex-navy.[52]

The passage of a revised National Insurance Act, 1920, ended the Treasury grants (which covered a maximum three-fifths of the capital costs of new sanatorium construction), thereby increasing the financial burden on local authorities to provide sufficient beds for tuberculosis

---

49 GRHB, E2\4\42, County of Aberdeen MOH, 'Annual Report on Tuberculosis, 1922', 6.

50 'So many soldiers and sailors have been discharged on account of their suffering from tuberculosis, or have been found to be suffering from tuberculosis after demobilisation, that the institutional accommodation in some areas has been taxed to its utmost. Ex- servicemen, it may be mentioned, have priority of admission to institutions over civilians. The total number of soldiers and sailors invalided owing to tuberculosis, or afterwards found to be suffering from tuberculosis aggravated by or attributable to service in the Forces, amounts to almost 40,000, and of these, 25,000 have received or are now receiving institutional treatment.' GRHB, E2\4\35, County of Aberdeen MOH, 'Annual Report on Tuberculosis, 1919', 46.

51 Figures taken from *Report of the Interdepartmental Committee* [...] *for the Provision of Residential Treatment for Discharged Soldiers and Sailors Suffering from Pulmonary Tuberculosis and for their Re-introduction into Employment* [...] (HMSO, 1919), 7. J.M Winter, *The Great War and the British People* (1986), 276, cites a figure of 65,000, while L. Bryder, *Below the Magic Mountain: A Social History of Tuberculosis in Twentieth Century Britain* (Oxford: Clarendon Press, 1988), 70, suggests 58,000.

52 GRHB, Aberdeen, E4\1\4, Banff County, 'Medical Officer of Health Annual Report, 1919', 4.

cases in their area. However, the Treasury grant of 50% of net annual expenditure by local authorities on tuberculosis treatment remained (Hobhouse grant), and was augmented by a compensatory annual grant fixed at £44,712. The new legislation ended the duplication of services, whereby the local Tuberculosis Officer was often also the medical expert controlling institutional admissions for local Insurance Committees. It also meant that insured patients were not paying twice for care through their insurance contributions and through their taxes and local rates. This had been the case since the 1912 arrangement to allow local authorities to provide institutional accommodation for all tuberculous cases (both insured and non insured).

In 1921, full administrative control of tuberculosis schemes passed to local authorities,[53] although in Scotland there was no equivalent of the Public Health (Tuberculosis) Act for England and Wales of that year. One consequence of this disparity was that few tuberculosis 'after care committees' were set up in Scotland. Such committees were required components of local authority schemes elsewhere, but were not compulsory for Scottish local authorities. A number of other changes followed as a result of the transfer of tuberculosis schemes to Scottish local authority control in 1921. One casualty was Sir Robert Philip, whose role as 'expert adviser' in the 'Edinburgh Scheme' was taken over by a full-time Medical Director appointed by Edinburgh Corporation.[54] Also the end of capital grants for sanatorium construction had repercussions for the relationship between Scottish local authorities and the SBH.

In the immediate post-war years, both the Ministry of Health and the SBH came under wholesale pressure from organisations such as the British Legion to set up village settlements (for treatment and

53 Under this legislation, 'the most elaborate scheme was developed in Wales, where the service was conducted by the King Edward the Seventh Welsh National Memorial Association.' C. Webster, *The Health Services since the War, vol. 1: Problems of Health Care – The NHS before 1957* (HMSO, 1988), 77–78

54 'Medical opinion in Edinburgh was far from supporting the change. It really amounted to replacing a policy of vision and initiative by one of respectable routine.' 'The Edinburgh Tuberculosis Scheme 1887–1937', *EMJ*, 44, (1937), 292.

occupational therapy) specifically for ex-servicemen. New sanatoria for ex-service personnel were opened, but not with state funding. The Tor-na-Dee Sanatorium near Aberdeen was opened during the war for service personnel, and a 26-bed sanatorium reserved exclusively for ex-service cases on the Island of Lewis, was opened in the 1920s. The Scottish Branch of the British Red Cross Society funded both. The government policy was that state-funded tuberculosis accommodation should cater for the whole community.[55] More emphasis was given to making a scheme of vocational training widely available to tuberculous ex-servicemen resident in sanatoria funded by the state through the Ministry of Pensions and the Treasury.

Vocational training measures were up and running in England considerably earlier than in Scotland. In April 1922, a Ministry of Health Circular listed retraining courses for seven occupations which were provided at a number of institutions (including sanatoria in Ilkley, Birmingham, Kent and Liverpool). Retraining was provided in outdoor pursuits such as market gardening and rural carpentry, as well as skilled craftwork including jewellery, watch, clock and china repairing. The courses were designed to give men increased opportunities in looking for work in suburbs, country towns or large villages, by providing vocational training in occupations suitable for their condition.[56]

The SBH contacted Scottish local authority Tuberculosis Officers in October 1923 to announce the extension of state-funded vocational re-training at sanatoria to Scotland. For ex-service personnel to qualify for the scheme they had to convince the Ministry of Pensions that their tuberculosis was attributable to, or aggravated by, war service. The ex-service person had also to be certified by a TO as unable to follow his or her pre-war occupation as a result of the disease.[57]

Some general Scottish sanatoria already operated occupational re-training, including Hairmyres in East Kilbride, Lanarkshire, and the

55 PRO, PIN 15/29, 'Village Settlements for Ex-Servicemen', 24 April 1924.

56 PRO, MH 55/132, Ministry of Health Circular 307 (England), 29 April 1922.

57 PRO, MH55/166, SBH, Tuberculosis Circular 8/23, 'Tuberculous Ex-Servicemen – Vocational Training', 26 October 1923.

Polton Farm Colony in Edinburgh. Hairmyres received state grants for its existing vocational scheme. A letter from the Treasury to the SBH Secretary on 10 October 1921 referred to '[...] the grants proposed to be made in aid of the special facilities of vocational training which are being provided at Hairmyres Sanatorium.'[58]

The vocational retraining made available at Hairmyres Colony included gardening, forestry work, poultry farming, pig-keeping, general farming and a guinea-pig department (which employed two patients and which raised animals for scientific experimentation at Lanarkshire County Laboratory). Industrial retraining was also provided at the institution workshops, formally opened in October 1923, (for those who had been carpenters or painters prior to admission), and in the motor, carpentry, boot-repairing and basket-making departments. In the industrial workshop (where the intention was to retrain patients to offer them suitable industrial employment upon release), it was noted '[...] in spite of the industrial depression, a considerable number of the trainees have been able to obtain employment in the occupation for which they have been trained'.[59] Trainees in the basket-making and woodwork departments were encouraged to take City and Guilds examinations. Other local authorities attempted to introduce a limited measure of retraining. In 1930, Argyll County Sanatorium was awarded a small grant by the County Council to allow convalescent patients to undertake hand work in basket making and rug making.[60]

Related to vocational training and retraining of adult tuberculosis cases was the provision of schools for tuberculous children in some of the larger institutions. The Edinburgh scheme led the way in 1905 with an open air school for children at the Royal Victoria Hospital. Schools were later opened at Robroyston in Glasgow (the former smallpox hospital with 448 beds, transferred for use as a tuberculosis

58 PRO, MH55/162, letter from B.P. Blackett, Treasury to John Jeffrey, Secretary, SBH, 8 October 1921.

59 Clydesdale District Council, Lindsay Institute, Lanark, County of Lanark Archives, Lanark County, 'Medical Officer of Health Annual Report, 1926', 202.

60 Argyll and Bute District Archives, CO6/9/1/32, Argyll County, 'Medical Officer of Health Annual Report, 1930', 51.

institution in 1920), Hairmyres in Lanarkshire, City Hospital, Aberdeen, South East Counties Sanatorium, East Fortune near Edinburgh, and Glenafton Sanatorium, Ayrshire. Robroyston employed four full-time teachers, Hairmyres three, and the rest one teacher each. Teachers' salaries and other school costs were met by the respective local authority tuberculous schemes and not by the Education Authorities.[61] By 1928, Hairmyres open-air school accommodated 90 children.[62]

In 1928, a joint meeting was held between the SBH, local Medical Officers of larger local authorities and members of the Scottish Branch of the British Legion. The conference decided that the numbers of tuberculous ex-service personnel willing to live in a village settlement was too few to make such a scheme viable. An alternative proposed by the SBH was for a broad 'after-care' scheme. The scheme's intention was to set up carefully selected tuberculous ex-service men in small businesses in their home areas, placing families of tuberculous service personnel in more suitable houses, and in sending the children of affected service personnel to residential homes for a time. The scheme seemed to be an extension of existing SBH arrangements for other tuberculosis sufferers and their families. It was met with a cautious response by the British Legion.[63]

The rationale behind the retraining scheme was clear. Money would be saved if some ex-servicemen (the initial number in the English scheme was 1,000) could be successfully retrained to take up an alternative occupation by which they could support themselves. The costs to the State of such an arrangement was less than continuing to pay war pensions to these tuberculous ex-servicemen for the rest of their lives. Similar reasoning applied as the scheme was extended to cover other convalescent cases with a hope of returning to the job market.

---

61 SBH, *Eighth Annual Report, 1926* (Edinburgh, HMSO, 1927), 63, [Cmd 2881].
62 SBH *Tenth Annual Report, 1928* (Edinburgh: HMSO, 1929), 204, [Cmd 3529].
63 Ibid., 206.

Conflict between SBH and Local Authorities over Institutional Tuberculosis Care

> The general policy of the Local Government Board for Scotland, now merged in the Scottish Board of Health, was to press forward all methods of prevention and treatment according to the needs of the case, and not to rely on any single type of institution.[64]

Despite this statement from SBH member William Leslie Mackenzie, the SBH policy at this time concentrated on plans for sanatorium construction, sometimes in the face of municipal reluctance. The issue of sanatorium provision in Scotland was raised at the inaugural meeting of the Scottish Board of Health on 18 July 1919. Item 10 on the first agenda was a discussion on whether to proceed with the building of a new sanatorium at Muirburn in Lanarkshire. The local authority view was that there was no need for a new sanatorium due to the number of tuberculosis beds which were available in the county (e.g. Hairmyres Sanatorium was officially opened in June 1919 with 260 beds). However, the feeling of the meeting was that the hands of the SBH were tied since the LGBS had advocated the combination of authorities to administer the new sanatorium and had also concurred in the selection of the site for a new sanatorium.[65] Yet within a few months, in February 1920 the plans for Muirburn were set aside by the SBH in view of the opening of Hairmyres Sanatorium. Instead the Lanark Combination of Burghs was advised to consider a scheme for the whole area to provide specialist services for non-respiratory tuberculosis. There remained a pressing need for more tuberculosis beds in the area.[66] For example, continued Lanarkshire bed shortages in the 1930s and 40s, led Coatbridge Burgh to send tuberculosis

64 PRO, PIN 15/27, 'Memorandum on the Present Position in Scotland' produced as part of an investigation into the question for village settlements for ex-servicemen in Scotland by W. Leslie Mackenzie, medical member of the SBH, (Undated, 1919?).

65 NAS, HH1/472, SBH minutes of first meeting, 18 July 1919.

66 Lanark County, Medical Officer of Health Annual Reports, 1919–48, passim.

patients to spare capacity institutional accommodation in the county of Argyllshire.

Other joint county boards expressed post-war reluctance towards building sanatoria. In August 1919, the SBH received a resolution from the Joint Sanatorium Board of Stirling County and Burghs and Clackmannan County and Burghs stating their decision not to proceed meantime with the building of a joint sanatorium for central Scotland.[67] The joint sanatorium board of the three local authorities in central Scotland combined soon after the issue of LGBS guidelines to local authorities for the 'Prevention, Detection and Treatment of Tuberculosis.' The site chosen for construction by the Joint Board was at Barr Wood, on the Denny/Stirling Road, 300 feet above sea-level. The plan was for a 100-bed sanatorium, principally for respiratory tuberculosis patients, to be built at a cost of £20–25,000, offset by a Government grant of £9,000. In 1916, before construction work could begin, the Joint Board was instructed by the LGBS to defer any building until peacetime. During the war, temporary accommodation for respiratory tuberculosis patients was found in sanatoria in Bridge of Weir, Perth and Peebles. In 1919, the joint Stirlingshire and Clackmannanshire Sanatorium Board discovered that building costs for the planned sanatorium had steeply risen. As an interim measure, the three local authorities gained the approval of the (soon to be replaced) LGBS to use beds in local Fever Hospitals (seven of the eight local Infectious Diseases Hospitals were used, including those at Stirling, Falkirk and Bannockburn) to house tuberculous patients in the area. Given this solution and the additional hurdle of the great costs involved in the projected new sanatorium, the Joint Board took the decision not to proceed with the new construction for the present. The familiar post-World War One theme of economy was crucial to the Joint Board's thinking, although some concern was expressed about the efficacy of sanatorium treatment.[68] The SBH response was abrupt. The SBH was '[...] not satisfied that the reasons for delay

67 NAS, HH1/472, SBH, agenda of SBH meeting, 29 August 1919.

68 NAS, HH1/472, SBH, undated papers attached to agenda of SBH meeting, 29 August 1919.

were adequate and did not see why their previous decision [...] should be departed from.'[69]

Other local authorities questioned the SBH emphasis on sanatorium construction. The 1919 Annual Aberdeenshire County Tuberculosis Report revealed doubts about the efficacy of continuing to pump money into sanatoria construction: 'One must acknowledge that the Utopian ideas which were entertained some years ago concerning the eradication of tuberculosis by means of Sanatoria have not been realised [...].'[70]

The financial burden on local authorities posed by sanatorium construction made them reluctant to build. To help overcome this difficulty, a SBH circular of November 1919 announced the Treasury decision to double the available capital grant up to the amount of £180 per bed to local authorities, subject to a maximum grant of three-fifths of the total cost. The increased grant was made available on condition that authorities submitted construction proposals no later than 30th June 1920 and that the works be completed within two and a half years.[71] This circular presaged the planned removal of sanatorium benefits (individual and local authority) under the revised 1920 National Insurance Act. It put in place a strict timetable for last-minute state subvented sanatoria construction. One area that benefitted from the new arrangements was the Joint Perth burgh and county board whose proposal for a new 100-bed sanatorium was approved by the SBH in December 1919.[72]

In late 1920, the Joint Stirling/Clackmannanshire Board (under pressure from the SBH to find more permanent accommodation) purchased the private Ochill Hills Sanatorium which had been under lease to Glasgow Corporation.[73] The sanatorium had accommodation

69 NAS, HH75/1, SBH minutes, 26 August 1919.

70 County of Aberdeen, MOH, 'Annual Report on Tuberculosis, 1919', 43.

71 GRHB, E4\1\4, Banff County, 'Medical Officer of Health Annual Report, 1919', 6.

72 NAS, HH75/1, SBH minutes, 8 December 1919.

73 Ochill Hills sanatorium was a former private sanatorium which had been let by Glasgow City Corporation for many years. Stirling Regional Archives, SC3/3/26, Stirling County, Medical Officer of Health Annual Report, 1921', 34–35.

for over 100 beds and was taken over by the Joint Board in May 1921. The sanatorium was converted from male-only accommodation to enable the admission of female and child patients.[74] Other Scottish counties gained SBH approval for similar take-over arrangement, rather than foot the bill for new, purpose-built, sanatoria. South Eastern Counties Joint Counties Board (covering seven counties) opened the 199-bed East Fortune Sanatorium in 1923 after converting buildings on the site of the former East Fortune Aerodrome.

Tuberculosis arrangements proved particularly difficult in remote areas of Scotland. But this did not prevent the SBH from questioning some of the less acceptable solutions reached. For example, in 1926 the town of Elgin in North East Scotland came under close questioning for their arrangements to send advanced tuberculosis cases to Aberdeen or Inverness rather than make their own local provisions:

> What arrangements are proposed as regards the conveyance of patients to hospital? It would obviously not be in the interests of the patients or of public health that acute and highly infectious cases should travel by train and it seems to the Board that it would be necessary to convey practically all patients by ambulance.[75]

Orkney island council had taken no action to set up a tuberculosis scheme or make sanatorium provision in the County (covering six small local authorities) until the SBH contacted it August 1920. The local MOH Dr. Heddle had been pressing for local Tuberculosis provision since 1912. Owing to the great cost involved, the Council decided not to build a new sanatorium, but secured the disused wartime Scapa Seaplane Station for conversion into a tuberculosis sanatorium.[76] It was not until 1922, after some debate with the SBH, over the arrangements for sanatorium provision at the former seaplane station, that the Tuberculosis Scheme for Orkney was

74 SC3/3/27, Stirling County, 'Medical Officer of Health Annual Report, 1922', 48.

75 NAS, HH75/24, SBH, Divisional Committee II minutes, 6 April 1926.

76 Orkney Archives, CO7/1/1, County of Orkney, 'Annual Report by the County Medical Officer, 1920', 9.

operational – even then the County Tuberculosis Pavilion at Scapa, with beds for 12 patients, was not opened until Autumn 1924. The Orkney Tuberculosis Scheme when it was finally launched appeared to be a comprehensive service. It included arrangements for District Medical Officers to notify the County MOH of tuberculous cases in their area. Notification was followed by a personal visit to the patient by the County TO. The TO also held a consultation with the patient's general practitioner over forms of treatment. The County TO could also make discretionary provisions for additional food and drugs at a maximum level of ten shillings (50 pence) per week for patients. Serious cases were admitted to Scapa Pavilion under the direction of the TO. The Orkney arrangements allowed District Nurses, where available, to act also as Tuberculosis Nurses.[77]

Other remote regions gradually obtained sanatorium provision. The Isle of Lewis (off the north west coast of Scotland in the County of Ross and Cromarty) was the site for a British Red Cross-sponsored sanatorium in Stornoway reserved for ex-service men. The Island had a high incidence of the disease. Lewis, untouched by tuberculosis until the middle of the nineteenth century, had a mortality level of 242 per 100,000 in 1905 (far above the Scottish average of 217).[78] Tuberculosis was introduced to the Island through contact with 'outsiders' through the fishing industry and return of people who had migrated to the mainland for work. The epidemic proportions of the disease can partly be accounted for by lack of immunity in a population previously untouched by the disease. By 1920, local MOH and Tuberculosis Officer for the District, Agnes Ellen Porter (later Miller)[79] estimated the Lewis notification rates to be 'about ten times

77 CO7/1/3, County of Orkney, 'Annual Report by the County Medical Officer, 1922', 16–17.

78 For more on the history of tuberculosis in Lewis, see R.S. Doig [MOH in Lewis, 1930–66], 'A Century of Tuberculosis on the Isle of Lewis in the Western Isles', Ph.D. Thesis, University of Glasgow, 1965.

79 Ellen Porter had served as a doctor with Elsie Inglis as part of the Scottish Women's Hospitals staff at Valjevo in Yugoslavia in 1915. She was MOH, Tuberculosis Officer and School Medical Officer for Lewis between 1920 and her resignation in 1925. For more on Porter see, see Catriona Macdonald 'The

as much tuberculosis in Lewis as in the average county'.[80] In 1920 the Scottish average death rate for tuberculosis stood at 124 per 100,000. of the population. In Lewis the death rate was 193. In 1924, it was estimated that 1,000 of the Island's 28,000 population had the disease.[81] In that year the Treasury agreed to make a special release of money from the Highlands and Islands Medical Service Fund to provide a sanatorium for the Island, since the Islanders themselves could not generate sufficient income from rates to make their own provision.[82] A similar special HIMS grant was provided for the Shetland Islands in 1925 to secure sanatorium provision at Lerwick. The Shetland Isles was almost as severely affected by the disease as Lewis. The death-rate for tuberculosis (all forms) in the Shetlands was 199 (per 100,000) for the years 1920–4, compared to the Scottish average of 119 for the same period.[83] A 24-bed sanatorium was opened in Lerwick in 1928.

Convinced that poor housing was aiding the spread of the disease in Lewis, Porter, the Island Medical Officer, called for an increase in preventive measures for tuberculosis. Porter wanted housing improvements,[84] especially the construction of chimneys and windows that could be opened. She also recommended the treatment and isolation of chronic cases. The Lewis Sanatorium had 26 beds for ex-service men only and Porter estimated a further 50 beds were required for the treatment of other tuberculous patients in the District. 'The chronic case [...] left as he is, spitting on the floor of the black house,

---

White Plague – A Study of Tuberculosis on the Isle of Lewis 1850–1950' M.Phil. dissertation, University of Glasgow, 1996.

80 HHBA, Ross and Cromarty County, 'Medical Report, 1920', [see section – Lewis District Report on Public Health and Tuberculosis], (Dingwall, 1921), 20.

81 SBH, *Sixth Annual Report, 1924*, 57.

82 Ibid.

83 SBH, *Seventh Annual Report, 1925*, 61–2.

84 The traditional 'black house' was a long, low building built of stone with a turf roof, here both humans and animals were housed together, often without partitions to divide the two. With no windows, there was no hope of through ventilation, allowing the smoke from peat fires to accumulate. For more on housing in the Isle of Lewis, see Macdonald, 'The White Plague – A Study of Tuberculosis on the Isle of Lewis 1850–1950', 1996.

where no precautions are taken to prevent infection, is a danger to the community, and he is useless to the community, while his ill-health continues.'[85] Porter's calls may have had some impact. In 1928, a 24-bed extension to the Red Cross sanatorium (with all beds available to the general public) was opened on Lewis.

The tuberculosis rate for the Island of Lewis (with a population of 28,400) continued to make up the majority of cases notified in the County of Ross and Cromarty (population 70,300) for the next two decades. More tuberculosis beds for Lewis inhabitants were opened up in 1932 when the British Red Cross Society terminated their lease on Lewis Sanatorium and handed the institution over to Ross and Cromarty County Council.[86] These measures of expanded sanatorium care made few inroads into high Lewis tuberculosis rates. In 1945, of 109 respiratory cases notified in the County of Ross and Cromarty, 70 came from the Island of Lewis. The figures for non-respiratory cases were 18 from Lewis out of a total of 36 notified cases.[87]

In the years between 1919 and the early 1920s, the SBH was pulled in various directions regarding their policy towards sanatoria construction. At one level, they had inherited an active policy of Joint Sanatoria projects from the LGBS, meantime they were faced with the post war economic and medical reality that sanatoria were expensive capital projects with questionable medical outcomes. Local authorities were pressed into action by the SBH to provide sanatoria. The local authorities which had most success in providing sanatoria were those which acted in combination with other authorities to increase the numbers of beds and range of services available. In the longer term, this experience influenced the 1936 Report by the Committee on Scottish Health Services (Cathcart Report). The idea of combination was taken a step further, with a recommendation to reorganise local authority tuberculosis schemes on a regional basis in order to provide a more comprehensive, (and cost-effective) range of treatments. 'The

85 Ross and Cromarty County, 'Medical Report, 1920', [see section – Lewis District Report on Public Health and Tuberculosis], 21.

86 DHS, *Annual Report, 1932* (1933), 77.

87 HHBA, County of Ross and Cromarty, 'Medical Officer of Health Annual Report, 1945', 18

reorganisation which we propose [...] would remove part if the criticism that is directed at present against sanatorium policy on the ground that the results are not commensurate with the expenditure.'[88] Such proposals lay in the future, in the early 1920s the SBH was itself coming under pressure from the Treasury to cut back on overall Scottish expenditure on tuberculosis provision.

The Development of Inter-War Local Authority Tuberculosis Provisions

The SBH's emphasis on sanatoria provision placed a heavy burden on small and rural authorities in the 1920s. (Local authority funding arrangements were later altered under the 1929 Local Government Act).[89] The possible solution of creating Joint Sanatorium Boards to provide larger authorities to fund new tuberculosis institutions, could on occasion prove counter-productive if local authorities worked to a different agenda than the SBH. Under the powers of the Local Government (Scotland) Act, 1929 the opportunities for joint local authority ventures increased. Any two or more local authorities could combine for any purpose in which they were jointly interested.

The best known of these joint local authority public health initiatives was the North East Regional Scheme. In 1930, the county councils of Aberdeen and Kincardine combined with the burgh of Aberdeen to provide public health services to cover a population of 347,000. The ground-breaking scheme actually commenced before the passage of the Local Government Act, 1929. In 1925, Aberdeen County Council combined with the County Education Committee to bring all the public health services in Aberdeenshire under a single health committee and therefore under the control of a single Medical Officer of Health. In 1927, the city of Aberdeen parish council gave Oldmill Hospital to the town council for use as a general hospital. The

88 DHS, *Committee on Scottish Health Services Report*, 205.

89 See chapter two for more on the Local Government Act, 1929.

newly opened Woodend Hospital set 100 beds aside for tuberculous cases.

The tuberculosis scheme for the North East region was designed for both the prevention and treatment of the disease. A regional Medical Officer devoted full time to tuberculosis was assisted by divisional medical officers. The Regional Scheme pooled close to 270 tuberculosis beds, (144 for respiratory and 124 for other forms of the disease). Two city institutions offered radiological facilities to the whole region, something that the counties of Aberdeen and Kincardineshire would not have been able to supply to their inhabitants without the existence of the Regional Scheme.[90]

Harry Rae, MOH for the north-east commented favourably on the city of Aberdeen figures for 1934. The total tuberculosis rate was 64 in the city of Aberdeen, compared to a Glasgow figure of 100, Edinburgh's 84 and Dundee's 80, (the all Scotland figure was 75). Rae put forward two reasons why 'so far as tuberculosis is concerned, Aberdeen stands in a distinctly favourable position.'[91] He felt that Aberdeen on the whole had less poverty, malnutrition, poor housing and overcrowding than the three other largest cities in Scotland. He also identified the anti-tuberculosis work in the city as a contributing factor (albeit of indeterminate worth). The stress of the scheme was prevention of the disease, or at least of an advanced stage of the disease. In the North East, this was chiefly done by the speedy segregation of identified cases in hospitals, sanatoria, or in outdoor shelters. Waiting lists for institutional admissions were short in the region. In 1925, in Aberdeenshire, there was little difficulty in obtaining the immediate admission of early or advanced respiratory cases, while provisions for non respiratory cases meant that no such cases had been refused institutional treatment in the fifteen years since the establishment of the Aberdeen County Tuberculosis Scheme in 1912.[92]

---

90 DHS, *Committee on Scottish Health Services Report*, appendix VI, 403.

91 GRHB Archives, GRHB, E1\1\40, Aberdeen City, 'Medical Officer of Health, Annual Report, 1934', 36.

92 GRHB, E2\4\35, County of Aberdeen, MO, 'Annual Report on Tuberculosis, 1925', 31.

Even in 1948 on the eve of the NHS, and after World War Two had put great strain on local authority health services, tuberculosis waiting lists in the city of Aberdeen were described as minimal.[93] The usual period between notification and hospitalisation was fourteen days. The use of periodic radiographic examinations to identify 'early' (treatable) cases was actively pursued by the city Public Health Department. This work was reliant on the co-operation of medical practitioners in the city. The work of general practitioners in encouraging young tuberculosis 'contacts' to attend the tuberculosis clinic for examination was described as 'invaluable' by Aberdeen MOH in 1935.[94] Another unique aspect of the regional scheme, was the existence of a 'preventorium' at Linn Moor Convalescent Home, Culter. The Home was open to pre-tuberculous and non-infectious respiratory tuberculous children aged between 3 and 13 years of age. The regimen included remedial physical exercise for the children aimed at improving the muscular, circulatory, respiratory, and locomotory functions of children admitted, to improve their overall chances of resistance to 'acute tuberculosis.'[95] Aberdeen's vigorous anti-tuberculosis policy was apparently rewarded by reduced mortality rates. The City of Aberdeen MOH Report for 1936 recorded a fall in the total tuberculosis death-rate in the city from 115 per 100,000 of the population in 1926 to 49 in 1936. Years later, during the war, the Aberdeen regional scheme was still held up as a model arrangement in the medical press.[96]

Elsewhere in Scotland, only 10 of 31 Scottish counties had tuberculosis dispensaries by 1939. Tuberculosis dispensaries, like

93 GRHB, E1\1\40, Aberdeen City, 'Annual Report of the Medical Officer of Health, 1940–45', 17.

94 GRHB, E1\1\40, Aberdeen City, 'Annual Report of the Medical Officer of Health, 1935', 35.

95 GRHB, E2\4\35, Aberdeen County, 'Annual Report of the Medical Officer of Health,1919, 58–60. The remedial and graduated exercises were also offered to adult non-respiratory cases, both at dispensaries and at patients' homes. See SBH, *Sixth Annual Report, 1924*, 58–59.

96 G. Lissant Cox, 'Co-ordination and Regionalisation of Tuberculosis Services in England, Wales and Scotland', *Public Health*, vol. 54, No. 9, (June 1941), 159 and 162.

infant and maternal welfare centres, were deemed impractical in rural areas with a dispersed population. By 1943, this figure had actually fallen to eight in the 31 Scottish counties. The death-rate in rural areas of Scotland varied enormously. In lowland counties mortality was often as much as 30–50 less per 100,000 of population than in urban areas. Meanwhile, in the Highlands and Islands it was ranged between 80 and 100 per 100,000 in 1943, when the Scottish aggregate figure was 83.[97]

In areas where it was not considered practicable to establish dispensaries, the local TO carried out an initial examination of the patient and any subsequent medical supervision at the patient's home. In very remote or sparsely populated areas where it would have been impossible for the individual TO to keep in regular touch with all tuberculosis patients, general practitioners were often paid by local authorities to make personal visits. Local authorities could also defray the cost of home nursing. Such visits were often supplemented by the attendance of voluntary nurses and health visitors.[98]

Inter-War Tuberculosis Mortality and Local Authority Preferential Housing Schemes

> It is impossible to prove that the anti-tuberculosis campaign has been the main factor in accelerating the decline in the mortality from tuberculosis as shown in the published statistics, but an even heavier burden rests on those who maintain that it has had no effect.
> (SBH, *Tenth Annual Report, 1928* (Edinburgh: HMSO, 1928), 200)

The major problem for all tuberculosis schemes in the period before World War Two was the inability of medicine to successfully treat the disease. In 1920, Sir George Newman, Chief Medical Officer of the Ministry of Health reported that three quarters of all British and

97 Clayson, 'Modern Trends in Preventive Medicine and Social Aspects of Tuberculosis', 210–211.

98 DHS, *Committee on Scottish Health Services Report*, 202.

German sanatorium cases were dead within five years of treatment.[99] An Aberdeenshire County survey revealed that of 90 cases treated institutionally in 1914, 47 or 52% had died before the end of 1922 – that is within eight years of treatment. (See table 5.3 for full details). Three of the deaths were not directly due to tuberculosis. One patient committed suicide, another died of heart disease and a third of rheumatic fever. A further eight patients could not be traced. The findings were not completely bleak. At the end of 1922, 23 of the sample 90 patients (26%) showed no signs of active respiratory tuberculosis and were engaged in full-time work.[100]

1914	13
1915	12
1916	5
1917	5
1918	4
1919	5
1920	1
1921	2
1922	0

Table 5.3 Mortality Rates among 90 Aberdeenshire Tuberculosis Patients, 1914–1922[101]

Figures for Glasgow revealed that 73% of all sputum positive cases notified between 1935 and 1938 died within five years of notification, the figure rising to 83% after nine years.[102] In 1937, for all notified adult tuberculosis cases in Britain, the death rate was 60%

99 'First Annual Report of the Chief Medical Officer of the Ministry of Health, 1919–20', (HMSO, 1920), 94.

100 GRHB, E2\4\42, County of Aberdeen, MOH, 'Annual Report on Tuberculosis, 1922', 46.

101 Ibid.

102 *Report of the Scottish Health Services Council's Committee on Tuberculosis* (Edinburgh, HMSO, Edinburgh, 1951), Appendix 14a, 60, cited in McFarlane 'Tuberculosis in Scotland', 150.

within 5 years of notification. These rates show no improvement over those for 1919/20.

In the inter-war years, the treatment for tuberculosis included x-ray and ultra-violet ray therapy ('artificial sunlight') for tubercular joints, glands and skin. Surgical intervention in the shape of Artificial Pneumothorax – ('collapse therapy') was also practised on selected 'early' cases of respiratory tuberculosis. The Tuberculosis Officer for Edinburgh, and Dr Rhodes, senior lecturer in Bacteriology at Edinburgh University laid plans to introduce the Bacille Calmette-Guerin[103] (B.C.G.) vaccine in Edinburgh in the autumn of 1939, as a consequence of a visit by to Dr. Guerin at the Pasteur Institute in Paris. However, the scheme was shelved due the outbreak of World War Two.[104] In 1948, plans were belatedly announced to introduce the B.C.G. vaccine into use in Edinburgh, targeting children and tuberculosis nurses.[105] The real breakthrough in successfully treating tuberculosis in Scotland was not made until the 1950s when the B.C.G. vaccine was finally made widely available in Scotland.

In the absence of a widely recognised 'cure' for tuberculosis, sanatoria treatment continued into the inter-war period. This was despite criticism of such treatment as ineffective both in the medical press and among public health appointees.[106] The need for an

103 The B.C.G. vaccine was first isolated in 1908 by Leon C.A. Calmette and Camille Guerin in Paris and made into a vaccine in 1921.

104 LHBA, Edinburgh, LHB16/2/21, 'Annual Report of the Medical Officer of Health, Edinburgh, 1939', 3.

105 LHB16/2/32, 'Annual Report of the Medical Officer of Health, Edinburgh, 1948', 4.

106 'It is too much to expect that the mortality from tuberculosis will be greatly diminished by Sanatorium treatment, but it can be confidently asserted that the economic value of a large number of sufferers will thereby be enhanced and maintained, and that the educational aspect of treatment will ultimately act as a prophylactic measure and as a means of raising the general health of the community.' County of Aberdeen, MOH, 'Annual Report on Tuberculosis, 1919', 44. The limitations of sanatorium care were reinforced in an article published in the *Practitioner* by R.R. Trail, Medical Director of Papworth Village Settlement in 1947: 'The end results of residential treatment and consequent return to the conditions of normal life and industry are well known: 60 per cent of those with moderately advanced disease at admission are dead

alternative, preventive medical approach (with the emphasis on the individual), was stressed amongst certain local authorities. For example, in Aberdeenshire in 1920, great stress was laid on the preventive aspects of public health activity:

> As a result of public health propaganda, the public are beginning to take a greater interest in health matters. In the first years of the County [Tuberculosis] Scheme, it was very difficult to get 'contacts' to come to the Dispensary for periodic examination, but now it is quite common for parents voluntarily to ask for the examination of 'contact' children.[107]

The massive public investment in institutional care combined with the failure to identify more efficacious forms of treatment meant that for the SBH there was little alternative to sanatoria. Sanatoria played a public health role in removing 'open' cases from their homes and workplaces. More broadly, the triumph of institutional treatment for tuberculosis was secured at a time when the personal health services in general were expanding at the expense of a more environmental emphasis of an earlier period of public health provision.[108] Poor housing and poor living conditions were identified as crucial factors in the spread of tuberculosis, but although not inexpensive, sanatorium treatment was preferred, as a cheaper alternative to a massive house building programme.

The economic argument i.e. that sanatoria treatment enabled people to return to the workforce, albeit doing different types of work, rather than leaving them chronically debilitated and drawing upon public funds was a strong one. Yet, long-term institutional treatment, fresh air, sunlight and conservative surgery when combined were no better than palliative measures.

---

within five years, and most of them within two years of the date of discharge. Yet this country is spending at least £12,000,000 a year on tuberculosis.' R.R. Trail, 'Advances in the Treatment of Tuberculosis', *The Practitioner*, vol. 159, no. 952, (October 1947), 296.

107 GRHB, E2\4\35, County of Aberdeen MOH, 'Annual Report on Tuberculosis, 1920, 17.

108 See C. Webster, 'Origins of Social Medicine in Britain', *Society for the Social History of Medicine Bulletin*, (June 1986), 53, and J. Lewis, *What Price Community Medicine?* (Brighton: Harvester Wheatsheaf, 1986), 9.

The pattern of sanatorium patients returning on their release to the unsuitable home conditions that had contributed to the onset of the disease in the first instance was long established. There were some initiatives to re-house tuberculosis sufferers. Following the lead of Sheffield in 1928, Glasgow began a policy of re-housing tuberculosis patients in 1929. Ten per cent of Glasgow's new housing stock was set aside for tuberculous families. By 1949, 1,849 Glasgow families with a tuberculosis family member had been re-housed.[109]

The 1936 DHS Cathcart Report noted that some other Scottish local authorities practised similar schemes.[110] The 1937 Annual Report of Lanark County Council noted that the local scheme for re-housing families affected by tuberculosis was still in operation, and during the year, 22 families were re-housed. Also, a further 26 families with tuberculosis sufferers were re-housed under 'Decrowding and Improvement' Schemes.[111] Not every local authority was in a position to operate such a scheme. In Dundee a scheme was unveiled in 1935 to allow the Housing Factor (Officer) for the City to maintain a special list of tuberculous families with the intention of giving them particular consideration in house allocation. In 1936, the MOH for Dundee noted that the proposal had been shelved because there were not sufficient available houses in Dundee.[112]

The principle of re-housing families containing a tuberculosis sufferer was eventually written into the National Health Service (Scotland) Act of 1947. Section 27 of the Act stated that a proportion (estimated at not less than one in ten) of permanent houses available for letting by the local health authority were to be allocated to tuberculous families for re-housing 'so long as the need remains'. This

109 See Bryder, *Below the Magic Mountain*, 90.

110 DHS, *Committee on Scottish Health Services Report* , 201.

111 Lanark County, 'Annual Report of the Medical Officer of Health, 1937', 8.

112 'It would appear that we will have to wait until sufficient houses have been erected under the Housing (Scotland) Act, 1935, to deal with overcrowding.' Dundee District Archives, City of Dundee, 'Medical Officer of Health Annual Report, 1937', 17.

provision was to be administered by the local MOH, with information passed on the National Assistance Board of all such re-housing.[113]

The Rising 'Costs' of Tuberculosis

The cost of institutional tuberculosis care mounted throughout the inter-war period. Scottish spending on general tuberculosis services rose from £100,000 to £600,00 in the decade between 1918–1928. Tuberculosis services accounted for 52% of the total expended on the four main public health services in Scotland in 1931. (See table 5.4). The level of expenditure was relative to what was considered the great scourge of the disease, particularly among young adults (of prime working age). In 1934, over 34,000 cases were identified, and in that year the disease was responsible for 3,702 deaths, equal to 5.8% of the total deaths in Scotland, and accounted for about one-third of the total deaths among those aged between 15 and 24.[114] Within tuberculosis expenditure, institutional provision swallowed the vast majority of the funds. In 1928, the SBH estimated that 85% of its total tuberculosis expenditure was spent on institutional services.[115]

Tuberculosis	52%
Maternal and Child Welfare	23%
School Medical Service	18%
Venereal Disease	7%

Table 5.4 Proportional Percentage Expenditure on Four Selected Scottish Public Health Services, 1931[116]

113 Lanark County, 'Annual Report of the Medical Officer of Health, 1948', [Survey of new NHS (Scotland) legislation], 201.

114 DHS, *Committee on Scottish Health Services Report*, 203.

115 SBH, *Tenth Annual Report, 1928*, 201–2.

116 H.J. Rae, 'Some Local and General Problems in Tuberculosis Administration', *EMJ*, 1931, 152.

In Scotland, sanatoria provision (as with National Insurance) was weighted towards the adult male worker. Overall, the identification of institutional deaths as a proportion of all tuberculosis deaths was traditionally viewed by the SBH/DHS as a monitor for the success of municipal tuberculosis schemes. The higher the percentage of deaths in institutions of all tuberculosis deaths the more successful the scheme was viewed in identifying cases and ensuring the tuberculous were separated from the general public.

Table 5.5 shows that in selected burghs in the 1930s the number of male tuberculosis deaths in institutions invariably outnumbered that of females. A possible factor would be the reluctance of females to leave home and family for the long-term stays which were often the result of sanatorium admission. The Borders town of Dumfries seemed to be the exception to the rule, in that 45% of females who died from tuberculosis between 1932–37 were institutionalised as opposed 32% of males. This was repeated in 1939 when 100% of female tuberculosis sufferers died in institutions compared to only 20% of males. However, the respective number of cases involved make these percentage figures misleading. In 1932–37, 65 males and 42 females respectively died of tuberculosis in Dumfries, while in 1939, 5 males and 2 females died of tuberculosis in the town.

Local tuberculosis death rates could be affected by particular circumstances. The tuberculosis rates for Coatbridge in Lanarkshire were higher than for Scotland as a whole between the years 1912 and 1938 (see table 5.6). An exception was the non-respiratory rate for 1938 which was at 9 in Coatbridge and 17 for the whole of Scotland. An official DHS report compiled from Coatbridge returns suggested the high rate of casual labour in the area, with incomers already suffering from the disease arriving to work in the town, as a possible explanation for the above average tuberculosis incidence. Other possible causes suggested were the age and sex distribution of the population, the nature of the local industries, and economic factors.[117]

117 North Lanarkshire Council, Coatbridge Public Library Archives, DHS, 1938 report to Cordiner, MOH, Coatbridge, 20 November 1939.

Burgh	Total Deaths				Institutional Deaths				Percentage Institutional Deaths			
	1932–37		1939		1932–37		1939		1932–37		1939	
	M	F	M	F	M	F	M	F	M	F	M	F
Arbroath	22	24	3	3	18	15	2	2	81	62	66	66
Aberdeen	278	187	43	25	170	63	23	11	61	33	53	45
Dundee	312	320	55	54	188	81	32	21	60	22	58	39
Ayr	68	65	13	7	32	25	6	4	47	38	46	57
Kilmarnock	59	53	13	5	40	17	7	0	69	32	53	0
Clydebank	120	94	11	13	77	46	3	8	64	49	27	61
Dumbarton	45	39	4	4	23	6	2	1	51	15	50	25
Dumfries	65	42	5	2	21	19	1	2	32	45	20	100
Dunfermline	44	44	10	6	25	13	6	4	56	29	60	66
Kirkcaldy	61	44	9	6	35	13	4	1	57	29	44	16
Inverness	46	38	8	6	33	16	6	3	71	42	75	50
Airdrie	33	35	6	9	19	8	3	6	59	22	50	66
Coatbridge	90	93	19	12	36	13	5	1	40	14	26	9
Glasgow	3154	2484	538	434	1737	993	254	195	55	39	47	44
Hamilton	54	58	9	14	37	16	3	3	68	28	33	21
Motherwell	92	112	23	21	55	31	8	3	59	27	34	14
Rutherglen	63	45	8	5	34	21	3	1	53	46	37	20
Edinburgh	992	797	163	122	528	233	75	33	53	29	46	27
Greenock	216	164	40	36	93	47	24	10	43	28	80	29
Paisley	199	151	40	34	126	62	22	19	63	41	55	55
Falkirk	71	64	14	6	45	18	9	4	63	28	64	66
Stirling	41	16	4	7	16	7	2	1	39	43	50	14
Perth	69	53	5	6	20	23	5	3	28	43	100	50
Total	6194	5022	1043	837	3408	1776	505	336	55	35	48	40

Table 5.5 Institutional Deaths from Tuberculosis in Selected Scottish Burghs, 1932–1937 and 1939[118]

118 Figures taken from Register General for Scotland Annual Reports, passim.

The Coatbridge population was 43,056 in 1939. There were 14,268 male workers in the town in 1931, and of these 4,749 were metal workers, 1,283 were miners or quarriers, and 1,139 in transport and communication. Of the 3,855 employed females, 1,185 were engaged in personal service (782 were indoor domestics) and 374 were textile workers. Perhaps most crucially the town was seriously over-crowded: 'Coatbridge at [the] 1931 census occupied an unfavourable place from the point of view and 1 and 2 apartment houses.'[119]

	Scotland		Coatbridge	
Period	Respiratory	Non Respiratory	Respiratory	Non Respiratory
1912–1915	109	59	112	89
1916–1920	98	47	99	71
1921–1925	80	35	87	47
1926–1930	67	28	74	45
1931–1935	59	22	69	30
1936	55	18	67	30
1937	56	18	76	45
1938	52	17	82	9

Table 5.6 Tuberculosis Mortality Rates: Scotland and Coatbridge, (per 100,000 population), 1912–1938[120]

The main conclusions of the 1936 *Committee on Scottish Health Services Report* (Cathcart Report) relating to tuberculosis suggested that there were major failings within the existing services. In the eight-point conclusion[121] to the section of the report on tuberculosis, the DHS Committee stressed that the great decline in mortality from the disease since the later nineteenth century was not enough, and 'intensive effort' was needed especially among adolescents and young adults. Another key finding was that tuberculosis schemes should be

119 DHS, 1939 report to Cordiner, MOH, Coatbridge, 26 April 1940.

120 Figures obtained from DHS, 1938 report to Cordiner, MOH, Coatbridge, 20 November 1939.

121 DHS, *Committee on Scottish Health Services Report*, 206.

regarded as supplementary to preventive measures, such as improved housing, feeding and general hygiene, and control of the milk supply.[122]

There was a further call for a regional basis for tuberculosis care to allow the most advanced techniques to be made available to a wider population. The Cathcart Report findings proposed the creation of a more comprehensive medical service for tuberculosis treatment. However, it also acknowledged a continued role for the voluntary sector: The Report commended 'the educational and other work of the National Association for the Prevention of Tuberculosis should continue to be encouraged.'[123] The Cathcart Report called for regionalisation of health services. It was not alone. The North East Regional Medical Scheme and the Highlands and Islands Medical Service (along with the Gloucestershire Medical Services Scheme) were held up as role models in the 1937 Political and Economic Planning Report on the British Health Services.[124] The success of the Aberdeen Regional Tuberculosis Scheme may be inferred from a comparison of Scottish and Aberdeen (city and county) tuberculosis rates for the period 1938–1945 (see table 5.7).

---

122 The Cathcart Report also stated that: '[...] the extension of medical services and the rehousing of families where a member is suffering from tuberculosis will facilitate the home treatment and after-care of tuberculosis patients and the supervision of contacts.' For more on the Cathcart Report's tuberculosis recommendations see points 2 and 4 of the conclusions and recommendations on tuberculosis in DHS, *Committee on Scottish Health Services Report*, 206.

123 Point 8 of the conclusions and recommendations on tuberculosis in DHS, *Committee on Scottish Health Services Report*, 206.

124 PEP, *Report on the British Health Services* (1937), 23, 363:392.

Wartime Arrangements and Breakthroughs

1. Local Services

By the outbreak of World War Two administrative provision for tuberculosis had been extended to incorporate a statutory local authority public health service for the identification, notification and treatment of the disease – as far as that was available at the time.[125] This, at least, was the official view contained in the DHS 'Outline of Scottish Services – Health' submitted to the Committee for Social Insurance and Allied Services (Beveridge Committee) in August 1941. However, the comprehensive service the DHS memorandum described (if in fact, it existed in this form) was not enough to cope with the impact of wartime circumstances on the disease rates. In particular, respiratory tuberculosis mounted throughout the war years and in the immediate post-war years. Respiratory tuberculosis rates rose from 4,567 in 1939 to 7,215 in 1943 (an increase of almost 37%). The overall tuberculosis rates made grim reading too. Notifications rose from 7,565 in 1938 to 9,048 in 1942. Death rates per 100,000 rose from 69 to 82 over the same period.[126] The 1941 DHS Memorandum outlined a broad ranging service, yet, there appears to have been little advance from the model tuberculosis scheme established by Philip in Edinburgh over 50 years before, except perhaps in the expansion of the scheme to cover the majority of the Scottish population. By 1941, there were 5,000 beds for tuberculosis cases in Scottish hospitals and sanatoria with 43 tuberculosis dispensaries in operation.

125 'The main features of the tuberculosis schemes in operation at the present day are notification of the disease, disinfection of premises, the provision of dispensaries, isolation and treatment – sanatoria for early cases, and hospitals for isolation of advanced cases.' PRO, CAB 87/76, Committee for Social Insurance and Allied Services, August 1941, Memorandum by DHS 'Outline of Scottish Services – Health', 8.

126 DHS, *Summary Report, 1944* (1945), 18.

The range of services outlined in the DHS submission to the Beveridge Committee may have appeared comprehensive. But no dispensary arrangements existed in the counties of Angus, Argyll, Banff, Berwick, Bute, Caithness, Dumfries, East Lothian, Fife, Kirkcudbright, Orkney, Shetland, Sutherland, and Wigtown. That is in 14 of the 22 single county authorities of Scotland in 1941. The most remarkable case was that of Fifeshire, which had no dispensary provision for a population of 201,476. It did however, possess institutional care at Glenlomond Sanatorium. Fife, had an average tuberculosis rate 27% less than the average Scottish rate throughout the period 1900–1950.[127] In contrast to Fife, Stirlingshire had four dispensaries for a population of 110, 988, as did Dumbartonshire with a population of 88, 509. Several other counties combined for public health purposes, but of these, Perth and Kinross and Moray and Nairn had no tuberculosis dispensary facilities. The same was true of the joint authority combining Inverness County and burgh. All of the single burgh authorities had at least one dispensary, Glasgow with a population of 1,119,863 had five, and Edinburgh with a population of 446,817 had four.[128]

2. Service Personnel

Added wartime pressure on tuberculosis beds was caused by the spread of the disease among service men and women. Prevention of the spread of the disease amongst service personnel was discussed in June 1940 and a suggestion that mass radiography be introduced to screen all recruits was proposed. However, mass radiography was considered impractical on the grounds that trained medical personnel were not readily available and that its introduction would prolong the medical examination of recruits. A small-scale trial radiographic

127 For more on this apparent contradiction see S. Patterson, 'The Control of Infectious Diseases in Fife c. 1855–1950', University of St Andrews, Ph.D. Thesis, (1989), 413.

128 Lissant Cox 'Co-ordination and Regionalisation of Tuberculosis Services in England, Wales and Scotland', 158.

screening of recruits to the Navy and Air Force was conducted in early 1941.[129]

Treatment of service and ex-service personnel in World War Two was integrated with general tuberculosis provision through the Emergency Hospital Scheme.[130] The Hospital Scheme was established at the beginning of the War under the general Emergency Medical Service. This wartime scheme meant that both civilians and service people were catered for under direct Government control and funding. All hospitals and sanatoria were forced to release tuberculous cases into the community in order to give priority to expected military casualties. In Stirlingshire, tuberculosis patients were discharged to clear the hospitals to allow air-raid precautions to be carried out. They were mostly re-admitted later.[131] The temporary discharge of tuberculous patients at the outset of the war was counter-acted by an initiative to free up civilian hospital beds. This was achieved through the construction of temporary huts for military casualties: 'As these huts came into commission, tuberculosis accommodation, which at present was reserved rather wastefully for casualties, would be released.'[132]

In 1942, the DHS set up clearing centres under the Emergency Hospital Scheme where service personnel diagnosed as tuberculous could be taken out of military hospitals and await admission to a sanatorium.[133] The impact of tuberculosis on service personnel in local communities was, as in World War One, keenly felt. For example, in the County of Argyll of twenty cases of respiratory tuberculosis identified in the county between August and October 1942, seven

129 PRO, MH/1184, Minutes of a Committee on the Protection of Young Industrial Workers, 16 January 1941. See also Clayson, 'Modern trends in preventive and social aspects of tuberculosis', 217–8.

130 See chapter seven for more on the emergency medical services.

131 Stirling Regional Archive, SC3/3/44, Stirling County, 'Medical Officer of Health Annual Report for the Years 1938, 1939, 1940', 30.

132 PRO, MH55/1183, Minutes of Standing Advisory Committee on Tuberculosis, 26 October 1939.

133 DHS, *Summary Report, July 1945–December 1946* (Edinburgh: HMSO, 1947), 7, [Cmd 7453].

were service personnel. Between March and July 1944 of 23 respiratory cases identified, thirteen were service personnel.[134]

Institutional tuberculosis provision still remained in the hands of local authorities through sanatoria built by the authorities (partially funded by central government). In addition, local authorities could make arrangements to pay voluntary hospitals to secure the admission of more advanced cases to these hospitals for treatment. Domiciliary care, including extra allowances of nourishing food, could be granted to patients on the recommendation of local authority Tuberculosis Officers. The trend on the eve of the war was towards centralising treatment in larger institutions, fully equipped with x-ray equipment and operating theatres. Smaller local sanatoria were increasingly used for convalescent tuberculosis patients – where the 'treatment' chiefly consisted of rest, fresh air and nourishing food.[135]

3. Wartime Increase in Tuberculosis Levels and Pressure on Beds

During and after World War Two there was a sharp increase in the incidence of tuberculosis in Scotland. This was in contrast to the position elsewhere in Britain which experienced a sharp increase 1940/1 followed by a reduction to pre-1938 levels thereafter. Some historians have suggested that the policy of discharging large numbers of infectious cases into the community in the first weeks of the war accounted for the marked increase in incidence in the following two years.[136] This explanation may account for the increase at the beginning of the war in England and Wales. Here, the pre-war decline in tuberculosis resumed after 1941, following the decision to readmit all discharged tuberculosis patients to hospitals, but in Scotland

134 ABDA, Oban, CO6/3/71/1, Argyll County, MOH Quarterly Reports, 6 November 1942 and 15 August 1944.

135 Committee for Social Insurance and Allied Services, August 1941, Memorandum by DHS 'Outline of Scottish Services – Health.'

136 Titmuss, *Problems of Social Policy*, 254–255, Bryder, *Below the Magic Mountain*, 229.

incidence rates continued to rise until well after the war.[137] The number of deaths in Scotland from all forms of the disease was about 11% higher in 1945 than in 1938, and continued to rise into 1946 and 1947. The increased mortality rates hit children and young adults particularly hard. During 1946/7 the death rate in the age group 15–25 was 30% higher than it had been in the depression years 1931–3. For children aged 5–15 the death rate in 1946/7 was about 10% higher than in 1931–3.[138] Overall death rates rose from 2,581 in 1938, to 3,389 in 1947. The wartime increase in tuberculosis is underlined by the significant rise in notifications from 4,793 in 1938, to 7,943 in 1947. The wartime rise in tuberculosis morbidity was at the time linked to the sudden release of tuberculosis patients into the community. Indeed, Walter Elliot, Minister of Health in December 1939, admitted that the scheme of releasing tuberculosis patients to clear beds for expected service casualties had gone farther than planned.[139] In the city of Aberdeen, the rise in respiratory death rates from 38 (in both 1938 and 1939) to 50 in 1940 was alarming. Meanwhile, the respiratory death rate in Aberdeen County rose only slightly from 25 in 1939 to 26 in 1940 (see table 5.7). This difference was put down to the fact that 'the County of Aberdeen was on the whole better able to find alternative accommodation for its tuberculosis patients discharged from the City hospitals at the outbreak of war.'[140] Patients from Aberdeenshire housed in the City

137 'The Annual Report of the Victoria Tuberculosis Trust for 1946–1947', noted that while in England a progressive fall in deaths occurred after the war-time increase in 1941, the position in Scotland was different. The Report was cited in City of Dundee, 'Medical Officer of Health Annual Report, 1947', 72.

138 Titmuss, *Problems of Social Policy*, 255.

139 'At the beginning of the war it had been necessary to clear beds in preparation for an unforeseeable emergency. This had admittedly gone further than the Ministry had intended, but it could not be done without giving a wide discretion which had in some cases led to anomalies. It was his firm policy that actively infectious cases should not be returned to their homes. Where they had been sent home they should be sought out and brought back to the institution.' PRO, MH55/1183, Meeting of the Standing Advisory Committee on Tuberculous Services in Wartime, 13 December 1939.

140 J. Mackintosh, 'Tuberculosis in Young Children', *Public Health*, vol. 56, no. 5, (February 1943), 54.

and Woodend Hospitals in the city of Aberdeen were transferred to the County Hospital, Strichen, and to Newhills Sanatorium, Bucksburn. Aberdeen had a nationally recognised regional tuberculosis scheme, but even here, it was clear that World War Two had an adverse effect on tuberculosis rates. Aberdeenshire Tuberculosis Clinics were severely curtailed during the war. Inverurie Clinic was closed completely, while Clinics at Huntly, Fraserburgh, and Peterhead were held only once every four weeks.[141] In the county of Aberdeen, respiratory notifications rose from 18 in 1938 to 29 in 1941 and to 30 in 1945. The rise may have been connected with the arrival of over 14,000 evacuees, mainly children, in Aberdeenshire on 3 September 1939.[142]

	TB (all forms)			Respiratory			Non Respiratory		
Year	Sco.	Ab. city	Ab. shire	Sco.	Ab. city	Ab. shire	Sco.	Ab. city	Ab. shire
1938	69	48	37	52	38	19	17	10	18
1939	70	47	38	54	38	25	16	9	13
1940	82	61	46	62	50	26	20	11	20
1941	85	61	42	62	48	29	23	13	13
1942	82	65	45	61	46	28	21	19	17
1943	83	62	40	58	46	25	25	16	15
1944	82	69	37	58	48	20	24	21	17
1945	79	52	42	60	43	30	19	9	12

Table 5.7 Tuberculosis Mortality Rates: Scotland, Aberdeen and Aberdeenshire, (per 100,000 population), 1938–1945[143]

141 GRHB, E2\4\20, County of Aberdeen, 'Annual Report of the Medical Officer of Health, 1940–1945', (1946), 26.

142 This figure was reduced to 6,535 by October 1939. See Mackintosh, 'Tuberculosis in Young Children', 54.

143 See Ibid., 54 and GRHB, E1\1\45, Aberdeen City, 'Medical Officer of Health Annual Report, 1940–1945' (1946), ii, v, and GRHB, E2\4\20, County of Aberdeen, 'Medical Officer of Health Report, 1940–1945', (1946), 28.

The Emergency Medical Service as a whole involved a policy of expansion of available beds, estimated at an increase of between 38–40,000 for the whole of Great Britain. In October 1939, Minister of Health Walter Elliot, felt that such an increase should augment, at any rate temporarily, the number of tuberculosis treatment centres around the country. He also believed the creation of a unified medical service due to the wartime emergency should be taken as an opportunity to expand the institutional treatment of non-respiratory cases.[144] Yet, an increase in deaths and notifications began to occur at a time (1940) when in total there were more tuberculosis beds available than ever before. Aside from the disruption of local authority tuberculosis schemes, wartime circumstances helped contribute to the mounting incidence of tuberculosis. Particular wartime developments which could have spread tuberculosis included the deterioration of housing stock, and an increase of overcrowding (housing repairs and building were suspended due to needs of wartime). The use of thick blackout materials hampered house ventilation. Other consequences of the war, such as long hours of work for an enlarged workforce, and limited diet, all had some impact on the spread of the disease. Many of these factors such as housing deterioration and limited diet carried on in to the immediate post-war period, when tuberculosis figures continued at a high level.

In Glasgow, the 1,700 beds available at the beginning of World War Two were considered adequate by the city's MOH, until an 'outbreak' of tuberculosis occurred which led to additional beds being made available under the Emergency Hospital Scheme.[145] In Coatbridge, Lanarkshire, the tuberculosis pavilion at Coathill Hospital with 28 beds (always full and often with a waiting list) was at first given over along with the rest of the hospital to wartime service.

144 PRO, MH55/1183, Minutes of Standing Advisory Committee on Tuberculosis, 26 October 1939.

145 MacGregor, *Public Health in Glasgow 1905–1946*, 98.

> At the recent emergency, the whole hospital was classed as IV and the tuberculosis patients sent home, some to very unsuitable conditions. By 26 October 1939, 19 of the beds had been re-occupied by tuberculosis patients.[146]

Hairmyres Sanatorium in East Kilbride, (also Lanarkshire) which had been reserved for wartime casualties in 1939, was gradually re-opened to civilian casualties by the DHS. In October 1942, 23 beds were re-opened to male civilians.[147]

In Coatbridge, alternative means were found to provide beds for tuberculosis sufferers by buying up spare capacity in other areas of Scotland. In August 1942, John A.C. Guy, MOH for the County of Argyll, responded positively to an approach by Robert Cordiner, Coatbridge MOH, to allow patients from Coatbridge to transfer to Argyll County Sanatorium at Oban at a cost of £3 per week.[148] Co-operation between two local authorities is not surprising given the wartime emergency. Coatbridge Burgh was already in the habit of sending tuberculosis cases elsewhere. In peacetime, respiratory tuberculosis patients were sent to Bridge of Weir Sanatorium in Renfrewshire and non-respiratory tuberculous children to the privately run 96-bed St. Andrew's Sanatorium, Millport, Isle of Cumbrae, Argyllshire. The Oban Sanatorium arrangement was not open ended: Coatbridge Burgh paid £3 per bed and did not receive a quota of beds at Oban Sanatorium – only when beds were at spare capacity were Coatbridge patients to be accommodated. Argyll County Council

146 North Lanarkshire Council, Coatbridge Public Library Archives, DHS, 1939 report to Cordiner, MOH, Coatbridge, 20 November 1939.

147 Letter from Andrew G. Reekie, Senior Assistant County Medical Officer, Hamilton, Lanarkshire to Cordiner, MOH, Burgh of Coatbridge, 28 October 1942.

148 'With the early cases in this county which require pneumothorax treatment being admitted to institutions outwith the County, the County Sanatorium is not receiving a large number of cases and there are quite a few empty beds. In view of the difficulty in obtaining beds for patients and *the increase in wartime of the disease* [author's emphasis] I think it would only be right that this Local Authority should give every facility to do what it can to admit cases from such places as the Burgh of Coatbridge.' Coatbridge Public Library Archives, Letter from Argyll County MOH, John A.C. Guy, to Argyll County Council Public Health Committee, 21 August 1942.

retained the right to discharge any Coatbridge patient for any breach in sanatorium discipline. In the event, the maximum number of patients admitted from Coatbridge at any one time was four. More often the figure was one or two.[149]

A more revolutionary plan for securing extra beds came with the Supplementary Medical Service Scheme which was developed in 1941/2 under the auspices of Secretary of State Tom Johnston. Patients were transferred from voluntary hospital waiting lists to emergency wartime hospitals. The scheme was extended to include a general screening programme for industrial workers, including hospital admission where necessary. It was clearly designed with the early identification of tuberculosis very much as a priority:

> I approached the general practitioners in the Clyde area and obtained their agreement to co-operate, without extra payment, in proposals designed to watch specially the health of workers between the ages of 15 and 25, so that earlier diagnosis of tuberculosis – and other diseases – could be secured.[150]

4. Central Government Action

The chronically debilitating nature of tuberculosis on the workforce gave rise to special wartime government measures. The health of the industrial worker was of great concern during wartime, when 'home front' effort was as important to the successful campaign as military might. In April 1943, a Tuberculosis Maintenance Allowance Scheme (directly funded by the Treasury as a war service) was introduced throughout Britain. This measure was in a similar vein to the special examination and hospital arrangements sponsored by the DHS in the Supplementary Medical Service Scheme to be discussed in chapter seven. The Allowance Scheme, first announced in October 1942, was targeted at those respiratory tuberculosis sufferers 'with a possibility

149 See ABDA, Oban, CO6/3/71/1, Argyll County Council MOH Quarterly Reports, 1942–1944, passim.

150 PRO, MH79/526, War Cabinet Home Policy Committee, HPC (42), January 1942, Memorandum by Scottish Secretary Tom Johnston, 'Prevention and Control of Tuberculosis.'

of restoration to working capacity'.[151] The allowance scheme made provision for both loss of earnings and the financial support of dependants for those agreeing to treatment. In addition to the maintenance allowances, discretionary allowances were made to assist in the payment of rent and rates, hire purchase repayments, and life assurance premiums. Thirdly, special payments, for example, for the provision of domestic help, or for travelling expenses incurred in visiting the patient in hospital, were also made. For those eligible for payments, the allowances were not means tested. The allowances were administered in Scotland by the DHS.[152] By this scheme, sufferers were encouraged to seek early treatment without loss of income, the pay off for the Government was the hope of a speedy return to the workforce for tuberculosis sufferers and the avoidance of further spread of the disease in the workplace.[153]

Local authorities operating the new scheme employed extra staff. In Glasgow, maintenance allowances were paid fortnightly through the Public Health Department. The Medical Officer of Health identified appropriate cases.[154] The unfair element to the Scheme was that it targeted early case respiratory tuberculosis sufferers, those

151 Allowances were granted only to those who had a reasonable prospect of being made fit for work, within approximately two years.

152 Following a recommendation by the Medical Research Council's Committee on Tuberculosis in Wartime, the DHS issued regulations to all Scottish local authorities regarding the payment of maintenance and other allowances to persons undergoing treatment for respiratory tuberculosis and their dependants in DHS Circular No. 36A/1943, 22 April 1943.

153 'You will remember that we have hitherto justified the cost of these allowances being met as a war service on the grounds that the removal from industry of persons suffering from tuberculosis with a view to their early cure and return and to prevent the infection of others is an important contribution to the man-power problem arising out of the war. It does not seem to us likely that the end of the war in Europe will substantially ease that problem [...]. In all the circumstances, we feel that there is still a case for continuing these allowances and for regarding them as a war service and we hope that you will agree.' PRO, MH55/1145, Letter from H.H. George, Ministry of Health, to E. Hale, Treasury, 16 November 1944.

154 Mitchell Library, Glasgow, Strathclyde Regional Archives, Glasgow Corporation Minutes, 15 June 1943, 1052.

chronic and advanced cases who were not in a position to give up employment and seek treatment to enable them to return re-invigorated to the workforce were not included. Non respiratory cases were similarly excluded. Local authorities condemned the limitations of the maintenance allowances.

> It is perhaps difficult, on general principles, to justify this invidious distinction, for the dependants of a sufferer from, say, tuberculosis of the spine or kidney, are just as liable to suffer acute economic hardship during his treatment as are those of the consumptive who is eligible for the benefits of maintenance allowances.[155]

It awaited the reform of National Insurance in 1946 to provide disability benefits for all tuberculosis patients.

It is noteworthy that there was no mention of seeking to tackle tuberculosis through the improvement of the housing stock of the country in these new initiatives. This contradicted an 1942 'Memorandum on Tuberculosis' outlined the Ministry of Health's policy priorities:

> The basis of the Minister's policy is to put more emphasis on preventive measures. As a long-term measure the improvement in housing conditions must be a chief factor to this end. But preventive action must also include the earliest possible ascertainment and treatment of individual cases of tuberculosis.[156]

The effects of low grade, overcrowded housing conditions on the spread of the disease, well known for decades, were not considered as pressing as the necessity of encouraging a healthy wartime workforce. The payment of Maintenance Allowances was postponed to tie in with the launch of mass radiography, which itself was delayed 'because the mass radiography sets would not be available until April [1943]'.[157]

155 LHBA, LHB16/2/28, 'Annual Report of the Medical Officer of Health, Edinburgh, 1946', 51.

156 PRO, MH55/1145, undated, unsigned, Ministry of Health Memorandum 'Tuberculosis', [1942?].

157 PRO, MH55/1145, memorandum on 'Tuberculosis Allowances', from J.H. Henderson, DHS, to T. Lindsay, Ministry of Health, 24 November 1942.

During World War Two, the Scottish administrative input into tuberculosis policy was a consultative one. For example, the DHS view was that the Tuberculosis Maintenance Allowances Scheme should not be put off, simply to coincide with the commencement of mass radiography. The implied connection between the two was questioned by J.H. Henderson, Secretary of the DHS, in a memorandum to the Ministry of Health in November 1942.[158] The DHS query fell on stony ground as the two tuberculosis initiatives were launched at the same time in April 1943. Although the Ministry of Health was apparently leading the way in terms of policy on tuberculosis allowances and mass radiography, distinct Scottish policies for preventive care were still being implemented by the DHS. The Supplementary Medical Service Scheme to preserve the health of Scottish industrial workers is probably the best such wartime example.

As the decision to grant maintenance allowances for tuberculosis sufferers and their dependants was announced and mass radiography launched, both notification levels and death-rates from tuberculosis were on the increase. Scottish waiting lists for tuberculosis beds were also mounting. In 1942, 771 patients were on the waiting list for a bed, by 1946 this had more than trebled to 2,324.[159] Longer waiting lists led to further spread of the disease as 'open' cases remained at home. Part of the problem lay in the chronic shortage of tuberculosis nurses identified by the Minister of Health in his October 1942 Radio broadcast.[160] In 1944, the DHS Summary Report stated that the difficulty in supplying more tuberculosis beds was due to the

158 'In view of the Ministerial publicity that has been given to the whole scheme I imagine that the Secretary of State would not wish to hold up the allowances scheme until mass radiography can be begun and frankly I fail to see what essential connection there is between the two.' Ibid.

159 Waiting lists for beds remained high after the end of the war. The waiting list stood at 2,877 at the end of 1949, and only slowly decreased, down to 148 at the end of 1955. See PRO, MH55/1186, Joint Tuberculosis Council, 'Definition of Tuberculosis', [Scottish] National Campaign against Tuberculosis, minutes of meeting, February 1956.

160 Health Minister Brown included a special plea to the women of Great Britain to '[...] join in the attack on consumption, that black thief of Life and Happiness, let me hear from you.' See text of Minister of Health, A.E. Brown's BBC Address to the Nation on 'Consumption', 6 October 1942

difficulty in finding staff, not beds. In March 1944, there was a waiting list of over 1,400 tuberculous patients, 1,200 of whom were suffering from respiratory tuberculosis.[161] In 1947, efforts were made to increase hospital accommodation for tuberculosis by enlisting the services of part-time nurses and employing ward orderlies. There was even an experiment in one hospital of running a ward on a hostel system by the patients themselves, with only nursing supervision.[162] By 1948 in Scotland, there was a reported 30% absolute shortage of sanatorium nursing personnel, that is a shortfall of 297 nurses.[163]

Post War Developments

The wartime Tuberculosis Maintenance Allowances scheme was maintained in the immediate aftermath of the war to avoid there being a gap between the payment of allowances under the scheme and the impending transfer to a universal system of benefits. Local authorities continued to administer the allowances until 4 July 1948. The next day, 5 July 1948 was the designated 'appointed day' for the great change over in health and welfare services. From then on, the National Assistance Board assumed responsibility for making financial provision for (all) tuberculous patients in need of financial help.[164]

Despite new state initiatives and medical breakthroughs there was still the problem to be faced of a Scottish tuberculosis rate which had risen during the war years and was continuing in an upward spiral post-war. In 1947, there were 10,117 cases of tuberculosis notified in

161 DHS, *Summary Report, 1944* (1945), 54.

162 DHS, *Annual Report, 1947* (1948), 8, [Cmd 7453].

163 'Tuberculosis in Scotland' commentary in *Public Health*, vol. 61, no. 12, (September 1948), 234. The Inverness County MOH reinforced this view in his annual report in 1948, when he noted that a shortage of sanatorium beds was being experienced due to a shortage of nursing staff. Highland Regional Archive, HRA C/CI/3/5/1, County of Inverness, 'Medical Officer of Health Annual Report, 1948', 15.

164 DHS, *Annual Report, 1948* (1949), 23, [Cmd 7659].

Scotland, a rise of over 400 from the 1946 figure of 9,713. About 35% of all Scottish respiratory and 24% of all non-respiratory cases in 1947 were housed in the city of Glasgow. Other industrialised west of Scotland areas also showed increased incidences of all forms of tuberculosis in the two years after the end of the war.[165] Lanark County Council placed much of the 'blame' for the increase upon the habits of young adults. Faced with an increase in respiratory tuberculosis deaths from 893 in 1940 to 1,749 in 1946, the view of Andrew G. Reekie, Medical Officer of Health for the County, was that young adults of both sexes were especially prone to develop dangerous tuberculosis by overdoing their social life. His advice was to work hard during the week and get to bed early and let youth have its fling at the weekend when the week's work is done. After stressing what adolescents could do to help themselves, only then did he turn to other factors such as bad housing conditions, inadequacy of hospital facilities (due to staff shortages) and the possibility of increased public awareness of the disease due to mass radiography schemes.[166]

The introduction of screening and incentives towards early treatment did not have an immediate impact on tuberculosis mortality. In 1948, it was estimated that 9.5% of all deaths in Glasgow were due to tuberculosis. Medical discoveries in the post-war period only gradually began to contribute to the reduction of tuberculosis death rates. Chemotherapeutic breakthroughs began with the limited use of streptomycin in some parts of the country in 1947. Dundee recorded one of the earliest uses of the drug in 1947.[167] In 1948, streptomycin was successfully used in the city of Aberdeen to save 'several cases of generalised tuberculosis who otherwise would almost certainly have died'.[168] Similar dramatic claims were made for use of the drug in

165 DHS, *Annual Report, 1947*, 8.

166 Lanark County, 'Medical Officer of Health Annual Report, 1946', 8–9.

167 'The year must rank as one of the most notable in the history of the anti-tuberculosis campaign in the City because it saw the introduction for the first time of a therapeutic agent (streptomycin) which has an unequivocally beneficial action against the tubercule bacillus in certain cases.' DDA, City of Dundee, 'Medical Officer of Health Annual Report, 1947', 71.

168 GRHB, E1\1\47, Aberdeen City 'Medical Officer of Health Annual Report', 1948, v.

Aberdeenshire.[169] Streptomycin was made widely available in Britain in 1949.

A post-war development arising from the creation of the National Health Service was the establishment of a co-ordinated after-care and rehabilitation scheme. Under the provisions of the Disabled Persons (Employment) Act, 1944, local health authorities were empowered to appoint Disablement Resettlement Officers to liaise with Tuberculosis Officers.[170] A new special education and propaganda campaign was to be carried out by Tuberculosis Officers and Nurse Health Visitors, designed for patients, their families and the general public.[171] But here again, some continuity with pre-war tuberculosis policy was evident, in that the campaign was to be conducted in close co-operation with the voluntary NAPT. Even at this time of the systematic entry of the state into public health, there was still a clear role to play by voluntary organisations.[172] With the passing of the National Health Service (Scotland) Act, 1947, central funding was put in place for tuberculosis services and the way was paved to place local tuberculosis services under regional control, as recommended by both the Cathcart and PEP Reports ten years earlier.

169 GRHB, E2\4\23, County of Aberdeen, 'Medical Officer of Health Annual Report, 1948', 34.

170 Lanark County, 'Medical Officer of Health Annual Report, 1948', 202.

171 Ibid., 203.

172 According to Geoffrey Finlayson, the 'mixed economy of welfare', where the state and voluntary agencies played component parts in the delivery of welfare services was not removed by a process of linear progression, in the course of the twentieth century. However, the mix undoubtedly altered in favour of the state: Finlayson, 'A Moving Frontier: Voluntarism and the State in British Social Welfare 1911–1949', *Twentieth Century British History*, 1/2 (1990), 185.

Conclusion

> After allowing for the indirect effects of improved housing, food and environmental conditions generally, [tuberculosis care], has very tangible results to its credit over the last twenty years, reflected in the improvements in the rate of mortality from the disease.[173]

This was the official DHS view on the operation of tuberculosis schemes in Scotland. It ignored the fact that no medical breakthrough had been made in the prevention or cure of the disease, neither did it take into account the increased rate of tuberculosis which occurred during, and continued after, World War Two.

The official emphasis on maintaining and reinforcing sanatoria provision in the inter-war period meant that attention was deflected from wider social factors such as poor nutrition and the lack of adequate housing. Voluntarist and local authority alternatives, such as after-care committees and focusing on the welfare of the dependants of tuberculosis sufferers were not pursued very far. Health policy as it developed in these years led to the triumph of curative over preventive measures in the attack on tuberculosis. The latter was too costly and suggested a comprehensive, co-ordinated health service. The non-implementation of the 1936 DHS Cathcart Report recommendations, proved as much. However, the position was altered dramatically with increased wartime intervention, specifically with the introduction of the Supplementary Medical Services Scheme in Scotland 1941/2, and the provision of Tuberculosis Maintenance Allowances and Mass Radiography for the whole of Britain from April 1943.

Local authority response to the disease was by no means unified. For example, this chapter has illustrated a varying range of experience in different parts of Scotland, with respect both to tuberculosis rates and in local authority provisions to counter-act the effects of tuberculosis on the community. However, there are grounds for believing that the SBH/DHS was attempting to deal with a deep-rooted problem in a pragmatic fashion. Increasing the number of

173 DHS, *A National Health Service* (1944), [Cmd 6502], 60.

sanatoria and hospital beds in the face of central Government cut backs and local authority reluctance in the early 1920s was only one aspect of its policy towards the scourge of tuberculosis.

The 1936 Cathcart Report (and other related DHS reports in the 1930s and 1940s into infant and maternal mortality) reveal there was a clear understanding of the deep rooted nature of the problems caused by poverty, and over-crowded, slum housing. These same reports also stressed that owing to relative poverty levels, there was less public health spending in Scotland than in England and Wales. It is arguable that in default of a massive injection of capital to tackle the environmental problems of the country, the policy of institutional expansion (with the emphasis placed on local authority effort in this field) was no more than a panacea. The cure lay beyond the remit of the DHS to initiate and finance.[174]

174 In support of this view of DHS policy and priorities, it appears more than coincidental that one of the first acts of the newly-appointed advisory Scottish Health Services Council established as part of the NHS in Scotland in 1948 was the creation of a 'Committee on Tuberculosis'. See DHS, *Annual Report, 1948*, 26.

6: National Health Insurance

> The National Health Insurance Scheme has not won a place in the popular imagination commensurate with its magnitude and its importance. Of all the means yet put into operation for the prevention of and cure of sickness and for the alleviation of want and distress in the households of the workers that follow upon the loss of earning power through illness, National Health Insurance is incomparably the widest-reaching and the most effective.
> (SBH, *Sixth Annual Report* (Edinburgh: HMSO, 1925), 138, [Cmd 2416])

Introduction

The fluctuations in the fortunes of National Health Insurance in many ways mirror the wider development of Scottish health provision and policy implementation in the first half of the twentieth century. Initially, the drive towards health insurance (influenced by the successful model of social insurance in Germany) came in the first years of the twentieth century, when the health of the nation commanded public and government attention.[1] Other European countries considered similar health insurance schemes around this time. For example, Sweden, which passed its first Sickness Fund law in 1890, expanded its health insurance provision in 1910.[2]

Britain's 1911 National Health Insurance legislation introduced payments of medical benefit and a basic general practitioner service, free of charge, to one-third of the nation.[3] The 1920s and 1930s, saw a

1 See chapter one for more details on the findings of the *Report of the Inter-Departmental Committee on Physical Deterioration* in 1904 and other government enquiries.
2 Immergut, *Health Politics*, 194.
3 Contributions towards National Insurance were levied from July 1912, meanwhile medical and sickness benefits were paid out from January 1913. By

great growth in the number of health insurance claimants. The increase in sickness claims suggests a deterioration of the state of the nation's health in the depression years. Although the evidence is by no means clear-cut, the fact that chronic cases were a particular drain on health insurance funds provides an indication of how far sustained economic depression undermined the general health of the population.[4] Whiteside has argued that while unemployment, particularly for sustained periods, carried risks of physical and mental deterioration, another side effect was the raising of the standard of 'employability'. Whiteside's view was that '[...] sickness was not so much caused by unemployment, but revealed by it.'[5] Inter-war diagnostic improvements led to the earlier detection and more widespread recognition of ailments, particularly those illnesses related to psychiatric disorders.[6] Whether there was more ill health or simply better recording of it is difficult to determine. What is clear is that the 1930s DHS Morbidity Statistics Scheme uncovered worryingly high levels of illness and chronic incapacity among Scots workers for the first time.

Health insurance claims were another indicator of the health of the adult population. Indeed, investigations into false claims for health insurance (as an alternative to unemployment or transitional means tested benefits) found the numbers of such claims to be smaller than expected. This suggests that health insurance claims were recording

---

1921, insured male and female workers accounted for almost nine-tenths of the male and female working populations of Scotland. The overall number of insured workers in Britain covered by the scheme in 1913 was fifteen million.

4 Whiteside has made the point that for those who support a 'pessimistic' view of the inter-war health of the nation, mounting claims for sickness and disablement benefit in the inter-war period are more suited to their argument than many other health figures which record declining mortality and morbidity statistics. For example, Whiteside notes that by the mid-1930s 'while rates of disability had more than doubled since the armistice fewer than 1 in 10 of these claimants could be deemed capable of any work at all.' See N. Whiteside, 'Counting the Cost: Sickness and Disability among Working People in an Era of Industrial Recession, 1920–1939', *Economic History Review*, vol. XL, No. 2 (1987), 230 and 243.

5 Ibid., 245.

6 Ibid., 238.

genuine cases of sickness in the depression years. Whether every claimant for health insurance would have made these claims at times when work was plentiful is another, separate, matter. The main thing is that the illnesses complained of by applicants were both increasing in number and discovered to be overwhelmingly genuine.

Mounting health insurance claims from the mid-1920s provoked a policy of increased monitoring, not only of the insured workforce accused of 'malingering', (especially married women), but also of general practitioners working under the National Health Insurance scheme. Some such 'panel' doctors were charged with over-generous certifying of patients as unfit for work in order to maintain large lists of insured workers – the so-called practice of 'lax certification'. In Scotland, the SBH plans devised to tackle these issues differed from the approach the Ministry of Health. This difference in policy led to friction between the two government health agencies.

As in many others areas of social policy, the need for 'economy' in government expenditure dominated the administration of National Health Insurance in the inter-war years. Previous chapters have shown how the policy of 'economy' impacted heavily on provisions for tuberculosis, infant and maternal welfare and school health. Health insurance fared no better.[7] The health insurance scheme, administered as it chiefly was by industrial insurance companies concerned with running at a profit (as well as Friendly Societies aiming to maximise members' benefits, and trade unions protecting specific occupations), was a particular hostage to fortune. The role of the state in National Health Insurance was that of regulator, supervising the scheme and auditing the accounts of the approved societies. Government involvement was designed, as far as possible, to minimise national

7 The Second Annual Report of the Ministry of Health published in August 1921 stated that financial restrictions would limit any health expenditure in the near future. The Report noted that the need meantime for a thorough investigation of the whole field of existing health services in order to have a well-prepared plan of action when the needs for economy lessened. As the economic difficulties continued long-term, the reforming zeal which led to the suggestion of extended medical services in the Dawson and MacAlister Reports (produced respectively by the Ministry of Health and SBH Consultative Councils on Medical and Allied Services) were quietly shelved.

expenditure on the scheme. Within three years of the end of World War One, cost savings dominated the government attitude to health insurance.[8] The national scheme, (which in 1928 covered over 16.5 million workers out of a total population of 45 million)[9] was on a scale far outweighing the services provided in other areas of personal health considered elsewhere in this book.

National Health Insurance was distinctive for reasons other than its sheer scale and the involvement of private insurance companies in its administration. It was a compulsory scheme for workers earning below a fixed annual sum (first set at £160 – the lower level for income tax eligibility – in 1911). It involved contributions from employers, employees and the Exchequer. This amounted to a more all-encompassing scheme than any so far described in regard to other (non-compulsory) areas of public health provision.

The involvement of private agencies notwithstanding, health insurance was administered in Scotland by Scottish agencies. At times, this involved independent initiative which was at odds with policy developments in London (as the issue of 'lax certification' will highlight). The Scottish Insurance Commission administered National Health Insurance from the enactment of the 1911 legislation until the end of 1918. The Commissioners' duties were assumed by the SBH between 1919–1928 and by the DHS after 1929. Other distinct Scottish developments, such as the 1930s Morbidity Statistics Scheme, had wider implications for the role of the government agencies in monitoring health trends, and led to a questioning of how far the bounds of state intervention should reach.

The importance of pressure groups, including representatives of the medical profession, has previously been noted in the creation and moulding of a distinct Scottish health administration. The role of the

8 A policy of national restriction was introduced from July 1921 to tackle the economic problems of the country, including high unemployment.

9 In Scotland, there were 1.76 million insured workers from a population of around 4.8 million in 1928. SBH, *Tenth Annual Report, 1928*, 18. The precise number of insured workers in 1928 was 16,577,000. Of these 13,908,000 were in England and 906,000 in Wales. By 1942, 25 million workers were under the scheme. See PRO, PIN4/29, memorandum on numbers entitled to Medical Benefit as certified by the Government Actuary.

medical profession within the scheme of health insurance was crucial. The resistance of representatives of the profession, both to a perceived increased central control of their rights to practise, and towards alterations to conditions of service, is pertinent to any discussion on health insurance administration.

Inter War Scottish Morbidity Statistics

Scotland produced detailed information on morbidity patterns among the insured workforce in the 1920s, initially on a small scale. A selection of morbidity statistics based on the examination work of District Medical Officers appeared regularly in the annual reports of the Scottish Board of Health from 1925. These data were expanded into special case studies of, for example, the incidence of heart disease and bronchitis among the Scottish insured workforce. Between 1930–1937 Scotland's innovative Morbidity Statistics Scheme produced detailed annual reports of morbidity patterns of workers. These revealed a high incidence of ill health among Scotland's insured workers. For example, in the year ending June 1933, a total of 18 million days were lost due to sickness. This accounted for 400,00 separate cases of illness, leading to an average of 227 cases of certified illness per 1,000 insured workers. The 1932/33 figures were much higher than those for 1931/2 and 1933/4, due in part to an influenza epidemic.[10] The following year (1933/34), overall rates had fallen to 16.9 million days lost. The chief cause of the fall was due to the decline in the incidence of influenza (accounting for a total of 600,000 working days lost in 1933/34 compared to 1.7 million in the previous year). Loss of days due to other diseases had risen, with tonsillitis, scarlet fever, erysipelas, diphtheria, and rheumatism leading the way in causing incapacity among insured workers.[11] In the Report for 1933/34, tonsillitis was second only to influenza in accounting for

10 DHS, *Annual Report, 1933*, 14.

11 DHS, *Annual Report, 1934* (Edinburgh: HMSO, 1935), 113, [Cmd 4837].

incapacity in the workforce, amounting to over half a million working days lost.[12] In 1936/7, morbidity figures rose markedly. A total of 26.7 million working days were lost due to illness (a new high for overall stoppages through sickness). Of these, 1.9 million working days were lost due to an influenza epidemic. For this report year, the average number of days lost per insured worker through incapacity was 14.92. The average was reached by combining the average for men of 14.13 days, with the level of 15.60 days for single women and just over 21.27 days for married women.[13]

The annual reports revealed that the main causes of sickness among Scottish insured workers in the 1930s were: droplet infections (including influenza), respiratory conditions, accidents and septic states, rheumatism, gastric upsets of all kinds and degrees, and ill-defined states of ill-health under the headings of debility, anaemia and neurasthenia. The results of a three-year DHS investigation revealed an unsuspected amount of long-term or chronic sickness with close to 19% of male and over 9% of female insurance claimants diagnosed as permanently incapable of work (see table 6.1). In 1936/7, 1.7% of the insured population was continuously ill throughout the whole twelve-month period. The broad implications of these findings helped shape distinctive Scottish health policies in the 1930s and 1940s.

12 DHS, *Annual Report, 1935* (Edinburgh: HMSO, 1936), 132, [Cmd 5123].

13 Mitchell Library, Glasgow, D. 458635, DHS, *Report on Sickness Statistics for the Insured Population of Scotland for the year from 1st July 1936 to 30th June 1937* (Edinburgh: HMSO, 1939), 12.

	Numbers			Percentage		
Prognosis	Male	Female	Total	Male	Female	Total
Early Recovery	1919	1763	3682	47.3	60.0	52.6
Relapsing Incapacity	963	581	1544	23.7	19.8	22.1
Prolonged Incap., but poss. return to work	404	306	710	10.0	10.4	10.1
Permanent Incapacity	755	273	1028	18.6	9.3	14.7
Not Stated	19	13	32	0.4	0.4	0.5
Total	4060	2936	6996	100	99.9	100

Table 6.1 Prognoses of 6,996 Cases of Incapacity Lasting at Least Three Months, 1943[14]

The Scheme of National Health Insurance 1919–20

At the transfer of functions from the National Health Insurance Commission (Scotland) to the Scottish Board of Health in 1919, 1,275,029 members of the Scottish population were covered by the scheme. The number of approved societies operating health insurance in Scotland was 245.[15] The Final Report of the National Health Insurance Commission for Scotland for the period 1917–1919 contained a mixed review of the history of the Scottish scheme.[16] Great faith was placed on possible future developments of health insurance arrangements under the new Scottish Board of Health. The

14 Figures obtained from DHS, *Health and Industrial Efficiency: Scottish Experiments in Social Medicine* (Edinburgh: HMSO, 1943).

15 The spread of membership was uneven across the approved societies. 76% of the British population were insured by 2.5% of societies, while 65% of societies insured only 2% of the population.

16 Summary of 'Final Report of the National Health Insurance Commission (Scotland)' in *The* [Scottish] *Poor Law and Local Government Magazine*, 30 (Glasgow, 1920), 273–275.

SBH would, it was hoped, draw upon the invaluable experience gleaned from the Commissioners' operation of health insurance since its creation in 1911.[17] Looking at the benefits available, while maternity benefit was found to be highly popular, there were clear expressions of dissatisfaction by the Commissioners at the limited medical treatment generally on offer to workers. The Commissioners acknowledged public pressure at the time of transfer to the Scottish Board of Health, to extend the scope of health insurance to provide a broader range of services for Scottish workers. The Commissioners put this public pressure down to changing times. They felt it was not a criticism of how health insurance had operated, but recognition of how far public expectations had increased with regard to the State promotion of national well being. The Commissioners also expressed uneasiness about lack of panel practitioner care in certifying illness. They believed that the employment of medical referees would be the best way of eradicating this problem. In drawing attention to the matter of 'lax certification' in their final report, the Commissioners highlighted an issue which loomed large in discussions on controlling the cost of health insurance throughout the inter-war period.

In 1920, a revision of health insurance payments fixed sickness benefit at 15 shillings (75p)[18] per week for men and 12 shillings (60p) for women. This benefit, along with basic medical treatment from a medical practitioner, payable after the fourth day of sickness, was available for up to 26 weeks in a year to all workers who earned less than £250 per year (raised from the original £160 income threshold). Medical treatment continued throughout the life of the worker, while sickness benefit ceased when the worker reached the retirement age (initially set at 70 in 1911, reduced to 65 after the passage of the Contributory Pensions Act, 1925). Maternity benefit was raised in 1920 to a lump sum of 40 shillings (£2) (from the original 30 shillings

17 The views of the Insurance Commissioners on the coming of the Scottish Board of Health were no doubt tempered by the fact that two of the Commissioners, Sir James Leishman and Dr John C McVail, moved to the new six-person Board respectively as Vice Chairman and Medical Member.

18 It had been set at 10 shillings (50p) in the original National Insurance Act, 1911.

[£1.50] in 1911), payable at child-birth to an insured woman or uninsured wife of an insured working man. Women whose husbands were not insured received a double maternity benefit out of their own insurance. Under the National Health Insurance (Amendment) Act of 1920, sanatorium benefit, which had been part of the original legislation and provided for the institutional treatment of tuberculous workers, now passed into the remit of local authorities.[19] When implemented, this relieved approved societies of the payment of an annual sum of around £500,000.

The scheme of National Health Insurance was funded by weekly contributions from the state[20], the employer (set at 5d in 1920) and the employee (also 5d in 1920).[21] Workers had a free choice of approved society and of practitioner (although both could and did reject applicants). After the initial 26 weeks payment, the chronic sick could claim disability benefit at half the initial rate (set at 7 shillings and sixpence in 1920 for both men and women). The health insurance scheme was administered by Friendly and Industrial Assurance Societies and by some trade unions. (Table 6.2 lists the membership levels of the various types of societies in Scotland in 1912 and 1922).

19 See chapter five on tuberculosis for more discussion of this piece of legislation.

20 The Exchequer did not pay a fixed sum per insured person. Although stated by Chancellor of the Exchequer, Lloyd George in 1911 to be 2d per week, it amounted to two-ninths of the benefits paid to workers. This fraction remained the same after the Cabinet review of health insurance in 1920, but was reduced to one-seventh in 1926 (one-fifth for insured women). Hence, when wealthy societies paid additional benefits to their members, the amount paid by the government increased proportionally. See Gilbert, *British Social Policy 1914–1939*, 258.

21 The 1911 Health Insurance levels were set at 3d per week for employers, 4d for male and 3d for female workers.

Class of Society	Male	Female	Total	Year 1912	1922
				% of Total	
1. Friendly Soc. with branches	347,00	120,00	467,000	32.4	27.2
2. Centralised Friendly Soc.	242,00	125,000	367,000	23.2	21.4
3. Industrial and Collecting Soc.	406,000	303,000	709,000	34.5	41.4
4. Trade Unions	140,000	14,00	154,000	9.4	9.0
5. Employers' Provident Funds	7,000	10,000	17,000	0.4	1.0
Total	1,142,000	572,000	1,714,000	99.9	100

Table 6.2 Membership of Approved Societies in Scotland, 1912 and 1922[22]

The regulations of all health insurance societies were subject to official approval before they were accepted into the scheme. Once 'approved', societies paid designated 'panel'[23] doctors to administer medical care. Doctors prescribed medicines and certified workers as unfit. Initially, there was no limit on the numbers of insured workers a panel practitioner could take on. But in 1920, revised terms of panel practice set a maximum of 3,000 patients for a single-handed practice. Local panel committees could reduce the maximum number, and in some areas it was fixed at 1,500. In 1923, the maximum figure was reduced to 2,500. Only basic general practitioner services were covered by the scheme. However, some of the wealthier approved societies offered additional benefits to their members. Additional benefits were estimated at an equivalent of between 1 (5p) and 5 shillings (25p) per week. These payments were on top of the health insurance flat rate in the first valuation of approved societies in 1918).[24] Additional benefits most frequently included the provision of

22 SBH, *Fourth Annual Report, 1922* (Edinburgh: HMSO, 1923), 58, [Cmd 2156].

23 So-called because workers could choose freely from a list (or 'panel') of those doctors in any specific area who had agreed to participate in the National Health Insurance scheme, up to the maximum number of patients any one doctor was able to administer.

24 SBH, *Second Annual Report, 1920*, 199

ophthalmic and dental services, although increased cash payments were also made.[25] The number of workers covered by the universal health insurance scheme rose steadily. There were 11.5 million workers covered by the scheme in Britain in 1912. This rose to 13.5 million by 1922, and to 20.3 million by 1938 (the total population was 47.5 million in 1938). The number of women covered by the scheme rose from 3.7 million in 1912 to 7.1 million in 1938.[26]

In Scotland in 1913 the number of insured workers under the scheme was 1,450,000 with 1,800 general practitioners involved as panel doctors. By 1936, the scheme covered 1,900,000 Scots workers and involved over 2,000 doctors. This allowed for an average of about 805 insured workers per Scots panel doctor in 1913, rising to 950 panel patients per doctor in 1936. The national average in 1913 was 850, rising to 940 in 1936. Of course, there would be many regional variations within these figures. In 1944, Scottish Secretary of State Tom Johnston informed the House of Commons that the panel doctor-insured patient ratio was one doctor per 930 of the insured population in Bridge of Allan, (the Stirlingshire spa town). In contrast, the figure for the Clyde port of Greenock, was one doctor per 3,535 of the insured population.[27] The respective level of service provided is not difficult to imagine. Although the ratio of patients to panel doctors was initially lower in Scotland, the tendency was towards a closer correlation between the size on panel practices around Britain, as the number of patients increased in the inter-war years.

At national level, the National Health Insurance Joint Committee was responsible for the central administration of the scheme. The Joint Committee was made up of the Minster of Health, the Scottish Secretary, the Minister of Labour for Northern Ireland and a Welsh

25 Approved societies were subjected to a quinquennial valuation. If a society had surpluses identified by the valuation, part of the surplus could then be assigned for use as additional benefits for members. In 1936, the Cathcart Report stated that about one-third of insured Scots were not entitled to additional benefits. DHS, *Committee on Scottish Health Services Report* [Cathcart Report], 215. By 1938, societies catering for Britain as a whole offered additional benefits to 88% of male members and 81% of female members.

26 Whiteside, 'Counting the Cost', 230.

27 HOC debates, 17–3–44, vol. 397 col. 621.

MP. In England and Wales, the day to day running of the scheme was the responsibility of a group of civil servants in the Health Insurance Division of the Ministry of Health, under the leadership of Controller, Sir Walter Kinnear.[28] Since the SBH administered health insurance in Scotland, the system of control was devolved. Below the Scottish Secretary and the administrative structure of the SBH, there were 54 local Insurance Committees in Scotland (each local committee was represented on the Scottish Association of Insurance Committees). The Insurance Committees were bodies appointed for each county (or combination of counties) and large burghs by the insured population (acting through their approved societies), the SBH, local health authorities, and local medical practitioners.[29]

The role of the state within the health insurance scheme was to arrange for the collection of stamped insurance cards and to credit the accounts of approved societies based on membership levels and claims made. It also supervised financial safeguards put in place to maintain the solvency of the individual approved societies. Periodic valuations were carried out by the Government Actuary, followed by a decision on how much surplus each society could use to offer additional benefits to their own members. The General Medical Benefit Fund also defrayed the costs of the medical benefit paid out to members and the costs of panel practitioners' salaries. However, in

28 Walter Kinnear was born in 1872. He was educated at University College, Dublin. In 1911 he became Deputy Chairman of the Irish Insurance Commission, a post he held until 1919. In 1919 he was appointed Controller of Insurance and Pensions at the newly created Ministry of Health, a post he held until his retirement in 1936. He was knighted in 1918. He died 4 April 1953.

29 The statutory membership of Insurance Committees consisted of three-fifths representatives of insured workers (appointed by approved societies operating in the area), one fifth nominated by the Burgh or county council, and the final fifth of members appointed by the SBH. Each of the Insurance Committees had a medical service sub-committee to oversee the work of panel doctors and chemists. For each of the 54 insurance areas there was also a local medical committee to deal with complaints against panel doctors supplying medical services. Some of the larger Scottish insurance areas had pharmaceutical committees to deal with complaints against chemists dispensing panel prescriptions. Panel doctors had their own professional committee, the panel committee, as did chemists in the pharmaceutical committee.

Spring 1922 the government, faced with economic crisis, withdrew its annual grant of £1.7 million towards the cost of medical benefit, throwing an added financial burden on the approved societies.

Inter-War Health Insurance

There were several attempts to modify the scheme of national health insurance in the inter-war period. For example, the SBH Consultative Council on Medical and Allied Services Interim Report (the MacAlister Report) recommended that National Health Insurance should extend its scope to cover dependants of the insured and all those of the same economic status as those currently insured.[30] The recommendation of the MacAlister Report found an echo in the report of the Royal Commission on National Health Insurance (set up in July 1924 after disputes over the level and funding of doctors' capitation fees). The Royal Commission was under the Chairmanship of Lord Lawrence of Kingsgate. The Commission considered whether the scheme of health insurance should be expanded to include cash allowances and medical treatment for dependants and whether to extend maternity benefit to cover medical and midwifery services as well as the existing cash payment.

The Commission findings stressed that any future developments in National Health Insurance would tend towards the creation of a unified health service.[31] The Commission produced two reports in 1926.[32] The Majority Report recommended that the health insurance medical service should be expanded beyond general practitioner care

---

30 SBH, *Consultative Council on Medical and Allied Services Interim Report* [the MacAlister Report], (1920), 19.

31 The Report of the Royal Commission on National Health Insurance concluded: '[...] whatever may be the changes which are made in the insurance scheme in the near future, the trend of the development will be towards a unified health service [...].' cited in DHS, *Committee on Scottish Health Services Report*, 163.

32 *Royal Commission on National Health Insurance Report* (HMSO, 1926), [Cmd 2596].

to include specialist and institutional treatment. Both Majority and Minority Reports recommended that health insurance should be widened to include the provision of medical care at childbirth and to offer dental and ophthalmic treatment as a basic right (and not as a privilege of membership of a wealthy approved society). The Reports also recommended that laboratory services be included in the health insurance scheme. The Majority report ruled out including dependants for the time being due to prohibitive costs, but favoured the rationalisation of administrative units, strengthening of government controls and pooling of approved society profits to spread the payments of additional benefits more evenly. The Minority Report recommended the abolition of approved societies on the grounds that many societies were out to maximise profits, not protect workers. The Minority Report findings also favoured the municipalisation of health insurance alongside other local authority health services, with the work of approved societies passing to local government control. It also recommended that profits from administering health insurance should be made available to all insured workers in the form of additional benefits and not confined to those whose societies were fortunate by size and relative health of membership to run at substantial profits. The recommendations of the 1926 Royal Commission, like those of the 1920 SBH McAlister Report ran aground due to economic restrictions.

District Medical Officers

From 1921, claims for sickness and disablement benefits for all groups of approved society members increased. Claims mounted in areas most seriously affected by high unemployment. The 1924 SBH Annual Report clearly linked the 'heavy' incidence of sickness that year to unemployment. The problem, as stated by several of the SBH-appointed District Medical Officers (DMOs) was that unemployment caused a general lowering of vitality, which increased susceptibility to illness and triggered longer periods of (chronic) incapacity. Two District Medical Officers were quoted in favour of the introduction of some form of 'Convalescent Benefit' to be paid to insured workers to allow them time in a convalescent home away from poor housing conditions in order to speed up recovery time.[33] The Report of another DMO outlined a range of occupations, which, while not recognised as 'dangerous trades', contributed towards serious incapacity. Miners, ironworkers, and those in the shipbuilding trades were susceptible to bronchial and heart disease due to the demanding, physical nature of their work.[34]

District Medical Officers were first appointed by the SBH in 1920. Two senior DMOs were appointed for Western and Eastern Districts (based in Glasgow and Edinburgh respectively). Three junior District Medical Officers were appointed with bases in Glasgow (South Western District), Aberdeen (Northern District) and Dundee (Eastern District). By March 1926 there were seven District Medical Officers covering slightly amended geographical areas. Taking up their posts on 16 May 1921, the DMOs acted as medical referees in cases referred to them on questions of incapacity of insured workers, and as consultants in giving second opinions in matters of diagnosis and treatment. The need for second opinions in certification of illness was highlighted by the SBH in a memorandum issued on the subject in August 1920. A four-page appendix to the memorandum listed over 30 cases of panel doctors fined for irregular certification. Fines ranged between £1–£10. One doctor fined £10 had granted 45 certificates at one time to a single patient. It was found that the doctor failed to examine the (presumably chronically ill) patient on most of the dates written on the certificates. The doctor admitted to acting irregularly, but had done so due to the 'deserving character of the case'.[35]

DMOs combined clinical consultative work with administrative duties within the SBH. They investigated the supply of drugs under

33 SBH, *Sixth Annual Report, 1924*, 181.

34 Ibid, 181.

35 GRHB Archives, GRHB D2/3/1, SBH, 'Memorandum in regard to the administration of the parliamentary grant in aid of Medical Benefit', August 1920 [ICB No. 9 1920].

Medical Benefit, examined prescriptions and advised Panel Committees and others on questions affecting prescribing generally. Other duties included inspecting panel practitioners records, and, if necessary, the issue of medical certificates.[36] Related work undertaken by the DMOs included the examination of disabled soldiers as to their fitness for training and acting as referees under the Blind Persons Act.[37] After the Scottish Board of Health's reorganisation as the Department of Health for Scotland in 1929, the District Medical Officers were re-titled Regional Medical Officers (RMOs). By 1934, RMO duties included examining applicants for admission to Ministry of Labour Training Centres and assessing insured workers for the Home Office in connection for claims for disability arising from asbestosis and silicosis.[38]

It cost an estimated £20,600 per year for the SBH to employ District Medical Officers. £4,000 of the sum came from fees paid by the approved societies.[39] The SBH hoped insurance societies would make use of the new District Medical Officers, at a small charge per case, rather than rely on existing private arrangements for obtaining medical refereeing. The SBH also expected that the appointment of DMOs would guarantee that insured workers could be satisfied that their case would be given the fullest medical consideration.[40]

The work of the SBH District Medical Officers became an invaluable aid to monitoring both the practices of panel doctors in signing off patients and also in conducting further examinations of claimants whose benefit claims were deemed suspect by approved societies. The creation of the referral mechanism of District Medical

---

36 SBH, *Second Annual Report, 1920*, 195.

37 Report on 'District Medical Officers for Scotland', *Poor Law and Local Government Magazine*, 31, (1921), 111. According to McLachlan, ed., *Improving the Common Weal*, 179, their role was eventually expanded into a general advisory function and a means of contact between the SBH and individual practitioners.

38 DHS, *Annual Report, 1934*, 113.

39 Sometime before 1929 this was revised to make approved societies bear the whole cost of the District Medical Officer Scheme. See DHS, *Annual Report 1929*, 150.

40 SBH, *Second Annual Report, 1920*, 195–6.

Officers had a deterrent effect on some medical benefit claims. For example, the SBH noted in 1922 that approved societies were learning from experience the types of case suitable for further investigation and to refer doubtful cases early to DMOs rather than wait until benefits had been paid for a long time.[41] In 1923, approved societies referred 19,040 cases to DMOs, and a further 297 cases were referred by individual panel practitioners. Of these, 8,519 (44%) examinations upheld the opinion of the certifying panel doctor. 4,367 (23%) of cases were reversed and certificates not supplied. A further 6,451 cases (33%) were not examined. The breakdown of the one-third of cases not examined included 13% who 'declared off' before examination, 16% who failed to attend, and 4% were not examined for unspecified other causes.[42] The number of cases examined by DMOs (Regional Medical Officers after 1929) peaked at close to 60,000 in 1932, thereafter it fell to under 52,000 in 1933, and fell by a further 8,000 to 44,870 in 1934.[43] The referral system represented only a small fraction of the total number of individual claimants in any given year. For example, there were 400,000 separate cases of illness in the year ending 1933, of these 13% were referred to Regional Medical Officers.

A key aspect of the work of DMOs envisaged by the SBH at their inception in 1920 was the plan to keep records and statistics of cases examined, as an aid to treatment and for administrative purposes. The SBH vision of medical records differed from that of the Ministry of Health at this point. An SBH discussion on medical records acknowledged that there were benefits in having a committee to oversee the collection and collation of uniform medical records from panel doctors in both England and Scotland as the Ministry of Health proposed. The Board's view was because of the SBH's 'separate status', any such committee should be a joint venture (or 'international' as it was described in SBH minutes).

The autonomy of the SBH from London control was implicit in the discussions on the issue of medical record keeping by panel

41 SBH, *Fourth Annual Report, 1922* (Edinburgh: HMSO, 1923), 65.

42 SBH, *Fifth Annual Report, 1923*, 102.

43 DHS, *Annual Report, 1934*, 112.

doctors. The Board's view, expressed by medical member J.C. McVail, of the possible application of such medical information gathering differed from that of the Ministry of Health. 'The Board felt that too much emphasis was being put on the possible administrative and statistical uses of the records and too little on their value as an aid to treatment.'[44] In fact, the SBH drafted its own amended terms of reference for the Ministry's proposed joint committee, which it sent to the Ministry for consideration. The Board's recommendation placed 'the remedial value of the patient of maintaining a scientific record of his case' before the 'clinical, administrative and statistical purpose which such records might advisedly be adapted to serve.'[45] Later discussion between the Ministry of Health and the Medical Research Council seemed to signify a change in priorities by the Ministry towards the proposed introduction of medical records.[46] The discussion over medical records and their purposes became an academic one. Within a year, the proposal was 'temporarily' shelved as an economy measure.[47] Nevertheless, the episode revealed the desire for autonomy of action by the Board members, and also demonstrated the influence of 'expert' opinion in the direction of SBH policy.

The strong support within the SBH for medical record keeping by panel practitioners demonstrated in 1919/20 by the Board did not

44 NAS, HH75/1, SBH minutes, 1 December 1919.

45 Ibid.

46 At a national level there was some discussion between the Ministry of Health and Medical Research Council around the time of the introduction of the reforming National Insurance legislation in 1920 (which revised Medical Benefit Regulations) about the possibility of requiring panel practitioners to systematically record insurance cases. The belief was that such record keeping would help fill gaps in current medical knowledge and allow more emphasis to be given the preventive aspects of national health insurance provision. No action was taken to enforce such a requirement in 1920. For more on this see, for example, Sir James Mackenzie and the staff of the St Andrews Institute for Clinical Research, 'Memorandum on some of the Medical Aspects of the National Health Insurance Acts', 16, published as an Appendix to the *Inter-Departmental Committee on Insurance Medical Records* [Rolleston Committee], (HMSO, 1920), [Cmd 836].

47 SBH, Sec*ond Annual Report, 1920*, 146.

disappear. In 1925, some preliminary conclusions on health trends among the insured Scots workforce were made by the SBH. These were based on 14,042 claimants examined by DMOs in that year. In total, 22,515 cases were referred that year to DMOs, however 38% of cases – 8,473 people – failed to show up for their examinations. The careful records kept of these 14,000 plus examinations allowed the SBH to identify some of the larger causes of incapacity in three (unidentified) regions. In the second sample region (described as partly agricultural, partly industrial – probably Aberdeenshire) of the 3,000 patients examined, 286 (9.5%) were found to be suffering from some form of heart disease.

A summary of DMOs' findings appeared as a distinct section in the 1925 SBH Annual Report. The summary report noted with some concern the increased incidence of heart disease across Scotland. According to the summary, the Scottish death rate from heart disease outstripped the mortality rate for all forms of tuberculosis (the death toll from heart disease was 7,374 and the tuberculosis figure was 5,389).[48] The DMO findings, although small-scale, helped provide more information on causal factors in the increased incidence of heart disease. The plan to use health insurance practitioner and DMO records for the purposes of research into general health trends and to monitor morbidity among the Scottish working population as a whole was placed on a more systematic level after the launch of the Morbidity Statistics Scheme in 1929. The creation of this scheme followed concern over mounting incapacity levels and will be discussed later in this chapter.

48 SBH, *Seventh Annual Report, 1925*, 242, 258.

Healthy or Hungry? Mounting Claims for National Health Insurance

Increasing health benefit claims in the 1920s did not reveal the full picture of morbidity patterns among the general population. Health insurance covered the insured worker, but no dependants[49] (unlike Unemployment Insurance which was expanded to include dependants' allowances in 1921). Hence, while mounting sickness benefit figures may suggest a link between rising unemployment and a tendency to ill health in the inter-war period, they do not present the whole picture. Increased sickness benefit claims do however, shows a growing dependency on state benefits among the (eligible) workforce.[50] This dependency was more in evidence in Scotland than in England and Wales. Partly this was due to differences in the system of Poor Relief in Scotland (in operation until 1929). The Scottish Poor Law did not give the able bodied unemployed a right to parish relief, but those deemed too sick to work were entitled to benefits. Unemployed Scottish workers, who were outside the scope of unemployment insurance, were understandably keen to be classed as eligible for sickness benefit. When that form of entitlement ran out, they would then be eligible for parish relief as a member of the sick poor.

The link between incapacity levels and the vagaries of industrial employment became all too clear during the General Strike in May 1926 and its aftermath. There was a sudden increase of sickness benefit claims among insured workers from May 1926. The SBH noted that the increase could not be tied to any epidemic or other exceptional illness, and was confined to industrial areas. During the months June to December 1926, there were four times as many male cases referred to DMOs as there had been in the corresponding months of 1925 in an attempt by approved societies to uncover false claims for sickness benefit.

49 Unemployment Insurance provided for dependants from time to time. Payments for dependants were introduced in 1921, but were removed again in the 1930s.

50 Whiteside 'Counting the Cost', 232.

The SBH view was that panel doctors, sympathetic to the plight of workers, were supplying certificates of ill health to strikers and the unemployed.[51] In July 1926, the SBH issued a circular to all panel practitioners warning them not to allow the employment status of sickness benefit applicants to cloud their professional judgement.[52] The official belief was that panel doctors had allowed sickness benefit to turn into a form of 'dole'.[53] Not surprisingly, the approved societies felt the same way. The *British Medical Journal* noted that 'some societies said they were fairly sure that there was a large number of doubtful claims lodged for sickness and disablement.'[54] The Scottish Miners' Federation Approved Society also issued a circular to their district agencies describing the situation as a 'an utter collapse from the normal standard of certification'. The Miners' Federation circular compared the 1926 experience to that which occurred during a previous miners' strike in 1921.[55] The continued high levels of sickness benefit claims after 1926 and the lingering suspicion that panel practitioners were reluctant to disallow false claims, will be dealt with in a later section on panel practice.

The Government Actuary's Report for 1930 examined sickness claims between 1921–1927 from a sample of approved society records. The Report revealed that almost half of all working class households used National Health Insurance sickness or disablement benefits to supplement ordinary family income.[56] The Report showed men's sickness claims to have risen 41 per cent between 1921 and 1927 and disablement claims had risen 85 per cent in the same period. The figures for married women's claims had risen 106 per cent between 1921 and 1927, while disability claims for this group rose 159 per cent over the same period.[57]

Morbidity patterns among uninsured dependants, women without employment, children and the elderly, often the most susceptible

51 SBH, *Eighth Annual Report, 1926*, 16.

52 SBH/National Health Insurance Joint Committee, Circular 3041C, July 1926.

53 Gilbert, *Social Policy*, 289.

54 *BMJ*, 1926 (2), 132.

55 Ibid.

56 Gilbert, *Social Policy*, 290.

57 Ibid.

sections of working class families, were not recorded in health insurance statistics. Yet, other vulnerable elements in society did appear in health insurance returns. Married female workers featured heavily in health insurance claims. High claim levels led to special scrutiny of this group of insured workers due to their high claim levels. Married women were suspected of 'malingering', perhaps claiming benefits due to pregnancy or recent childbirth, rather than suffering from specific illnesses. This suspicion, in evidence before World War One, reached higher levels in the 1920s.

In 1923, claims from single and widowed women members of the National Amalgamated Approved Society were 91 per cent of the expected level. For married women, claims were running at 125% of expectation for the year.[58] In 1927, referrals of patients claiming incapacity to District Medical Officers highlighted the greater claims by females than males. According to the SBH 1927 Annual Report, while women accounted for 33% of the Scottish insured population they accounted for 57% of referrals. This may have been due to the belief by approved societies that women were more likely to be 'malingering' and women were therefore referred proportionally more often for second examinations than male workers. Of the women examined in 1927, 40% were found capable of some work. The comparable figure for men was 33%. Moreover, 41% of all referred women failed to turn up for the DMO examination or signed themselves off sickness benefit before the appointment date, compared to 34% of men.[59] Due to these figures, the SBH generally regarded women's claims as more suspicious than men's. The belief was that women worked until benefit entitlement accrued and then claimed sickness payments while still carrying out household duties, rather than continue in insurable employment. Many more women than men were in part-time or irregular work which paid the same or little more than sickness benefit, and therefore women were (consciously or unconsciously) choosing to claim benefits rather than work to earn a small income.

58 Ibid., 288.

59 SBH, *Ninth Annual Report, 1927*, 265.

The SBH did not take into account the inequalities of income that confined women to irregular, poorly paid work or to household duties and living on an income inadequate to maintain dependants. Between 1928–1930, women's insurance claims were almost double that of males, while married women's claims outstripped all male claims by three to one. Married women's benefits had been cut once in 1915, in 1932 they were cut once again, from 12 shillings (60p) per week to ten shillings (50p) per week. Disability benefit was similarly reduced from 7 shillings and sixpence (37.5p) to five shillings (25p) per week. The right to claim benefit was also more strictly monitored. The official view that women were excessive claimants clearly lay behind these moves.

In reproving tones similar to the debate on maternal mortality levels in the 1930s, the impression given by government agencies was that malingering women were to blame for the high rate of female National Health Insurance claims.[60] This controversial issue re-emerged during debates on the passage of the National Health Insurance and Contributory Pensions Act, 1932. Approved societies – through their representative in parliament, R.J. Meller[61] – put forward a motion to create a new class of insurance for married women. The measure was designed to force women to re-qualify for health insurance upon marriage by paying 26 weeks contributions before any entitlement became due. Such women would also be ineligible for maternity benefit for a year and disability payments for two years. This amendment was defeated before it came to a vote[62], however, the level of payments to both married and single women were reduced in the new legislation, operative from January 1933. James Maxton, Independent Labour MP for Glasgow Bridgeton, alleged that the tone of the debate gave the impression that there was a sort of tacit conspiracy between panel doctors and married women to get more out

60 For more on 'blaming' mothers see chapter three on infant and maternal welfare.

61 Conservative MP for Mitcham, Chair of the Consultative Council on Health Insurance and former executive of the Prudential Insurance Society.

62 HOC debates, 21–6–32, vol. 267, col. 933–936.

of the National Health Insurance funds than they were entitled.[63] Maxton challenged this opinion and went on to say that the one figure in the country's aggregate vital statistics which had not shown any improvement for a long period was maternal mortality.[64]

However tempting to contemporary official opinion, the ill health of the women worker could not simply be put down to malingering or lack of alternative income. The view of the Chief Medical Officer for the Ministry of Health, Sir George Newman, in 1932, was that over every five year period 250,000 women became virtually incapable for work due to the ravages of difficult childbirth and the aggravation of illnesses due to frequent pregnancy.[65] The 1933/34 DHS Report on Incapacity among Insured Workers stated that heavier incapacity levels among married women were not unexpected. The 1933/34 Report noted that married women were more frequently subjected to the major and minor 'upsets' associated with childbearing and to the disabling effects of gynaecological conditions. A further factor identified by the Report to account for higher incapacity among married women workers was that married women in the insured population were 'by no means representative of married women in the general population'.[66] This comment is not developed, but it suggests that the official view was that married women workers (from lower social classes) brought illness upon themselves by taking the decision to enter the workforce.

The DHS 'Morbidity Statistics Scheme' inaugurated in 1930 gave the Department a unique series of detailed information about the distribution of disabling sickness among the Scottish insured population. The first DHS *Report on Incapacitating Sickness among the Insured Population of Scotland* (as the printed morbidity statistics findings were called) for 1930/1 uncovered '[...] an extraordinary

63 HOC debates, 11–5–32, vol. 265, col. 1981.

64 HOC debates, 11–5–32 vol. 265, col. 1981–1982. Maxton's comments here are reminiscent in content, if not in tone, of his 'murderers' allegation levelled at those who supported SBH budgetary cuts in milk and meals to mothers and babies which he made in June 1923. See chapter three for more on this issue.

65 Cited in Webster, 'Healthy or Hungry Thirties?', 123.

66 DHS, *Report on Sickness Statistics for the Insured Population of Scotland for the year from 1st July 1933 to 30th June 1934* (Edinburgh: HMSO, 1935), 4.

amount of invalidism' among the insured working population as a whole.[67] The 1930/1 Report revealed that female disability claims exceeded those for males by 13 per cent. Married women showed an incapacity rate from all causes twice as high as that for males. The incidence of anaemia among women was 35 times higher than among men. Women were also more likely to suffer from debility and nervous debility. Women were 9 and 5 times respectively more likely than men to suffer these illnesses. The incidence of women suffering diseases of the bladder and the kidney was 8 times higher than for men, and women were 5 times more likely to fall prey to valvular heart disease. Women also were 3 times as likely as men to fall ill to diseases of the veins and neurasthenia. Women (both single and married) had lower rates for hernia, gastric and duodenal ulcer, accidents, and pneumonia than the corresponding male rates.[68]

Generational, Regional and Occupational Incapacity Trends in the 1930s

The nature of sickness benefit claims changed in the decade between the mid 1920s and mid 1930s. The age profile altered between the earlier period and the later, more young workers were in receipt of health benefits in the 1920s and older workers in the 1930s. This may have been due to the maturing of the insured workforce. Steady increase in the number of claims with age was a pronounced feature of the sickness rates of both men and women. The number of older workers entitled to health insurance benefits naturally increased with the passage of years since the implementation of National Health Insurance coverage in 1913.

There was also an identifiable regional imbalance in the incapacity rate of Scottish workers during the 1930s. The lowest rates

67 DHS, *Annual Report, 1931*, p. xv.

68 DHS, *Report on Sickness Statistics for the Insured Population of Scotland for the year from 1st July 1930 to 30th June 1931* (Edinburgh: HMSO, 1932), 25.

of incapacity uncovered in 1930/1 occurred in the sparsely populated rural counties of Inverness, Ross and Cromarty, Argyll, Orkney, Zetland, Perth and Bute, and in the burghs of Greenock, Inverness and Rutherglen. The heaviest incidence of sickness was experienced in the eastern industrial (mining) counties of the Lothians, Stirling, Clackmannan and Kinross, and in the burghs of Dunfermline in the east, Aberdeen in the north-east, and in the heavy industrial towns of Airdrie, Coatbridge, Hamilton (all Lanarkshire) and Kilmarnock in Ayrshire. The absence of three of the four largest cities in Scotland: Glasgow, Edinburgh and Dundee, from the list of unhealthiest burghs is, perhaps, surprising. (The presence of a proportionately larger middle class in these major cities might go some way to explaining this phenomenon.) In fact, compared to the Scottish averages for incidence per 1,000 workers, and duration of incapacity, these three large burghs did relatively well (see table 6.3).

The DHS Report on Incapacitating Sickness for 1933/34 again showed a disproportionately high rate of sickness in the mining areas of Scotland, contrasting with conspicuously low levels in the highland rural districts.[69] Some of the highest incapacity rates occurred in the mining areas within Lanarkshire, East, West and Mid Lothian, Ayrshire, Fife and Stirlingshire. Miners were two to three times more likely to contract injuries, septic and inflammatory skin conditions, rheumatic conditions, anaemia, gastritis and tachycardia than other workers. Miners were 75% more likely than other male workers to fall victim to bronchitis, pneumonia, and diseases of the veins and cardiac debility.[70]

69 DHS, *Report on Sickness Statistics for the Insured Population of Scotland* [...] *1933 to* [...] *1934*, 26–7.

70 Ibid., 47.

Burghs	Incidence per 1,000 insured workers	Average duration (in days)
Airdrie	309.55	47.90
Coatbridge	258.46	58.55
Dundee	191.25	57.55
Dunfermline	308.12	42.39
Edinburgh	191.01	41.33
Glasgow	200.34	49.85
Greenock	169.59	48.42
Hamilton	282.49	49.42
Inverness	185.67	44.65
Kilmarnock	282.85	41.74
Rutherglen	188.97	40.26
Scotland	210.60	47.03

Table 6.3 Comparison of Sickness Experience in Selected Scottish Burgh Insurance Committee Areas, 1930/1[71]

The DHS recognition of the peculiar health difficulties of the mining industry led to a special case study of morbidity among miners over the period 1 July 1930–30 June 1933. This study was included in the 1933/34 Incapacity Report. Over the three-year period there were 133,280 cases of illness and 6 million days of incapacity among Scottish miners. The special survey found that the higher frequency of incapacity among miners (405 cases per 1,000 miners compared to 190 cases per 1,000 male workers) accounted for an annual average incapacity per miner of 18 days, while for other male workers the rate was 8.7 days.[72] The ill health among miners was given added significance because of the large numbers employed in mining in Scotland (8% of the workforce in 1921).[73]

71 DHS, *Report on Sickness Statistics for the Insured Population of Scotland* [...] *1930 to* [...] *1931*, 35.

72 DHS, *Report on Sickness Statistics for the Insured Population of Scotland* [...] *1933 to* [...] *1934*, 44.

73 Foster, 'A Proletarian Nation? Occupation and Class since 1914', 203

A further development was the increased number of chronically ill workers who made claims during the 1930s (see table 6.4). The DHS Incapacity Report for 1935/6 discovered that 40% of days lost among the insured Scottish population were attributable to chronic cases (those incapable of work for twelve months or more).[74] Of the 30,754 chronic cases considered in the 1935/6 report: 17.01% of cases were aged under 35, 44.85% were aged 35–55, and 38.14% cases were aged over 55. Two-thirds of all chronic cases were suffering from one of the following five illnesses: nervous diseases (mostly insanity), rheumatism, disease of the circulatory (nervous) system, tuberculosis and bronchitis.

Year	Number of Cases	Rate per 1,000 insured workers
1930/1	23,835	13.5
1931/2	22,887	12.9
1932/3	26,059	14.7
1933/4	27,224	15.6
1934/5	29,504	17.3
1935/6	30,410	17.6
1936/7	30,754	17.2

Table 6.4 Chronic Cases among Scotland's Insured Population, 1936/7[75]

The significance of other illnesses fluctuated. Between July 1936 and June 1937 an influenza epidemic caused on average one day of incapacity for every insured Scottish worker. Among other features, age of claimant was less important than type of employment. Those claimants who had previously been employed in domestic service and mining were most at risk of chronic disability.[76] Since domestic servants were ineligible for unemployment benefits, as one of the

74 DHS, *Report on Sickness Statistics for the Insured Population of Scotland for the year from 1st July 1936 to 30th June 1937* (Edinburgh: HMSO, 1939), 58.

75 Ibid, 8.

76 DHS, *Annual Report, 1937*, 116–117.

'uninsured trades', it is perhaps not surprising that this particular occupation was much in evidence in sickness claims. The Scottish findings on these occupational groups were broadly supported by the findings of a Ministry of Health Disability Committee in the later 1930s.[77]

Successive 'Incapacitating Sickness of the Insured Population in Scotland' (ISIPS) reports led the DHS to the conclusion that malingering due to straitened economic circumstances was not a feature of Scottish morbidity. Scottish workers were not prone to dramatic morbidity patterns. The ISIPS reports showed that influenza epidemics could push up figures from year to year, meanwhile underlying trends identified around 50% of recorded incapacity being due to minor complaints, such as upper respiratory infections. This discovery, coupled with the confirmed trend of increasing chronic incapacity accounted for much of the increase in claims. Prompted by such findings the calls for tightened certifying practices which had been so much in evidence in the late 1920s tailed off in the 1930s. The rising levels of chronic incapacity revealed by the ISIPS reports and mounting disability payments gave rise to a wider consideration of the role played by social conditions in disease causation among Scots workers. In 1936, the DHS conceded that '[...] general factors such as diet, housing, occupational conditions will all require evaluation before a satisfactory explanation is forthcoming.'[78] These comments hint at a need to move health policy towards more preventive measures and away from simply treating the sick. Such measures of 'social medicine' were more clearly debated during and after World War Two.[79]

The chronic incapacity rate, especially the numbers suffering from chronic illness at relatively young ages, suggests that despite the improvements in health care for infants and children in Scotland since the beginning of the twentieth century, many were reaching adulthood with a legacy of physical deficiency. Many insured Scottish workers

77 See Whiteside, 'Counting the Cost', 235.

78 DHS, *Report on Incapacitating Sickness in the Insured Population of Scotland during the year 1st July 1934–30th June 1935* (Edinburgh: HMSO, 1936), 5–6.

79 For more on 'social medicine' see chapter seven.

in their twenties, thirties and forties were being laid low by the illnesses or physical defects which ailed them in childhood. In the 1930s, the DHS was not in a position to act positively on the morbidity statistics and launch campaigns for early diagnosis and preventive treatment, e.g. physiotherapy or convalescence. Despite increased awareness of trends in chronic incapacity and employment-specific illness achieved by the Morbidity Statistics Scheme, no new policy initiative was undertaken by the DHS in these years. The DHS, like other government departments, remained cost conscious. However, the outbreak of World War Two and the need for preserving a healthy workforce enabled the DHS (with years of statistical evidence to hand) to undertake a number of pioneering health promotion schemes.[80]

'Panel' Practice

In the early years of the twentieth century, the medical profession focused its opposition on what it regarded as increasing government intrusion in to the practice of medicine and over-regulation of public health provision. Such intervention was regarded by many general practitioners as an attempt to reduce their independent position as providers of health care, to the role of government agent or medical civil servant. In Immergut's thesis the conflict was between the 'buyers' and 'sellers' of medical services. As buyers of medical services, governments aim to reduce the cost of these services. Medical practitioners as sellers wish to maintain as wide a market as possible for their services to keep both income and professional status buoyant.

Medical practitioner resistance to health insurance pre-dated the creation of the Ministry and Scottish Board of Health. By World War One, health insurance and the realities of panel practice were established features of medical practice. By the mid-1920s, Scottish

80 See chapter seven for more on these wartime schemes.

panel practitioners had four basic duties. Most crucially, panel doctors were obliged to give, on request, sickness certificates to incapacitated insured workers. Secondly, the doctor was obliged to keep a record of the nature and duration of each illness certified, and to transmit yearly summaries for each patient treated under the scheme to the SBH. Thirdly, doctors had to provide proper surgery and waiting-room accommodation. Finally, panel doctors were to furnish patient reports to District Medical Officers, where requested, for further investigation (and also to make reports available to municipal Tuberculosis Officers in cases suspected of suffering from the disease).[81]

The routine work of insurance medical practitioners could be placed under strain by the extreme demands of insurance patients (or occasionally, by their employers). In March 1926 a case was referred to the SBH for investigation. Dr J.W.I. of Tongue in the Highland county of Sutherland became involved in a vicious slanging match with the employer, (Mr. M.) of one of his panel patients, J.G., who lived in the nearby village of Dornoch. Mr. M. was critical of the level of care and attendance provided for his chauffeur, J.G. The patient, J.G., was suffering from cold in the lungs. Dr. J.W.I. attended him for this illness. Within a few days J.G. also developed a dental problem. Despite several requests from his employer, Mr. M., Dr. J.W.I. did not attend the chauffeur for this second ailment for over two weeks. Mr. M. then sent a letter to the doctor requesting he attend the chauffeur as soon as possible. It was clearly not the first time that Dr. J.W.I. had received such a summons from this particular employer. This request brought a stinging response from the Highland doctor:

> I beg to point out to you that although J.G. has the misfortune to be your employee, I am not [...]. I thought that from past experience that by now you should be thoroughly conversant with the National Health Insurance Act, but yet you have apparently not assimilated the fact that a doctor is not a travelling dentist. I do not know of any clause in the National Health Insurance Act which empowers an employer to summon a medical practitioner unless he is doing so at the request of the insured person. If, however, you are acting as J.G.'s messenger you are filling the only position for which I think you are suited.[82]

81 SBH, *Sixth Annual Report, 1924*, 149.

82 NAS, SBH 75/24, SBH minutes, 14 March 1926.

In response to this letter, Mr. M. had his solicitor contact the SBH with a request that disciplinary action should be taken against Dr. J.W.I. The Board referred the matter to its National Health Insurance Committee for adjudication. The Board also issued a letter of reprimand to Dr. J.W.I criticising his improper conduct and lack of professionalism: 'it is not in the interests of the medical service of insured persons that a communication in the terms used by you should have been made.'[83] Two months later the SBH decided not to take action against Dr. J.W.I. However, the Board recommended that an SBH Medical Officer, Dr. Shearer, should visit Dr. J.W.I. on his next tour of the district to 'impress upon him the gravity with which the Board regard his conduct in this case'.[84]

An issue of perennial concern for panel doctors was their pay level under the National Health Insurance scheme. Pay disputes began even before the scheme was put into operation in 1913. Under the terms of the 1911 Insurance Act, each panel practitioner received between 8 shillings and sixpence and nine shillings (capitation fee) for each insurance contributor s/he had on their list, depending on whether the doctor dispensed his or her own medicines. Other payments included a mileage allowance to panel practitioners in rural areas and subventions to those practising in isolated areas with small populations. Throughout the early 1920s payment levels for panel doctors continued to be the subject of much wrangling between the profession and the government.[85]

---

83 Ibid.

84 NAS, SBH 75/24, SBH minutes, 28 May 1926.

85 In early 1920, payment to panel practitioners was raised to 11 shillings (55p) per panel patient year to take account of inflation. However, the mounting financial crisis which affected unemployment insurance and severely curtailed the housing programme, also took its toll on health insurance. Capitation fees were reduced after 1 January 1922 to 9 shillings and sixpence (47.5p) per patient. Panel doctors' capitation fees remained at 9 shillings until reduced by 10 per cent under the National Economy Act, 1931. The cut was restored in 1935 and the figure stayed at 9 shillings until January 1942 when it was raised to 9 shillings and 9 pence (48p). The capitation fee was raised again in 1943 to ten shillings and sixpence (52.5p) with the promise a further review at the end of the war. The Spens Committee recommendation for a new capitation level of 15 shillings and sixpence (77.5p) was accepted by the BMA at the end of 1946.

Panel practice based as it was on payment by numbers on a practitioner's list, rather than by results, generally encouraged a perfunctory standard of service for insured patients. Moreover, one survey of inter-war medical incomes has suggested that the average panel practitioner derived a declining share of income from panel practice, with an increasing share coming from private practice.[86] While 'average' figures must be treated with caution, this evidence does at least suggest that there was no incentive for panel practitioners to improve the standard of their care. This was far removed from the original intention 'to provide for insurance against loss of health and for the prevention and cure of sickness.' Anne Digby has suggested that negotiations regarding health insurance between the BMA and the state often were dominated by rates of remuneration rather than practical health matters.[87] Meanwhile, inter-war medical developments such as routine laboratory testing of patient samples were beyond the remit of most panel practice.

In 1926, the Medical Officer of Health for Aberdeen, John Parlane Kinloch,[88] in an address to the Scottish Association of Insurance Committees accused the Insurance Commissioners (and by inference the medical practitioners they directed) of failing to recognise the differences between ameliorative and preventive care. Using the example of rheumatic heart disease, which a study had found to be the greatest cause of loss of working days in Aberdeen,

---

86 A. Digby and N. Bosanquet, 'Doctors and Patients in an Era of National Health Insurance and Private Practice, 1913–1938', *Economic History Review*, 1/1 (1988), 75.

87 A. Digby, 'Medicine and the State, 1901–1948', in S.J.D. Green and R.C. Whiting, eds, *The Boundaries of the State in Modern Britain* (Cambridge: Cambridge University Press, 1996), 217. Peter Bartrip contradicted this view in *'Themselves Writ Large': A History of the BMA 1832–1966* (BMJ Publishing Group, 1996), 214. Bartrip commented: '[...] the BMA was not preoccupied with the question of the capitation rates available to its members. Rather, while remaining in favour of a scheme restricted to the less well off sections of society and opposed to any form of state intervention between patients and their practitioners, it also took an expansive and progressive view of the future of national health insurance.'

88 John Parlane Kinloch later became Medical Officer for the SBH. See chapter two for more on Parlane Kinloch.

Parlane Kinloch suggested that by the time treatment was given the adult worker, the best that could be hoped for was an amelioration of the disease. However, if the disease were treated at its onset in childhood, a recovery would be the rule rather than the exception. According to Parlane Kinloch, prevention rather than amelioration was the key.[89]

This theme of continuity in care was again explored by the DHS during the passage of the Local Government (Scotland) Act in 1929.[90] In 1936, the Cathcart Report suggested that more emphasis should be given to the panel practitioner 'as an adviser in health as well as in sickness'.[91] The Cathcart Report's stress on prevention as well as treatment in health insurance medical treatment was not the end of the matter. Although ten years apart, both Parlane Kinloch's view and the Cathcart Report raised the wider question of the standard of health care provided by panel doctors. According to the DHS Cathcart Report in 1936, only a very limited degree of supervision was given to the quality and nature of treatment provided by insurance practitioners.[92] The prevailing attitude was for doctors to provide the minimum treatment necessary to keep patients on their list. There were no incentives to introduce modern curative procedures or for panel practitioners to keep up with new developments in medicine for their panel patients.

In an attempt to improve the standard of panel practitioners, the DHS introduced an experimental postgraduate training scheme in 1937. Following the success of the trial, a comprehensive scheme was launched in 1938. During 1938, twelve two-week courses were run for panel practitioners. The courses were offered at the four Scottish medical schools (Edinburgh, Glasgow, Aberdeen and Dundee). 251 Scottish doctors attended the courses (400 had applied), as did five English insurance practitioners. Eight other Scottish panel doctors attended courses at the British Post-Graduate Medical School at Hammersmith in London. Course fees were paid by the DHS direct to

89 *GMJ*, (1926), 324.

90 See chapter four on school health for more on this topic.

91 DHS, *Committee on Scottish Health Services Report*, 220.

92 Ibid., 216.

the medical schools. The doctors received travel and subsistence payments while training. The cost of hiring a full-time locum for each participant in the courses was also covered by the DHS. The total cost of the scheme was £6,653. The money was defrayed from the residue of the unclaimed proceeds of the sales of NHI stamps.[93] This initiative was a case of too little, too late. During the war criticism of the standard of care provided by panel doctors re-emerged.[94]

Panel Practice and 'Lax Certification'

> You, Sir, are interested in statistics, forms, and figures, whilst our interest is simply in some sick man or woman.
> (NAS, HH3/17, Letter for Dr J.G. Gilruth, Leith, to John Jeffrey, Secretary, DHS, 1 February 1932)

As health insurance claims mounted in the mid 1920s, fresh official attempts were made to curtail the 'problem' of panel doctors' open-handed certification of unfitness to work. By the late 1920s, the DHS were in advance of the Ministry of Health in developing ways to control panel practitioners who were accused of 'lax certification'.[95] The problem had been noted on previous occasions. For example in 1923, a Scottish doctor was removed from the panel list and reported to the General Medical Council for lax practices. 'The offence consisted mainly in the lax issuing of certificates and prescriptions,

93 DHS, *Annual Report, 1938* (Edinburgh: HMSO, 1939), 148–149, [Cmd 5969].

94 Panel practice was compared unfavourably to that of private practice by social investigator, GDH Cole, Director of the Nuffield Social Reconstruction Survey. See Honigsbaum, *The Division in British Medicine*, 174. Muriel Ritson of the DHS refuted this differentiation in her evidence to the Beveridge Committee in July 1942. CAB, 87/81, Committee on Social Insurance and Allied Services, [Beveridge Committee], memorandum number 114, 20 July 1942.

95 Scotland and Ireland followed different methods of inspecting the record of panel practitioners to England and Wales and this led the DHS down a separate path when the issue of lax certification became a pressing one to health insurance administrators.

the filling in of these forms being left on occasion to the discretion of the clerkess employed at the doctor's surgery.'[96] The problem was more widespread than individual cases of irresponsibility. In 1925, the SBH Annual Report commented 'there is still [...] an undesirably large volume of "loose certification"'.[97]

Claims for sickness and disablement benefit rose between 1926 and 1927. The high level in 1926 had been viewed by the SBH as a 'one-off' event caused by the General Strike. However, as the numbers claiming benefits under National Health Insurance increased the following year, the Board expressed a sense of disquiet and fear for the financial stability of health insurance if high claim levels persisted. The SBH reacted by expanding benefit claim monitoring by DMOs and reminding panel practitioners of the dangers of over certification.[98]

In 1927, joint meetings were held between practitioners in the industrial regions of Scotland and a small group of official representatives. These included an official from the SBH, one or more District Medical Officers and an official representative from the BMA. The SBH representative addressed each meeting, this speech was followed by a general discussion of the issues of insurance certification. In addition, a SBH representative, accompanied by one of the District Medical Officers, made over 150 personal visits to practitioners whose certification during the General Strike and the continued miners' strike (between May and December 1926) was regarded as unsatisfactory. Some practitioners interviewed appeared not to understand their responsibility in certifying workers as 'incapable of work'. Evidence was also uncovered of practitioners issuing certificates in the knowledge of, or in fear of, losing these patients from their lists to rival practitioners who may have been more free in granting illness certificates. After discussion with the SBH Consultative Council on Health Insurance, the right of insured people to change their panel practitioner without any restriction was amended in 1927. For those wishing to change practitioner while remaining in

96 SBH, *Fifth Annual Report, 1923*, 113.
97 SBH, *Sixth Annual Report, 1924*, 179.
98 SBH, *Ninth Annual Report, 1927*, 17.

the same area, this was to be done in writing and a fourteen-day hiatus was to be observed between consultations with new and former panel practitioner. This brought Scotland into line with English practice.[99]

A joint advisory committee was also formed in 1927 to consider cases of negligence (failure to provide appropriate treatment, incomplete or wrong advice or the refusal to visit patients) by panel practitioners. The advisory committee included a Medical Officer appointed by the SBH (to chair), and a member of the BMA Insurance Acts Sub-Committee (Scotland) to represent the profession. The great rise in claims for health insurance in the wake of the General Strike led the SBH to put a squeeze both on claimants and on their panel doctors. As a consequence of the 1927 investigations, the Joint Committee devised a scheme the following year to discipline lax practitioners which involved the local insurance committee medical services sub-committee imposing an appropriate fine. In order to gather better information on certification, the SBH (DHS from 1929) developed a more rigorous procedure for overseeing the work of panel doctors under the auspices the District Medical Officers. These activities continued over the next two years of administrative re-organisation. From May 1930, monitoring duties fell to the re-organised Regional Medical Officer service. Panel practitioners were sent a memorandum by the DHS stating the need for doctors to co-operate with the RMOs in certification and supervision of claims. The DHS hoped that closer linking of hospital, clinic and panel practitioner services would be obtainable under the Local Government reform to the benefit of insured persons and insurance funds.

Under the new monitoring arrangements District (later Regional) Medical Officers visited practitioners to examine their 'live register' of all cases in receipt of incapacity certificates. The RMO would go over the live register, discuss any special cases with the practitioner, and call up for examination any case mutually agreed upon. The patient concerned would then be sent a letter from the RMO asking her/him to attend for an examination, but not stating that the

99 Ibid., 269.

practitioner was concerned in the decision.[100] Whiteside has described the methods used by Medical Officers as the 'bullying'[101] of panel practitioners.

One Leith doctor assessed the activities of RMOs in 1932 not as bullying, but as generally ineffective and unhelpful. Dr John Gilruth[102] wrote a letter of complaint to DHS Secretary John Jeffrey in February 1932 on the subject. Gilruth felt that the reason large numbers of patients were signing off after reference to RMOs, but before being examined, was due to the number of cases of minor ailments referred to RMOs, between the second and third week of benefit. This period was the time when a patient would ordinarily have been signed off in any case. Gilruth denied it was because the patient and her/his doctor was afraid of a second opinion. Gilruth felt that RMOs were turning down patients who had been certified as 'unfit for work' by the doctor on the grounds that the patient was 'fit for light work'. Gilruth's view was that doctors were asked to certify whether a patient was fit or unfit for work, not whether that patient was fit or unfit for 'light work'. A patient was either capable or incapable of work, there were no 'degrees of fitness'.[103]

As part of the stricter monitoring of sickness certification RMOs also paid visits to some of branches of approved societies to stress the need for constant supervision of claims and the early use of RMOs as medical referees in doubtful claims for sickness benefit.[104] The DHS also monitored the expenditure of approved societies for lax practices. The Department believed there was ample evidence that many

---

100 'Glasgow Burgh Panel Committee / Glasgow Burgh Local Medical Committee Bulletin', No. 18, 30 June 1930, 1.

101 N. Whiteside, 'Private Agencies for Public Purposes', *Journal of Social Policy*, 12/2 (1983), 178.

102 John Grant Gilruth was a Leith general practitioner. He graduated MB, ChB from Edinburgh University in 1917. He was Medical Officer at Leith Dockyard and served as a naval surgeon between 1915–1919.

103 NAS, HH3/17, Letter from Dr Gilruth, Derby Street, Leith to John Jeffrey, Secretary, DHS, 1 February 1932.

104 PRO, PIN4/29, 'Note for the Joint Committee by the DHS in connection with consideration of Report by the Government Actuary on the Sickness and Disablement Experience of a group of Societies in the period 1921–27', 26 February 1930.

approved societies and individual branch officials did not fully appreciate the importance of using all available information when considering each claim for sickness benefit. For example, past history of claims could easily be checked (if societies had kept good records – the DHS found that in some cases societies could only find past records after long searches). In summary, the DHS charge was that lax practices were as likely from the approved society in administering a claim for sickness or disability benefit as they were from the panel doctor in certifying the claim.[105]

The Ministry of Health approach to panel practitioners was less direct to that employed by the Department of Health for Scotland. Although an agreement to investigate procedures for disciplining 'lax practitioners' was agreed in June 1930, it took some time for disciplinary measures to be put in place. The Ministry issued circulars drawing the attention of insurance practitioners to the dangers of lax certification in 1931. The Ministry also conducted a series of 'educational' interviews with practitioners to inculcate better care in certification. Yet by 1933, the debate had moved on only so far as to whether identified cases of lax certification were to be referred to Panel Committees or whether warning letters were to be issued by the Minister of Health.[106] In June 1934, a Memorandum to the Ministry from A.R. Roache, District Medical Officer in Leeds, expressed grave fears that the problem of lax certification was getting out of hand. He noted that (as far as he knew) there had not even been one case of disciplinary action against English panel doctors charged with lax practice. Roache noted that some doctors had been visited two or even three times, the Ministry had also written to some, yet no real improvement had been evident. Roache felt that many panel doctors would do nothing to 'take steps, which they hold to be inimical to their financial interests' unless compelled to do so.[107]

---

105 DHS, *Annual Report 1929*, 148.

106 PRO, MH62/47, Ministry of Health minute, 'Action in respect of Lax Certification', 20 March 1933.

107 PRO, MH62/47, Memorandum to Ministry of Health from A.R. Roache, Divisional Medical Officer of Health, North Eastern Division, Leeds, 20 June 1934. The Ministry of Health and the BMA struggled to form an appropriate advisory committee to consult regarding action over lax certification in

Meanwhile in Scotland, close monitoring of certification seemed to reap a dividend by 1930. The DHS Annual Report for that year noted that claims for male disablement benefit and female sickness and disablement in 1930 were lower than for the previous two years (male sickness benefit claims were at a lower level than in 1928, but were greater than in 1929). The question posed in the DHS Report was whether there was less sickness in 1930, or whether there were other factors at work, '[...] such as greater care in certification and/or more effective supervision of claims'.[108]

Yet even after the 1929 initiative and encouraging 1930 figures, the DHS continued to make veiled references to lax certification by panel practitioners. In 1934, the DHS speculated on the level of expenditure by approved societies not only on actual incapacitating illness, but also on claims made by people who were not really incapable of work, 'although they have obtained medical certificates of incapacity'. This allegation was linked to comments on a pilot scheme initiated by Dundee approved societies in 1932. Here, approved societies sent their own sick visitors to make regular health checks on claimants. The juxtaposition of the two reports identifying continued 'lax certification' by panel practitioners on the one hand and describing the close monitoring of insurance claimants in Dundee suggests that, for the DHS at least, the solution to the former lay in the wider implementation of the latter scheme.

The Dundee scheme provided three full-time sick visitors (to cover an insured population of 40,000). The sick visitors visited every claimant for sickness benefit in the city within a few days of their claim.[109] The DHS held up the Dundee scheme as useful exercise. 'An appreciable reduction' in the average number of days' incapacity per insured person in Dundee was noted in 1937. As a result of 13,000 visits paid by the approved society-funded sick visitors during 1937, 55% of those visited ceased to claim benefits.[110]

England. See correspondence and memoranda in PRO, MH62/46. See also Eder, *National Health Insurance and Medical Practice in Britain*, 296–307.

108 DHS, *Annual Report, 1930* (Edinburgh: HMSO, 1931), 119.

109 DHS, *Annual Report, 1934*, 111–112.

110 DHS, *Annual Report, 1937*, 118.

A further attempt to deal with the lax certification issue was the 1934 formation of a new joint committee representing the DHS, the BMA and the Scottish Association of Insurance Committees. The Committee decided to suspend judgement on the issue until RMOs carried out a special twelve-month investigation in co-operation with panel doctors.[111] As with incapacitating illness itself, the problem of lax certification was a chronic one.

'An Outside Policy' – The Ministry of Health and DHS Clash over 'Lax Certification', 1929/30

> You may rest assured that we have no desire to work otherwise than in close collaboration, but we could not accept the situation that the Secretary of State for Scotland, in the making and alterations of Regulations, is to be in the position of having an outside policy forced on him without full consultation with the Scottish interests concerned.
> (PRO, MH62/46, Letter from John Jeffrey, Secretary, Department of Health for Scotland, to Sir W. Arthur Robinson, Ministry of Health, 2 August 1929)

In the course of 1929/30, the issue of 'lax certification' brought the DHS into direct confrontation with the Ministry of Health. Between 1928 and the beginning of 1929, the Ministry of Health negotiated with the BMA Insurance Acts Committee regarding a disciplinary procedure for insurance doctors who were identified as lax in granting certificates of unfitness for work. The sticking point in negotiations revolved around the BMA desire for doctors to be judged by their peers in what they regarded as an issue of professional competence. Once agreement had been reached between the Ministry and the BMA, the Insurance Acts Committee of the BMA felt that a Britain-wide policy and procedure was essential. The committee did not believe that panel practitioners would agree to any measure of investigation (by District Medical Officers) into cases of lax certification identified by the approved societies, without this wider

111 DHS, *Annual Report, 1934*, 121.

agreement.[112] Initially, the Ministry broadly accepted this view and believed that any anomalies in existing Scottish regulation of lax certification should give way to the new Ministry proposals which had been a long time in the making.[113]

The point of discrepancy between the two schemes was the inclusion of Insurance Committees in the adjudication process on doctors charged with lax certification. This was already the practice in the Scottish scheme. Insurance Committees included representatives of all interested bodies in the functions of health insurance legislation. These, of course, included lay interests. The DHS felt that the Scottish procedures developed in 1927/8, using existing National Health Insurance Regulations, and which included a role for the Insurance Committees worked reasonably well.

The desire of the London-based BMA Insurance Acts Committee was to have a purely medical professional body judge the conduct of other medical professionals. The preferred Ministry option was to have a small advisory committee of representatives of approved societies and insurance committees whom the Minister would consult before making a decision on cases of lax certification. The DHS view, as expressed in official correspondence by DHS Secretary John

---

112 For example, a letter from G.C. Anderson, Deputy Secretary of the BMA to Ministry of Health Secretary, Michael Heseltine, 11 July 1929 stated that the Scottish Sub-Committee of the BMA Insurance Acts Committee had been told to inform the SBH (DHS) that: 'the matter is not one in which a different practice in Scotland as compared with England and Wales can be agreed to, and unless the Board agrees to adopt what is arranged with the Ministry of Health the whole proposals will be dropped so far as the profession is concerned.' PRO, MH62/46.

113 This was due to difficulties in getting the BMA Insurance Acts Committee to acknowledge there was a possibility of practitioners making erroneous certification judgements, let alone deciding on a possible method of disciplining such lax professionals. 'We have spent at least eighteen months in persuading the Insurance Acts Committee [of the BMA], not that any doctor ever gives certificates which he ought not to give, but that, if there were such a doctor, it would be right to take money off him, and this is the object we all have in common.' PRO, MH62/46, Sir W. Arthur Robinson, Departmental Secretary, Ministry of Health, to John Jeffrey, Secretary, Department of Health for Scotland, 30 July 1929.

Jeffrey, was that investigation of lax certification had been addressed in Scotland in 1927. Jeffrey believed there was no need to change existing Scottish procedure (which had been agreed with Scottish BMA representatives) to facilitate the introduction of a new British-wide measure. In fact, this was not the first occasion in which Secretary Jeffrey had stressed the independence of Scottish insurance procedures.[114]

A crucial issue in the late 1920s discussions on measures to deal with 'lax certification' for the DHS was that the Department felt it was being railroaded into the Ministry scheme without any consultation period. This was also a matter of contention for other representative insurance agencies. A motion by Henry S. Keith at the annual meeting of the Scottish Association of Insurance Committees in Ayr in September 1929, deprecating the lack of involvement of insurance committees in the negotiations to revise medical benefit regulations between the MH and the BMA in London, was unanimously passed. Keith (Hamilton Burgh Representative) commented: 'He was led to believe that the Department of Health in Edinburgh rather resented the attitude of the English [sic] Ministry of Health in entering into

114 A distinctly Scottish approach to health insurance had appeared years earlier. In July 1919 the SBH issued a memorandum on planned changes in health insurance for 1920. John Jeffrey initialled the memorandum. Jeffrey was then Joint Secretary to the SBH, (and a former Secretary to the Scottish Insurance Commission). He stated that although there were clear advantages in adjusting terms of panel practitioner service 'by means of international conferences' between representatives of the medical profession in both England and Scotland, with central government and insurance committees, a Scottish dimension was essential. Jeffrey's view was that the application of new principles towards panel practice in Scotland should be the subject of a Scottish conference between the SBH, Scottish medical profession representatives and Scottish insurance committees. As regards new health insurance regulations, the SBH 1919 memorandum recommended that the Board should be allowed more latitude to provide machinery specially adapted to suit Scottish conditions – notwithstanding that such Scottish machinery of administration could differ from that developed for England. NAS, HH3/3, SBH, 'memorandum on the question of negotiations with medical practitioners and chemists in regard to arrangements for medical benefit', 24 July 191.

negotiations without consulting them at all.'[115] Sir Henry Keith's inside information had clearly come from the horse's mouth. For, at the end of the day's business a complimentary dinner was given to the SAIC guest of honour for that year's meeting, none other than DHS Secretary, John Jeffrey,

In August 1929, Jeffrey wrote to Sir W. Arthur Robinson, Permanent Secretary at the Ministry of Health. Jeffrey pointed out that negotiations between the BMA Insurance Acts Committee and the Ministry had begun in January 1928, yet the first the DHS heard of the new proposals was December 1928. Even then it was not until April 1929 that papers produced as a result of the BMA/MH discussions were forwarded to the DHS. Jeffrey's (not unreasonable) point was that if the success of the whole measure hinged on the adoption of the English arrangement in Scotland then it seemed strange that the DHS was being faced with a *fait accompli*. In other words, the DHS was being asked to adopt a measure in which it had no input, although the DHS had been operating its own procedures against lax certification for two years within existing NHI Medical Benefit Regulations.[116]

> It seems unfortunate that the British Medical Association evidently regard themselves as certain of receiving the acquiescence of the Ministry in the suggestion made in their latest letter [and] that this Department and the Insurance Acts Sub-Committee are to be coerced into measures which have been settled without consultation with us.[117]

The possibility that the BMA had undue influence over the Ministry hinted at by Jeffrey was challenged from within the Ministry itself. At the end of August 1929 Michael Heseltine, Assistant Secretary at the Ministry of Health, sent a personal letter to BMA Secretary Alfred Cox. Heseltine described the difficulty in reaching a Britain-wide solution was due to the fact that the DHS already had a procedure in place to deal with lax certification and questioned

---

115 Lothian Health Board Archives, Edinburgh, LHB24 8/17, 'Transactions of the Scottish Association of Insurance Committees Seventeenth Annual Meeting, 1929', 28.

116 PRO, MH62/46, Letter from John Jeffrey, DHS, 2 August 1929 to Sir W. A. Robinson, Ministry of Health.

117 Ibid.

whether it was desirable or necessary to upset existing practice for the sake of having a single procedure for lax certification throughout Great Britain.[118]

The DHS resistance to what it regarded as the imposition of a lax certification policy by the Ministry was ultimately successful. A Memorandum issued by the Ministry of Health to the Secretary of the Association of Welsh Insurance Committees in February 1930 made this clear. The memorandum noted that a proposed regulation on the issue of certificates by medical practitioners would apply to England and Wales, but not to Scotland, which had its own distinct regulations.[119] The DHS policy on lax certification was developed within existing National Health Insurance Regulations and throughout the policy-making process was subject to joint consideration by all interested parties (including the Scottish Insurance Acts Sub-Committee of the BMA). This helps explains why it remained untouched by the Ministry's initiative. However, lax certification remained an issue for as long as panel practice continued to operate.

The Morbidity Statistics Scheme

> The problem revealed by study of the morbidity statistics of the insured population is one of the great problems confronting public health.
> (DHS, *Seventh Annual Report, 1935* (Edinburgh: HMSO, 1936), 132, [Cmd 5123])

The increased monitoring of Scottish panel doctors in the late 1920s indirectly helped launch the DHS 'Morbidity Statistics Scheme' in September 1929. Arising as a consequence of the desire to tighten up on lax certification by Scottish insurance practitioners, this measure

118 PRO, MH62/46, personal letter from Michael Heseltine, Ministry of Health to BMA Secretary, Alfred Cox, 31 August 1929.

119 PRO, MH62/46, unsigned extract of memorandum from Ministry of Health to the Secretary of the Association of Welsh Insurance Committees, Newport, Monmouthshire, 27 February 1930.

seemed to be a step towards a more preventive system of health provision in Scotland. While discussing possible procedures for the investigation of lax certification, DHS Secretary John Jeffrey put forward the suggestion that the opportunity be taken to obtain full certification details from panel practitioners including descriptions of illness, which could be used for research purposes.[120] The proposal, at a DHS meeting on 'medical certification' on 21 June 1929 came to fruition shortly after in the DHS's Morbidity Statistics Scheme.

The cost of administering the scheme (which included payments to the approved societies for ensuring complete returns from panel practitioners at a rate of a halfpenny per each completed return) was offset by using surplus funds saved from medical benefits. In particular, money saved in prescription costs in Scotland was used for this purpose (the Scottish insurance practitioners were recognised as 'more economical' in their habits than their counterparts in England). The relative thrift in Scots prescribing allowed funds to be diverted into the Morbidity Statistics Scheme. In fact, Scottish cost-saving was one reason put forward by Ministry Health Insurance Controller, Sir Walter Kinnear, in 1930 for not considering the implementation of a Morbidity Statistics Scheme for England – there was no similar pool of funds with which to finance a comparable English scheme.[121] In his unveiling of the 'Morbidity Statistics Scheme', John Jeffrey, stressed the importance of the scheme to the future planning of Scottish health services.[122] The scheme coincided with the setting up of a Scientific Advisory Committee on Medical Administration and Investigation (later Research), which was to act in a consultancy capacity regarding areas for special investigation.[123]

The administrative change that led to the creation of the Department of Health for Scotland in 1929 may have eased the passage of the Morbidity Statistics Scheme. The removal of the old

120 PRO, MH 62/46, DHS minutes, 21 June 1929 discussion on 'Medical Certification'.

121 PRO, PIN4/41, Ministry of Health memorandum on Scottish Morbidity Statistics Scheme, 17 March 1931.

122 *Scotsman*, 30 September 1929, 10.

123 PRO, PIN4/41, Letter from DHS to BMA regarding 'Terms of Service – Summary Cards [for Insured Practitioners]', 10 November 1930.

six-member Scottish Board of Health allowed for the gradual emergence of top ranking full time administrators. Although this did not happen overnight,[124] the new Department structure gave more authority for policy formulation to those, such as Jeffrey, already well established in Scottish health administration.[125] John Jeffrey had previously been Secretary to the Scottish Insurance Commission and then Secretary to the SBH from 1919–1928. As Departmental Secretary to the DHS, Jeffrey was responsible only to the Secretary of State for Scotland. Muriel Ritson, former women member on the SBH, as Woman Assistant Secretary continued her special interest in insurance in the DHS as Controller of Pensions and Insurance. Both Ritson and Jeffrey played an instrumental role in the creation of the Morbidity Statistics Scheme.[126] Ritson's close involvement in this policy initiative fits well with Dowding's analysis of the civil service hierarchy: 'Assistant Secretaries handle the minutiae of policies and they are perhaps the civil servants who are most directly concerned with producing detailed policy advice.'[127]

As noted earlier, a selection of morbidity statistics based on the examination work of District Medical Officers had appeared regularly in the annual reports of the Scottish Board of Health from 1925. The usefulness of these findings in allowing special case studies of particular diseases (heart disease and bronchitis among them) and in tracing patterns of morbidity and incapacity encouraged the Board, later Department to expand their investigations. Early plans to publish information regarding incapacitating sickness levels stuttered over lack of comprehensive data (District Medical Officers whose detailed records were used for case studies published in SBH annual reports examined only a small fraction of the total number of sickness claimants). In 1929, the new DHS put together plans to secure complete returns from panel practitioners which would allow a more

124 See chapter two for more discussion on changes in Scottish health administration.

125 Later, in 1933, Jeffrey was promoted to Permanent Under-Secretary of State for Scotland, the highest post in the Scottish civil service.

126 NAS, HH3/9, DHS memorandum on the 'proposed scheme for linking morbidity statistics and the control of certification', 24 April 1930.

127 Dowding, *The Civil Service*, 28.

detailed bank of data on sickness statistics to be compiled. The statistical studies analysed the sickness experience of over 1.7 million of the Scots population in work, aged between 16 and 65 (young workers aged between 14 and 16 became part of the wider insurance scheme at a later date). For the first time, the health problems of adult life where given specific, systematic attention.

In an address to one of the approved societies, (the High Court of the Ancient Order of Foresters) in 1930, Labour Scottish Secretary of State, William Adamson stressed the need for whole hearted team work from all Scottish agencies involved in health insurance. He believed co-operation was the key to discovering why there was an increasing number of claims for National Insurance. Adamson concluded by expressing the hope that the new statistical information might afford some solution to the quandary of mounting claims and spiralling expenditure.[128] By the year ended June 1931, the DHS estimated expenditure on cash benefits on health insurance to amount to approximately £2 million.[129]

The Morbidity Statistics Scheme launched by the DHS in 1930 had a dual purpose: it was part of the wider process of monitoring health insurance claims, and was motivated by a desire to track patterns of morbidity which could influence future DHS health planning. The method of collecting information was via approved societies passing all first and final certificates of illness to the DHS. For each cause of incapacity, details were recorded for reputed cause of the illness, the dates of onset and termination, the final outcome (death or recovery), year of birth, sex, occupation, and (for women only) marital status.[130] An annual summary report on 'Incapacitating Sickness of the Insured Population in Scotland' (ISIPS) – was then produced by the DHS to give the comparative experience around Scotland. The statistical guide allowed the Department to single out practitioners whose certification methods compared unfavourably with

128 *GMJ*, (1930), 136.

129 NAS, HH3/16, DHS circular issued to panel practitioners, 'Morbidity Statistics Scheme: Certification', January 1932.

130 DHS, *Report on Sickness Statistics for the Insured Population of Scotland* [...] *1930 to* [...] *1931*, 3.

their local colleagues. Initial certificates were also passed onto Regional Medical Officers who could then pay additional visits to patients in doubtful cases within a day or two of the certificates being issued. RMOs also would pay visits to a sample of certified cases to make checks on overall certifying practice by panel doctors.

In 1932, the DHS announced that the 'Morbidity Statistics Scheme' (MSS) was working smoothly. The DHS hoped that data compiled under the initiative would shed light on problems of public health, particularly once full census figures for 1931 were available to put the statistics of sickness among the population, by age, sex, locality and occupation into a wider context. However, in the 1934/55 ISIPS Report, the DHS gloomily noted that five years of investigations had merely spelled out the magnitude of problems confronting preventive medicine across all age groups in the insured population.

More generally, the statistics allowed the DHS to follow trends in incapacity, assess the causes in any variations in the trend, and by using detailed case studies help in approaches to solving specific problem areas.[131] Although the MSS had the dual purpose of monitoring for 'lax' certification as well as tracking patterns of incapacity, the annual reports served a third purpose – it convinced the DHS that 'malingering' was not a widespread phenomenon among those claiming benefits. The ISIPS reports showed the depth of genuine incapacity among Scots workers in the 1930s.

Special investigations were mounted with the co-operation of general practitioners and others.[132] In July 1933, a special inquiry into valvular heart disease was inaugurated. Panel practitioners were issued with special forms to record relevant heart cases. The aims of the investigation were to review the treatment methods of general practitioners, to compare varieties of treatment at various stages of the disease, and to produce data sufficient to evaluate treatment methods. The DHS annual report for 1934 noted that the enquiry was still on going. Most returns from practitioners had been diligently produced,

131 DHS, *Report on Incapacitating Sickness in the Insured Population of Scotland* [...] *1934 to* [...] *1935*, 4.

132 DHS, *Annual Report, 1932*, 14.

but '[...] some practitioners, however, display a want of interest or a carelessness that render the return valueless for the purpose of the inquiry'.[133] In 1935, plans were laid for future panel doctor investigations into tonsillitis and quinsy.

According to the DHS Annual Report for 1935, the ISIPS findings emphasised the need to conserve adult health and to provide suitable opportunities for rehabilitation of workers. The need for a reorientation of Scottish health policy towards a more preventive system was stressed.[134] Meanwhile, the 1936 ISIPS Report revealed the findings of a five-year statistical study to show that much sickness was attributable to environmental factors – bad housing, poor diet, poverty and unhealthy working conditions.[135] The view of the *Glasgow Medical Journal* was that such detailed statistical surveys simply reinforced the need for better health planning to prevent the health of Scottish working population deteriorating further.[136] The intention of the ISIPS to aid future planning of Scottish health policy was given particular emphasis during the sitting of the Cathcart Committee between 1933 and 1936. The annual ISIPS reports which were released most years in the 1930s can be seen as an indication of a new trend towards the preservation of health rather than the treatment of ill health through state intervention. Such a trend was further confirmed by the findings of the Cathcart Report. However, the idea of 'social medicine' which these reports implied was still some way from fulfilment.

Despite the range of opinions in support of a more preventive slant to state health provision, there was no great sea change in Scottish health policy. The DHS annual report for 1936, published after the Cathcart Report was released, referred to increasing public expectations in health standards. These, it was alleged, increased the tendency of some Scots to stay off work when ill and to remain away from work for longer in an effort to regain full health. In other words,

133 DHS, *Annual Report, 1934*, 122.

134 DHS, *Annual Report, 1935* (Edinburgh: HMSO, 1936), 18.

135 DHS, *Report on Sickness Statistics for the Insured Population of Scotland* [...] *1934 to* [...] *1935*, 5.

136 *GMJ*, (1936), 238.

the benefits of health insurance had led to what today may be described as a 'dependency culture'. These sort of comments are a long way removed from earlier official 'approval' for workers reducing the chances of spreading infection by staying off work. Now the belief was such trends merely slanted the figures for ill health among the population: '[...] incidence of incapacitating sickness could convey a fallacious impression of national deterioration.'[137] In this sense, the downplaying of pessimistic health trends by the DHS was part of a much wider contemporary (and subsequent historical) debate about the health of the population during the economic depression of the 1930s.

In April 1938, an important alteration in National Health Insurance was the extension of coverage to juvenile workers from the time they left school until they became fully insured aged sixteen. Under the operation of the National Health Insurance (Juvenile Contributors and Young Persons) Act, 1937, medical treatment was provided for young workers aged fourteen and fifteen. Juvenile contributors and their employers each paid 2 pence per week into the scheme, with coverage beginning immediately the first payment was made. The scheme was announced to the general public in a short BBC Radio broadcast at the beginning of April 1938. The number of juvenile contributors by the end of 1938 was 133,500, and slightly more than half were boys.

Provision in the new legislation allowed for medical information from a teenager's school health record to be passed on to their panel practitioner. This meant that previous medical history could be taken onto account during current medical supervision.[138] It also underlined the increasing importance given to the use of medical statistics (pioneered in the MSS) as a prospective aid to preventive medicine. The new legislation was an attempt to fill a void in the health supervision of young persons from birth until adult worker. The pre-sixteen workforce presented a small, but obvious gap in the recording of medical statistics.

137 DHS, *Annual Report, 1936*, 12.
138 DHS, *Annual Report, 1938*, 14.

The role of panel practitioners in Scotland underwent a considerable change during World War Two. In the most immediate sense, war service stretched panel practice coverage as doctors were called up for war service, leaving colleagues to take on additional panel cases to plug the gaps. Of the 501 panel practitioners on the Insurance Committee list for Glasgow Burgh in 1939, 71 were called up for war service, of whom one died on active service and two following their discharge.[139]

A scheme for the protection of practices was put into operation at the outbreak of the war, which ensured that absent doctors received a retainer from the income of the practice left behind. Deputies to absentee practitioners were appointed where possible. The scheme of medical benefit was maintained by spreading panel patients among the lists of doctors who remained. Insured workers whose doctor was called up to war service were permitted to transfer to any other panel practitioner in their locality for the duration of the war. However, it is clear that many insurance patients would be inconvenienced by the reduction in the number of doctors available for consultation. The effects of war also caused changes in the system of National Health Insurance. After the chaos of the Blitz on Clydeside in 1941, the DHS agreed to a suggestion – from the BMA Insurance Acts Sub-Committee (Scotland) – to extend 'temporary residents' cover' from a period of three months to six months. This allowed insured workers who had lost or left their homes to maintain their right to panel care while they found accommodation elsewhere.[140]

The outbreak of World War Two heralded a number of other changes in the health insurance scheme. One of the most obvious was the reduction in the number of eligible insured workers paying into scheme due to the enrolment of hundreds of thousands of workers into

139 'Annual Report for the Insurance Committee for the Burgh of Glasgow, 1946', 5.

140 'Glasgow Burgh Panel Committee/Glasgow Burgh Local Medical Committee Bulletin', No. 36, 31 December 1941, 5.

the armed forces. This placed additional burdens on the approved societies to continue to fulfil their commitments with a much-reduced income from insured workers. There were also government attempts to counter-act the ill effects of wartime conditions on the insured population. At the beginning of 1942, levels of sickness benefit were increased by three shillings (15p) per week (offset by a penny increase in both employee and employer payments into the scheme). In addition, the level of eligibility for workers was raised to take account of wage and price rises during wartime. Non-manual workers earning between £250 (the previous threshold) and £420 were now within the range of compulsory insurance.

In June 1941, the Government launched a survey of the Health Insurance and Contributory Pensions Schemes under the auspices of the Committee on Social Insurance and Allied Services chaired by Sir William Beveridge. The Beveridge Committee's Report published at the end of November 1942 contained the notable Assumption B: 'Comprehensive health and rehabilitation services for prevention and cure of disease and restoration of capacity for work, available to all members of the community.' Although the wartime coalition government did not pledge to enact Beveridge's recommendations, his findings soon became accepted components in the future plans of all the political parties. The recommendations of the Beveridge Report placed the National Health Insurance scheme (and the approved societies) on a road to extinction. A Social Insurance White Paper was issued in 1944 which became the model for the 1946 Insurance Act. By this measure, the Labour government dissolved the partnership between the state and the approved societies. The new Insurance Act assimilated the existing health and unemployment insurance schemes and set out a uniform basic rate of benefit. It also introduced new dependants' allowances. In the same year, the medical service aspects of health insurance were subsumed in the National Health Service Act, with the Scottish NHS legislation following on a year later.[141]

During the war there was less information on levels of sickness among insured workers. This was due to the discontinuation of the

141 See chapter seven for discussions on the formulation of the National Health Service.

Department's annual reports on incapacity. The Summary DHS Report for 1939–1941 provided little detail on the functioning of health insurance in wartime and the general level of sickness in Scotland during the first three years of war. The Summary Report noted only that there was a sharp increase in sickness claims at the beginning of 1940 due to an influenza epidemic at that point. Indeed, all further attempts at comprehensive central recording of workers' ill health, including the annual DHS Incapacity Reports, came to an end due to wartime disruption.[142] However, the ground-breaking surveys on morbidity statistics found a wartime legacy both in the creation of the Supplementary Medical Service and the launch of research into the rehabilitation of injured servicemen and debilitated workers between 1939–1943.[143]

Wartime circumstances opened up a new range of opportunities for panel doctors, for example, general practitioners were eligible for appointment as visiting medical officers in auxiliary hospitals opened up under the Emergency Medical Service.[144] The development of a more preventive role in public health for general practitioners through the unique Scottish Supplementary Medical Services scheme for the first time forged a closer relationship between general practitioners and Regional Medical Officers, through practitioner referral of incapacitated industrial workers. RMOs, under a reconstituted wartime Regional Medical Service,[145] were no longer primarily viewed as an intrusive, judgmental presence in the panel surgery. Previously there had been very few panel cases referred by panel

142 DHS, *Summary Report for the period 1st January 1939 to 30 June 1941* (Edinburgh: HMSO, 1941), 18–19, [Cmd 6308].

143 For more on this area see DHS, *Health and Industrial Efficiency: Scottish Experiments in Social Medicine.* This report included a summary of factors responsible for long-term incapacity based on the 1937/8 incapacity reports. For more on this pamphlet see chapter seven.

144 McLachlan, ed., *Improving the Common Weal*, 184.

145 The Edinburgh, Aberdeen and Dundee regional medical services were fully occupied with Emergency Medical Service activity. The Glasgow (Western Divisional) office was sole the point of referral for all Health Insurance cases until 1943 when the service was reopened on a regional basis.

practitioners to RMOs for second opinions.[146] By 1943, the active co-operation of panel practitioners in the Supplementary Medical Service Scheme may be measured by the increased use of the terms 'debility' and 'industrial fatigue' on certificates of sickness. This caused some problems as a number of approved societies refused to recognise these terms as entitling payment of sickness benefit. After the RMOs took up the matter with the DHS on behalf of panel doctors, the Department notified approved societies that the diagnosis of 'debility' was adequate in wartime circumstances.[147]

The Supplementary Medical Service (also known as the Clyde Basin Experiment) aimed at extending medical facilities for, and rehabilitation of, insured industrial workers. It involved general practitioners at a crucial level of diagnosis and placed responsibility on them for referral of cases to hospital for specialist services.[148] The Clyde Basin Experiment is discussed in detail in the following chapter. However, the scheme is worth mentioning here in the context of its relationship with the health insurance scheme in Scotland. The Clyde Basin area, (that is, the City of Glasgow and the counties of Lanark, Renfrew and Dunbarton) housed 40% of Scotland's insured population. Much wartime industrial production was carried out in this area. The DHS recognised that it was important to safeguard the health of industrial workers in this part of Scotland by calling upon the full range of public and personal medical services which had come under central control for the first time due to the wartime emergency.

Special emphasis was given to the health of young industrial workers who were considered most at risk from the stresses of shift work of long duration and the irregular meal times which followed as a result. Once a patient had been identified as in failing health, they were then to be sent for examination by the RMO. The opinion of the RMO was the decisive factor in whether a patient was recommended

---

146 For example, in 1925 approved societies referred 22,231 insurance claimants to DMOs for second opinions. In contrast, panel practitioners referred 284 cases (about 1.3% of the total). See SBH, *Seventh Annual Report 1925*, 208.

147 'Glasgow Burgh Panel Committee/Glasgow Burgh Local Medical Committee Bulletin', No. 38, 31 December 1943, 6.

148 See chapter seven for more on the Clyde Basin Experiment.

for admission to one of the centrally-run Emergency Hospitals for observation and diagnosis, or instead, sent to a convalescent home for a period of rest before resumption of work. The responsibility for initiating the process of monitoring of insured war workers lay with panel doctors. In 1942, the DHS noted that a 'small but steady flow of cases' had been referred to the RMOs. Of the first 579 cases referred for examination, RMOs arranged for hospital or convalescent home admissions for 293 patients.[149] In the twelve months down to 31 March 1944, panel doctors referred 4,655 workers (2,256 men and 2,399 women) to RMOs for assessment. Of this number, 2,074 were admitted to hospitals and 1,033 were admitted to convalescent homes for treatment.[150]

The number of Scots covered by the National Health Insurance scheme peaked after the war to a level of 2,316,000 in 1947. The number of panel doctors had not quite reached pre-war levels, standing at 1,915 insurance practitioners, (aided by 145 assistants). The medical 'refresher courses' made available after the war for demobilised service medical officers were extended to insurance practitioners during 1947, thereby re-activating the postgraduate training of panel doctors which had begun in 1938. One hundred insurance practitioners attended University medical school courses in 1947.

The End of Panel Practice, 1946–8

The coming of the National Health Service had potentially immense implications for general practitioners employed under the National Health Insurance scheme. Existing Insurance interests were able to make representations to the DHS during the discussions on the NHS

149 DHS, *Summary Report for the year ended 30th June 1942* (Edinburgh: HMSO, 1942), 11.

150 DHS, *Summary Report for the year ended 30th June 1944* (Edinburgh: HMSO, 1944), 6, [Cmd 6545].

(Scotland) Bill. For example, the Joint Committee of the Association of Insurance Committees (Scotland) met with the Scottish Secretary of State Joseph Westwood, on 15 February 1946 in Edinburgh to discuss proposals for the new health service, but their influence was clearly on the wane. Under the National Health Service (Scotland) Act, 1947, the principle of the capitation fee for practitioners remained, and only the application (free treatment open to all members of the public) was changed. Doctor's fears for the introduction of a salaried service were not realised. Basic salary for general practitioners (plus the capitation fee) was provided under the new legislation only for the purpose of aiding new doctors setting up in practice and to attract general practitioners to unpopular areas. To represent NHS doctors' interests, the former local Panel Committees evolved into Local Medical Committees, statutory bodies elected by local practitioners. The new Local Medical Committees mainly had advisory and consultative functions.

In 1948, National Health Insurance medical arrangements were superseded by the arrival of the NHS, and the 2.3 million insured workers were joined by the remainder of the Scottish population (together adding up to an estimated total of 5,120,000 in December 1948) under the new general practitioner services. 97% of Scottish doctors (2,364 practitioners) joined NHS lists, an increase of 449 doctors from the last year of National Health Insurance in 1947. In 1948, remuneration (capitation) levels were set at eighteen shillings (90p) per head per year based on 95% of the estimated total civilian population of Britain.

After 1948, the Regional Medical Service (which administered the work of the RMOs and their expanding body of staff) continued. The shift away from monitoring lax certification by doctors and towards co-operation with local practitioners noted during the war, was maintained. The Regional Medical Service served both NHS general practitioners and the new Ministry of National Health Insurance, wherever a second opinion on 'capacity for work' was desired. The emphasis was no longer on weeding out false claims by watching over panel practitioners, but in aiding the assessment of working capacity, when requested by the doctor. Regional Medical Office staff also assessed applicants for admission to the Disabled

Persons Register which had been set up under the Disabled Persons (Employment) Act of 1944.

As with the introduction of health insurance between 1911–13, the BMA orchestrated a campaign against the new health services legislation.[151] Again, as with health insurance in 1911, member support for BMA opposition to the coming health service was less strident in Scotland than elsewhere in Britain. By the end of 1949, only 2% of Scottish general practitioners remained outside the NHS.[152] Reflecting the total coverage of the population provided by the NHS, the number of patients assigned per doctor was greater than under National Health Insurance, 4,000 as opposed to 2,500–3,000.

Conclusion

Scottish National Health Insurance arrangements, while devolved in terms of administration, generally followed central government direction. For example, insurance legislation when enacted referred to the whole of Britain. There were no distinctive legislative measures for Scotland as was the case for other health services such as infant and maternal welfare and school health. However, within the administration of health insurance there was room for independent Scottish initiative. This happened most obviously in two linked aspects of health insurance policy.

The procedure developed by the DHS at the end of the 1920s to monitor and discipline panel practitioners was distinct from, and challenged by, the Ministry of Health. The DHS successfully defended this policy, drawing heavily upon its long-standing administrative distinctiveness and by criticising the Ministry's own consultation processes. The creation of the Morbidity Statistics Scheme followed on from the DHS initiative in monitoring the certifying practices of panel doctors. The MSS was an important short

151 See chapter seven for more on the coming of the NHS.

152 McLachlan, ed., *Improving the Common Weal*, 189.

and longer-term development. The ISIPS reports produced between 1930 and 1937 revealed the nature and extent of incapacity among the insured Scottish workforce. It also provided, an indication of how far heavy industrial employment (especially in mining), combined with poor environment under-pinned Scotland's relatively poor health indices. The level of detailed information on morbidity patterns for a mass section of the population provided by the MSS was unique in Britain. Yet, when made known, the findings were not immediately acted upon by the DHS. However, the increased importance of ensuring a healthy workforce with the advent of war elevated the MSS findings to a matter of national concern.

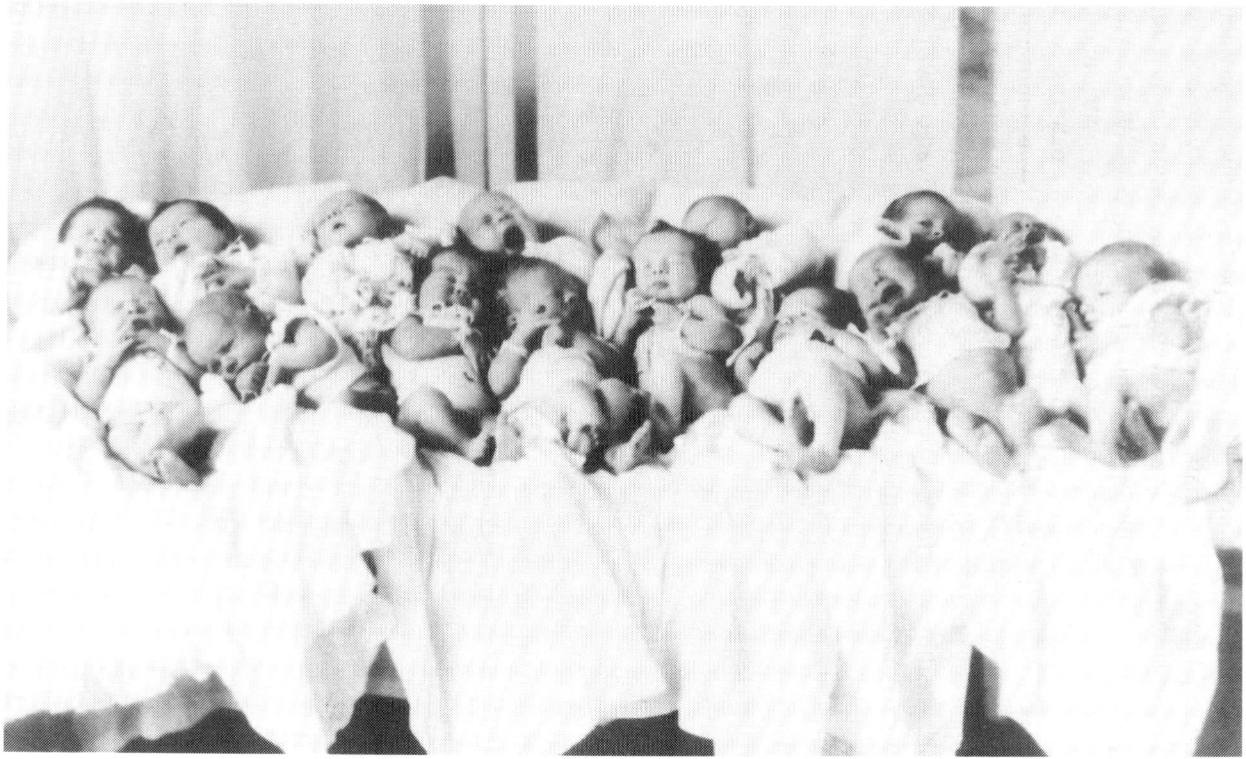

‘A Day’s Catch’ at the Simpson Maternity Hospital, Edinburgh, 1933
© Edinburgh City Museums, Huntly House Museum, Canongate, Edinburgh

7: Wartime Health Services and the Creation of the National Health Service

What the government propose is that there should be an all-in service, providing a complete range of personal health services for every man, woman and child; that there should be a general practitioner service open to everybody; that there should be a consultant and specialist service, where necessary, for everyone; that there should be treatment in hospital, including maintenance while there [...].
(Scottish Secretary of State, Tom Johnston, speaking to the Commons on the publication of the White Paper *A National Health Service* (HMSO, London, 1944), [Cmd 6502], HOC debates 17 March 1944, vol. 398, col. 622–623.)

Introduction

This chapter continues the themes identified in chapters one and two. It examines the administrative changes brought about between 1939–1948 on the Department of Health for Scotland. Scotland's population and its health services were both immeasurably affected by Britain's participation in war. Warfare had an impact on health levels. Chapter five has shown how tuberculosis rates increased during the war. The war situation also allowed further discovery of high levels of chronic incapacity among Scotland's workforce. The health of young workers gave particular cause for concern.

The future health care of Scotland's people was much debated and finally determined in the years between 1942 and 1948. The creation of the National Health Service is discussed in the context of inter-war health policy discussions. Although the National Health Service was a unique development in the history of health care introduced for the whole of Britain, it is important to compare the new service and its bureaucracy to inter-war Scottish health administrative practice and policy initiatives, especially the 1936 DHS Cathcart Report. Yet, the influence of wartime experiences on the new health proposals has to be considered. War, or recent experience of it, had already given rise to a re-evaluation of the State's role in the personal health of its citizens in both the Boer and First World Wars.

The role of war as a factor in social change is an argument most associated with the work of Richard Titmuss.[1] However, the Titmuss view has to be balanced by a consideration of the cumulative effects of health policy developments before and during the war on post-war policy. How far wartime administrative changes were simply a response to the emergency situation or the herald of increased state intervention in the nation's health is a key issue to be addressed. In other words, was 'warfare to welfare' the policy lurch Titmuss indicated, or were the new services merely a logical continuation of the various planning proposals brought forward by the DHS, (and PEP and the BMA) in the 1930s, discussed earlier in this book? Against this, how crucial was the role of the 1945 Labour government in the achievement of an expanded state medical service by 1948?[2] Meanwhile, as Finlayson noted, while the frontiers of the state expanded in wartime, they still left room for voluntary activity, for example in the organisation and billeting arrangements of the wartime evacuation movement, principally undertaken by the Women's Voluntary Services.[3] These are all issues to be considered in

1 'Paradoxically, when human lives are cheapest, the desire to preserve life and health is at its highest. Wasted and neglected lives become "manpower" and the injured limbs of miners are discussed at Cabinet level.' Titmuss, *Problems of Social Policy*, 474.

2 Immergut has questioned the inevitability of social reform under liberal democracies. The crucial question in any debate on the welfare state is when and why democratic processes result in an extension of social rights. In the 1940s, Titmuss, Beveridge and others such as T. H. Marshall, viewed the welfare state in Britain as an inevitable step in the advance of democracy. These assumptions came to be challenged in the 1970s and 1980s. It is not clear to revisionists that democracy invariably results in the growth of social programmes. See Immergut, *Health Politics*, 2.

3 G. Finlayson, 'A Moving Frontier: Voluntarism and the State in British Social Welfare 1911–1949', *Twentieth Century British History*, 1/2 (1990), 204. The WVS also had a part to play in the co-ordination of and publicity for another

examining the policy developments and health outcomes of the work of the DHS between 1939 and 1948.

The Department of Health for Scotland underwent a series of rapid changes in the course of the war. The organisation of the Emergency Medical Service, the Emergency Hospital Scheme, the Government Evacuation Scheme, the administration of First Aid Posts, Ambulance Services and the Emergency Relief Organisation for the care of the homeless, were all major tasks for which the Department assumed responsibility. The DHS also administered the pioneering Supplementary Medical Service for the treatment and rehabilitation of industrial war workers. Preparatory work was also undertaken for post-war developments in the health service, including the setting up of small special branches within the DHS to discuss possible future changes in the Department's responsibilities. In 1945, the first such alteration took place with the removal of 520 staff from the DHS (from the division of National Health Insurance and Old Age Pensions, including Controller of Pensions, and former member of the Scottish Board of Health, Muriel Ritson) to the newly-created Ministry of Pensions.[4]

Exceptionally, hospital services are considered in this chapter, since the development of the wartime hospital service is closely related to the coming of a state-sponsored comprehensive health service in Scotland. While hospitals are not generally considered in this study of health policy and the personal health services, the coming of the NHS was to some extent influenced by central and Scottish governmental policy responses to a unique series of difficulties in hospital provision during the wartime emergency.

---

voluntary agency, the Scottish National Blood Transfusion Association which was set up in March 1940.

4 NAS, DHS SOE 1/234, DHS, Departmental Handbook No. 1 'The Organisation and Functions of the Department' (1946), 10. The staff of the DHS was reduced from 1,234 to 714 by this single measure.

In the months before the outbreak of World War Two, there was a common belief that there would be huge numbers of civilian wounded if war came. These fears came from the recent use of aerial warfare in Abysinnia and Spain, and the experience of air raids on the south east of England in World War One. In the Spring of 1938, the DHS surveyed the hospitals in Scotland and investigated what use might be made of hotels and public schools to see where beds could be obtained for air-raid casualties. As a result of this, and equivalent surveys elsewhere around Britain, the Emergency Medical Service (EMS) was established in Autumn 1938. Through the related Emergency Hospital Scheme, the EMS greatly increased hospital accommodation, expanded the provision of specialist facilities and services, and brought together the various types of hospital authority on a regional basis.

John Colville, (Scottish Secretary of State between 1938–1940), held joint discussions with Prime Minister Neville Chamberlain, Health Minister, (and former Scottish Secretary of State), Walter Elliot, and with local authorities. Colville sought to co-ordinate plans for an Emergency Medical Service, evacuation, and air raid precautions for the estimated 35,000 daily casualties which were expected in the first three weeks of war.[5] Overall, the DHS was responsible for twelve services[6] as diverse as recruitment and

5 A further 17,500 fatalities per day were estimated in the worst case scenario put forward by the Minister for Co-ordination of Defence. For more on the issue of wartime hospital accommodation see PRO, CAB 27/659, EHO 1 (39) 2, cited in Levitt, *The Scottish Office – Depression and Reconstruction*, 355–357.

6 PRO, MH79/90, DHS, Civil Defence Emergency Schemes – 'Summary of Government War Plans (Scotland)', 18 March 1939. The twelve services were, The Emergency Hospital Service, First Aid Posts, Ambulance Services, Recruitment and distribution of doctors, dentists, pharmacists, nurses, Establishment and supervision of Civilian Medical Boards, Public Health and Sanitary Services, Bacteriological Services, Burials, Billeting, Payment of Pension Orders, Emergency Relief for those made homeless by bombing, and the Emergency Repair of war damage to property.

distribution of doctors, billeting and the emergency repair of war damage to property. For the first time, close co-operation between the four Scottish Departments (Health, Home, Education and Agriculture and Fisheries) was essential. The concentration of the majority of the staff from the four Departments in a single building at St. Andrew's House took place in September 1939 – just in time for the task which lay ahead.[7]

The Civil Defence Act of 1939 (Section 50) laid responsibility on the DHS to prepare hospital facilities for civilian casualties as a result of enemy action. Later responsibility was accepted by the Scottish Secretary of State for the treatment of service personnel in the event of their numbers being too great for the service hospitals to cope. Before the Civil Defence Act, the DHS had supervised the work of local authorities, now it held chief responsibility for administering and operating the emergency services required.

The immense scale of the task to be undertaken is clear from Supplementary Estimate made by the DHS to the Treasury in 1939 to 'provide for measures to deal with casualties and disease, evacuation of the civilian population, and other services, in the event of war'.[8] Of the £2,239,150 requested (and sanctioned for payment by the Treasury eight days later), £1.5 million was requested for supplementary 'temporary' hospital accommodation, £188,000 for local authorities to adapt existing hospitals and £102,000 was allocated for payment to voluntary hospitals for the use of their facilities. £20,000 was set aside for the Emergency Nursing Services and £215,000 to local authorities for planning and implementing civilian evacuation measures. The sum asked for also included £330 for the preparation of vital emergency registers of doctors, dentists, pharmacists and opticians.[9] These proposals were made under the provisions of the 1939 Civil Defence Act in preparation for the expected 'total war' that lay ahead. The

---

7 A small liaison office remained in London at Fielden House playing an important wartime communications role between the DHS and central Government. For more on the centralisation of the Department's staff in Edinburgh see chapter two.

8 PRO, T160/880, DHS Supplementary Estimate to the Treasury, 11 July 1939.

9 Ibid.

expected number of casualties never arrived and by 1941, pioneering schemes were put into operation by Colville's successor as Scottish Secretary of State, Tom Johnston,[10] to make civilian use of the increased hospital and nursing home capacity which had been created.

DHS Special Wartime Arrangements

A potentially serious public health problem to emerge in World War Two was the increased incidence of diphtheria. Increased mortality from the disease between 1939 and 1941 forced the DHS to launch a massive propaganda campaign to promote immunisation in 1941/2. The immunisation programme had positive results. The average death rate from diphtheria in Scotland in the years 1935–9 was 430. In 1940 it rose to 675 and in 1941it was 517. In 1942 it fell markedly to 290. It continued to decline, and was down to 126 by 1945. At 30 June 1941, 40% of school children had been immunised[11], by June the following year the figure was 73% of school children and 58% of pre-school children (792,000 children in total had been immunised). The overall incidence of the disease fell from 15,069 cases in 1940 to 5,679 in 1945.[12] In 1944, the death rate from diphtheria in Glasgow was 65 – all of them young children who had not been immunised.[13] By 1947, this had fallen to 13.[14] Not all areas recorded a wartime increase in diphtheria. For example, in Aberdeenshire, a successful Diphtheria Immunisation Scheme had been launched as early as 1935. By 1945, it was estimated that over 95% of children in the county of Aberdeen

10 See chapter two for more on Tom Johnston's career.

11 DHS, *Summary Report 1939–1941* (Edinburgh: HMSO, 1941), passim.

12 Sir A.S. Macnalty, ed., *The Civilian Health and Medical Services*, vol. II [History of World War Two: United Kingdom Medical Services], (HMSO, 1955), 238, 264–5.

13 Corporation of Glasgow Medical Officer of Health, 'Summary of Health Statistics, 1944', reported in *GMJ*, 1945 (1), 104.

14 Corporation of Glasgow Medical Officer of Health, 'Summary of Health Statistics for 1947', reported in *GMJ*, (1948), 69.

had been immunised and re-immunised, leading to a low death rate of 0.7 per 100,000 of the population in 1945.[15]

Hospital beds across Scotland were cleared of civilian cases in the first months of the war to prepare for expected military casualties. For example, in Aberdeen city, practically all tuberculosis patients were discharged from hospitals in the city and either sent home or re-housed in less satisfactory conditions in cottage hospitals in Aberdeenshire.[16] The mass discharge of tuberculosis patients in Aberdeen and around Britain had a bearing on increased tuberculosis deaths after 1940.[17]

There was a steady development of the Emergency Medical Service and its Hospital Scheme in the early period of the war. New 'base hospitals'[18] were built for the DHS by the Ministry of Works at Ballochmyle in Ayrshire, Law in Lanarkshire, Killearn in Stirlingshire, Bridge of Earn, Perthshire, Stracathro in Angus, Peel, Selkirkshire and Raigmore in Inverness. The new hospitals provided 7,038 additional beds. Hutted annexes were added to many existing hospitals to add a further 8,526 beds to the Emergency Hospital Scheme total. Two converted hotels (owned by the London, Midland and Scottish Railway) at Gleneagles, Perthshire, and Turnberry, Ayrshire provided an additional 910 beds (initially for convalescent troops). Large country houses were converted to cottage hospitals to provide a further 3,600 beds.[19] A DHS Hospitals Division was set up on 12 September 1939 to administer the new hospital service and a large hospitals supply branch was later established to serve the new hospitals. Voluntary hospitals were supported directly by the DHS

15 Grampian Regional Health Board Archives, GRHB E2\4\20, Aberdeen City MOH, 'The Health and Sanitary Conditions of the County of Aberdeen during the Second World War 1940–1945', (1945), 1.

16 J. Mackenzie, 'Tuberculosis in Young Children', 54.

17 See chapter five on Tuberculosis for more on this issue.

18 'Base' hospitals were those in areas believed to be relatively safe and suitable for the immediate reception of patients in their own localities as well as for the continued treatment of casualties transferred from more dangerous areas.

19 PRO, MH76/603, DHS, Office Committee memorandum on '"Demobilisation" of the Emergency Hospital Scheme, Scotland – Concentration of Stores', 18 December 1943.

from the beginning of the war. However, the voluntary hospital authorities continued to run their own institutions, acting as the Department's agents. At the start of the war, Scotland had 35,331 hospital beds (21,248 in voluntary and 14,083 in local authority hospitals). By the end of the war the total had risen to 48,101, with the net additional 12,970 beds remaining in use after the war ended. The extended hospital and convalescent system created during the war helped shape the peacetime health services.

In March 1941, the two-day bombing of the port of Clydebank on the outskirts of Glasgow caused destruction beyond the abilities of the local authority and wartime emergency services to cope. The main lesson from the two nights' massive destruction was to the necessity of giving immediate aid to local authorities in terms of evacuation assistance and housing of homeless. But in May 1941, the bombing of the Clydeside port of Greenock showed that local authority services, even when supplemented by DHS assistance within hours, were insufficient given the communications, transport and morale problems caused by large scale bombing. There was no second night's bombing in Greenock and no further major bombing of Scotland, but this did not prevent the continued reassessment of contingency planning for any future air raids. The DHS assumed responsibility for air-raid shelters in January 1941 and improvements were gradually undertaken as a result of the bombings of Spring 1941 to the drying, ventilation, sanitation, seating, lighting and bunking facilities. The Scottish Home Department in conjunction with the Home Office took over the local authority Auxiliary Fire Service to form a comprehensive National Fire Service to cope with any future bombing campaigns. Meanwhile, a memorandum from the DHS asked local authorities to make certain that their plans for relief of those made homeless by enemy attack would actually work even under the severest pressure, by arranging large-scale rehearsals to test emergency relief systems.[20]

In early 1941, Prime Minister Winston Churchill reconstructed the National Government cabinet. This led to changes in the Health Offices of State. Tom Johnston was appointed Scottish Secretary of

20 *BMJ*, 1941 (1), 976.

State, while his predecessor, A. Ernest Brown,[21] became Minister of Health. Joseph Westwood[22] appointed Parliamentary Under Secretary of State in 1940 continued in post until 1945 (when he became Secretary of State). Tom Johnston's tenure as Secretary of State marked a period of pioneering wartime activity that helped shape the future National Health Service in Scotland. Johnston's strong social conscience and long-term commitment to meeting the needs of the working class have been demonstrated on several occasions in this book through his speeches in the House of Commons in particular on nutrition and school health. In addition, by this time he had moved away from a specifically 'Home Rule' stance (as described in chapter one) and towards the possibilities of socio-economic planning for Scotland to be achieved through a consensual approach. Harvie described Johnston's position as a move '[...] towards administrative rather than legislative devolution'.[23] Johnston, placed in the highest office in Scotland by the Coalition Government at a time of national emergency, rose to the challenge and in particular used the wartime situation to energise and invigorate the Scottish health services.

---

21 Alfred Ernest Brown, was Liberal MP for Leith from 1927–31 and National Liberal for the same constituency from 1931–45. English-born and educated in Torquay, he served as a Liberal MP for Rugby in 1923. He served as Parliamentary Secretary in the Ministry of Health between 1931–2 and then as Secretary to the Mines Department from 1932–5. He was Minster of Labour between 1935–40 and also Minister of National Service from 1939–40. He served as Scottish Secretary of State between 1940–41 and became Minister of Health in 1941 where he remained until 1943. In that year he became Chancellor of the Duchy of Lancaster where he remained until 1945. Finally, he served briefly as Minister of Aircraft Production May–July 1945.

22 Joseph Westwood was elected Labour MP for Stirling and Falkirk in 1935. He had previously served as Labour MP for Peebles and South Midlothian from 1922–1931. Westwood left school aged 13 and worked as a miner from the age of 16. He was political organiser of the Scottish Miners between 1918–29. In 1931 he served for a year as Parliamentary Under Secretary of State for Scotland, a post he was reappointed to between 1940–45. He served as a member of the Committee on Scottish Health Services (Cathcart Committee), 1933–1936. He was Scottish Secretary of State between 1945–47. He was sacked by Prime Minister Clement Atlee in 1947 and replaced by Arthur Woodburn.

23 Harvie, *No Gods and Precious Few Heroes: Scotland 1914–1980*, 101.

Given the freedom to expand Scottish administrative devolution in the wartime situation, Johnston sought the advice of former holders of the office of Scottish Secretary of State. With Churchill's approval he created the 'Advisory Council on Post-War Problems', to help plan for the peace in Scotland. The council consisted of the remaining living former Scottish Secretaries, A. Ernest Brown (then Minister of Health, Colonel Sir John Colville (a leading industrialist), Walter Elliot, Sir Archibald Sinclair (then Liberal leader and Air Minister), and Robert Munro (by this time Lord Alness). Secretary to the Council was Thomas Macrae. The Council was an influential political tool in Johnston's negotiations with central government since it included experienced representatives of the coalition interests of Conservative, Labour, Liberal and National Liberal. The Council met monthly from September 1941 until the end of 1942, thereafter it met irregularly until February 1945, when the Wartime Coalition government itself was coming to an end. The Council vetted all proposed Scottish legislation. Where the Council gave its approval, Cabinet implemented the legislation with minimal discussion. In addition thirty-two special sub-committees launched enquiries into a wide range of issues affecting Scotland's social and economic life. Johnston viewed these arrangements as the highpoint of devolved Scottish government for over two centuries: '[...] we had got Scotland's wishes and opinions respected and listened to, as they had not been [...] since the Union.'[24]

Tom Johnston's time as Scottish Secretary of State resulted in a number of pioneering health initiatives. In 1941, he presided over the introduction of the voluntary hospitals' waiting list scheme. Scotland was short of hospital beds at the outbreak of war and the wartime pressures exacerbated the problem.[25] In effect, this wartime measure

24 T. Johnston, *Memories* (Collins: 1952), 169.

25 Scotland's hospital bed shortage had been a constant feature of the inter-war period. In 1926, the SBH Hospital Services (Scotland) *Committee Report on the Hospital Services of Scotland*, 34–35 found a shortage of 3,600 beds in voluntary hospitals and a lack of coverage and co-ordination in Poor Law Hospitals. It recommended an extension of local authority responsibility to include the Poor Law hospitals. Yet, even after 1929, the new local authorities implemented the clause in the Local Government (Scotland) Act which allowed

made possible the transference of waiting patients from voluntary hospital waiting lists to emergency war hospitals. With an estimated shortage of 3,600 beds in Scotland at the beginning of the war, the need for such an extension of the EMS hospitals' work was clear. Although executor, Johnston was not the originator of the special hospital beds arrangements for Scotland. As early as October 1939, the then Secretary of State John Colville, raised the possibility of allowing: 'ordinary sick persons in those areas who are in urgent need of hospital treatment which cannot be obtained elsewhere'[26] to enter the EMS hospitals as required. By this, Colville intended the EMS hospital provision to cover rural patients who in normal times travelled into the large cities for treatment that they could not obtain locally. The new measure allowed such cases to attend EMS hospitals (which often were situated outside supposed danger zones). The opening of the EMS hospitals in all the civil defence areas of the country greatly increased the number of beds available in Scotland. In 1941, 2,000 voluntary hospital waiting list cases were treated under the Emergency Hospital Scheme. In 1942, this figure rose to 8,000.[27]

Although the hospital waiting lists scheme was already under consideration in the DHS before Johnston's appointment as Secretary of State, it was Johnston who secured the co-operation of both the voluntary hospitals and general practitioners for this unique measure. He offered to take patients from the long voluntary hospital waiting lists at 30 shillings per patient (irrespective of length of stay) charged to the voluntary institutions for treatment at the new, unused hospitals. The initial take-up of this scheme, which was at first restricted to short-stay surgical patients was poor, hence in January 1942, Johnston extended it to include all but chronic cases. In March 1945, he referred to the scheme as having had a considerable effect in reducing the waiting lists and of its immense benefit to thousands of patients.[28] By

muncipalisation of former Poor Law hospitals only slowly. Glasgow, and especially Aberdeen, were notable exceptions to this rule, having put municipal hospital services into operation by the mid-1930s.

26 HOC debates, 18–10–39, vol. 352 col. 888.

27 *GMJ*, 21 1943 (1), 18.

28 *BMJ*, 1945 (1), 718.

the middle of 1945, a total of 32,826 patients had been taken off voluntary hospital waiting lists to be treated in the EMS hospitals.[29]

The Clyde Basin Experiment and Recuperative Treatment of War Workers

> How to reduce health breakdown to a minimum, [...] how to restore one who has been sick to the greatest measure of working capacity compatible with any residual disability; how to integrate medical and industrial care to ensure that determined efforts are made to obtain for the individual work consistent with his talents and his physical capacity – these are the problems.
> (DHS, *Health and Industrial Efficiency: Scottish Experiments in Social Medicine* (HMSO, Edinburgh, 1943), 56)

In January 1942, Johnston extended Scottish wartime experiments in 'social medicine' with the launch of the Supplementary Medical Service, also known under the title 'Clyde Basin Experiment'. 'Social medicine' meant an increased role for the state not only to correct existing ill health, but also as the means of engineering a more healthy society. In other words, this signaled a move from curative to preventive medical provision.

Such a pioneering Scottish measure set the scene for much that was envisaged under the National Health Service, what Lowe has described as '[…] state intervention [which] was not a mere corrective for market failings but the means of engineering a more equal and fair society'.[30] The Clyde Basin Experiment was a revolutionary proposal to permit the DHS to use the Emergency Hospital Scheme hospitals situated in the Clyde Valley as centres for the recuperation of hard-pressed industrial workers. Taking advantage of the wartime expansion of beds, Johnston insisted that the under-used Emergency Hospitals, in the Clyde Valley, and later all EMS hospitals throughout

---

29 DHS, Committee on Scottish Health Services, *Summary Report for the year ended 30 June 1945* (HMSO: Edinburgh, 1945), [Cmd 6661], 15.

30 R. Lowe, *The Welfare State in Britain since 1945* (2nd ed., 1999), 19.

Scotland, should extend their facilities for specialist services to civilian war workers. The solution was an obvious one according to Johnston's memoirs: 'it was obviously foolish to have well-equipped hospitals often standing empty and their staffs awaiting Civil Defence casualties – which, thank God, never came – while war workers could not afford specialist diagnosis and treatment.'[31]

The Clyde Basin Experiment (CBE) was a unique experiment in preventive medical care involving the close co-operation between family doctors, consultants and hospital services. Unlike the fragmented local control of the EMS in England and Wales, the Scottish Secretary of State had complete control of the EMS, including the hospital scheme, this allowed for the creation of an integrated scheme of referral, examination, rehabilitation and hospital stays distinct to Scotland. The CBE was initially confined to young industrial workers in West Central Scotland aged 15 to 25 in a debilitated state. One early intention of the scheme was to tackle the growing wartime incidence of tuberculosis.[32] Later, the scheme was extended to cover workers of all ages in all Scottish counties (except the Highlands). Under the CBE arrangements, doctors referred their own panel patients for assessment to Regional Medical Officers. Consultants examined patients if further examination was required they were then admitted to an EMS hospital, or sent for convalescence to one of the auxiliary hospitals. The London-based medical press referred approvingly to the Scottish experiment:

> The Englishman may well have begun to wonder why Scotland has been able to initiate a number of experiments in social medicine since war began, and the Department of Health in the opening pages of a pamphlet describing these experiments acknowledges that the accommodation available in EMS hospitals has made much of the work possible. The Clyde Basin experiment, for example – remarkable because it is directed to maintaining the health and efficiency of young civilian workers – was made practicable because beds were available at

31 Johnston, *Memories*, 152.

32 PRO, MH79/526, War Cabinet, Home Policy Committee HPC (42), memorandum by Scottish Secretary of State Tom Johnston, 'Prevention and Control of Tuberculosis', (no day) January 1942.

two base hospitals – Law and Killearn – in addition to convalescent-home accommodation.[33]

Details of the Clyde Basin Experiment were supplied by the DHS for the information of the War Cabinet's Inter-Departmental Committee on Social and Allied Services (Beveridge Committee) in July 1942. In a memorandum entitled the 'Health of War Workers', the preventive element of the scheme was given great emphasis:

> The experiment is designed to safeguard the health of young war workers – largely by preventive measures. It was inaugurated by the Secretary of State issuing to all 'panel' doctors in the area of the Clyde basin a letter in which he appealed for their help in protecting the health of the workers, especially those between the ages of 15 and 25. He suggested that doctors should take the chance whenever possible of overhauling young patients, and intimated that, to help them with those cases, the Department's Regional Medical Service was available.[34]

In December 1942, Johnston took questions on the CBE in parliament. He confirmed that he had 'the entire concurrence of the medical practitioners for the scheme.'[35] The co-operation of general practitioners in the CBE may be inferred by the fact that by the war's end in 1945, over 22,000 patients had been referred by general practitioners to Regional Medical Officers for assessment regarding possible convalescent treatment.[36] The construction of wartime emergency hospitals facilitated the development of new screening and preventive care of the workforce through the CBE.[37]

---

33 *BMJ*, 1943 (1), 789. Report on the DHS pamphlet, *Health and Efficiency: Scottish Experiments in Social Medicine* (1943).

34 PRO, Cab 87/81, War Cabinet Inter-Departmental Committee on Social and Allied Services, Memoranda Papers, file 100–129, memorandum 112 – DHS 'Health of War Workers', 20 July 1942.

35 HOC debates, 8–12–42, vol. 385 col. 1420.

36 Macnalty, ed., *The Civilian Health and Medical Services*, 288–91.

37 Further preventive health measures for workers also came in late 1942 in the shape of state-funded allowances to tuberculosis workers to encourage them to seek early and sustained treatment for the disease. For further discussion of tuberculosis allowances see chapter five on Tuberculosis.

In September 1943, the DHS published a report, *Health and Industrial Efficiency.*[38] The Report outlined the advances in social medicine in Scotland during the war to date. The report noted: '[the] growing recognition of the essential relationship between health and industrial efficiency is one of the valuable outcomes of war, one of the present gains that surely must not be lost in times of peace.'[39] The report continued the pioneering statistical work of the DHS Incapacitating Sickness of the Insured Population Reports 1930–1937 described in the previous chapter, and included a summary of factors responsible for long-term incapacity for work in the years 1937/8. The Report concluded that chief contributors to this long-term incapacity were mental and nervous disorders, rheumatism and diseases of the respiratory and circulatory systems. These summary findings made a logical starting point for an investigation into wartime health and industrial efficiency. The investigation was most obviously concerned with the discovery that on the eve of the war, 22% of chronically incapacitated insured Scots workers were under the age of 35.[40]

The DHS *Health and Industrial Efficiency* report also examined the health and working experience of 1,000 men and women invalided out of the Armed Forces into civilian life. 27% of those invalided out of the armed forces were still unemployed six months after their discharge, and only one-third had been able to return to their former employment. The report concluded with a case study of the rehabilitation work carried out at the Gleneagles Fitness Centre for Miners. The Fitness Centre was set up at the beginning of 1943 after a

---

38 DHS, *Health and Industrial Efficiency: Scottish Experiments in Social Medicine*. The 1943 Report was the result of a joint effort. Input came from Peter L. McKinlay and John Gilmour of the DHS medical administrative staff who were responsible for the medical arrangements behind the Clyde Basin Experiment. DHS Regional Medical Officers compiled the incapacity figures. DHS Deputy Chief Medical Officer, T. Ferguson, assisted by A.E. Ferguson, carried out the enquiry into the health and experience of those invalided out of the armed forces. The co-ordinator of the various enquiries was Sir Andrew Davidson, CMO of the DHS between 1942–48. Davidson took over from James MacAlister Mackintosh who served as CMO from 1939–1942.

39 DHS, *Health and Industrial Efficiency* (1943), 5.

40 Ibid., 7.

joint approach to the DHS from the Ministry of Fuel and Power and the Miners' Welfare Commission and described in the report as a 'a valuable complement to existing health services'.[41] 314 cases were admitted to the centre between January and June 1943 staying for an average of six weeks. It is no coincidence that miners were some of the first recipients of the new rehabilitation services. The importance of mine workers, a significant section of the Scottish workforce in peacetime, was crucial in wartime. Moreover, the DHS were already aware of miners' incapacity due to the investigations carried out under the auspices of the Morbidity Statistics Scheme.

The findings of the 1943 Report on the incapacity of the workforce were along the same lines as those uncovered by the DHS ISIPS reports (1930–1937) discussed in the previous chapter. Now though, against a background of warfare and a 'manpower' shortage action swiftly followed. A wide-ranging rehabilitation programme for Scotland's industrial workers was launched. The Ministries of Health and Labour belatedly introduced recuperative treatment for industrial workers in England and Wales in May 1944. But the scheme was not so extensive as the CBE, applying to factory workers and miners only in establishments were there was medical supervision by industrial medical officers, who could recommend workers for examination at Emergency Medical Services hospitals. English and Welsh workers in need of convalescence were accommodated at one of thirteen convalescent homes affiliated to the hospitals – stays were normally limited to two weeks.[42]

The emphasis given to the importance of convalescence in the DHS wartime report in some respects brings the story full circle to the recommendations of the SBH MacAlister Report of 1920. The MacAlister report proposed the introduction of convalescent homes not simply for those recovering from illness, but also as a form of rest cure for those physically or emotionally exhausted.[43] The 1943 Report's examination of the Clyde Basin Experiment concluded that

41 Ibid., 54.

42 C.L. Dunn, *The Emergency Medical Services vol. 1 – England and Wales* [History of World War Two – UK Medical Services], (HMSO, 1952), 149.

43 SBH, *A Scheme of Medical Service for Scotland* (1920).

most of the civilian workers treated were suffering from debilitating illnesses such as anaemia, stress and anxiety strains which had been exacerbated by people continuing to work even when unfit to do so. The DHS Report concluded that the CBE had demonstrated the need for recuperation facilities. It recommendation that the experiment should become a permanent resource for industrial workers. 'The removal of fears of serious illness by complete medical overhaul provides the reassurance so helpful in expediting recovery.'[44]

In October 1943, the Office Committee of the DHS decided that the CBE should continue until the introduction of a 'comprehensive health service'. The DHS memorandum on the 'Demobilisation of the Emergency Hospital Scheme' commented: 'that the kind of service now given under the Supplementary Medical Service should become a permanent feature of preventative [*sic*] medical service. These matters will require consideration by the Department, Hospital Authorities and the Treasury.'[45]

Interim Measures at the End of World War Two

Tom Johnston retired from politics in 1945. In July 1945, the incoming Scottish Secretary of State, Joseph Westwood, recognising the importance of the extended hospital facilities which had been introduced during the war, pledged to continue to make the additional beds available for the use of the Scottish population. Joint Under Secretary of State for Scotland, Commander Thomas Dunlop Galbraith[46] further pledged that the wartime hospitals would have a

44 DHS, *Health and Industrial Efficiency* (1943), 7.

45 PRO, MH76/603, DHS Office Committee on the 'Demobilisation' of the Emergency Hospital Scheme: Scotland, 13 October 1943.

46 Galbraith was educated at Glasgow Academy and Royal Naval Colleges, Osborne and Dartmouth, Galbraith entered the Royal Navy in 1903 and remained in active service until 1922. He qualified as a Chartered Accountant in 1925, joining the family firm Walter and WB Galbraith, CA, Glasgow, where he remained a partner until 1970. He was elected National Conservative MP for

secure place in the permanent hospital system of Scotland in conjunction with the introduction of the National Health Service.[47]

In mid-1946, the DHS announced that the EMS hospitals would continue to be administered by the Department until the NHS was set up. The EMS was regarded as an integral part of what had become (although initiated by wartime requirements) a single comprehensive service under the general control of a central authority (the DHS). This policy had evolved as the needs of additional wartime bed accommodation were replaced with a desire to reduce civilian waiting lists. The next step, a scheme of screening and preventive care of the workforce seemed a logical, albeit bold, progression. Yet, it was not clear that these wartime ventures would become post-war policy. The DHS was careful not to look beyond immediate need in their Emergency Medical Service provision.[48]

From mid-1941 the DHS conducted internal discussions on the possible post-war system of health administration. The DHS set up a small 'office' committee to monitor wartime developments. Perhaps learning the lessons of the limited policy initiatives which followed the radical recommendations of the 1936 Cathcart Report, DHS

Glasgow, Pollok in 1940 serving until 1955. He was Joint Parliamentary Under Secretary for Scotland in 1945 and again 1951–55. He was Minister of State at the Scottish Office, 1955–58. From 1959–67 he was Chairman of the North of Scotland Hydro-Electric Board.

47 'It will be the aim of the Department of Health to integrate these new hospitals with the permanent hospital system of the country. The precise method of doing so will be considered in relation to the post-war development of the hospitals general.' Galbraith, HOC debates, 12–6–45, vol. 411 col. 1578.

48 'Purely war-time problems of hospital policy, such as the devising of arrangements for treating patients on voluntary hospital waiting lists in Emergency Scheme new hospitals [...] are of interest in the present connection only in so far as their solution may prejudice post-war developments. Until the main lines of post-war policy emerge, however, the Department have sought to avoid any such prejudice in the arrangements that have been made, and have refrained from any action that might reasonably have been held to undermine the present position of voluntary hospitals.' PRO, CAB 87/76, Inter-departmental Committee on Social Insurance and Allied Services, DHS Memorandum 'Outline of Scottish Services – Health', (no day) August 1941, 11.

bureaucrats were keen not to pre-empt the decisions of central government. Again, the 'state-autonomist' theory, as described by Dowding, whereby interested agencies influence government only when their views coincide[49] has clear resonance for the role of the DHS immediately after the war. What Immergut has identified as an 'executive-centred' approach to policy implementation[50] left the DHS as a peripheral agency post-war. Central planning was the keystone of the in-coming Labour administration. The DHS retreated into a more reserved position after the war, in contrast with the dynamic policy initiatives it implemented during the 1939–45 period. However, many of the DHS's wartime services, including the priority given to the rehabilitation of industrial workers and the executive predominance of the Scottish Secretary, were enshrined in the new NHS legislation enacted in 1947 and in operation from 1948.

In Scotland, the EMS and its Hospital Scheme were unrivalled successes. A unitary, centrally administered hospital service was not attempted in the EMS elsewhere in Britain. The result was that when a 'national health service' was proposed to include all hospitals, there was less resistance to this in Scotland than elsewhere and the integration was made more painlessly.[51] The work of the EMS hospital services showed both the medical profession and the public that a State-run hospital service could function smoothly.

---

49 Dowding, *The Civil Service*, 4.

50 Immergut, *Health Politics*, 24, 28–9.

51 'Overall, the measure of Scottish control of Scottish health affairs enjoyed by the Department under its ministers proved to be a major factor in the relatively smooth development of the National Health Service in Scotland.' Gibson, *The Thistle and the Crown*, 114.

The increase in state-sponsored health care in evidence through the EMS carried on the tradition of high-level public health involvement that was begun in 1913 with the Highlands and Islands Medical Service. By World War Two, the HIMS had developed into a comprehensive health service for those entitled to coverage: 'The scheme applies to "crofters, cotters, dependants of insured persons and others in like circumstances on whom the doctor's usual fee would be an undue burden".'[52] HIMS payments (via Treasury funds) to general practitioners for subsidised treatment of patients in 1939 stood at five shillings (25p) for a first visit, and 3/6 (17.5p) for subsequent visits.

Wartime extension of services in the Highlands and Islands included a large Emergency Hospital built for wartime needs, incorporating facilities for orthopaedics and dermatology. A full-time obstetrician was appointed to the Royal Northern Infirmary, Inverness. This appointment was primarily made to provide for evacuated expectant mothers, but the obstetrician also acted as an adviser to the whole northern area. A full-time surgeon was also appointed in Oban under the auspices of the Emergency Medical Services scheme.

By 1941, the HIMS covered an eligible population of 327,437 with 176 doctors for the area. The Scheme did not cover the sick poor, who were the responsibility of local authorities, but it did cover the insured working population of the region, through special arrangements with the DHS Insurance Division. Although the HIMS started out as a scheme to provide a subsidised general practitioner service in the Highlands and Islands, it quickly expanded into areas of hospital, clinic and nursing care, and later to laboratory, dental and ophthalmic services. For example in 1914, there were 107 nurses working under the scheme, only 47 of whom were fully trained. By 1941, there were 200 nurses subsidised by the HIMS, 185 fully trained, including those with midwifery qualifications. Also by World War Two, full-time resident consultant surgeons were in practice in five areas of the Highlands and Islands. The air ambulance service,

52 PRO, CAB 87/76, DHS, 'Outline of Scottish Services', August 1941.

first introduced in the 1930s, was extended in wartime to cover Shetland and Lewis, and continued as an essential link between the remote islands and lowland hospitals.

Such measures continued the improvement of the range of care provided by the scheme far beyond that first envisaged in the 1912 Dewar Report. According to a later official account of medical services in the area, the HIMS was immensely popular among the medical profession. During the discussions on the coming of the National Health Service doctors requested that they be allowed to continue to work directly under the DHS under the aegis of the Secretary of State for Scotland.[53] Indeed, when it came, the NHS (Scotland) Act, following on from HIMS practice, included special payments for doctors in remote areas of the country, to supplement the income derived from general practitioners' patient lists. The official Second World War record of Scottish health services commented that the HIMS provided a small-scale illustration of what might be achieved in the national field through the agency of a comprehensive health service.[54]

'Social Reconstruction' and Health Issues

On 9 October 1941, Ernest Brown by now Health Minister, announced the outlines of the Government's proposed post-war hospital policy.[55] A comprehensive hospital service, organised on a regional basis, was proposed. The proposed hospital service was to be based on both local authority and voluntary hospital funding was to be supported by Treasury grant and patient contribution. Two weeks later the *Glasgow Herald* welcomed the government's proposals: '[...] the conviction

53 Scottish Home and Health Department 'General Medical Services in the Highlands and Islands' – [Report of a Committee appointed by the Secretary of State for Scotland], (Edinburgh: HMSO, 1967), 12.

54 Macnalty, ed., *The Civilian Health and Medical Services*, 296.

55 HOC debates, 9–10–41, vol. 374 col. 1116–20.

had been growing that the adequate hospital service necessary to public health can be provided only through the closest possible co-operation between the voluntary and statutory systems.'[56] Following Brown's announcement, a DHS survey was carried out in 1942 of all Scottish hospitals in each of five proposed hospital regions. The information gained in the 1942 survey proved useful to the Regional Hospital Boards which were set up by the NHS (Scotland) Act of 1947.

In January 1942, Sir Hector Hetherington (Principal of Glasgow University) was appointed by the DHS to chair a committee which was charged with making 'recommendations within a policy aimed at the post-war development of a comprehensive and co-ordinated hospital service in Scotland on a regional basis'. The Hetherington Committee was also asked to consider the future administration of the EMS hospitals and suggest arrangements to secure the future co-operation of voluntary, local authority and EMS hospital services. The Hetherington Report,[57] published on 13 October 1943, recommended a partnership between voluntary and statutory hospitals. The Hetherington Report assumed that the dual voluntary and statutory hospital system would continue after the war. However, the Report also recognised that closer co-ordination would be required if the comprehensive hospital system then under Government debate[58] was to come about. The financial independence of voluntary hospitals was no longer regarded as viable in the Report. The Report recommended that public grants should be made available after the war, and that in order to receive such aid, the voluntary hospitals would have to abolish hospital charges and also liase with regional hospital authorities and fit their programmes of care to a regional policy. To this end, the Hetherington Report followed the 1936 DHS Cathcart Report in recommending the establishment of five advisory Regional Councils, whose areas would be based in Edinburgh, Glasgow,

---

56 *Glasgow Herald*, 25 October 1941, 4b.

57 DHS, *Report of the Committee on Post-War Hospital Problems in Scotland* (Edinburgh: HMSO 1943), [Cmd 6472].

58 Change was expected following the convening of the (Beveridge) Committee on Social and Allied Services in June 1941, which reported at the end of 1942.

Aberdeen, Dundee and Inverness. These regional arrangements continued to operate the existing Emergency Medical Service districts (themselves based on an existing pre-war, albeit relatively inactive, regional hospital committee structure): South Eastern, Western, North Eastern, Eastern and Northern, although slight amendments were made with the regional borders in the new arrangements.

The Hetherington Report stated the view that honorary medical service in the voluntary hospitals could not survive, and in future, it recommended that hospital staff should be paid according to a uniform salary scale. the Hetherington Committee proposed a contributory system of a payment of 3 pence a week, to finance the new co-ordinated regional hospital services. This income would only cover a fraction of the costs and it the Committee further recommended that 60% of the running costs would come from the government in the form of a grant from a central hospitals fund. Any remaining costs were to come from local rates and Exchequer grants. Direct state funding of hospitals – not a completely free hospital service – was the essential point of the Report.[59]

The Report's recommendations for state subsidies and the ending of 'hotel' charges (i.e. paying accommodation charges, but not the cost of treatment), for voluntary patients went further than those contained in the 1942 Beveridge Report. Tom Johnston welcomed the Hetherington Report as crucial in the wider context of the possible nationalisation of the health services:

> The Report contains many important recommendations affecting the future of the hospital system of Scotland. Those recommendations are now being considered in connection with the Government's examination of the whole question of a new *national health service* [author's emphasis].[60]

Johnston supported the findings of the Report in the War Cabinet in October 1943. His view was that so-called 'hotel' charges for in-patient care were strongly opposed by public opinion, the local

59 DHS, *Report of the Committee on Post-War Hospitals Problems in Scotland*, 33–35.

60 HOC debates, 13–10–43, vol. 392 col. 910.

authorities and the voluntary hospitals in Scotland.[61] When the NHS Bills were introduced in 1946 by the Labour government, proposals for hospitals went beyond both the Beveridge and the Hetherington Reports recommendations, and a free hospital state hospital service was introduced.

In addition to the discussion on the future shape of the post-war hospital service, attention was given to the overall direction of health policy within a wider movement for reconstruction. Within the Ministry of Health, discussions had taken place over the expansion of general practitioner services to include the whole population. Meanwhile, the BMA too, actively participated in debates on post-war social reconstruction.[62] The BMA Medical Planning Commission was drawn together during 1940 and held its first meeting in May 1941. The MPC sought a wide range of views. Among its original 67 members were representatives from the Scottish Royal medical corporations, the Society of MOsH, the Medical Women's Federation, and observers from the DHS and Ministry of Health).[63] The remit of the MPC was 'to study wartime developments and their effects on the country's medical services both present and future.' The MPC published a draft interim report (in fact, its only report) in June 1942.[64] The interim report, as the title of the Commission suggests, emphasised planned future health services, in particular through co-operation between and integration of statutory and voluntary medical services. This echoed the planning concerns raised in the DHS Cathcart Report of 1936. The MPC Interim Report was clearly an attempt by the broad spectrum of medical professionals to add their

61 PRO, CAB 87/13, PR (43) (76), Committee on Reconstruction Priorities, Memorandum, Secretary of State for Scotland, Tom Johnston, 'National Health Services', 12 October 1943. See also memoranda dated 29 July 1943 and 29 October 1943.

62 As did the much smaller Socialist Medical Association, which issued a report *Whither Medicine?* in 1940 which recommended a unified medical service organised on a regional basis with doctors receiving salaries.

63 For more on the MPC see P. Bartrip *'Themselves Writ Large': The British Medical Association 1832–1966*, 227–232

64 *BMJ*, 1942 (1), 'Medical Planning Commission Draft Interim Report', 20 June, 743–53. This was the only Report published by the MPC.

views to the ongoing debate on plans for state health care.[65] The creation of the Emergency Medical Service had shown a possible future direction for state medicine and many within the medical profession sought to avoid this possibility.

The MPC Interim Report proposed a comprehensive health service, with general practitioner, specialist and hospital services under regional control. It also emphasised preventive health care through the notion of 'positive health', and envisaged general practitioners working in group practices at health centres in a part-time salaried service. This radical proposal still allowed general practitioners a unique, independent role in the health services. The emphasis on the individual practitioner as the central component of any unified health service was nothing new. Similar proposals were contained in the MacAlister Report of the SBH's Consultative Council on Medical and Allied Services in 1920.[66] The MPC sent out copies of its interim report in September 1942 to member medical organisations to gauge their reaction. In response to a question on the future coverage of a new health service, the RFPSG view was that direct state medical provision should be made only to those who were presently within the scope of the National Health Insurance scheme and their dependants and those of similar economic status.[67]

The presentation of the Report on Social Insurance and Allied Services to parliament at the end of November 1942 dramatically changed the climate of the discussions on the future shape of a comprehensive health service. Underlining the Second World War vogue for planning through a centralised state, Finlayson described the Beveridge Report as the 'apogee of this drive towards greater planning in the social services'.[68] The Beveridge Report, with its assumption that a new comprehensive medical service would cover the total

---

65 Virginia Berridge has suggested that 'the radical nature of its proposals proved an embarrassment to the BMA and it was quickly buried.' See Berridge, 'Health and Medicine' in Thompson, ed., *Cambridge Social History of Britain – Social Agencies and Institutions*, 236.

66 SBH, *A Scheme of Medical Service for Scotland*, (1920).

67 RCPSG, 1/1/1//17, RFPSG minutes of meeting, 2 November 1942.

68 G. Finlayson, *Citizen, State and Social Welfare, 1830–1990* (Oxford: Clarendon Press, 1994), 256.

population, rendered the work of the MPC, and its interim proposal for a continuation of private practice to cover around 10% of the population, as largely 'irrelevant'.[69] The Beveridge Report was able to find a path through the overlapping, incongruous and unwieldy system of health and unemployment insurance, pensions and statutory and voluntary medical provision and produce a plan to resolve the complex issue of social welfare with radical, yet straightforward and relatively cost-efficient proposals.

Among the members of the Beveridge Committee was Muriel Ritson, representative of the Department of Health for Scotland, and who had been an original member of the Scottish Board of Health on its formation in 1919.[70] At the first meeting of the Beveridge Committee in July 1941, she jointly raised a question of the scope of the Committee in relation to the health services:

> Miss Ritson [DHS] and Mr. Hamilton Farrell [Ministry of Health] raised the question of the public health services. Their Departments already had in hand a survey of the future of the health services, and, therefore, there was a danger of overlapping. Should not the Committee confine itself to cash benefits?
>
> The Chairman [Beveridge] agreed that the Committee should not go into the details of the public health services. But there was a close relation between the development of health insurance and the health services generally. He therefore thought that the Committee should be made aware of the points of contact between the insurance schemes and the general health services.[71]

In fact, the recommendations of the Beveridge Committee went far beyond identifying 'points of contact' between insurance schemes and health services. The medical section of 'Assumption B' of the Report recommended a 'national health service' to:

> [...] ensure that for every citizen there is available whatever medical treatment he requires, in whatever form he requires it, domiciliary or institutional, general, specialist, or consultant, and will ensure also the provision of dental,

69 Bartrip, *'Themselves Writ Large': The British Medical Association 1832–1966*, 231.

70 See chapter one for more on the career of Muriel Ritson.

71 PRO, CAB 87/76, SIC (41), Interdepartmental Committee on Social Insurance and Allied Services, minutes of first meeting, 8 July 1941.

ophthalmic, and surgical appliances, nursing and midwifery, and rehabilitation after accidents.[72]

Not until the Beveridge Report appeared in late 1942, did the government's intention with regard to general practitioner care within a new comprehensive health service come into public view. The Beveridge Report, and various popular versions, had become an overnight success.[73] As a result, in February 1943, the coalition wartime National Government extended the commitment it had earlier confined to hospital care, to the point where it covered the health services as a whole. Yet, the Government did not commit itself to the implementation of the Beveridge Report or the expenditure which was involved in its proposals. Indeed, the coalition's commitment was, according to Kevin Jeffreys, the result of an 'artificial consensus' between the Conservative and Labour members of the wartime coalition, as the former felt that reconstruction and forward-looking welfare proposals were necessary policies following the wave of popular support which greeted the Beveridge Report. Coalition white papers on National Insurance, employment policy and health reform were regarded by the Labour Party as no more than something on account.[74] Despite the lukewarm Coalition government response to the Beveridge Report in parliament, events overtook the government's adopted position. The popularity of the Report coupled with the back-bench revolt against the government ensured that future post-war reconstruction plans incorporated its main principles.

72 Ibid., paragraph 427

73 According to Webster: 'Beveridge became the touchstone for a new social order.' Partly, this was due to the coincidence of the Report's publication in late 1942 with a renewed sense of optimism due to allied force victories at El Alamein a few weeks earlier. *BMJ*, 17 October 1992, 901. For more on the public response to the Report see, Paul Addison, *The Road to 1945: British Politics and the Second World War* (Quartet, 1977), 217–219.

74 K. Jeffreys, 'British Politics and Social Policy during the Second World War', *Historical Journal*, 30 (1987), 127.

Consultation and the Scottish Medical Advisory Committee

The creation of the Scottish Medical Advisory Committee (SMAC) in February 1943 by Tom Johnston was an attempt to bring medical professional opinion into the discussions on the future form of state health arrangements. As part of the consultation process, he set up SMAC to: 'advise on the medical aspects of problems relating to the health of the people.'[75] The remit of the Committee was to consider the pressing medical questions of the day and voice the opinions of the Scottish medical profession. The National Government had committed itself to setting up a co-ordinated and comprehensive health service, by early 1943, but the details of the service remained to be settled by consultations between Government Departments, local authorities, voluntary hospitals and the medical profession. Of course, the degree of interest group influence over policy formulation was determined by the political context of the dispute. The move from wartime situation to peacetime practicalities altered the balance of power in favour of the state.

The convening of SMAC in February 1943 under the chairmanship of Sir John Fraser allowed Johnston access to expert medical advice. It was also a concession to pressure by the Scottish medical profession to have a voice in the coming changes in health service arrangements. Johnston conceded 'I find there is in the profession a general desire for a regularly constituted Committee to advise the Department on the many problems with a medical interest which are confronting the country to-day.'[76] One of the first tasks of the Scottish Medical Advisory Committee was to discuss the Beveridge Report with the Scottish Secretary of State.[77]

---

75 *GMJ*, (1943), 53.

76 HOC debates, 16–2–43, vol. 386 col. 1574.

77 Home Secretary, Herbert Stanley Morrison announced the forthcoming meeting between Johnston and SMAC in parliament. 'My Right Hon. Friend, the Secretary of State for Scotland, who has already done a fair amount of unification of the health services in Scotland, will to-morrow meet his Medical Advisory Council in order to discuss the Beveridge Report with them.' HOC debates, 18–2–43, vol. 386 col. 2245. Morrison was Labour MP for South

Among the 14 members of SMAC were Professor E.P. Cathcart[78] and Sir John Boyd Orr[79] – both of whom produced Reports of great significance for Scottish health services policy in 1936 and 1943, respectively. (Boyd Orr and Cathcart were both also members of the Ministry of Health Advisory Committee on Nutrition). In 1944, Cathcart chaired a SMAC sub-committee investigation into rehabilitation. The sub-committee reported in 1946. Its conclusions were that as far as possible, there should be continuity of patient supervision during the whole process of primary medical treatment and rehabilitation, and that a planned programme of increased activity should be followed until the patient was fit enough to resume ordinary employment or alternative work.[80]

The role of the new Scottish Medical Advisory Committee was discussed in Cabinet in October 1943 in relation to the draft White Paper on the proposed National Health Service. A Joint Memorandum from A. Ernest Brown and Tom Johnston in October 1943 suggested two central Medical Advisory Committees, one for England and Wales and one for Scotland, should advise the government on any general medical questions affecting the National Health Service. The memorandum proposed that the Advisory Committees be allowed to publish any advice given to government.[81] Since SMAC had been in operation for eight months, it seemed that in this instance the Ministry of Health was playing catch up with the DHS.

Hackney in 1923–4, 1929–31, and 1935–45. He was later MP for East Lewisham 1945–51 and for South Lewisham from 1951–9. Morrison served as Minister of Transport from 1929–31 and then Minister of Supply in 1940. Under the wartime coalition he served as Home Secretary and Minister of Home Security 1940–45. He became Deputy Prime Minister and Leader of the House of Commons in 1945, positions he held until the end of the Labour Government in 1951.

78 See chapter two for biographical details of Edward Provan Cathcart.

79 See chapter four for more on the career of John Boyd Orr.

80 DHS, *Rehabilitation: Report of a Sub-Committee of the Medical Advisory Committee (Scotland)*, (Edinburgh: HMSO, 1946).

81 PRO, CAB 87/13, PR (43) (73), Committee on Reconstruction Priorities, Joint Memorandum, by Minister of Health, Ernest Brown and Secretary of State for Scotland Tom Johnston, 'National Health Service: Matters Provisionally Agreed and Outstanding Points', 9 October 1943.

Tom Johnston also continued the smaller eight-member DHS Scientific Advisory Committee (SAC) chaired by Boyd Orr. The remit of SAC was: 'to advise the Secretary of State for Scotland on the application of the results of scientific research to public health administration and to promote medical investigations designed to assist the Secretary of State in the discharge of his responsibilities for the health services in Scotland.' It was the practice of SAC to delegate special investigations to expert sub-committees to which non-members of SAC were co-opted. For example, in 1935, the clinical sub-committee of SAC compiled the 1935 Report on Maternal Morbidity and Mortality in Scotland. In 1943, the SAC sub-committee on infant mortality reported under the name of SAC chair, Boyd Orr.[82]

The work of SAC continued in a more formalised way the DHS-sponsored scientific investigations by Boyd Orr and others, which produced the late 1920s investigations into milk feeding discussed in chapter three. Johnston was not only interested in the opinions of the Scottish medical experts. His interest in the wider aspects of reconstruction for Scotland led him to create the Scottish Advisory Council on Post War Problems, (featuring Johnston and all the surviving ex-Scottish Secretaries mentioned earlier). In convening such heavy-weight Committees and commissioning comprehensive reports, including the Hetherington Report, Johnston wanted to secure the widest of all opinions with which to go before the Cabinet, armed with a representative Scottish 'voice' for planning the future health administration of the country.

82 See chapter three for more on this report and the convening of the sub-committee.

Debate on the Future Shape of a National Health Service

In Government discussions on a new health services Bill after 1942, it was proposed that the central organisation of the Scottish health service should parallel that of its counterparts in England and Wales. However, authority was to be devolved. The Scottish Secretary of State was to be directly responsible to parliament for the administration of the new health service, exercising powers through the DHS. From early in the discussions, Tom Johnston stressed the differences between Scotland and England and Wales and brought these before the War Cabinet Committee on Reconstruction Priorities:

> My colleagues have before them a paper by the Minister of Health dealing with proposals for a new national health service. I have had parallel discussions with the various Scottish bodies concerned and I am in general agreement with the proposals in the paper but there are certain special Scottish aspects (some of them requiring rather a different approach) to which I think it necessary to draw the Committee's attention.[83]

The DHS was involved in a long series of discussions and consultations in relation to the development of the proposals for the NHS in Scotland. The creation of the Scottish Medical Advisory Committee in February 1943 allowed the Scottish medical profession to express their views, and related discussions were held with the local authorities, the voluntary hospitals and ancillary medical services. Perhaps due to Johnston's overtures to the Scottish medical profession through SMAC, throughout the move towards a national health service, better relations were maintained with the Scottish profession than elsewhere in Britain. This was also partly owing to the distinct nature of Scottish health administration. Central funding of health care provision, including an element of salaried practice, had been a feature of Scottish medicine since the creation of the Highlands and Islands Medical Services Board in 1913. Johnston's view, expressed before

83 PRO, CAB 87/13, PR (43) 45, Committee on Reconstruction Priorities, memorandum by Tom Johnston, 'National Health Services', paragraph 1, 29 July 1943.

the Cabinet, was in favour of central control of general practice conducted directly by the DHS through the office of the Scottish Secretary of State. Johnston thought this was a solution acceptable for all concerned in the Scottish health services.[84]

At the time of the Cabinet discussion on 'National Health Services' in July 1943, a future comprehensive health service seemed likely to be a municipal service. In this model, the local authority would constitute the unit of control with medical care under the supervision of local Medical Officers of Health. Such a service would have been a logical expansion and extension of the system of health care in Scotland as it had developed since the passage of the Local Government Act of 1929 and the enactment of the Scottish Maternity Services legislation of 1937. The running of hospitals through Regional Boards had continuities with the successful wartime arrangements and had been suggested in the DHS Hetherington Report. As Johnston pointed out, the circumstances in Scotland already lent themselves to a three-tier administration (that is, separate hospital, clinic and general practitioner services) with a co-ordinating centre. Johnston based his opinion on the successful wartime operation of the CBE.[85] The main proposal to emerge from the 1943

84 Ibid., paragraph 5.

85 'Under this scheme general practitioners throughout the industrial belt refer industrial workers with incipient medical conditions to the regional medical officers of the Department of Health for Scotland, who arrange, where necessary, for diagnostic examinations by consultants and for admission to hospital. General practitioners are unanimous in their praise of the efficiency of this scheme in bringing them into close and effective contact with consultants and the hospitals. My proposal envisages an extended development of this successful co-operation, in which the regional medical officers could serve as the co-ordinating link between the general practitioner and the consultant and hospital services. I am satisfied that this machinery, together with the Regional Hospital Councils and the Medical Services Committee [...] would be sufficient to secure an effective co-ordination between the three parts of the service. In any event I personally would rather sacrifice some degree of apparent unity to get our reforms introduced in an atmosphere of goodwill.' See PRO, CAB 87/13, PR (43) 60, Committee on Reconstruction Priorities, memorandum by Tom Johnston, 'General Practitioner Service', 14 September 1943.

Cabinet discussions was that general practitioners would be employed in group practices at state-funded health centres.

On 17 February 1944, the Ministry of Health and the DHS jointly issued a White Paper entitled a *National Health Service*.[86] The White Paper was not a statement of government policy. It was a discussion document, intended to stimulate public debate and accelerate progress towards an agreement on the nature of the legislation to follow. The White Paper stated for the first time that a national health service would be free and open to all. Such a suggestion had already been raised at one level in Scotland. The DHS Hetherington Report of 1943 ruled out payments towards the cost of patients' maintenance in hospital.[87]

The 1944 Health Service White Paper jointly released by the Ministry of Health[88] and the DHS, outlined a system of consultation between the Scottish Secretary of State and interested health groupings. The White Paper proposed that the Scottish Secretary of State would in future be advised by a Scottish Health Services Council (to be largely composed of members of the medical profession). A proposed Scottish Central Medical Board, to be charged with 'the day-to-day administration of the general practitioner service'[89] also appeared set to be dominated by medical professionals. Despite

86 Ministry of Health and Department of Health for Scotland, *A National Health Service* (HMSO, London, 1944), [Cmd 6502].

87 PRO, CAB 87/13, PR (43) (76), Committee on Reconstruction Priorities, memorandum, by Tom Johnston, 'National Health Services', 12 October 1943, See also memoranda dated 29 July 1943 and 29 October 1943. See also Johnston's comments on hospital funding during the March 1944 Commons debate on the National Health Service White Paper. 'It always appeared to me not very dignified for a great nation to provide partly for its hospital service by funds secured by the activities of students dressed up as Red Indians, stage Highlanders, nigger minstrels, Mickey Mouse, Lady Godiva and Charlie Chaplin, all holding tin cans below the noses of the charitably disposed.' Scottish Secretary of State Tom Johnston in the Commons debate on the MH/DHS White Paper on the National Health Service, HOC debates, 17–3–44, vol. 398 col. 628.

88 Henry Willink replaced A. Ernest Brown as Minister of Health in November 1943.

89 MH/DHS, *A National Health Service*, 42.

provisions for professional consultation, the contents of the White Paper excited the organised opposition of the Scottish medical profession. For example, the Royal College of Physicians of Edinburgh formed a sub-committee to discuss the implications of the new discussion document. The RCPE also made successful overtures to its two 'sister Scottish corporations' to collaborate in opposition to the White Paper.[90] The BMA, representing wider medical opinion, felt the profession was to be deprived of playing anything other than an advisory role in the new comprehensive health service.

During a debate on the 1944 White Paper in the RCPE, one member spoke out against it urging 'that the medical profession should not become a part of the Civil Service, and that the old relationship between the family doctor and his patients was in danger of being destroyed'.[91] Attempts were made by the organised medical profession to revise the Health Services White Paper in subsequent negotiations with the government in a specially convened negotiating committee. Concessions gained by the negotiating committee by February 1945[92] were rapidly overtaken by the break-up of the wartime coalition government in May 1945. The calling of a general election soon followed. At the July 1945 election both the Conservative and Labour parties' supported the idea of a national health service. Respective interpretations of what such a service would entail diverged.

---

90 See RCPE Minute Book 16, RCPE quarterly meeting, 18 July 1944, and RCPSG Minute Book 1/1/1/17, RFPSG, meeting 3 July 1944.

91 Speech by A. Graham Ritchie. RCPE Minute Book 16, quarterly meeting, 2 May 1944.

92 According to former RCPE President Charles MacNeil who represented the College on the negotiating committee: '[...] considerable progress had been made with consideration of the general practitioners' part of the scheme, there was much more to be done as regards the Hospital and Specialist services.' See RCPE Minute Book 16, quarterly meeting, 6 February 1945.

The change in Government as a result of the Labour landslide at the July 1945 election brought a dramatic shift in direction for the planned comprehensive health service for the nation. Since 1934, the Labour Party had been pledged to a free and comprehensive health service, operated by a full-time salaried staff, with the creation of health centres and administered under reorganised regional authorities. A state-controlled health service was now planned. For the first time, a Labour government had the majority to ensure that a radical approach to social welfare could be implemented. The motivations and impact of the Labour Government 1945–51 on Britain's welfare arrangements have given rise to a keen historiographical debate.

According to Jeffreys, it was the breakthrough of the massive Labour victory in 1945 and the distinctive approach to social welfare of the new government that shaped the state welfare programme of 1945.[93] In this theory, the creation of the National Health Service and other welfare reforms post-1945 were not moulded by the experiences of the inter-war years and the patchwork of health services which had then developed. Nor were they the result of pressure for change due to the common experience of warfare – 'the new emphasis on the social needs of ill people' – as Titmuss had argued.[94] In Jeffreys' view there was less consensus among the parties during the war than previously thought.

Others, notably Charles Webster, have supported Jeffreys' viewpoint. Webster, writing on the occasion of the fiftieth anniversary of the NHS, cast doubt upon a Whig interpretation on the coming of the National Health Service.[95] Lowe too, has stressed the innovation

93 Jeffreys, 'British Politics and Social Policy during the Second World War' 144.

94 Titmuss, *Problems of Social Policy*, 472.

95 'The process of incremental growth operating over the course of more than a century has sometimes fostered the impression that by the start of the Second World War a comprehensive health service was so near to accomplishment that its final institution represented an inevitability.' C. Webster, *The National Health Service: A Political History* (Oxford: Oxford University Press, 1998), 3.

displayed by the post-1945 Labour government's approach to social welfare.[96] The work of Jeffreys, Webster and Lowe contrasts with the 'incrementalist'[97] argument put forward by Paul Addison. Addison saw the policies of the Labour Party in government from 1945 as the culmination of trends in social policy developed under the wartime Coalition government, rather than as a distinct new beginning.[98]

Looking at the Scottish evidence, previous chapters have shown that the DHS had promoted extended state medical services since the 1930s via the publication of the 1936 Cathcart Report and the annual release of gloomy findings on the 'Incapacitating Sickness of the Insured Population in Scotland' (ISIPS). While such publications opened up a debate, they did not result in much legislation (the expansion of maternity services in 1937 was the exception). Indeed, it was only under emergency wartime arrangements that the DHS was able to put innovative Scottish health initiatives such as the Clyde Basin Experiment into operation. However, the title of this measure underlines the apparent transitory nature of this and other wartime 'experiments', such as the related rehabilitation measures for industrial workers. There was no inevitability about the permanent expansion of emergency wartime measures into peacetime practice, as the DHS was clearly aware. The DHS had exercised bureaucratic autonomy in wartime to the benefit of the industrial workforce and those on hospital waiting lists, but they were not in a position to pre-

96 'In the early postwar years, it was the ideas of democratic socialists which gave the British welfare state its unique international reputation [...] these ideals [of democratic socialists] also infused the welfare legislation of the 1945–51 Labour governments and provided the logic for further advances [...].' Lowe, *The Welfare State in Britain since 1945* (2nd ed., 1999), 19.

97 Incrementalism, according to Lowe, '[...] stresses, over time and at all levels, the complex mixture of rationality and realism, short-term expediency and planned development, that determines policy.' Ibid., 51.

98 'The Atlee governments of 1945 to 1951 completed and consolidated the work of the Coalition by establishing a peacetime managed economy, and the expanded welfare state envisaged by Beveridge. To some extent they also exercised the right to go beyond the Coalition framework and implement specifically Party ideas. But this was often because the Left of the Party, which had strongly opposed many of the Coalition policies managed to exert itself successfully.' Addison, *The Road to 1945*, 273.

empt the decisions of central government. As with the publication of the Cathcart Report, a decade earlier, the DHS role was one of informing the debate rather than dictating it.

The National Health Service Bills introduced by the new Minister of Health, Aneurin Bevan, in March 1946 and in December 1946[99] by Scottish Secretary of State Joseph Westwood[100], differed markedly from the 1944 White Paper proposals of the wartime National Government. Both government Bills sought to nationalise all hospitals and remove existing statutory health services such as tuberculosis schemes from local authorities. The Bills also sought to emphasise the development of health centres, centralise control over the distribution of doctors around the country and introduce payment of general practitioners.

Yet, the new proposed structure of the National Health Service perpetuated some of the weaknesses of the old system of health care. Most obviously, the creation of a tripartite structure of hospitals, general practitioner services and a (much reduced) local authority service, did nothing to achieve the co-ordination of services called for in the inter-war SBH MacAlister and DHS Cathcart Reports, among others. Yet, this aspect of the proposals reflected Johnston's aims stated in Cabinet in September 1943. One criticism of the NHS Bill expressed by the RCPE in May 1946 (in a unanimous resolution forwarded to the professional negotiating committee for further discussions with the DHS and the Ministry of Health) related to the planned separation of health services for children. 'The college is opposed to and regrets the disintegration of the Maternity Services threatened in the Bill, and still more the absence of provision for linking together the personal services dealing with children.'[101] More recent criticism of the NHS legislation has reinforced this view of a

99 The National Health Service (Scotland) Bill was published on 6 November 1946 accompanied by a White Paper (Edinburgh: HMSO, 1946), [Cmd 6946].

100 Joseph Westwood, Labour Scottish Secretary of State was appointed in July 1945. He succeeded 'caretaker' Scottish Secretary of State, the 6th Earl of Rosebury, who held the office briefly in 1945.

101 RCPE Minute Book 16, quarterly meeting, 7 May 1946.

deficient health structure, unable to fully address the needs of preventive as well as curative health services.[102]

Among the general public, there was widespread approval for the proposed new state health service. Scottish parliamentary opposition to the Bill surfaced in the House of Commons during its Second Reading on 10 December 1946. Westwood, who introduced the Bill, stressed both the comprehensive nature of a publicly-sponsored health service and its Scottish roots:

> The Bill which is now before the House – a Bill drafted and directed towards providing for Scots people a comprehensive Health Service – places for the first time on public authorities – central and local – the responsibility for seeing to the provision of all facilities needed for the health of the whole population.[103]

Westwood[104] built on Johnston's wartime proposal to rest central responsibility for health services, not as in England and Wales, under the local authorities, but in the office of the Secretary of State for Scotland. This not only made sense administratively, but also, coincidentally, helped allay the Scottish medical profession's long-time fear of local authority control. The Conservative view was that too much power was going to be placed in the hands of the Scottish

102 'The National Health Service as established on its tripartite basis in 1948 was recognisably the inheritor of nineteenth and early twentieth-century relationships between medicine and the state.' V. Berridge, 'Health and Medicine', 241.

103 HOC debates, 10–12–46, vol. 431 col. 999.

104 'Local authorities have not hitherto been concerned with the general practitioner service, and in Scotland they have not pressed for any part of this responsibility in future. I feel therefore, that progress could best be made with the development of Health Centres by adhering to the White Paper proposal that the provision, equipment and maintenance of Health Centres in Scotland should be the direct responsibility of the Secretary of State, instead of being the responsibility of local authorities as in England and Wales. The Secretary of State will be empowered to delegate any of his functions in this connection to a local authority. This was accepted both by the Scottish local authorities and by the medical profession in Scotland in the discussions following on the White Paper.' PRO, CAB 129/5, CP (45) 345, memorandum by Joseph Westwood on the National Health Services in Scotland, 15 December 1945.

Secretary.[105] The Conservative press also disagreed with the Scottish Bill: '[...] the danger of too much centralisation in St. Andrew's House, with remote control by the Treasury which provides much of the cost, is latent in the scheme.'[106] This aspect of the Scottish Bill differed from the NHS Bill for the rest of Great Britain, which devolved much control for health centres and ambulance services to local authorities. The small size of Scottish authorities made the provision and administration of such services impractical at the local level.

Another crucial difference in the Scottish Bill was the integration of the Scottish teaching hospitals with other local hospitals in the new Regional Hospital Board management structure. During the debates on the Scottish Bill, Conservative amendments were put down in an attempt to keep the teaching hospitals independent, as was the case in the NHS arrangements for the rest of Britain:

> The great infirmaries in Scotland are being reduced to the level of minor institutions; they will not be anything like as efficient for their patients. This may well be disastrous for their position as centres of the great schools of medicine.[107]

This amendment was successfully resisted. Westwood gave the case for the merger. He correctly predicted that the creation of a bigger group of hospitals would help eliminate the old difference in prestige between the two types of hospitals and raise the standard of the former municipal hospitals.[108]

---

105 James Reid, Conservative MP for Glasgow Hillhead and former Lord Advocate (1941–5), moved an amendment to the Bill. Reid's amendment stated: 'This House, while welcoming the idea of a comprehensive Health Service for Scotland, declines to give a Second Reading to a Bill which concentrates so large a proportion of the control of the service in the hands of the Secretary of State.' HOC debates, 10–12–46, vol. 431 col. 1013.

106 *Scotsman*, 7 November 1946, 4 col. b. See also *Glasgow Herald*, 11 December 1946, 3 col. a.

107 James Reid, HOC debates, 10–12–46, vol. 431 col. 1021.

108 'Hospital services are developing in such a way as to make a new and comprehensive authority with a large area and resources behind it a practical necessity [...]. There is no possible chance, I submit, of securing all these

Opposition to the Bill also came from the Labour backbenchers. Some MPs believed that Westwood had granted too many concessions to the medical profession. William McLean Watson[109] stated:

> The proposed representation of the professional classes on the various bodies to be set up is a very much larger proportion than is justified. I dare say that the agitation that has been carried on by the doctors and others has had its effect on my Right Hon. Friend, and that he has gone as far as he possibly can to placate those various interests.[110]

Ex-Scottish Secretary of State and Health Minister, Walter Elliot[111] asked why the recommendation of the Hetherington Report for grants to the voluntary hospitals which would leave them under the control of the voluntary hospitals board 'had been thrown overboard'.[112] His complaints were described as 'frivolous' and 'facetious'.[113] Elliot viewed the recommendations of the Hetherington Report selectively. For example, the Report's recommendation for Regional Hospital Boards that would assume the direction of both municipal and voluntary hospitals was taken up in the national health legislation.

The NHS (Scotland) Bill proceeded through the Commons along Party lines, with a clear Labour majority. In the 1947 Cabinet re-shuffle, Arthur Woodburn replaced Westwood as Secretary of State for Scotland.[114] Woodburn oversaw the final implementation of the new Scottish health service.

---

developments so long as the general hospital is a voluntary one and infectious disease is the responsibility of a local authority.' HOC debates, 10–12–46, vol. 431 col. 1005–6.

109 William McLean Watson, Labour MP for Dunfermline 1922–31 and 1935–50. See chapter two for further biographical details.

110 HOC debates, 10–12–46, vol. 431 col. 1025.

111 For more on Walter Elliot's career see chapter one.

112 HOC debates, 10–12–46, vol. 431 col. 1036.

113 HOC debates, 10–12–46, vol. 431 col. 1042.

114 Arthur Woodburn, Labour MP for Clackmannan and East Stirling from 1939–70. Educated at public school in Edinburgh, Woodburn studied at Heriot Watt College in the city. From 1919 he lectured at the Edinburgh Labour College in History, Economics and Finance. He became President of the National Labour Colleges in 1937 and was Secretary of the Scottish Labour College. He was Secretary of the Scottish Labour Party from 1932–39. From 1941–45 he served

The Influence of the 1936 Cathcart Report on the NHS (Scotland) Act, 1947

During his introduction to the Second Reading of the NHS (Scotland) Bill in December 1946, Westwood made great play of the continuities of the new measure with the recommendations of the 1936 Committee on Scottish Health Services Report (Cathcart Report). Westwood had been a member of the Cathcart Committee: 'That Committee gave me an insight into health administration in Scotland and the opportunity of getting a grounding for the work which I have to do in this House now, to get this Bill through in time.'[115]

The NHS (Scotland) Bill did not include the Cathcart Report's recommendation for a continued contributory health scheme (albeit extended to dependants and administered by local authorities rather than approved societies). However, Westwood stressed that both the 1936 Report and NHS Bill recommended the introduction of a 'comprehensive health service'. Westwood and six others on the 18-member Cathcart Committee had signed a reservation to the main report stating their belief that it was essential to have a comprehensive general practitioner service available to all. This reservation was included at the end of the published report.[116]

In relation to hospital services, Westwood acknowledged that the Cathcart Report had envisaged a continuity of the voluntary system, but it had stated that there should be no extension of financial commitments to the voluntary sector. In the intervening period voluntary hospitals had become an increased burden on the State without any great growth in central control over the grant-aided but independent voluntary hospitals. The Cathcart Report recommended

as Parliamentary Private Secretary to Tom Johnston, Scottish Secretary of State. He then served as Secretary to the Ministry of Supply from 1945–47. From 1947–50 he was Scottish Secretary of State, replacing the sacked Joseph Westwood.

115 HOC debates, 10–12–46, vol. 431 col. 997.

116 'But if the state is to care for the health of its citizens, its care should be comprehensive.' DHS, *Committee on Scottish Health Services Report*, 360.

that Scotland's hospitals should form a unitary service and should be subject to regional policy directives.[117] Again, Westwood saw a parallel between the Cathcart recommendations of 1936 and the NHS (Scotland) Bill of 1946.

Westwood also emphasised the strong continuity in Scottish health policy for the Highlands and Islands. Westwood identified the Highlands and Islands Medical Service as a direct predecessor of the NHS. 'I am often asked what will become of that service in future under proposals contained in this Bill [...]. What, in fact, is happening is that the Bill is extending to all Scotland many features hitherto operating in the Highlands and Islands.'[118] It was noted that not a single representation against the NHS (Scotland) Bill had been received from doctors working in the HIMS. By implication, those already working in a state medical service saw the benefits of the new proposals for the whole country.

The 1936 Cathcart Report recommendation (and that of the 1920 MacAlister Report) that the general practitioner should be the key of any reorganised health service was ignored in the 1947 Act. The Cathcart Report's call for a co-ordinated service was also overlooked – the new NHS was split between general practice, the hospital service and the local authority service, with only a passing reference made for the need for liaison between the separate agencies. Speaking to the Glasgow Southern Medical Society[119] in 1949, E.R.C. Walker, Secretary of the Scottish BMA, felt the National Health Service (Scotland) Act bore little resemblance to the Cathcart Report. The Reports emphasis on the importance of the general practitioner in delivering health care had disappeared: 'It is inconceivable that, had the legislation been based on the Cathcart Committee Report, anything like the present Act would have resulted.'[120]

117 HOC debates, 10–12–46, vol. 431 col. 999.

118 Ibid., col. 1011.

119 The Glasgow Southern is a medical society dominated by general practitioners (and has been since its formation in 1844). Walker's comments were, therefore, likely to be well-received. For more on the Glasgow Southern Medical Society see J. Jenkinson, *Scottish Medical Societies: Their History and Records, 1731–1939* (Edinburgh: Edinburgh University Press, 1993), passim.

120 E.R.C. Walker, 'The Forgotten Report', *EMJ*, 56, (1949), 499.

Walker felt that the NHS (Scotland) Act was 'befogged and bedevilled by the irrelevancies of doctrinaire politics'[121] and sadly ignored the Cathcart Report's findings and hinted at DHS compliance with consultants to secure the Act's passage:

> It seems to be considered necessary with our present legislative machinery that a Scottish Act of Parliament must so closely resemble its English counterpart as to be distinguishable only by the faint Caledonian flavour of its language. There is little doubt in my mind that it was principally conceived in the minds of Whitehall [...] I think I can detect – and this is rather curious – a definite flavour of Harley Street. Indeed, in bitter moments, I have wondered if N.H.S. stood for Nationalised Harley Street![122]

Walker's comments show his firm adherence to the BMA Party line of opposition to the new nationalised health service. However, it also reflected the widely held view that general practitioners' claims for a key role in the new health service had been largely overlooked in favour of pacifying consultants' desire for hospital pay beds. General practitioners were not alone in their sense of being largely overlooked, so too, were local authorities. Municipal government had been responsible for the administration of the personal health services since the beginning of the twentieth century. They had also assumed control of the former Poor law hospitals after 1929. Now, the local authorities were left with little more than a rump of ancillary services: among them were maternity and child welfare, domiciliary midwifery, health visiting and district nursing services, home helps, and vaccination and immunisation programmes.

121 Ibid., 498.

122 Ibid., 500.

Within the medical profession, hospital consultants were won over to the new proposals through the offer of payment of salaries for NHS work and the freedom to take on private patients. This manoeuvre also split the BMA opposition to the proposed new health service. The BMA's Scottish Division opposed many of the new proposals. Yet it also acknowledged that the HIMS, the nearest thing to a complete medical service in Britain, and the operation of the Maternity Services (Scotland) Act of 1937, provided sound Scottish examples of a wide ranging health service. The Scottish BMA acknowledgement of the merits of state health provision is less surprising when it is noted that these particular services were centred on the general practitioner (with the support of other services including specialist and nursing provision).

Two plebiscites to assess BMA members' views on the new health service arrangements were held in December 1946 and May 1947. The second plebiscite, in May 1947, showed a majority of Scots doctors in favour of the NHS, but a majority of those in England and Wales against. By the time of the second plebiscite, 37% of all Scottish general practitioners had already signed up for service under the NHS. The corresponding figure in England was 26%. Although a majority of BMA members rejected the new health service, the majority was not overwhelming enough[123] to keep up their protest, particularly since the NHS legislation had passed into law and was a few months from being put into operation. In view of the turning tide of medical opinion, there was some criticism of the BMA's intransigent negotiating position from within the Scottish medical profession in January 1948. Charles MacNeil, RCPE representative on the medical negotiation committee on the NHS legislation, expressed his personal opinion doubting: 'the political wisdom of the advice being given by the British Medical Association and that to be

123 The final plebiscite showed 10,906 for the new legislation and 12,550 against. By contrast, 1893 Scots doctors voted for the legislation and 1341 against. See *BMJ*, 1948 (1), 893.

successful very strong political and public support would be required in favour of their case.'[124] MacNeil's views were echoed by RCPE Fellow J.S.M Hamilton, who 'stressed the fact that the attitude of the British Medical Association had always been that of an opponent'.[125]

The less hostile attitude of Scottish practitioners in general was noted in 1947 by new Scottish Secretary of State, Arthur Woodburn. Woodburn noted that: 'Prior to the time the Scottish doctors became associated with the BMA there was every indication that the Scottish doctors were willing to co-operate with us, but a conflict of loyalties seemed to have arisen.'[126] However, there were many among the Scots medical profession who opposed the NHS. For example, an extremely provocative motion was put forward for discussion at an extraordinary meeting called by the Royal Faculty of Physicians and Surgeons in Glasgow less than six months before the 'Appointed Day' for implementation of the NHS:

> The Royal Faculty of Physicians and Surgeons views with apprehension the failure of the Minister of Health to reach agreement with the Negotiating Committee of the Profession and urges Parliament to amend, in the public interest, those parts of the National Health Service Act and of the National Health Service (Scotland) Act which are totalitarian in conception, inimical to freedom and contrary to the ideas of justice as understood in this country.[127]

The motion was later considerably watered down before it was passed by the Glasgow medical corporation and released to the press. The final view was that the new legislation would not operate in the best interests of the public and impair the quality of the medical treatment of the country). Such comments reveal the bitter opposition of a section of the Scots medical profession to the health service.

In general, this study has followed the 'state-autonomist' (or 'executive-centred') theoretical model of policy development as the most convincing explanation as to how health policy in the period 1919–1948 was influenced by external agencies. Such outside

---

124 RCPE Minute Book 16, RCPE extraordinary meeting, 22 January 1945.

125 Ibid.

126 See D. Hamilton, *The Healers: A History of Medicine in Scotland* (Edinburgh: Canongate, 1987 ed.), 260 for non annotated quotation from Woodburn.

127 RCPSG 1/1/1/17, RFPSG extraordinary meeting, 27 January 1948.

influence could come in many guises, from 'expert' members of the Scottish Board of Health, from scientific advisors or via the organised medical profession. In the state autonomy model, policy may be influenced only where there is no clear policy preference set in stone within government (which helps explain the occasions when distinct Scottish health measures were enacted), or when pressure group opinion ties in with policy decided upon by government. However, in the negotiations for the creation of the National Health Service, while this model has some merit, there does seem to be more evidence of bargaining involved.

In order to bring the whole medical profession, (under protest) into the Labour government's view, concessions were made to win over one section of the medical profession (by granting consultant rights to private practice). In this instance, the 'pluralist' model of the state, wherein policy develops as a result of bargaining and negotiation between various sets of pressure groups and civil servants within Departments must be considered.[128] In support of this analysis it may be noted that is his 1993 study of the British welfare state after 1945, Lowe stated that 'pluralism represents the values that were most prevalent in post-war Britain'.[129] It could then appear that the advent of the National Health Service marked a shift in the theory of policy formulation. However, as noted by Mackintosh in his study of the British cabinet, the decision to make concessions to the BMA lay with the government. The government did not bend to the will of the BMA.[130] Moreover, even if some concessions were granted by the state towards one element within a single pressure group, this does not necessarily mark the triumph of a pluralist form of government.[131]

128 For further discussion of the 'pluralist' model of policy development see, Dowding, *The Civil Service*, 116 and Immergut, *Health Politics*, 19.

129 Lowe, *The Welfare State in Britain since 1945* (1st ed., 1993), 36.

130 '[...] the BMA wields little power in the sense that it is unable to bend a reluctant government to its will or thwart positive policies that have been endorsed by the electorate.' John P. Mackintosh, *The British Cabinet* (2nd ed., Methuen and Co., 1968), 558.

131 '[...] a consistent bias in favor of some social actors at the expense of others does indeed damage the pluralist claim that plural and balanced social pressures

Differences between the NHS Act of 1946 and the NHS (Scotland) Act of 1947

The NHS (Scotland) Act had certain distinctive features.[132] Overall, the Scottish Secretary of State was given the leading executive powers in the NHS (S) Act, as made clear in Section 1 of the Scottish Act of 1947.[133] The Scottish Secretary of State was also given ultimate sanction over other authorities involved in the administration of the NHS (S) Act.[134] Another key difference between the English and Scottish legislation was that the latter made no differentiation between teaching and non-teaching hospitals. All hospitals were under the administrative jurisdiction of Regional Hospital Boards. Scottish teaching hospitals played such a large and important part in the services of their regions that the hospital service would not have been

---

are the source of political decisions.' Immergut, *Health Politics*, 249, footnote. 25.

132 The National Health Service Act for England and Wales was enacted on 6 November 1946, the National Health Service (Scotland) Act followed six months later, on 21 May 1947. Papers for the Scottish NHS Act are in PRO, MH 77/158 and NAS, HH102/501–3.

133 'It shall be the duty of the Secretary of State to promote the establishment in Scotland of a comprehensive health service designed to secure improvement in the physical and mental health of the people of Scotland and the prevention, diagnosis and treatment of illness, and for that purpose to provide or secure the effective provision of services in accordance with the following provisions of the Act [...] The services so provided shall be free of charge, except where any provision of this Act expressly provides for the making and recovery of charges.' National Health Service (Scotland) Act, 21 May 1947, Section 1, Parts (1) and (2) .

134 Section 56, Clause 1 of the NHS (S) Act reads: 'Where the Secretary of State is of opinion on representations made to him or otherwise that any Regional Hospital Board, Board of Management, Executive Council, Ophthalmic Services Committee or local health authority, or the Scottish Medical Practices Committee or the Scottish Dental Estimates Board have failed to carry out any functions conferred or imposed on them by or under this Act, or have in carrying out those functions failed to comply with any regulations, schemes, proposals or directions relating thereto, he may after holding an inquiry make an order declaring them to be in default.'

complete without them: although containing only one-tenth of Britain's hospital beds, Scotland educated almost one-third of the medical students. The teaching hospitals in England and Wales were to be administered by Boards of Governors independent of the Regional Hospital Boards. Thus, the well-established voluntary teaching hospitals came under the NHS only in Scotland, with the consequence that in England the teaching hospitals maintained a separate existence to the NHS hospitals.

Differences between the two Bills had the potential to cause problems for the Ministry of Health. On 12 October 1946, an internal minute in the Ministry of Health reviewed the differences between the Scottish Bill and that for England and Wales, coming to the conclusion:

> Although [...] there is no individual point to which objection should be raised, I feel that there are points [...] which it might embarrass the Minister to have known publicly before our Bill, as amended by the Lords, has been dealt with by the Commons. There is always the possibility that some amendment may be forced on us in the Lords on a point on which the Scottish Bill differs from ours, and the consequent discussion in the Commons on the Lords' amendment might be distinctly difficult if the Scottish Bill was public property [...] My own view is that the Minister should insist that introduction and publication of the Scottish Bill should await the completion of the consideration of the Lords' amendments in the Commons, and should not be published immediately our Bill has left the Lords.[135]

Bevan acted on the civil service advice, and four days later wrote to the Secretary of State Westwood, asking that the Scottish Bill be delayed:

> When your National Health Service (Scotland) Bill proposals came up to the Social Services Committee you were good enough to say that the Bill would not be published until the Lords had finished with ours. I would be grateful if you would read this as 'until the Lords' Amendments have been considered by the Commons'. There is not much difference, of course, in point of time, but in the

135 PRO, MH77/158, internal memorandum (initialled JEP) on the differences between the Scottish NHS Bill and that for England and Wales, 12 October 1946.

> saving of trouble there might be a great deal and I should be much obliged if you could do this.[136]

Bevan was not prepared to see the debate on the London teaching hospitals re-opened by letting MPs see that the matter had been successfully arranged in Scotland to allow teaching hospitals to come under the remit of Regional Hospital Boards.[137]

Unlike the English arrangements which placed hospitals under Hospital Management Committees, Scottish hospitals were grouped under Hospital Management Boards, which in almost all cases had more than one hospital under their jurisdiction. The intention of this difference, suggested by Westwood, was to allow the Management Boards more autonomy than their English counterparts.[138] This autonomy was continued with regard to the redistribution of the endowments of voluntary hospitals. This was to be carried out by a Hospital Endowments Commission, and pending redistribution the money was to remain at the disposal of the responsible Board of Management instead of, as in England and Wales, being put in a national pool and redistributed.[139]

The Scottish Health Services Council set up by the 1947 Act was the official advisory body to the Scottish Secretary of State, it provided advice when requested, but could also initiate its own subjects for discussion. The Council of 35 included 18 medical practitioners, 4 lay persons with an interest in hospitals and 5 representatives from local authorities. There were also two pharmacists and a number of dentists and nurses and one midwife, on the council. Standing Advisory Committees could report direct to the Minister, but usually reported to the Council, which produced an annual report. Membership of the Council was for a three-year

---

136 PRO, MH 77/158, Letter from Health Minister, Aneurin Bevan to Scottish Secretary of State, Joseph Westwood, 16 October 1946.

137 PRO, CAB, 129/7 CP (46) 89, memorandum by Joseph Westwood to the Cabinet on the National Health Service in Scotland, 1 March 1946.

138 *BMJ*, 1948 (1), 39.

139 PRO, MH77/158, Cabinet Legislative Committee, memorandum by Scottish Secretary of State, Joseph Westwood, 'National Health Service (Scotland) Bill', 9 October 1946, par. 2 (v).

period.[140] A six-member Scottish Medical Practices Committee was also created to oversee the activities of medical professionals within the NHS, four of whom were to be medical practitioners.

The Health Services Councils, like the Consultative Councils before them (some of which continued to act as standing advisory bodies from their creation in 1919 down to World War Two),[141] were at first thought to be of great importance to the medical profession. Yet within a few years it was being alleged that whenever any really important issue arose, the Health Services Councils were overlooked in favour of separate ad hoc bodies – committees, working parties or Royal Commissions.[142] Such ineffectiveness was a point previously made by various of the Consultative Councils.[143]

The measure of Scottish control of Scottish health affairs already enjoyed by the DHS and enacted through local authorities was

---

140 The Health Services Council set up by the 1946 NHS Act for England and Wales, and answerable to the Minister of Health had a similar structure – a 35 member council, including 18 medical members.

141 See PRO, CAB 87/76, Interdepartmental Committee on Social Insurance and Allied Services, DHS memorandum, 'Outline of Scottish Services – Health', August 1941, 1, which cites the four Consultative Councils as the first item in a list of the Department's current standing advisory bodies.

142 R.J. Peters and J. Kinnaird, eds, *Health Services Administration: A Source Book* (Edinburgh: E&S Livingstone, 1965), 184.

143 The Scottish Health Service Council was augmented by Standing Advisory Committees representing the various branches of medicine, including hospitals, general practice, nursing, mental health, dentistry, pharmaceutical services and the Highlands and Islands, which acted as specialised bodies to provide advice as and when required by the Scottish Secretary of State. In addition, another layer of administrative control was provided by the Executive Councils (85 in Scotland) which were set up in defined areas to administer general medical, dental, ophthalmic and pharmaceutical services within the area. Each Council consisted of 25 members including 7 doctors, 3 dentists, 2 pharmacists, 8 local authority members and 5 members appointed by the Scottish Secretary of State. Local Health Executives took over from the former Local Health Committees which previously administered health insurance. By such measures, a clearly-defined mechanism was put in place for wide ranging consultation. The role of experts in providing information and guidance, so prominent under the Scottish Board of Health in 1919, was maintained in a more limited form under the National Health Service.

important in the relatively smooth launch of the NHS in Scotland. Scottish autonomy over health issues dated back long before the creation of the SBH in 1919 and continued beyond 1948. Paterson has gone as far as to say that Scotland 'had a welfare state of its own'.[144] Former Scottish Office civil servant George Pottinger[145] held a different view. Writing retrospectively, he saw the NHS legislation in Scotland as little different from that passed in England. Pottinger argued that since parliament had already approved the principle of a National Health Service it was extremely difficult for the Scottish Secretary of State to make any distinctive Scottish impression on the administration. He believed that Scottish health administrators were also finding the climate had changed in their relationship with Whitehall. Ministers were now less inclined to entertain proposals based on distinct Scottish conditions. Pottinger believed that some English Departments resented Tom Johnston's wartime achievements. Johnston's success according to Pottinger was due to the Scottish Secretary's influence over Churchill. Westwood did not enjoy similar influence over Atlee. Pottinger's view was that the Treasury was

144 '[…] the UK welfare state which emerged between 1910 and 1950 took a distinct form in Scotland, to such an extent that Scotland can be described as having had a welfare state of its own.' Paterson, *The Autonomy of Modern Scotland*, 103.

145 William George Pottinger was born in June 1916. He was educated at Edinburgh and Heidelberg Universities and Queens' College, Cambridge. He joined the Scottish Home Department in 1939. After an interruption for war service, he returned to the Scottish civil service. He served as Private Secretary to two Scottish Secretaries, Hector MacNeil and James Stuart. He was appointed Assistant Under Secretary of State in the Scottish Office in 1967. He became Under Secretary at the Scottish Department of Agriculture and Fisheries in 1970. His friendship with architect John Poulson brought his career to an abrupt end. Pottinger accepted gifts and payments from Poulson in return for providing him with inside information which it was later alleged gained Poulson work in Scotland. After a police investigation, both men were taken to trial in Leeds in 1973. Poulson was jailed for five years. Pottinger was found guilty of receiving £30,000 in gifts with an intent to corrupt and was also sentenced to five years imprisonment. The sentence was reduced to four years on appeal. Pottinger was stripped of his CBE and forfeited a large part of his pension. On his release he wrote a dozen books, including his *Secretaries of State for Scotland 1926–76* (1979). He died in January 1998.

unwilling to agree to anything that might give Scotland an advantage over Whitehall: 'The Treasury was excessively vigilant if not openly obstructive to Scottish initiative in the immediate post war period.'[146]

Perhaps Johnston's influence over health policy developments owed something to the fact that for most of the war, the DHS led the way in policy initiatives and practical responses to wartime health needs, increasing the Scottish Secretary of State's authority over Cabinet beyond what was usual. The personal authority of Johnston as a politician is worth considering in this respect. It may be, too, that the DHS, represented by Johnston, was able to influence government opinion, because at this point central government had no final policy set out regarding a peacetime health service.

The National Health Service (Scotland) Act was passed on 21 May 1947. A little over a year later, on 5 July 1948: the 'Appointed Day', the National Health Service came into operation, alongside other components of Labour's social service programme. For local authorities, the coming of the National Health Service was viewed as a mixed blessing. On the one hand, local authorities were relieved of a large rate burden. In Glasgow, it was estimated that between £3.5 to £4 million would be saved each year from the public budget due to the removal of hospital services and outdoor relief provision from the rates. However, this would be offset somewhat by the loss of the block grant (payable under the Local Government (Scotland) Act of 1929), which amounted to around £1.75 million per year. Aside from income, the range of health services by the Glasgow Corporation, like its municipal counterparts elsewhere, was drastically reduced. According to a report in the *Glasgow Herald* in August 1948 what remained was a small, but crucial, clutch of preventive health services:

> What is left to the municipality is still very considerable and takes the form mainly of preventive work. Authoritative opinion is that this is the most useful role the local health department can play. Freed from the heavy financial and administrative burdens of the hospitals and mental institutions, they will be able now to concentrate greater resources on means of raising the general standard of health of the citizens.[147]

146 See Pottinger, *The Secretaries of State for Scotland*, 104.

147 *Glasgow Herald*, 3 August 1948.

The rather idealised view has echoes of the hopes placed on the creation of the SBH itself thirty years before.

In terms of take up at least, both the Scottish people and the local medical profession enthusiastically accepted the new service. By the end of 1948, 94% of the Scottish population were on doctors' lists and only 2% of general practitioners were not in the NHS.[148] The overnight demand for spectacles and medical appliances caused a drain on the Exchequer, but to the new Scottish Secretary of State, Arthur Woodburn, this was not due to people playing the system, but was a demonstration of the absolute necessity of a National Health Service in the first place:

> In considering the present very large demand I think we have to remember, first, that a good many people postponed the purchase of spectacles, dentures and other appliances until after July 5th and secondly, that we are now meeting, often once and for all, genuine needs which people were unable to afford before. For example, we have had one-legged patients coming for an artificial leg who never had one before. We have sometimes had the tragedy that it is now too late to fit limbs and all we can do is to supply them with wheeled chairs. I am sure that for many appliances we are now facing the peak of the demand but, whether that is so or not, the very magnitude of the demand is significant of the need for the new Service and of the gaps that formerly existed. There are, of course, abuses which it will take time and possibly some tightening up to eliminate, but in relation to the whole they are very small.[149]

---

148 'In Scotland, as in England, the new administrative organisation has been brought into being with remarkable smoothness. On the latest information I have, 94% of the population were on the doctors' lists at the end of October [1948]. Almost all the general practitioners, some 98%, were taking part in the Service and it is only in some of the cities that there are still a few doctors engaged entirely in private practice. Nearly all the 1,200 dentists in general practice in Scotland have joined the Service, nearly all the 1,800 chemists and 800 opticians are taking part. During the first four months of the new Service 10% of the population (about 500,000 persons) received glasses. All the hospitals in Scotland of any consequence, with the exception of three Roman Catholic mental deficiency institutions and a Red Cross Sanatorium, have been taken over – 425 in all, with 62,000 beds.' PRO, CAB, 129/31, CP (48) 308, memorandum by Scottish Secretary of State, Arthur Woodburn to the Cabinet, 29 December 1948.

149 Ibid.

The cost of the NHS to the Treasury was an immediate concern of Cabinet discussion on the Service within six months of its launch. Ironically, the issue of economy which overshadowed so much of inter-war state health and local authority health provision again became a dominant issue. However, post-war methods of dealing with the excess expenditure on the NHS are outside the scope of this study.

Conclusion

The Second World War gave fresh impetus to on-going investigations into the state of public medical care. Yet, the Beveridge Report – arising directly from the wartime coalition government's desire to plan post-war reconstruction – can be regarded as simply the culmination of a series of enquiries into the inter-war health services which questioned the limitation of existing health insurance to the adult working population. However, the impact of the Report went beyond this, it moulded and shaped the social welfare debate in such a way that the involvement of the state as guarantors and providers of health and social security gained immediate popular and political currency.

The fall out of the Beveridge Report and the spectacular success of the Labour Party in the 1945 election also led to a turn-round in health policy. Change came at a faster pace and took policy farther than could have been envisioned by the advocates of a state medical service in the mid to late 1930s. Dictated by the unique set of circumstances, the creation of the National Health Service was part of a wider programme of welfare and social security innovations under the new government. This programme seemed at surface level to herald a new 'pluralistic' concept of the state mediating between various interest groups in society to reconcile their differences and create a suitable, compromise, policy. This approach has been here questioned, particularly in view of the limited input of the organised medical profession into the make up of the service.

Various criticisms of Titmuss's theory on war as a factor in social change have been raised in this chapter. However, it is clear that the war brought social policy and welfare reforms to the forefront of the political stage in a way which had been noticeably absent for much of the inter-war period. World War Two also provided the opportunity to experiment with a much wider range of state health services, especially in Scotland. The DHS initiated an impressive set of wartime measures. These included the hospital 'waiting lists scheme', the rehabilitation schemes, follow-up enquiries into the rehabilitation of invalid service personnel, the opening of the special facility for miners at Gleneagles, together with the pioneering Clyde Basin Experiment. Together these initiatives heralded a move towards extended DHS health provision and a shift away from inter-war emphasis on personal medical services (with the stress on individual responsibility). Wartime events helped quicken the pace towards a policy of preventive medicine. Wartime experience had shown that co-operation and integration of health agencies was achievable.

Yet, in the wake of special DHS wartime measures, and the extensive discussions on a comprehensive post-war health service, which they partly fuelled, there was also clear continuity with pre-war DHS policy debates, if not with DHS practice. Inter-war reports on the health services, notably the Cathcart Report of 1936, had a role to play in informing the discourse on a new universal health care system. In Immergut's telling phrase: 'policy legacies and administrative capacities'[150] exerted their influence on the range of policies considered after the war.

The Scottish NHS legislation seemed a compromise between the need for a comprehensive health service that would obviously follow to a great extent the 1946 NHS Act for England and Wales, and the traditions of independent Scottish health policy. In particular, this was demonstrated in the shape of a more unified hospital system including the University teaching hospitals governed by Hospital Boards of Management with more devolved powers than the English and Welsh Hospital Management Committees. Finally, in a clear continuation of the devolved Scottish health policy that can be traced back to the

150 Immergut, *Health Politics*, passim.

creation of the SBH, overall administrative control was placed in the hands of the Scottish Secretary of State (in England administrative control lay with the local authorities). In this respect, some continuity can, therefore, be identified in Scottish health policy between the emergence of the DHS in 1929 (from the shadows of the expert-dominated SBH, 1919–28) down to the implementation of the National Health Service (Scotland) Act in 1948.

Conclusion

Scottish health policy and health concerns in the period 1919–1948 were both similar to those of the rest of Britain at this time, and distinctive. Scottish health concerns were distinct because Scotland experienced high levels of poverty and unemployment, combined with a reliance on over-crowded and insanitary housing in both urban and rural areas. Similar difficulties were experienced in other parts of Britain too, but as has been shown in many sections of this book, Scotland often suffered more severely. For example, Scotland's infant and maternal mortality rates invariably outstripped the levels recorded in England and Wales. In addition, rural Scottish areas (including the Highlands and Islands) and urban conurbations (particularly in and around Glasgow) suffered badly in Scotland's above average levels of tuberculosis morbidity and mortality.

During the inter-war years the Scottish Board of Health and its successor, the Department of Health for Scotland, faced similar concerns to those faced by the Ministry of Health. In fact, at critical turning points in health policy, namely the creation of the Ministry itself and with the foundation of the National Health Service, Scottish legislation followed that for England and Wales. However, there were many crucial areas where health policy formulators in Scotland pursued their own distinct agenda. Among the initiatives of the SBH/DHS were investigations into the benefits of free and subsidised milk for school children in the 1920s, the pioneering medical statistics scheme of the 1930s and the wartime Clyde Basin Experiment and related rehabilitation services. These policies were tailored to the particular needs of the Scottish population. Even before the creation of the SBH, the Highlands and Islands Medical Service was established as a special, state-subsidised, Scottish medical service. Between 1919–1948, the HIMS was expanded and adapted (as far as possible within financial constraints) to meet the changing expectations of the population of this region.

The SBH was created along the lines of the existing Scottish Boards, but differed in that it met in Edinburgh independently of the Whitehall-based Scottish Office. Executive control of health matters effectively rested in the hands of the six Board members. The Scottish Secretary, at a distance of over 400 miles and occupied by the concerns of the whole of Scottish executive government, left policy direction, as well as the day to day running of Scotland's health administration, to the SBH. It was this autonomy which Scottish Secretary Sir John Gilmour sought to remove from the Board and rest in the Scottish Office. Various reorganisation proposals in the 1920s attempted to channel the advice and opinion of Scottish health experts more directly into the office of the Scottish Secretary, through the filter of a formal civil service structure. Even so, the setting up of the DHS in 1929 did not bring an end to independent Scottish health initiatives. An autonomous bureaucracy of ten-years' standing could not be cast out overnight. Politicians came and went, but throughout the period 1919–1948 the work of medical experts or 'technocrats' within the SBH and DHS maintained active Scottish executive involvement in attempting to preserve the nation's health.

Many individuals made notable contributions to Scottish health developments between 1919–1948. These included career civil servants and administrators such as Muriel Ritson and John Jeffrey. Arguably, their endeavours were matched by the efforts of medical professionals and scientists who were appointed to or worked periodically under the auspices of the DHS: including John Parlane Kinloch, John Boyd Orr, and Dugald Baird. Although the autonomy of the Scottish health bureaucracy has been stressed throughout this work, clearly certain politicians appointed to the office of Scottish Secretary made a decisive impact in the direction of Scotland's health policy. Walter Elliot and Tom Johnston stand out in this role. It is no coincidence that both men had previously served as Parliamentary Under Secretaries for Scotland and therefore had experienced at first hand the workings of the SBH/DHS.

A number of unique SBH/DHS policies made a positive impact on the health of Scotland's population. Notable innovations included the SBH-sponsored scientific enquiries into the benefits of additional milk in the diet of school children. The positive results of this research were incorporated into local authority policy, taken further with the 1934 Milk Act, and finally, elevated to an issue of national priority in the wartime nutrition initiatives. In 1930, the creation of the unique Morbidity Statistics Scheme provided the DHS with detailed information on morbidity patterns for the Scottish insured workforce, amounting to one-third of the total population. The economic situation of the 1930s prevented the launch of health initiatives by the DHS to set about improving these damning statistics. The same reason lay behind the curtailing of the wide-ranging reorganisation of the Scottish health services expected in the wake of the publication of the Cathcart Report of 1936. Only the Maternity Services (Scotland) Act was introduced in 1937. Yet, subsequent events serve to indicate that within the DHS there was a strong will to implement what increasingly became known as 'social medicine' to improve the health of the population. This was demonstrated by the introduction by the DHS of a series of pioneering measures during World War Two, most notably the Clyde Basin Experiment, but also the setting up of rehabilitation services that were later incorporated into the NHS arrangements across Britain.

In terms of relationship with the centre, the DHS negotiated with both the Ministry of Health and the Treasury. Often in this period the debate was over spending levels. While these battles were hard-fought, they were not unique. Other spending departments too, had to negotiate with the Treasury over expenditure. On occasion, the Scottish health administration came into conflict with local authorities as they pursued different policy agendas. This occurred most notably during the 1920s in the strong resistance of a number of Scottish authorities to the pressure from the SBH to maintain a planned programme of tuberculosis sanatorium construction. Yet, the SBH also fought rearguard actions with the Treasury in order to defend local authority powers, for example, over the issue of local provision of milk for necessitous mothers and babies.

The Scottish health agencies worked in co-operation with various voluntary organisations throughout this period. Sometimes this could be in the form of a partnership, for example in the SBH work with the National Association for the Prevention of Tuberculosis most notably in parts of rural Scotland. Often it appeared that the intervention of the voluntary sector (such as the Carnegie Trust) was welcomed as a method of reducing the financial obligations of the state and local authorities, in particular with regard to providing health visitors, play areas, nurseries and feeding for mothers, infants and children.

Scottish health bureaucracy throughout the years 1919–1948 may be described as both dependent and independent. Even in areas where Scotland apparently followed London's lead, there was influential Scottish input into the eventual form of the legislation. Good examples of this were the creation of a separate SBH emerging in the wake of debates on the form of a Ministry of Health for England and Wales at the beginning of the period and with Scottish input into NHS legislation at the end. Scottish autonomy over health issues in this thirty year period (arguably at its highest under the SBH, 1919–28) was never completely subsumed to central control.

Yet, London held the purse strings. Policy initiatives may have been tailored to the particular health needs of Scotland's population, but often the SBH/DHS and the local authorities lacked the finances to make a real difference to the day to day health of the nation. The belief that Scotland's health problems were severe was demonstrated at every level. The activities of prominent individuals on the SBH (and later in the DHS) such as William Leslie Mackenzie and Muriel Ritson, among permanent staff, such as John Jeffrey, and among medical appointees and advisers, including Parlane Kinloch, Boyd Orr and Dugald Baird, all demonstrated a great desire to improve the nation's health, but too often in the period 1919–1948 their efforts were poorly rewarded. Among politicians, too, there was great interest shown in Scotland's health and health administration. Here contributions ranged from the emotive and informed interventions of backbench MPs such as Maxton and Drummond Shiels, to the tenure of Scottish Secretaries, with Elliot and Johnston the most prominent. Yet Scotland's morbidity and mortality patterns were not dramatically improved in the first half of the twentieth century. Nationally and internationally, Scotland's health failed to keep pace.

After 1948, health improvements were uneven. Mortality from tuberculosis fell markedly in the years after the War due to the widespread availability of effective drug therapy, but morbidity levels came down more slowly. Scotland also gained an unwelcome later-twentieth century association with the 'new' killing diseases, notably lung cancer and heart disease (the latter had already been the subject of DHS investigation and disquiet in the inter-war years). Both diseases can in part be related to Scottish lifestyle and environmental factors, dominated by poverty and poor diet.[1]

There was an improvement in life expectancy as the century wore on. Life expectancy in the years soon after World War One (1920–1922) was 56.4 years for Scotswomen and 53.1 years for Scotsmen. In the depression years (1930–1932) the average life span was 59.5 years for Scots females and 56.0 years for males. At mid-century (1950–1952) the relative figures were 68.7 years for women and 64.4 for men. By the years 1980–1982 the comparable rates were 75.2 for females and 69.1 for males. Latest figures released (1998–2000) show life expectancy at 77.1 for Scotswomen and 72.8 for Scotsmen. Although improving, the rate of increase has slowed since the 1970s.[2]

However, even in aspects of health where progress has occurred, such as life expectancy and in infant mortality, (which fell from 47.3 deaths per 1,000 babies in 1946–1950 to 5.6 deaths per 1,000 between 1996–2000)[3] class differences have remained. In 1948, IMR was two and a half times greater among the lowest social class than in the highest. In 1975, these ratios were unchanged. Into the twenty-first century the class divide remains. Overall, Scots adults die younger than English adults. Poorer Scots die younger than richer Scots. Poorer children weigh less, are shorter and less likely to receive immunisation and dental care than those from wealthier families.[4] In other words, generations of Scots living under the NHS or born in the decades after its creation still suffer the same inequalities in health standards which increasingly came to light in the first half of the twentieth century.

---

1 By 1976, Scottish consumption of cigarettes was 30% higher than for England and Wales. Hamilton, *The Healers*, 267.

2 For full figures see Register General for Scotland *Annual Report, 2000* (Edinburgh: Register General for Scotland, 2001), 64.

3 Ibid., 53.

4 Hamilton, *The Healers*, 268.

Appendix 1: Map of Scotland with pre-1996 Regions and Scottish Cities and Towns

Reproduced with permission of School of Town and Regional Planning, University of Dundee.

Appendix 2: British and Scotland-only Maternity and Child Welfare Legislation, 1907–1948

1907	Notification of Births Act [permissive]
1908	Education (Scotland) Act [permissive]
1911	National Health Insurance Act
1912	Report on the Highlands and Islands Medical Service
1913	Education (Scotland) Act
	Highlands and Islands (Medical Services) Act
1914	Public Health (Ophthalmia Neonatorum) Regulations
	Milk and Dairies (Scotland) Act [not operative till 1920s]
1915	Notification of Births (Extension) Act [compulsory]
	The Midwives (Scotland) Act
1918	Maternity and Child Welfare Act
	Midwives (Amendment) Act
	Ophthalmia Neonatorum (Scotland) Regulations [made notifiable]
1919	Scottish Board of Health Act
1927	The Midwives and Maternity Homes (Scotland) Act
1929	Local Government (Scotland) Act
1930	Education (Scotland) Act
1934	Milk Act
1937	Maternity Services (Scotland) Act
1938	Registration of Stillbirths (Scotland) Act
1942	Education (Scotland) Act
1945	Education (Scotland) Act
1946	Education (Scotland) Act
1947	National Health (Scotland) Act [implemented 1948]
1948	Nurseries and Childminders' Regulation Act

Appendix 3: Municipal Tuberculosis Provision in Glasgow, 1890–1925

1890 Local powers established to control milk as a medium in spread of Tuberculosis.

1896 Sub-Committee on Prevention of Tuberculosis formed as a branch of the Health Committee.

Washing and disinfection on death of Tuberculosis patients commenced.

Leaflets distributed from house to house to inform public on nature of Tuberculosis in man.

1897 Veterinary Surgeon appointed with the view to eliminating Tuberculosis Cows from the diaries in the City.

1899 Bacteriologist appointed.

Voluntary notification of Tuberculosis begun.

1901 £500 voted by Local Authority to funds of Bellefield Sanatorium, controlled by Glasgow Branch of National Association for Prevention of Consumption.

1904 £5,000 voted to the funds of Bellefield Sanatorium.

£5,000 voted to funds of Consumption Sanatorium of Scotland, Bridge of Weir.

1906 Dispensary opened in Sanitary Chambers, Glasgow, operated by Glasgow Branch of National Association for the Prevention of Consumption.

Local Authority formally agreed to the principle that Pulmonary Phthisis [Respiratory Tuberculosis] should be added to the diseases which are notifiable under the Infectious Diseases (Notification) Act.

1909 Five Parish Council Dispensaries made available for the purpose of district Tuberculosis Dispensaries.

1910	Dr MacGregor (now MOH) appointed to supervise Tuberculosis work [beginning of the Glasgow Tuberculosis scheme].
	Four visiting Nurses appointed.
	Compulsory notification commenced.
1912	Parish Council Dispensaries replaced by Public Health Department Dispensaries.
	Additional Tuberculosis Officers appointed.
	Ten additional Nurses appointed.
	Clerks and Dispensaries appointed.
	City area extended.
1913	Three of eight new pavilions, forming extension of Ruchill Hospital for treatment of Pulmonary Tuberculosis, opened.
1914	Bellefield Sanatorium purchased by Glasgow Corporation.
	Erection of Robroyston Hospital commenced.
1922	Erection of Mearnskirk Sanatorium commenced. (This institution will provide chiefly for treatment of children suffering from non-Pulmonary Tuberculosis).
1924	Extension of Bellefield Sanatorium.
1925	Light treatment commenced at Baird Street Reception House.[1]

1 'The Glasgow Tuberculosis Scheme' (Glasgow: Corporation of Glasgow, 1926), 10–11.

Bibliography

Primary Sources
in chronological order

Scotland, Government Reports

Select Committee on the Poor Laws, Scotland, 1869

Report of the Royal Commission on Physical Training (Scotland) (HMSO, 1903), [Cmd 1507]

Report of Departmental Commission on Poor Law Medical Relief in Scotland (1904), [Cmd 2022, Cmd 2008]

Scotch Education Department, W. L. McKenzie and A. Foster, *Report on a Collection of Statistics as to the Physical Condition of Children Attending Public Schools of the School Board of Glasgow* (HMSO, 1907), [Cmd 3637]

Report of the Royal Commissioners on the Poor Laws and Relief of Distress, Scotland [and Minutes of Evidence], (HMSO, 1909, 1910), [Cmd 4922]

Local Government Board (Scotland), F. Dittmar, J.C. McVail and T. Dewar, *Report to on the Administrative Control of Pulmonary Phthisis in Glasgow* (Edinburgh: HMSO, 1911)

Report on the Highlands and Islands Medical Service, to the Lords Commissioners of HM Treasury [Dewar Report] (HMSO, 1912), [Cmd 6559]

Report of the Royal Commission on Housing in Scotland (Edinburgh: 1917), [Cmd 8731]

Population of Scotland Rural and Urban (Edinburgh: HMSO, 1917), [Cmd 8731]

Local Government Board for Scotland Annual Report, 1918 (Edinburgh: HMSO, 1919), [Cmd 230]

Scottish Board of Health [SBH], *Annual Reports, 1919–1928* (Edinburgh: HMSO, 1920–1929)

SBH, Consultative Council on Medical and Allied Services, *Interim Report of a Scheme of Medical Service for Scotland* [MacAlister Report] (Edinburgh: HMSO, 1920), [Cmd 1039]

SBH, *Memorandum on School Health Administration* (Edinburgh: HMSO, 1920)

SBH, *Report on the Hospital and Nursing Services in Scotland* (Edinburgh: HMSO, 1920), [Cmd 699]

SBH, *Reports by Consultative Councils on a Reformed Local Authority for Health and Public Assistance* [Separate Reports by the Local Health Administration

and General Health Questions and the Highlands and Islands Consultative Councils] (Edinburgh: HMSO, 1923)
SBH, Hospital Services (Scotland) Committee, *Report on the Hospital Services of Scotland* (Edinburgh: HMSO, 1926)
SBH, *Maternal Mortality: Report of Maternal Mortality in Aberdeen 1918–1927* (Edinburgh: HMSO, 1928)
SBH/Scottish Education Department, *Joint Memorandum on the School Medical Service* (Edinburgh: HMSO, 1929)
Department of Health for Scotland [DHS], *Annual Reports, 1929–1948* (Edinburgh: HMSO, 1930–1949)
DHS, G. Leighton and P.L. McKinlay, *Milk Consumption and the Growth of School Children: Report on an Investigation in Lanarkshire Schools* (Edinburgh: HMSO, 1930)
DHS, *Incapacitating Sickness in the Insured Population of Scotland* [Reports for 1930–37] (Edinburgh: HMSO, 1932–1939)
DHS, Consultative Council on Medical and Allied Services, *Report on Hospital Services* (Edinburgh: HMSO, 1933)
DHS, Scientific Advisory Committee Clinical Sub-Committee, C.A. Douglas and P.L. McKinlay, *Report on Maternal Morbidity and Mortality in Scotland* (Edinburgh: HMSO, 1935)
DHS, *Committee on the Scottish Health Services Report* [Cathcart Report] (Edinburgh: HMSO, 1936), [Cmd 5204]
DHS, *Report of the Committee on Post-war Hospital Problems in Scotland* [Hetherington Report] (Edinburgh: HMSO, 1943), [Cmd 6472]
DHS, Scientific Advisory Committee Sub-Committee Report, *Infant Mortality in Scotland* [Boyd Orr Report] (Edinburgh: HMSO, 1943)
DHS, *Health and Industrial Efficiency: Scottish Experiments in Social Medicine* (Edinburgh: HMSO 1943)
DHS, *A National Health Service* (Edinburgh: 1944), [Cmd 6502]
DHS, *Scottish Hospitals Survey* (Edinburgh, HMSO, 1945)
DHS, *Rehabilitation: Report of a Sub-Committee of the Medical Advisory Committee (Scotland)* (Edinburgh: HMSO, 1946)
DHS, *Scottish Health Statistics* (Edinburgh: HMSO, 1958)
Scottish Health Services Council, *The Organisation of Laboratory Services* (Edinburgh: HMSO, 1958)
Scottish Home and Health Department, *General Medical Services in the Highlands and Islands* [Report of a Committee appointed by the Secretary of State for Scotland] (Edinburgh: HMSO, 1967)
Register General for Scotland, *Annual Report, 2000* (Edinburgh: Register General for Scotland, 2001)

Other Government Reports

Report of the Inter-Departmental Committee on Physical Deterioration (HMSO, 1904), [Cmd 2175]

Report of the Royal Commission on the Poor Laws and Relief of Distress (HMSO, 1909), [Cmd 4499]

Royal Commission on the Poor Laws and Relief of Distress [Minority Report] (HMSO, 1909)

Local Government Board, Arthur Newsholme, *Second Report on Infant and Child Mortality, Supplement to the 42nd Annual Report, 1913* [Cmd 6909]

Report of the Machinery of Government Committee [Haldane Report] (HMSO, 1918), [Cmd 9320]

Ministry of Health, Consultative Council on Medical and Allied Services, *Interim Report on the Future Provision of Medical and Allied Sciences* [Dawson Report] (HMSO, 1920), [Cmd 693]

Report of the Inter-Departmental Committee on the Form of Medical Record to be Prescribed under the Terms of Service of Insurance Practitioners contained in the Medical Benefit Regulations, 1920 [Rolleston Report] (HMSO 1920), [Cmd 836]

Report of the Royal Commission on National Health Insurance (HMSO, 1926)

Medical Research Council, Privy Council, H.C. Corry Mann, *Diets for Boys during the School Age* (HMSO, 1926)

Report of the Committee on Social Insurance and Allied Services [Beveridge Report] (HMSO, 1942), [Cmd 6404]

White Paper, *A National Health Service* (HMSO, 1944), [Cmd 6502]

Register General, *Statistical Review of England and Wales for the Year 1941* (HMSO, 1945)

Report of the Inter-Departmental Committee on the Remuneration of General Practitioners (HMSO, 1946), [Cmd 6810]

Ministry of National Insurance, *Family Guide to the National Insurance Scheme* (HMSO, 1948)

Report of the Inter-Departmental Committee on the Remuneration of Consultants and Specialists (HMSO, 1948), [Cmd 7420]

Report of the Inter-Departmental Committee on the Remuneration of General Dental Practitioners (HMSO, 1948), [Cmd 7402]

Report of the Working Party on Differences in Dispensing Practice Between England, Wales and Scotland (HMSO, 1948)

Statement on Personal Incomes, Costs and Prices (HMSO, 1948), [Cmd 7321]

Seventh Report from the Committee on Estimates 1948–1949 (HMSO 1949)

Ministry of Health, *Report of the Ministry of Health for 1949* (HMSO, 1950)

The Development of Consultant Services (HMSO, 1951)

Distribution of Remuneration among General Practitioners (HMSO, 1952)

Report of the Interdepartmental Committee on the Statutory Registration of Opticians (1952), [Cmd 8531]
Report of the Committee on the Internal Administration of Hospitals (HMSO 1953)
Report of the Committee on the Economic and Financial Problems of the Provision for Old Age (HMSO, 1954), [Cmd 9333]
Report of the Committee on General Practice within the NHS (HMSO, 1954)
Report on Internal Administration in Hospitals (HMSO, 1954)
Report of the Committee of Enquiry into the Cost of the National Health Service [Guillebaud Report] (HMSO, 1956), [Cmd 9663]
Report of the Committee on Recruitment to the Dental Profession (HMSO, 1956), [Cmd 9861],
Report of the Maternity Services Committee (HMSO 1959)
Final Report of the Committee on the Cost of Prescribing (HMSO 1959)
Central Office of Information, [Reference Pamphlet], *Health Services in Britain* (HMSO, 1974)
Department of Health and Social Security, *Inequalities of Health: Report of a Research Working Group* [Black Report] (Harmondsworth: Penguin, 1982)

Records Consulted, National Archives of Scotland, Edinburgh, (SBH/DHS files)

HH series:
HH1 – Scottish Home and Health Department files, 1841–1967: includes files on restructuring, SBH, 1922, SBH becomes DHS, 1928/1929, pay differentials SBH/MH
HH2 – LGBS miscellaneous files, 1885–1930
HH3 – National Insurance records, 1911–1955 includes, insurance morbidity and certification statistics
HH58 – Infectious diseases and public health – medical, sanitary and veterinary services 1919–1962
HH61 – Scottish local authority and voluntary health and welfare services, 1860–1986
HH62 – County Medical Officers Reports, 1891–1948
HH65 – Medical services files (Highlands and Islands), 1909–1966
HH75 – SBH minutes, 1919–1928
HH101 – NHS Administration files, 1891–1988

DD series (Scottish Office Environment Department files):
DD1 – General establishment files, 1912–74, including, DD1/11 SBH constitution and original appointments, DD1/12 – introduction of civil service administrative grade and staff reorganisation, SBH/DHS, 1920s, 30s, overview of departmental organisation

GD (Gifts and Deposits):

GD1/41 – Scottish National Milk and Health Association

GD1/1022 – Association of School Medical and Dental Officers of Scotland 1911–1983

SOE series (Scottish Office Central Services Department):

SOE1/234 – Scottish Office Departments: reorganisation and description of functions/Departmental Handbook 1 – Organisation and Functions of DHS, 1946

Records Consulted, Public Record Office, London

Cabinet papers:

CAB21 – World War One Cabinet papers

CAB24 – Cabinet papers on establishment of SBH, Ministry of Health, 1918

CAB26 – Cabinet Home Affairs Committee on setting up of MH/SBH, 1918/9

CAB87 – Beveridge Committee and Post-war Reconstruction, 1941/2

Housing and Local Government papers:

HLG 1 – General

HLG30 – Unemployed, Special Areas

Ministry of Health papers:

MH20 – Poor Law Government Offices, Registers of Correspondence, 1837–1920

MH55 – Maternity and Child Welfare, Scotland – Schemes and Regulations, 1919–1931, Tuberculosis treatment, 1915–48

MH56 – DHS/Rowett Institute Dietary Survey, 1937

MH58 – General Health questions, 1910–1972, includes professional registration, voluntary hospitals

MH76 – Reconstruction and the Emergency Hospital Scheme, 1943/4

MH77 – NHS (Scotland) Bill

MH78 – Establishment and organisation files, 1862–1972

MH79 – Wartime measures, war cabinet, food policy

MH101 – Government wartime evacuation scheme

Treasury papers:

T128 – Out-letters, Local Government Board, 1914–1919

T154 – Out-letters, Ministry of Health, 1919–1920

T160 – Financial estimates, 1921–1945

T161 – Correspondence between SBH and Treasury over expenditure limitations, 1921–28, papers relating to NHS (Scotland) Bill

Ministries of Pensions and National Insurance:
PIN2 – National Health Insurance Committees
PIN4 – Pensions and Insurance
PIN8 – Beveridge Committee
PIN15 – Treatment of tuberculosis

Ministry of Reconstruction:
RECO1 – Records, 1915–1920, includes papers on establishment of MH

Welsh Board of Health files:
BD2, BD11, BD18, BD35

Official Reports (Scotland)

British Hospitals Association, Executive Committee, *Considerations affecting the Service in Scotland*, in BHA, *A National Health Service* (1944)

British Medical Association, Edinburgh Branch, *Medical Institutions and Information* (Edinburgh: BMA, 1938)

Burgh of Edinburgh Insurance Committee, *Handbook for the Use of Medical Practitioners* (Edinburgh, 1929)

City of Edinburgh Charity Organisation Society, *A Social Survey of the City of Edinburgh* (Edinburgh, 1926)

Glasgow Burgh Panel Committee and Glasgow Division, BMA, *Notes on Hospital and Infirmary Arrangements in Glasgow* (Glasgow: Alex. MacDougall, 1932)

Mackenzie, W. Leslie *Report on the Physical Welfare of Mothers and Children, Scotland* (Carnegie United Kingdom Trust, 1917)

Scottish Branch of the British Hospitals Association, *Memorandum of a Scheme for the Regionalisation and Co-ordination of the Hospital Services of Scotland* (1942)

Transaction of the Scottish Association of Insurance Committees, 1919–1948

Young, J.A. *Report on the Evolution and Development of Public Health Administration in the City of Edinburgh from 1865 to 1919* (Edinburgh, 1919)

Official Reports (Other)

British Hospitals Association [BHA], *A National Health Service* (1944)
BHA, *A Plan for a National Hospital Service* (1946)
BHA, *Voluntary Hospitals Commission Report* (1937)
British Medical Association [BMA], *The Doctors' Case* (BMA, 1948)
BMA, *Draft Interim Report of the Medical Planning Commission* (BMA, 1942)
BMA, *A General Medical Service, 1930* (BMA, 1930 revised 1938)
BMA, *The Private Patient and the New Health Service*, (BMA, 1948)
Central Council for Health Education, *The Eleventh Annual Health Education Conference* (1938)
Nuffield Provincial Hospitals Trust, *A National Hospital Service* (1941)
Medical Practitioners Union, *Transition to a State Medical Service* (1942)
Political and Economic Planning [PEP], *Report on the Local Authority and Voluntary British Health Services: A S survey of Existing Health Services in Great Britain with Proposals for Future Development* (PEP, 1937)
Report on the International Congress on Infant Welfare (1906)
Royal College of Obstetricians and Gynaecologists, and Population Investigation Committee, *Maternity in Great Britain* (Oxford: Oxford University Press, 1948)
Socialist Medical Association, *The New Chapter* (1945)

Other Primary Materials

Aberdeen Burgh Insurance Committee Minutes, [Grampian Health Board Archives, Aberdeen – GRHB]
Aberdeen City, MOH Annual Reports, School Medical Officer Annual Reports, Tuberculosis Officer Annual Reports, 1919–1948, [GRHB]
Aberdeen County, MOH Annual Reports, School Medical Officer Annual Reports, Tuberculosis Officer Annual Reports, 1919–1948, [GRHB]
Aberdeen Education Authority Medical Reports, 1919–1925, [GRHB]
Arbroath Public Health Committee Papers 1889–1941, Medical Officer of Health Annual Reports, 1889–1936, [Angus District Council]
Argyll County Medical Officer of Health Reports, 1915–1944, [ABDA]
Argyll County, papers on wartime nurseries, communal feeding, NHS (Scotland) Act, [ABDA]

Argyll School Medical Officer of Health Reports, 1916–1929, [Argyll and Bute District Archives, Lochgilphead, ABDA]
Banff County Medical Officer of Health and School Medical Officer of Health Reports, 1918–1948, [GRHB]
Berwick County Medical Officer of Health Annual Reports, 1941–1948, School Medical Officer of Health Reports, 1920–1927, Child Welfare Committee Minute Books, 1919–1930, [Borders Regional Archive, Selkirk, BRA]
Caithness County Medical Officer of Health Annual Reports, 1939–1945, 1947–1954, and School Medical Officer of Health Reports, 1927–1930, 1947, [Highland Health Board Archives, Inverness, HHBA]
Clackmanann County Council Minutes, 1919, 1926, [Central Regional Archive, Stirling, CRA]
Coatbridge Burgh Public Health Department records 1919–1948, [South Lanarkshire Council Archives, Coatbridge]
Dundee Medical Officer of Health Annual Reports, 1913–1948, School Medical Officer of Health Reports, 1919–1930, Dundee Clerk's files – wartime nurseries for children, memorandum on Report Infant Mortality in Scotland, (1943), tuberculosis scheme records, [Dundee District Archives, Dundee, DDA]
Edinburgh Burgh Records of Insurance Committee, 1912–1954, [LHBA]
Edinburgh City Archives, Public Health series – maternity and child welfare schemes, nursery school, kindergartens 1914–1925, Edinburgh Day Nurseries Association, Tuberculosis general files, 1913–1920, 1923–1926, 1930–1936, [Edinburgh City Archives, Edinburgh, ECA]
Edinburgh Medical Officer of Health Annual Reports, 1918–1948, [LHBA]
Inverness County Medical Officer of Health Annual Report, 1924, [HRA]
Kincardine Central Committee for Maternity and Child Welfare, 1918–1929, [GRHB]
Lanark County Medical Officer of Health Annual reports, 1918–1948, [Lindsay Institute, Lanark]
Moray and Nairn County Medical Officer of Health, School Medical Officer of Health Reports, 1919–1948, [GRHB]
Motherwell and Wishaw Medical Officer of Health Annual Reports, 1936, 1937, [Motherwell Leisure Services]
Oban Burgh, Town Clerk's files, Maternity Service and Child Welfare: Approval of Scheme, 1917–1920, [ABDA]
Orkney County Medical Officer of Health Annual Reports, 1920–1935, School Medical Officer of Health Reports, 1921–1938, [Orkney County Archives]
Perth and Kinross Medical Officer of Health Annual Reports, 1918–1948, Joint County Council minutes, 1939–1944, [Perth District Archive]
Ross and Cromarty Medical Officer of Health Annual Reports, 1920–1948, School Medical Officer of Health Reports, 1920–28, 1939, 1941, [HHBA]
Rowett Institute, Aberdeen, British Nutrition Survey Test Results, 1937–1939, [Rowett Archive, Aberdeen]

Rowett Research Institute Aberdeen, Health Education Conference, 1946, [Rowett Archive]
Royal College of Physicians, Edinburgh, Minutes and Council Minutes, 1918–1948, [RCPE, Edinburgh]
Royal Faculty of Physicians and Surgeons, Glasgow, Minutes, 1917–1948, [Library, Royal College of Physicians, Glasgow]
Roxburgh County Medical Officer of Health Annual Reports, 1919–1932, [BRA]
Skye and Outer Hebrides School Medical Officer of Health Report, 1929, [Highlands Regional Archive]
Strathclyde Regional Archive, Glasgow Corporation Records: Minutes, 1918–1948, Glasgow Child Welfare Advisory Committee Minutes, 1920–1924, Corporation of Glasgow Public Health Department Pamphlets: 'Maternity and Child Welfare Schemes' (1917), 'Scheme for Maternity and Child Welfare' (1926), 'The Glasgow Tuberculosis Scheme', (1926), 'Maternity and Child Welfare Service: Instructions for the Guidance of Municipal Midwives', (1941), Corporation of Glasgow, 'The Health of the Mother and Child' (n.d.), [Mitchell Library, Glasgow]
Stirling Burgh Medical Officer of Health Annual Reports, 1919, 1930, 1946, [CRA]
Stirling Burgh School Medical Officer of Health Reports, 1919–1939, [CRA]
Stirling County Medical Officer of Health Annual Reports, 1915–1950, [CRA]
Sutherland County Medical Officer of Health Annual Reports, 1923–1948, School Medical Officer of Health Reports, 1921–1939, [HHBA]

Unpublished Collections of Private Papers

Addison, C., Papers, Department of Western Manuscripts, Bodleian Library, University of Oxford
Conservative Research Department Papers, 'Health and Physique of the Nation', Bodleian Library
Greenwood, A., Papers, (papers relating to membership of MH Consultative Council on General Health Questions), Bodleian Library

Newspapers, Periodicals and other Contemporary Printed Sources

Bellshill Speaker
British Medical Journal
Burgh of Edinburgh Panel Committee Annual Reports, 1929–1934, and other published papers, 1919–1944
Edinburgh Medical Journal
Glasgow Burgh Panel Committee Bulletin, 1922–1940
Glasgow Herald
Hansard: Published Parliamentary Debates, House of Commons and House of Lords
Lancet
Motherwell Times
Practitioner
Public Health
Scotsman
[Scottish] *Poor Law and Local Government Magazine*, 1911–1929
Stirling Observer
Transactions of the Scottish Association of Insurance Committees, 1920–1938

Secondary Sources

Scottish Works

[place of publication London unless otherwise stated]

Books:

Adam, A., Smith, D., and Watson, F., eds, *'To the Greit Support and Advancement of Health': Papers on the History of Medicine in Aberdeen* (Aberdeen: Aberdeen History of Medicine Publications, 1996)

Boyd, W., ed., *Evacuation in Scotland: A Record of Events and Experiments* (University of London Press, 1944)

Boyd Orr, J., *As I Recall: the 1880s to the 1960s* (McGibbon and Kee, 1966)

Boyd Orr, J., *Food, Health and Income: Report on a Survey of Adequacy of Diet in Relation to Income* (William Clowes and Sons, 1936)

Chalmers, A.K., *The Health of Glasgow 1818–1925: An Outline* (Glasgow: Bell and Bain, 1930)
Checkland O., and Lamb, M., eds, *Health Care as Social History: The Glasgow Case* (Aberdeen: Aberdeen University Press, 1982)
Coote, R., *A Companion of Honour: The Life of Walter Elliott* (Collins, 1965)
Currie, J.R., *The Mustering of Medical Services in Scotland 1914–1919* (Edinburgh: Morrison and Gibb, 1922)
Dickson, T., and Treble, J., eds, *People and Society in Scotland vol.III3 1914–1990* (Edinburgh: John Donald, 1994)
Dudley, H.A.F., *Aberdeen Royal Infirmary: The People's Hospital of the North East* (Bailliere Tindall, 1992)
Flinn, M.W., ed., *Scottish Population History from the Seventeenth Century to the 1930s* (Cambridge: Cambridge University Press, 1977)
Fraser, W. Hamish, and Morris, R.J., eds, *People and Society in Scotland, Volume II 1830–1914* (Edinburgh: John Donald, 1990)
Geyer-Kordesh, J., and Ferguson, R., *Blue Stockings, Black Gowns, White Coats: A Brief History of Women Entering Higher Education and the Medical Profession in Scotland* (Glasgow: Wellcome Unit for the History of Medicine, 1994)
Gibson, J. S., *The Thistle and the Crown: A History of the Scottish Office* (HMSO, 1985)
Glasgow Burgh Panel Committee, *Hints on Prescribing* (Glasgow: Alex. MacDougall, 1934)
Hamilton, D., *The Healers, a History of Medicine in Scotland* (Edinburgh: Canongate, 1987 ed.)
Harvie, C. *'No Gods and Precious Few Heroes': Scotland 1914–1980* (Edward Arnold, 1981)
Hutchison, I.G.C., *Scottish Politics in the Twentieth Century* (Basingstoke: Palgrave, 2001)
Jenkinson, J., *Scottish Medical Societies, 1731–1939: Their History and Records* (Edinburgh: Edinburgh University Press, 1993)
Johnston, T., *Memories* (Collins, 1952)
Kellas, J. G., *The Scottish Political System* (Cambridge: Cambridge University Press, 1975)
Knox, W., ed., *Scottish Labour Leaders 1918–1939: A Biographical Dictionary* (Edinburgh: Mainstream Publishing, 1984)
Levitt, I., *Poverty and Welfare in Scotland 1890–1948* (Edinburgh: Edinburgh University Press, 1988)
Levitt, I., *The Scottish Office – Depression and Reconstruction, 1919–1959* (Edinburgh: Scottish History Society, 1992)
MacGregor, Sir A.S.M., *Public Health in Glasgow 1905–1946* (Edinburgh: E.S. Livingstone, 1967)

MacKenzie, W. L., and Matthew, E., *The Medical Inspection of Children: A Text-book for Medical Officers of Schools, Medical Officers of Health, School Managers and Teachers* (Edinburgh & Glasgow, 1904).

McLachlan, G., ed., *Improving the Common Weal: Aspects of the Scottish Health Services, 1900–1984* (Edinburgh: Edinburgh University Press, 1987)

MacNair Wilson, R., *The Beloved Physician – Sir James Mackenzie* (John Murray, 1926)

Mair, A., *Sir James Mackenzie M.D. 1853–1925: General Practitioner* (Churchill and Livingstone, 1973)

Milne, Sir D., *The Scottish Office and other Scottish Government Departments* (George Allen and Unwin, 1957)

Munro, R., *Looking Back: Furtive Writings and Sayings* (Edinburgh: Nelson and Sons, 1930)

Mayes, M., *The Stormy Petrel: The Life of Dr Kate Fraser, 1877–1957* (Glasgow: Wellcome Unit for the History of Medicine, 1995)

Nottingham, C., ed., *The NHS in Scotland: The Legacy of the Past and the Prospect of the Future* (Aldershot: Ashgate, 2000)

Paterson, L., *The Autonomy of Modern Scotland* (Edinburgh: Edinburgh University Press, 1994)

Peters R.J., and Kinnaird, J., eds, *Health Administration: A Handbook* (Edinburgh: E&S Livingstone, 1965)

Pottinger, G., *The Secretaries of State for Scotland 1926–1976* (Edinburgh: Scottish Academic Press, 1979)

Smout, T.C., *A Century of the Scottish People 1830–1950* (Collins, 1986)

Smout, T C., ed., *The Search for Wealth and Stability* (Basingstoke: Macmillan, 1979)

Tocher, J.F., *The Book of Buchan* (Aberdeen: P. Scrogie Ltd and Aberdeen University Press, 1943)

Tough, A., *Medical Archives of Glasgow and Paisley: A Guide to the Greater Glasgow Health Board Archive* (Glasgow: Wellcome Unit Publications, 1993)

Turner, A., *Scottish Home Rule* (Oxford: Clarendon Press, 1952)

Wolfe, J.N., ed., *Government and Nationalism in Scotland* (Edinburgh: Edinburgh University Press, 1969)

Wood, I.S., *John Wheatley* (Manchester: Manchester University Press, 1990)

Scottish Periodical Articles:

Baird, D., 'Maternal Mortality in Hospital', *Lancet*, 8 February 1936, 295:298

Baird D., and Wyper, J.F.B., 'High Stillbirth and Neonatal Moralities', *Lancet*, 29 November 1941, 657:659

Blackden, S., 'From Physicians' Enquiry to Dewar's Report: A Survey of Medical Services in the West Highlands and Islands of Scotland, 1852–1912', part 1 and part 2, *Proceedings of the Royal College of Physicians, Edinburgh*, 28 (1998), 51:66, 207: 217

Cage, R.A., 'Infant Mortality Rates and Housing: Twentieth-Century Glasgow', *Scottish Economic and Social History*, 14 (1994), 77:92

Campbell, R.H., 'The Scottish Office and the Special Areas in the 1930s', *Historical Journal*, 22/1 (1979), 167:183

Chalmers, A.K., 'Infant Mortality', *Public Health* (1906)

Clark, J., 'The Rise and Development of Scottish Education', *Proceedings of the Royal Philosophical Society of Glasgow, 1909–1910*, XLI (1910)

Clayson, C., 'Modern Trends in Preventive Medicine and Social Aspects of Tuberculosis', *Edinburgh Medical Journal*, 50 (1943), 208:225

Davidson, R., '"A Scourge to be Firmly Gripped": the campaign for VD controls in inter-war Scotland', *Social History of Medicine*, 6/2 (August 1993), 213:235

Davidson, R., 'Searching for Mary, Glasgow: Contact Tracing for Sexually Transmitted Diseases in Twentieth-Century Scotland', *Social History of Medicine*, 9/2 (August 1996), 194:213

MacDonald, H.J., 'Boarding-Out and the Scottish Poor Law, 1845–1914' *Scottish Historical Review*, LXXV no. 2 (October 1996), 197:220

McKee, F., 'The Popularisation of Milk as a Beverage in the 1930s', *Proceedings of the Scottish Society of the History of Medicine, 1993–1994*, (1997), 50:58

McNeill, R., 'The Importance of Teaching Domestic Science as an Aid Towards the Improvement of Public Health', *Caledonian Medical Journal*, (1909), 4

Menzies, M.J., 'Maternity and Child Welfare in Scotland', *BMJ*, 1922 (2)

Mitchell, J., 'The Gilmour Report on Scottish Central Administration', *Juridicial Review*, (1989), pt. 2

Paterson, L., 'Scottish Autonomy and the Future of the Welfare State', *Scottish Affairs*, 19 (Spring 1997)

Pitman, J., 'The Sir Robert Philip Collection: The Fight against Tuberculosis', *Proceedings of the Royal College of Physicians, Edinburgh*, 18 (1988), 76:80

Rae, H.J., 'Some Local and General Problems in Tuberculosis Administration', *Edinburgh Medical Journal*, 38 (1931), 152:158

Reid, E.N., 'Airthrey Castle Maternity Hospital 1939–1948', *Proceedings of the Scottish Society of the History of Medicine, 1986–7* (1993), 14:16

Smith, D.F., 'Professor Cathcart's Military Physiology and Nutrition', *Proceedings of the Scottish Society of the History of Medicine 1993–1994* (1998), 41:50

Smith D.F., and Nicolson, M., 'The "Glasgow School" of Paton, Findlay and Cathcart: Conservative Thought in Chemical Physiology, Nutrition and Public Health' *Social Studies of Science*, 19 (1989), 195:238

Walker, E.R.C., 'The Forgotten Report', *EMJ*, 56 (1949)

Theses and Dissertations:

Doig, R.S., 'A Century of Tuberculosis on the Isle of Lewis in the Western Isles', Ph.D. Thesis, University of Glasgow, 1965
Ewan, J., 'Origins and Growth of the School Health Service Glasgow', University of Glasgow Ph.D. Thesis, 1956
Levitt, I., 'Welfare and the Scottish Poor Law 1890–1948', University of Edinburgh, Ph.D. Thesis, 1983
McDonald, C., 'The White Plague – A Study of Tuberculosis on the Island of Lewis 1850–1950', University of Glasgow, M.Phil. dissertation, 1996
McFarlane, N.M., 'Tuberculosis in Scotland, 1870–1960' University of Glasgow, Ph.D. Thesis, 1990
Patterson, S., 'The Control of Infectious Diseases in Fife c. 1855-1950', University of St Andrews, Ph.D. Thesis, 1989

Unpublished materials:

Fulton, W.F., 'General Practice – Then and Now' Inaugural Fulton Lecture, Royal College of General Practitioners, West of Scotland Faculty, 6 March 1990
Levitt, I., 'Scottish Housing Policy', Economic and Social History Seminar, University of Glasgow, 3 February 1994
Levitt, I., 'The Scottish Office and Labour Unionism, 1919–1959', Scottish History Society, University of Edinburgh, 4 December 1992

Other Secondary Sources

Books:

Abel-Smith, B., *The Hospitals 1800–1948: A Study in Social Administration in England and Wales* (Heineman, 1964)
Abel-Smith, B., and Titmuss, R.M., *The Cost of the National Health Service in England and Wales* (Cambridge: Cambridge University Press, 1956)
Abrams, M., *The Condition of the British People 1911–1945* (Victor Gollancz, 1946)
Addison, C., *Four and a Half Years: A Personal Diary from June 1914 to January 1919* [2 vol.], (Hutchinson and Co., 1934)
Addison, P., *The Road to 1945: British Politics and the Second World War* (Quartet, 1977)
Aldcroft, D.H., *The Inter-War Economy: Britain 1919–1939* (Batsford, 1970)
Alford, B.W.E., et al, eds, *Economic Planning, 1943–1951* (HMSO, 1992)
Allsop, J., *Health Policy and the National Health Service* (1984)

Andrzejewski, S., *Military Organization and Society* (Routledge and Kegan Paul, 1954)
Attlee, C., *As it Happened* (Heineman, 1954)
Barker, R., *Education and Politics* (Oxford: Clarendon Press, 1972)
Barker, T., and Drake, M., eds, *Population and Society in Britain 1850–1980* (Batsford, 1982)
Barry, J., and Jones, C., *Medicine and Charity before the Welfare State* (Routledge, 1991)
Bartrip, P., *'Themselves Writ Large': The British Medical Association 1832–1966* (BMJ Publishing, 1996)
Bellamy, J.M., and Saville, J., eds, *Dictionary of Labour Biographies* (Basingstoke: Macmillan, 1972)
Bevan, E., *In Place of Fear* (Heineman, 1952)
Berridge, V., *Health and Society in Britain since 1939* (Cambridge: Cambridge University Press, 1999)
Beveridge, Sir W., *The Pillars of Security* (Allen & Unwin, 1943)
Beveridge, Sir W., *Voluntary Action, A Report on Methods of Social Advance* (Allen & Unwin, 1948)
Birch, R.C., *The Shaping of the Welfare State* (Longman, 1974)
Blacker, C.P., *Neurosis and the Mental Health Services* (Oxford: Oxford University Press, 1946).
Bourne, A., *Health of the Future* (Harmondsworth: Penguin, 1942)
Bock G., and Thane, P., eds, *Gender Policies: Women and the Rise of the European Welfare states 1880s–1950s* (Routledge, 1994)
Brand, J., *Doctors and the State: The British Medical Profession and Government Action in Public Health* (Baltimore: Johns Hopkins, 1965)
Brend, W.A., *Health and the State* (1917)
Bruce, M., *The Coming of the Welfare State* (Batsford, 1968)
Bryder, L., *Below the Magic Mountain: A Social History of Tuberculosis in Twentieth Century Britain* (Oxford: Clarendon Press, 1988)
Brown, J., *The British Welfare State: A Critical History* (Oxford: Historical Association Studies, Blackwell, 1995)
Butler, D.E., *The British General Election of 1951* (Basingstoke: Macmillan, 1952)
Butler, D.E., *The British General Election of 1955* (Basingstoke: Macmillan, 1955)
Cairncross, Sir A., *Years of Recovery: British Economic Policy* (Methuen, 1985)
Churchill, Sir W., and Eade, C., eds, *War Speeches* (Cassell, 1944)
Clegg, H.A., and Chester, T.E., *Wage Policy and the Health Service* (Oxford: Blackwell, 1957)
Cooter, R., ed., *In the Name of the Child: Health and Welfare 1880–1940* (Routledge, 1992)
Craig, F.W.S., *British General Election Manifestos 1900–1974* (Basingstoke: Macmillan, 1975)
Cranshaw, L., *St Mark's Hospital London* (Kings Fund, 1985)

Crowther, M.A., *British Social Policy 1914–1939* (Basingstoke: Macmillan, 1988)
Crowther, M.A., *The Workhouse System 1834–1929* (Batsford, 1981)
Dale, H.E., *The Higher Civil Service of Great Britain* (Oxford: Oxford University Press, 1941)
Dalton, H., *High Tide and After: Memoirs 1945–1969* (Muller, 1962)
Dawson, Sir B., *The Nation's Welfare: The Future of the Medical Profession* (Cassell, 1918)
Digby, A., *Pauper Palaces* (Routledge, 1978)
Donnison, D., *The Politics of Poverty* (Oxford: Martin Robertson, 1982)
Donoughue, B., and Jones, G.W., *Herbert Morrison: Portrait of a Politician* (Weidenfield and Nicholson, 1973)
Dow, C.R., *The Management of the British Economy 1945–1960* (Cambridge: Cambridge University Press, 1970)
Dowding, K., *The Civil Service* (Routledge, 1995)
Dunn, C.L., *The Emergency Medical Services* [History of the Second World War – UK Medical Series], 2 vol., (HMSO, 1952, 1953)
Dwork, D., *War is Good for Babies and Other Young Children: A Story of the Infant and Child Welfare Movement in England 1898–1918* (Tavistock Publications, 1987)
Eckstein, H., *The English Health Service: Its Origins, Structure and Achievements* (Oxford: Oxford University Press, 1959)
Eckstein, H., *Pressure Group Politics, The Case of the British Medical Association* (Allen & Unwin, 1960)
Eder, N.R., *National Health Insurance and the Medical Profession* (New York: Garland Publishing Inc., 1982)
Farndale, J., *The Hospital Day Movement in Britain* (Oxford: Pergamon, 1961)
Ferguson S., and Fitzgerald, H., *Studies in the Social Services*, [History of the Second World War – UK Civil Series], (HMSO 1954)
Fildes, V., *Breasts, Bottles and Babies: A History of Infant Feeding* (Edinburgh: Edinburgh University Press, 1992)
Fildes, V., Marks, L., and Marland, H., eds, *Women and Children First: International Maternal and Infant Welfare 1870–1945* (Routledge, 1992)
Finlayson, G., *Citizen, State and Social Welfare in Britain, 1830–1990* (Oxford: Clarendon Press, 1994)
Fisher, N., *Iain Macleod* (Deutsch, 1973)
Floud, R., et al, *Height, Health and History: Nutritional Status in the United Kingdom, 1750–1950* (Cambridge: Cambridge University Press, 1970)
Foot, F., *Aneurin Bevan*, 2 vol., (Paladin, 1975)
Fraser, D., *The Evolution of the British Welfare State: A History of Social Policy since the Industrial Revolution* (Basingstoke: Macmillan, 1973)
Fraser, W.M., *A History of English Public Health 1834–1939* (Bailliere Tindall and Cox, 1950)

Freeman, H., and Farndale, J., eds, *Trends in the Mental Health Services* (Oxford: Pergamon 1963)
Fry, G.K., *Statesmen in Disguise: The Changing Role of the Administrative Class of the British Civil Service, 1853–1966* (Basingstoke: Macmillan, 1969)
Garcia, J., et al., *The Politics of Maternity Care* (Oxford: Clarendon, 1990)
Gilbert, B.B., *British Social Policy 1914–1939* (Batsford, 1970)
Gilbert, B.B., *The Evolution of National Insurance in Great Britain: The Origins of the Welfare State* (Michael Joseph, 1966)
Gilbert, B.B., *The Origins of National Insurance* (Michael Joseph, 1968)
Gladden, E.N., *Civil Services of the United Kingdom 1855–1970* (Frank Cass, 1967)
Godson, P.H., and J.H., *Education in the Second World War* (Methuen, 1976)
Goodman, N.M., *Wilson Jameson, Architect of National Health* (Allen & Unwin, 1970)
Gough, I., *The Political Economy of the Welfare State* (Basingstoke: Macmillan 1979)
Green, D.G., *Challenge to the NHS: A Study of Competition in America Health Care and the Lessons for Britain* (Institute of Economic Affairs, 1986)
Green, S.J.D., and Whiting, R.C., eds, *The Boundaries of the State in Modern Britain* (Cambridge: Cambridge University Press, 1986)
Hall, P., et al., *Change, Choice and Conflict in Social Policy* (Heineman, 1971)
Ham, C.J., *Policy Making in the National Health Service* (Basingstoke: Macmillan, 1981)
Hardy, A., *Health and Medicine in Britain since 1860* (Basingstoke, Palgrave, 2001)
Harley Williams, J., *Requiem for a Great Killer: The Story of Tuberculosis* (Health Horizon, 1973)
Harris, B., *The Health of the School Child: a History of the School Medical Service in England and Wales* (Open University Press, Buckinghamshire, 1995)
Harris, J., *Attlee* (Weidenfield and Nicolson 1982)
Harris, J., *William Beveridge: A Biography* (Oxford: Clarendon Press, 1977)
Harris, R.W., *National Health Insurance in Great Britain* (Allen & Unwin, 1946)
Hay, J.R., *The Development of the British Welfare State 1880–1975* (Arnold, 1978)
Henderson, P., *The School Health Services, 1908–1974* (HMSO, 1975)
Hill, C., *Both Sides of the Hill* (Heineman, 1964)
Hill, T.W., ed., *The Health of England* (Cape, 1933)
Honigsbaum, F., *The Division in British Medicine, A History of the Separation of General Practice from Hospital Care 1911–1968* (Kogan Page 1979)
Honigsbaum, F., *Health, Happiness and Security: The Creation of the National Health Service* (Routledge, 1989)
Honigsbaum, F., *Struggle for the Ministry of Health, 1914–1919* (Bell, 1970)
Hopkinson, T., ed., *Picture Post 1938–1950* (Harmondsworth: Penguin, 1970)
Immergut, E.M., *Health Politics: Interests and Institutions in Western Europe* (Cambridge: Cambridge University Press, 1992)
Jenkins, M., *Bevanism, Labour's High Tide* (Spokesman, 1979)

Jewkes, J., and S., *The Genesis of The British National Health Service* (Oxford: Blackwell, 1962)
Jones, K., *Health and Society in Twentieth Century Britain* (Longman, 1994)
Kelsall, R.K., *Higher Civil Servants in Britain from 1870 to the Present Day* (Routledge and Kegan Paul, 1955)
Kelsall, R.K., *Population* (Longmans, [sic], 1967)
Klein, R., *The Politics of the National Health Service* (Longman, 1983)
Lambert, R., *Sir John Simon 1816–1904 and English Social Administration* (McGibbon & Kee, 1963)
Land, A., Lowe R., and Whiteside, N., *The Development of the Welfare State 1939–1951: A Guide to Documents in the PRO* (PRO, 1992)
Le Gros Clark F., and Titmuss, R.M., *Our Food Problem and its Relation to our National Defences* (Harmondsworth: Penguin 1939)
Lesser, H., ed., *The Health Services* (Allen & Unwin, 1951)
Loudon, I., *Death in Childbirth: An International Study of Maternal Care and Maternal Mortality, 1800–1950* (Oxford: Clarendon Press, 1992)
Lewis, J., *The Politics of Motherhood: Child and Maternal Welfare in England 1900–1939* (Croom Helm 1980)
Lewis, J., *What Price Community Medicine? The Philosophy, Practice and Politics of Public Health since 1919* (Brighton: Wheatsheaf, 1986)
Lindsay, A., *Socialised Medicine in England and Wales: The National Health Service 1948–1961* (North Carolina: North Carolina University Press, 1962)
Lowe, R., *The Welfare State in Britain since 1945* (Basingstoke: Macmillan, 1993)
McCallum R.B., and Readman, A., *The British General Election of 1945* (Oxford: Oxford University Press, 1947)
McCleary, G.F., *Early History of the Infant Welfare Movement* (1933)
McCleary, G.F., *The Maternity and Child Welfare Movement* (1935)
MacFarlane A.and Mugford, M., *Birth Counts: Statistics of Pregnancy and Childbirth* vol.2 (HMSO, 1984)
Mackenzie, J.M., *Imperialism and Popular Culture* (Manchester: Manchester University Press, 1986)
Mackenzie, W.J.M., *Power and Responsibility in Health Care: The National Health Service as a Political Institution* (NPHT, 1979)
McKeown, T., *The Modern Rise of Population* (Edwin Arnold, 1976)
McKeown, T., *The Origins of Human Disease* (Oxford: Basil Blackwell, 1988)
McKeown T., et al, *Health, Society and Medicine: An Introduction to Community Medicine* (Oxford: Blackwell, 1984)
Mackintosh, J.M., *Topics in Public Health*, (Edinburgh: E.&S. Livingstone, 1965)
Mackintosh, J.M., *Trends of Opinion about Public Health 1901–1951* (Oxford: Oxford University Press, 1953)
Mackintosh, J.P., *The British Cabinet* (2nd ed., Methuen and Co., 1968)
Macleod, I., *The Life of Neville Chamberlain* (Basingstoke: Macmillan, 1961)

McNalty, Sir A.S., *The Civilian Health and Medical Services* 2 vol. [History of the Second World War – UK Civil Series], (HMSO, 1953, 1955)
McNalty, Sir A.S., *The Reform of the Public Health Services* (Oxford: Oxford University Press, 1943)
Marks, L.V., *Metropolitan Maternity: Maternal and Infant Welfare Services in Early Twentieth Century London* (Amsterdam: Rodopi Press, 1996)
Marks, L.V., *Model Mothers: Jewish Mothers and Maternity Provision in East London, 1870–1939* (Oxford: Clarendon Press, 1994)
Marland, H., ed., *Early Modern Midwives in Europe* (Routledge, 1994)
Marrack, J.R., *Food and Planning* (Victor Gollancz, 1942)
Mazumader, P.M.H., *Eugenics, Human Genetics and Human Failings: the Eugenics Society, its Sources and its Critics in Great Britain* (Routledge, 1992)
Mitchell, B.R., *British Historical Statistics* (Cambridge: Cambridge University Press, 1988)
Mitchell B.R., and Deane, P., *Abstract of British Historical Statistics* (Cambridge: Cambridge University Press, 1971)
Mitchison, R., *British Population Change since 1860* (Basingstoke: Macmillan, 1977)
Mommsen, W.J., ed., *The Emergence of the Welfare State in Britain and Germany, 1850–1950* (Croom Helm, 1981)
Morgan, J., ed., *The Backbench Diaries of Richard Crossman* (Hamilton/Cape 1981)
Morgan, K.O., *Consensus and Disunity: The Lloyd George Coalition Government 1918–1922* (Oxford: Clarendon Press, 1979)
Morgan, K.O., *Labour in Power 1945–1951* (Oxford: Clarendon Press, 1984)
Morgan, K.O., and Morgan, J., *Portrait of a Progressive: The Political Career of Christopher, Viscount Addison* (Oxford: Oxford University Press, 1980)
Mowat, C.L., *Britain Between the Wars 1918–1940* (Methuen, 1955)
Newman, Sir G., *The Building of a Nation's Health* (Basingstoke: Macmillan, 1939)
Newsholme, Sir A., *Fifty Years in Public Health* (Allen & Unwin, 1935)
Newsholme, Sir A., *The Last Thirty Years in Public Health* (Allen & Unwin, 1936)
Nicholas, H.G., *The British General Election of 1950* (Basingstoke: Macmillan, 1951)
Oakley, A., *The Captured Womb: A History of Medical Care of Pregnant Women* (Oxford: Blackwell, 1984)
Parry, N., and McNair, D., eds, *The Fitness of the Nation* (History of Education Society, 1983)
Pater, J.E., *The Making of the National Health Service* (Kings Fund, 1981)
Peacock, A., and Wiseman, D., *The Growth of Public Expenditure in the UK* (2nd ed., Allen and Unwin, 1966)
Peden, G.C., *British Economic and Social Policy: Lloyd George to Margaret Thatcher* (2nd ed., Oxford: Philip Allen, 1991)
Peele, G., and Cook, C., *The Politics of Reappraisal 1918–1939* (Basingstoke: Macmillan, 1975)
Peterson, O.L., *A Study of the NHS* (New York: Rockerfeller Foundation, 1951)
Poggi, A., *The Development of the Modern State* (Hutchinson, 1978)

Pimlott, B., *The Political Diary of Hugh Dalton 1918–1940, 1945–1960* (Cape, 1986)
Riley, D., *War in the Nursery: Theories of the Child and Mother* (Virago, 1983)
Riley, J.C., *Sick Not Dead: The Health of the British Workingman during the Mortality Decline* (Baltimore: Johns Hopkins University, 1997)
Robson, W.A., *The Development of Local Government* (Allen & Unwin, 1931)
Rosen, G., *A History of Public Health* (New York, M.D. Publications, 1958)
Ross, J.S., *The National Health Service in Britain* (Oxford: Oxford University Press, 1952)
Rowbotham, S., *Hidden from History: 300 Years of Women's Oppression and the Fight against it* (Pluto Press, 1973)
Ryan, J., with Thomas, F., *The Politics of Mental Handicap* (Harmondsworth: Penguin, 1980)
Seldon, A., *Churchill's Indian Summer. The Conservative Government 1951–1955* (Hodder & Stoughton, 1981)
Sissons, M., and French, P., *Age of Austerity 1945–1951* (Harmondsworth: Penguin 1964)
Smith, F.B., *The People's Health, 1830–1910* (Croom Helm, 1979)
Smith, F.B., *The Retreat of Tuberculosis, 1850–1950* (Croom Helm, 1988)
Smith, L., *Harold Wilson* (Hodder & Stoughton, 1964)
Stevens, R., *Medical Practice in Modern England* (New Haven, Conn.: Yale University Press, 1966)
Stevenson, J., *Social Conditions in Britain between the Wars* (Harmondsworth: Penguin, 1980)
Stevenson, J., and Cook, C., *Britain in the Depression: Society and Politics, 1929–39* (Basingstoke: 2nd ed., Longman, 1994)
Summerskill, E., *A Woman's World: Her Memoirs* (Heineman, 1967)
Taylor, A.J.P., *English History 1914–1945* (Oxford: Oxford University Press, 1965)
Thane, P., *Foundations of the Welfare State* (Longman, 1982)
Thompson, F.M.L., ed., *Cambridge Social History of Britain 1750-1950, vol. 3 – Social Agencies and Institutions* (Cambridge: Cambridge University Press, 1990)
Titmuss, R.M., *Birth, Poverty and Wealth: A Study of Infant Mortality* (Hamish Hamilton, 1943)
Titmuss, R.M., 'Community Care – Fact or Fiction?' in, H Freeman and J Farndale, eds, *Trends in the Mental Health Services* (Oxford: Pergamon, 1963)
Titmuss, R.M., *Poverty and Population, A Factual Study of Contemporary Social Waste* (Basingstoke: Macmillan, 1937)
Titmuss, R.M., *Problems of Social Policy,* [History of the Second World War – UK Civil Series], (HMSO, 1950).
Titmuss, R.M., 'War and Social Policy', in Titmuss, *Essays on the Welfare State* (Allen & Unwin 1958)
Townsend, P., *The Last Refuge, A Survey of Residential Institutions and Homes for the Aged in England and Wales* (Routledge, 1962)

Tracey, H., *The British Labour Party*, [in 3 vols.], (Caxton, 1948)
Wear, A., ed., *Medicine in Society, Historical Essays* (Cambridge: Cambridge University Press, 1992)
Webb, S., and Webb, B., *The Break Up of the Old Poor Law* (Longmans, 1909)
Webb, S., and Webb, B., *The State and the Doctor* (Longmans, 1910)
Webster, C., ed., *Biology, Medicine and Society 1840–1940* (Cambridge: Cambridge University Press, 1981)
Webster, C., *The Health Services Since the War Vol. 1: Problems of Health Care – The National Health Service before 1957* (HMSO, 1988)
Webster, C., *The National Health Service: A Political History* (Oxford: Oxford University Press, 1998)
Willcocks, A.J., *The Creation of the National Health Service* (Routledge and Kegan Paul, 1967)
Williams, A.S., *Women and Childbirth in the Twentieth Century: The History of the National Birthday Trust Fund 1920–1993* (Stroud: Sutton Publishing, 1997)
Williams, P.M., *The Diary of Hugh Gaitskell 1945–1956* (Cape, 1983)
Williams, P.M., *Hugh Gaitskell* (Cape, 1979)
Winter, J.M., *The Great War and the British People* (Cambridge, Mass: Harvard Press, 1986)
Winter, J.M., ed., *The Working Classes in Modern British History* (Cambridge: Cambridge University Press, 1983)
Woolton, Lord, *Memoirs* (Cassell 1959)

Other Periodical Articles

Apple, R., 'Constructing Mothers: Scientific Motherhood in the Nineteenth and Twentieth Centuries', *Social History of Medicine*, 8/2 (August 1995), 161:178
Atkins, P.J., 'White Poison? The Social Consequences of Milk Consumption, 1850–1930', *Social History of Medicine*, 5/2 (1992), 207:227
Ball, W.J., 'The Hospital Services of Cumberland and N. Westmorland', *The Hospital*, 1950
Bryder, L., 'The First World War – Healthy or Hungry?', *History Workshop Journal*, 24 (1987), 141:155
Chamberlain, G., and Williams, A.S., 'Ante Natal Care in South Wales 1934–1962', *Social History of Medicine*, 8/3 (December 1995), 480:488
Cherry, S., 'Before the National Health Service: Financing the Voluntary Hospitals, 1900–1939', *Economic History Review*, L, 2 (1997), 305:326
Collins, J.S., 'General Practice in England Today, A Reconnaissance', *Lancet*, 1950, (1)
Cox, A., 'Seven Years of National Insurance in Great Britain', *Journal of American Medical Association*, 2 (1921)
Crofts, W., 'The Atlee Government's Pursuit of Women', *History Today*, 36/8 (August 1986), 29:35

Crowther, M.A., 'Family Responsibility and State Responsibility in Britain before the Welfare State', *Historical Journal*, 25/1 (1982), 131:145

Crowther, M.A., 'Paupers or Patients? Obstacles to Professionalisation in the Poor Law Medical Service before 1914', *Journal of the History of Medicine*, 39 (1984), 33:54

Davies, C., 'The Health Visitor as Mothers' Friend: A Woman's Place in Public Health 1904–1915', *Social History of Medicine*, 1 (1988), 39:59

Dawson, Sir B., 'Medicine and the State', *The Medical Officer*, 23 (1920)

Digby, A., and Bosanquet, N., 'Doctors and Patients in an Era of National Health Insurance and Private Practice, 1913–1938', *Economic History Review*, XLI, (1988), 74:94

Dupree, M., 'Other than Healing: Medical Practitioners and the Business of Life Assurance during the Nineteenth and early Twentieth Centuries', *Social History of Medicine*, 10/1 (April 1997), 79:103

Dwork, D., 'The Milk Option, An Aspect of the History of the Infant Welfare Movement in England 1898–1908, *Medical History*, 31 (1987)

Finlayson, G., 'A Moving Frontier: Voluntarism and the State in British Social Welfare 1911–1949', *Twentieth Century British History*, 1/2, (1990), 183:206

Fox, E., 'District Nursing in England and Wales before the National Health Service: The Neglected Evidence', *Medical History*, 38 (1994), 303:321

Gayle, C.R., and Martyn, C.N., 'Dummies and the Health of Hertfordshire Infants 1911–1930', *Social History of Medicine*, 8/2 (August 1995), 231:256

Harris, B., 'Health, Height and history: An Overview of Recent Developments in Anthropometric History', *Social History of Medicine*, 7/2 (1994), 297:320

Harris, B., 'The Demographic Impact of the First World War: An Anthropometric Perspective', *Social History of Medicine*, 6/3 (1993), 343:366

Honigsbaum, F., 'The Inter-War Health Insurance Scheme: A Rejoinder', *Journal of Social Policy*, 12/4 (1983), 515:524

Hunter, J.B., 'Emergency Medical Service and the Future', *BMJ*, 1941, (1)

Illsley, R., 'Social Class Selection and Class Differences in Stillbirths and Infant Deaths', *BMJ*, 24 December 1955, 1520:1524

Jeffreys, K., 'British Politics and Social Policy during the Second World War', *Historical Journal*, 30/1 (1987), 123:144

Kermack, W.O., et al, 'Death-Rates in Great Britain and Sweden: Some Irregularities and their Significance', *Lancet*, 31 March 1934, 698:703

Labisch, A., 'History of Public Health, History in Public Health: Looking Back and Looking Forward', *Social History of Medicine*, 11/1 (April 1998), 1:13

Lewis, J., 'Family Provision of Health and Welfare in the Mixed Economy of Care in the Late Nineteenth and Twentieth Centuries', *Social History of Medicine*, 8/1 (April 1995), 1:16

Lewis, J., 'The Social History of Social Policy: Infant Welfare in Edwardian England', *Journal of Social Policy*, 9/4 (1980), 463:486

Loudon, I., 'Maternal Mortality: 1880–1950. Some Regional and International Comparisons', *Social History of Medicine*, 1/2 (August 1988), 183:228

Loudon, I., 'Obstetric Care, Social Class and Maternal Mortality', *BMJ*, 293 (6 September 1986), 606:608

Macaulay, H.M.C., Reflections on the Origins of the National Hospital Service, *Public Health*, 89 (1974)

MacDonagh, O., 'The Nineteenth-Century Revolution in Government: A Reappraisal' *Historical Journal*, 1/1 (1958), 52:67

Mackintosh, J., 'Tuberculosis in Young Children', *Public Health* 56/5 (February, 1943)

McKeown, T., and Record, R.G., 'Reasons for the Decline in Mortality in England and Wales during the Nineteenth Century', *Population Studies*, 16 (1962), 94:112

McKeown, T., and Record, R.G., and Turner, R.D., 'An Interpretation of the Decline of Mortality in England and Wales during the Twentieth Century', *Population Studies*, 29/3 (1975), 391:422

MacNicol, J., 'Eugenics and the Campaign for Voluntary Sterilisation in Britain between the Wars', *Social History of Medicine*, 2/2 (August 1989), 147:169

Marland, H., 'A Pioneer in Infant Welfare: the Huddersfield Scheme 1903–1920', *Social History of Medicine*, 6/1 (April 1993), 25:50

Marland, H., 'Questions of Competence: The Midwife Debate in the Netherlands in the early Twentieth Century', *Medical History*, 39 (1995), 317:337

Marwick, A., 'The Labour Party and the Welfare State in Britain 1900–1948' *American History Review*, 73 (1967), 380:403

Maurice, Major General Sir F., 'National Health: A Soldier's Study', *Contemporary Review*, 83 (1903), 41:56

Mitchell, M., 'The Effects of Unemployment on the Social Conditions of Women and Children in the 1930s', *History Workshop Journal*, 19 (1985), 105:127

Moeller, R.G., 'The State of Women's Welfare in European Welfare States', *Social History*, 19/3 (1994), 385:393

Moore, S.G., 'Infant Mortality and the Relative Practical Nature of Measures Directed at its Prevention', *Lancet* 1916, (1), 22, 29 April, 6 May, 849:853, 895:900, 941:948

Peden, G.C., 'The Road to and from Gairloch: Lloyd George, Unemployment, Inflation, and the "Treasury View" in 1921', *Twentieth Century British History*, 4/3 (1993), 224:249

Peden, G.C., 'The Treasury as the Central Department of Government, 1919-1939', *Public Administration*, 61 (1983)

Picken, R.F.M., 'The Comprehensive Health Service', *Public Administration*, 21 (1943)

Practitioner, 'The National Health Service Act in Great Britain. A Review of the First Year's Working', [extra edition], Autumn 1949

Prohaska, F., '"A Mother's Country": Mothers' Meetings and Family Welfare 1850–1950', *History*, 74 (1989), 52:58.
Pugh, M., 'Women, Food and Politics, 1880–1930', *History Today*, 41/3 (March 1991), 14:20
Ryan, M., 'Health Centre Policy in England and Wales', *British Journal of Sociology*, 19 (1968)
Ryle, J., 'Social Medicine', *BMJ*, 1942, (1)
Ryle, J., 'Social Medicine: Its Meaning and its Scope', *BMJ*, 1943, (2)
Stewart, J., 'Ramsey MacDonald, the Labour Party, and Child Welfare, 1900–1914' *Twentieth Century British History*, 4/2 (1993), 105:125
Stewart, J., 'Socialist Proposals for Health Reform in Inter-War Britain: The Case of Somerville Hastings', *Medical History*, 39 (1995), 338:357
Szreter, S., 'The Importance of Social Intervention in Britain's Mortality Decline c. 1850–1914: A Re-interpretation of the Role of Public Health', *Social History of Medicine*, 1/1 (1988), 1:37
Tannenbaum, S.L., 'Making Good Little English Children: Infant Welfare and Anglicisation among Jewish Immigrants in London, 1880–1939', *Immigrants and Minorities*, 12/2 (July 1993), 176:199
Thomas, E.G., 'The Old Poor Law and Medicine', *Medical History*, 24 (1980)
Thomas, J., and Williams, A.S., 'Women and Abortion in 1930s Britain: A Survey and its Data', *Social History of Medicine*, 11/2 (August 1998), 283:309
Webb, S., et al., 'Interim Report on the Committee of Enquiry on [...] the Working of the Insurance Act', *New Statesman*, special supplement, 14 March 1914
Webster, C., 'Beveridge after 50 years', *BMJ*, 305 (17 October 1992), 901:902
Webster, C., 'Conflict and Consensus: Explaining the British Health Service', *Twentieth Century British History*, 1 (1990), 115:151
Webster, C., 'Health, Welfare and Unemployment During the Depression', *Past and Present*, 109 (1985), 204:230
Webster, C., 'Healthy or Hungry Thirties?' *History Workshop Journal*, 13 (Spring 1982), 110:129
Webster, C., 'The Origins of Social Medicine in Britain' *Bulletin of the Society for the Social History of Medicine*, 39 (June 1986), 52:55
Welshman, J., 'In Search of the Problem Family': Public Health and Social Work in England and Wales 1940–1970', *Social History of Medicine*, 9/3 (1996), 447:466
Welshman, J., 'Physical Education and the School Medical Service in England and Wales, 1907–1939', *Social History of Medicine*, 9/1 (April 1996), 31:48
Welshman, J., 'School Meals and the Problem of Malnutrition in England and Wales 1900–1938', *Bulletin of the Society for the Social History of Medicine*, 40 (1987), 37:40
Whitehouse, Sir B., 'The British Tradition and the New Outlook', *BMJ*, 1942, (2)

Whiteside, N., 'Counting the Cost: Sickness and Disability among Working People in an Era of Industrial Recession, 1920–39', *Economic History Review*, XL, 2 (1987), 228:246

Whiteside, N., 'Private Agencies for Public Purposes: Some New Perspectives on Policy Making in Health Insurance between the Wars', *Journal of Social Policy*, 12/2 (1983), 165:194

Winter, J.M., 'Infant Mortality, Maternal Mortality, and Public Health in Britain in the 1930s', *Journal of European Economic History*, 8 (1979), 439:462

Wilson, G.S., 'Public Health Laboratory Services', *British Medical Bulletin*, (1951), 7

Woods, R.I., et al., 'The Causes of Rapid Infant Mortality Decline in England and Wales 1861–1921', *Population Studies*, 42 (1988), Pt. 1, 343–346, Pt. 2, 43, (1989), 113:132

Index

Studies in the History of Medicine

Edited by Charles Webster, All Souls College, Oxford

Studies in the History of Medicine provides an outlet for academic monographs devoted to both the social and the intellectual dimensions of the history of medicine. No limitations are imposed with respect to period or place, providing the approach adopted is analytical and historical. The series encourages investigations relating to previously neglected aspects of medicine and health care such as the history of nursing or other occupations associated with health care, case studies of particular disease and illness phenomena, health care in colonial and postcolonial settings, or indeed complementary medicine, dentistry or veterinary medicine. The monographs inevitably evaluate the impact of modern high-technology medicine, but they also give appropriate weight to health care as it relates to the elderly, the mentally ill or other vulnerable social groups. Except in special circumstances the series will not include general biographies, histories of individual institutions and organisations, or studies of parochial interest. The monographs included in this series reflect the leading edge of research in the now well-established and still expanding field of medical history.

Vol. 1 John Welshman. Municipal Medicine: Public Health in Twentieth-Century Britain. 2000. 339 pp.
ISBN 3-906766-40-3 / US-ISBN 0-8204-5327-7

Vol. 2 Jacqueline Jenkinson. Scotland's Health 1919–1948. 2002. 506 pp.
ISBN 3-906768-34-1 / US-ISBN 0-8204-5622-5

Vol. 3 Charles Webster. The Great Instauration: Science, Medicine and Reform 1626–1660. 2002. 670 pp.
ISBN 3-906768-37-6 / US-ISBN 0-8204-5616-0